Back in the USSR
1967-1970

A Russian Memoir

Genia Browning

Pamela Percy and Valerie Spargo
My grateful appreciation for all your support,
Not least for all the words you ploughed through
to produce this memoir.
Thank you

Book Design Christine Bone
Thank you for your time and enthusiasm

Copyright © Browning Books 2022
ISBN: 978-1-3999-1552-6

Produced by self-publishing company Lulu 2021

To order email browningbooks231@gmail.com

Sturgeon in newspaper

Here am I walking across Red Square sharing sturgeon out of a newspaper with Bernie. Bernie's wife, who is interpreting at some event in the Kremlin, procured it for him to collect from the holy of holies. The sturgeon is tender white meat that melts in the mouth. Never will I taste better.

Not something I'd imagined doing in my 20s when in 1967 I'd taken a two year contract to work on Radio Moscow.

Contents

1967   3
A chilly reception, but I survive
and celebrate the fiftieth anniversary of the USSR.

1968   47
Warmth enters with broadcasting and friendships.
A bizarre encounter with actor Robert Morley in Bukhara.
I discover how old pots become new in Samarkand.

1969-70   136
New Year celebrations, Misha takes me to a Yolka,
Good bye to Radio Moscow.
Back to the USSR. Hello Moscow University.

End Pieces

Of friends and colleagues	155
The influence of my political background.	161
Tentative reflections on the Soviet Union.	164
Revisiting some of my cultural experiences.	168

1968 on Kalinin Prospekt

1967

Why Moscow?

I had always intended to travel after I'd completed a couple of years teaching. I felt it incumbent on me to gain experience outside of education if I was going to be effective as a teacher. I was very aware of my limitations, confined by school, college and return to school.

I had not intended this would take place in the USSR. Originally I was going to North Vietnam. But the situation changed – not least the US intensified bombing of Hanoi. But I had already resigned from my teaching post. King Street, the Communist party (CP) headquarters which had recommended me to the Vietnamese, offered me alternative posts in Russia or Eastern Europe. I was tempted by Bulgaria having fallen in love with the culture, but thought that it would make more sense to go to the heart of the socialist states – the USSR.

I was enjoying my teaching in London's East End, half classes of girls for needlework, ideal for discussions. I had introduced Art needlework, embroidery and design in which the Asian and east European pupils excelled. The school was supportive, unlike the church school where I had done my probationary year. I was offered the bait of a post of responsibility if I stayed on the following year. Although I was tempted to take up the offer, arrangements had gone ahead for my contract in Moscow.

I was interviewed at the Soviet embassy; a formality given the CP had recommended me. Just my voice was recorded. The post was for the English section of Moscow Radio. This sounded interesting. I gave no thought to how this would be a black mark for the future[1].

And that was it, apart from being handed money in advance, presumably from the embassy, to purchase necessities.

Preparation
I received no preparation. No one thought to prepare me for life in the USSR. But neither did I seek advice. Later I discovered that British Council students were routinely prepared with dire warnings to avoid devious relationships and spy networks. "Spying was an obsession with everyone on the exchange" – writes one such student co-currently with me in Moscow, an obsession affecting their view of all whom they met[2], Not surprisingly there was no mention of such possibilities from the CP. Yet the Party hierarchy was well aware of the pit falls, just something they were not prepared to divulge. And such issues were not on my radar for I supported the Soviet Union in the cold war.

British Council students presumed the KGB was keeping tabs on them, I presumed they were not.

My own preparation was woefully inadequate. Naively I bought Mary Quant type boots and a new spring coat – light green which did not cover my knees. No hat.

It wasn't only the clothes choice that was naïve; I had no Roget's Thesaurus, not even a dictionary, and just one case for my two year stay.

And that was it. Supposedly ready at 26 years of age to start my contract at Moscow Radio.

---

1 The British Council refused financial support for my PhD. Initially the reason given was my age. My supervisor pointed out another of her students was older. She was then told the reason could not be divulged.

2 Sheila Fitzpatrick, A Spy in the Archives, MUP, 2013, p.84

What follows are selected sketches from the combined sources of notes, correspondence and memories from 1967 to 1970. Reminiscences have all the problems of the vagaries of memory. Thankfully they are anchored in the correspondence to my parents. My mother kept my letters and postcards; they remain for me now almost fifty years later, a picture of my experiences and responses to the USSR of the 1960s.

These combined sources are organised in two ways; a loosely chronological framework of 1967, 1968 and 1969 and some clusters under a common heading. 'Broadcasts' consists of programmes I produced for Radio Moscow and 'University' refers to my return to Moscow from 1969-1970 for a language course and each year ends with its collection of miscellaneous snippets entitled "Moscow Life".

My political background which led to me being in Moscow is located as an end piece, but equally can be read as an introduction if preferred.

Moscow arrival and flat

February 9th 1967. I'm met at the airport by Tanya, my radio nanny. She's an editor at Moscow Radio. There's snow on the ground already turning to a dirty grey slush and bitter winds. We go to *Hotel Ukraina* for a meal of *'kotlety po kievski'* (Chicken Kiev) - long before it becomes a staple of British supermarkets. Delicious. The hotel is my first encounter with one of Stalin's seven "wedding cake buildings" which dominate central Moscow. Tanya is horrified to see I'm hatless. Next morning she whisks me off to a 'valuta' store, where goods are sold for foreign currency, to buy a *shapka*, a padded Russian fur hat with ear flaps. A life saver. It lasted me for over thirty years. Mine is just common rabbit, but it does its job. Secretly I fancy the opulent red fox.

My home for the next two years is a self-contained flat. I'm pleased that I'm not in a foreigners' block, but in an ordinary block with only two flats for Radio Moscow employees, mine and an adjacent one. On my other side is a communal flat: three separate Russian families each allocated a bed sitter, the single bathroom and kitchen are shared between them.

My flat is generous: a large living room with a sofa bed, hall, separate kitchen, bathroom and toilet. I overlook *Sadovya Koltso* a main ring road. Moscow is built around three: the central one, this middle one and then the main one which rings the city. *Sadovya Koltso* means the garden ring. There are no gardens, but it is extremely wide, a major thoroughfare. There had been gardens, but Tanya tells me Stalin had them removed during the war to allow Russian tanks quicker access to the centre. And it still provides the tanks access for parades. In 1944, 57,000 German Prisoners of War were marched out of Moscow along this road. The pavements were packed with Russians - silent observers.

Across the road I look out on the US embassy. My flat is above a fabric and haberdashery shop. Apparently fabric stores are a favourite site for *terakani* – cockroaches are legion for seeking the warmth of radiators. Going to the toilet at night, turning on the light sends them into a frenzy of scurrying. I place glass jars on those too slow to escape and give them a slow death, until disposed of by the vacuum cleaner. Probably crueller than killing them outright, but I can't deal with the crunching noise they make. Eventually I employ a cockroach catcher to rid the flat of their presence.

As it is February, the windows remain sealed, just the small *fortochka* can be opened. So the heat from the radiators is too much for me – until I come to welcome the warmth after forays outside. My monthly bill for gas and electricity is just 5 Roubles[1]. The heating comes from rubbish disposal. My block like most surrounds an inner courtyard. It's a communal space. Even in the snow, young boys play ball games here. The courtyard is surrounded by various old buildings.

From the flat I can walk or take the bus to Red Square, or to Mayakovsky metro with its pillars of stainless steel on Gorky Street. I can also walk the side streets of Old Arbat and breathe in the character of an older Moscow. The Moscow Conservatoire is nearby. In the opposite direction turning left outside my building, is a bread shop on the corner of the road being transformed, Kalinin Prospekt, (now re-named as *Novii Arbat*, (New Arbat). The bread shop introduces me to unknown varieties of bread including loaves of rye and the white bread previously favoured by the Russian gentry. The window display of swans and wheatsheaves fashioned from dough with much artistry, invites entry.

---

1   Roughly 2R to £1.00

Weather wise my arrival in Moscow could not have been worse. Much of the snow on the main streets is melting leaving ugly dirty slush. Slippery slush. One day walking to work in only my first week, I slide, hitting the ground hard. I discover I have a coccyx. My Mary Quant style boots not surprisingly, proving quite unsuitable for these conditions.

However, I survive my first winter.

Red Square

Ensconced in my flat, I realise I've arrived. I'm actually in Moscow. The Red Square is a must. During the day, crowded as I first see it, I'm disappointed. But then I take a solitary midnight walk and its splendour is revealed. *Krasnii* means 'Red' but also 'beautiful' and it is; vast, with the magical Basil Cathedral, red brick Kremlin walls, and the gleaming white of the great bell tower topped by its golden cupola, and over all the movement of the floodlit red flags fluttering against the dark sky.

During my time here I experience Red Square in its various guises: tourist venue, shopping centre with department store Gum, its history captured in the History Museum and through Russian art, Surikov's depiction of the Streltsy's execution in front of St Basil's cathedral, the people addressing Boris in Mussorgsky's opera *Boris Godunov*; political with its memorial wall and not least Lenin's mausoleum, resting place of the revolutionary leader's embalmed body. This was not unexpected but the impact was greater. What I had not realised was the significant years of my contract. 1967 marked the 50th anniversary of the Revolution. Subsequently the 50th anniversaries of the Komsomol and the Red Army were celebrated. For each occasion there were parades, for which I was both participant and spectator and of the many rehearsals I witnessed when crossing the Square on my way to work. The mood of the Square responded to each event.

The Square's role of solemnity was apparent for Yuri Gagarin's funeral on March 30th 1968.

But there are other images:

The tanks parading across its width, the slogans, "Down with Imperialism", in stark conflict with the many posters and banners demanding peace.

Stopping to watch a rehearsal for one such event, I'm sitting next to an old man, head in his hands, he's chanting the Russian orthodox prayer. Behind us are the ancient towers of the Kremlin Cathedrals, whilst tourists in their fur coats swan around taking pictures, women posing in their contemporary clothed selves against a background of old Russia. The old man continues his chanting. The sun glints on the massive new statue of Lenin.

On another occasion, a female commander chest to the fore, medals proudly jangling, barks out marching instructions "Lev, lev, lev" (left, left, left) past St Basils, eyes left at the podium. She turns to inspect her charges- a column of small children, concentrating on left leg, right arm, right leg, left arm rehearsing for a coming parade.

Later, in November however, I was enthralled by the spectacular 50th anniversary parade of the revolution and felt so lucky that I was able to take part. In May the following year, I was privileged to be given a spectator's ticket for the May Day parade.

Over all, that early experience of the Square at midnight remains a vivid memory

Introduction to Radio Moscow

But now reality steps in – the start of my two year contract. Tanya takes me to Radio Moscow. Firstly I'm introduced to the English announcers, Doris and Tom who sit outside the recording studio together with the American section. The Americans are more vocal and friendlier than the English appear, I might come back with an American accent.

But to my consternation, I discover this is only a courtesy call, the Studio is not for me. I will not be broadcasting. Why was my voice recorded?

No. My place is in the Pool. This is a large room where at least thirty people are busy typing, translating articles from Russian to English. It seems the translators have been waiting ten years for a style editor: that is now me

Tanya introduces me. I feel a frosty silence. Who am I? I look younger than my 26 years. I have no reference books. The previous incumbent had been a middle aged man, well prepared. Tanya leads me to a desk at the front, my back to the majority of translators.

My role is to edit the translated articles. The majority of the translators are Russians who've learnt their English from various sources. Some acquired English as children when their families were posted abroad in the diplomatic service, as had one smartly dressed woman who had learnt English in China. The other nationalities include a young Iraqi political refugee[1] and a venerable Irishman who had come to support the young Soviet Socialist republic and remained, like his English, entrapped in his past.

I soon discover my role is made worse by the time factor. These are articles for broadcasting. Unfortunately, I'm a slow reader, working against time, on boring articles, in mangled English. Before long I acquire a propensity to see Russian syntax as the norm. As I gain more confidence there's a further problem. If I stray too far from the original translation, by re-writing a paragraph, or introducing an idiom, it is re-translated into Russian to check I haven't changed the meaning. I notice that not all translations reach me, it is soon evident that a) I am too slow, and b) not an editor.

So, my first few weeks do not bode well. My demoralisation in the pool is combined with unexpectedly experiencing several days as a patient in Moscow's No 1 hospital. The torn pieces of *Pravda* and *Izvestia* newspapers hanging from string in lieu of toilet paper prove a rude awakening to the Soviet health service. Subsequently in April I found it upsetting witnessing children being drilled in Red Square. Undiplomatically, I announce to the Pool, "How is all this militarism compatible with peace" ? Shocked silence. I escape for a reassuring cup of coffee. Later the Iraqi translator who had appeared to befriend me, got pleasure from relating the Pool's negative opinions of me, even questioning my political allegiance.

I am wondering how I am going to survive my two year contract.

Then in April, an American middle-aged man appears at the desk next to me. My saviour. He introduces himself as Bernie Cooper and apologises for having been on holiday when I arrived. Smooth talking, born in America, he is also known in

---

1 Who gave me this Iraqi recipe for Aubergine: Cut thin slices across. Fry aubergine (& marrow). Lay sliced potato underneath, then aubergine, then rings of onion, then sliced tomato & pepper, & garlic. Add water. Bake in oven until soft and well-cooked on a slow heat - approx. 45 minutes

Russia as Victor Kuprianov. Although his desk is in the Pool, he is an anomaly. He writes his own programmes directly in English, and broadcasts them himself both for the British and American sections. Yet he is neither in the editors' room where Tanya works, nor entirely with the announcers who keep to the recording area, for he spends time in the pool to write. He is particularly on friendly terms with the Americans and that is where he is most at ease. Whilst pleasant to all in the pool, the one person he associates with is Helen, quiet, hard-working, an accurate translator whose work I do not need to edit. They escape to the corridor for ritual cigarette breaks. Helen becomes my good and respected friend.

With Bernie's arrival a welcome ritual is established. On his morning appearance we visit the buffet on the third floor for an expresso with a slice of lemon. Lemon in black coffee, not tea?[2] I soon develop a taste for it. At some point this becomes two cups. When I need three before I feel ready for work, I realise I've become addicted and limit my intake. In retrospect long coffee breaks is not what I was being paid for, but no one chastised me, at least not to my face. And Bernie was his own man.

When scripts are wanted urgently by the announcers, I take them along myself so begin to know those broadcasting to the UK.

Doris is the chief British announcer. She rules the English section with a rod of iron. Despite her thirty years in Russia, her word on pronunciation and UK knowledge is law. I have to tread warily with her for many months before she shows some slight acceptance. She re-edits any script I'd edited for her. Eventually a heavy cold on my part leads to Doris unbending a little. She gives me advice on how to treat it, and even finds me some Vick.

Tom is the other native speaker. The atmosphere feels restrained between the two of them. He has lived here since the late thirties.

Yuri, a young Russian is the third regular announcer. A serious, ambitious, rather intense person, already going bald. He graduated from the prestigious Foreign Languages Institute and speaks correct English. The first time I hear him, I burst out laughing. He had delivered a piece on trade unions, but in excellent imitation of Lord Douglas Home. What trade unionist would take him seriously? I tell him it just won't do. But, his proudest achievement had been capturing the tones and pronunciation of the British aristocracy. I tried, in vain to explain to him that announcing an item on Trade Unions sounding like Lord Douglas Home, would not gain the sort of attention required.

Like many youngish Russian males, he has the confidence to believe that he knows best. Neither does he have a concept of social class, after all officially it doesn't exist in the USSR. He is eager to hear about Britain, and I give him all the help I can.[3]

Occasionally, Zena, a middle aged Russian woman also broadcasts. Someone told me she'd been brought up by Maxim Litvinov, Ambassador and Foreign Minister, and Ivy his English wife. Zena's parents had suffered in the Gulag, many offspring left as orphans were adopted by the comrades of those who perished.

---

2   Tea, whether with lemon or without, was taken through a lump of sugar, or sometimes jam spooned from a little saucer. The sweetness is more apparent this way. Lemons are often unavailable in the State shops, but usually available at the Radio's buffets.

3   It was thanks to Yuri though that I was barred from the radio on a return visit.

The Americans are fun. There are four of them: two women and two men. Both the women tower over me. Like Doris and Tom they have been at Radio Moscow for many years.

I find the announcer's area far more congenial than the Pool and manoeuvre as much time there as I can.

My neighbours

The family of three in the communal flat next door become close friends. The round faced smiling Lena is an office worker, her husband Yuri, tall and lanky works in a factory and Sasha their ten year old son, is pale and self-contained. All three are very welcoming. They are delighted I'm English as Sasha's secondary school specialises in English and I'm more than happy to have an excuse to converse with him. Lena has a lively mind with a wide range of interests. She puts up with my broken Russian in order to argue eagerly with me about politics, normally quoting from the Government paper *Izvestia*. She becomes a Party member and soon after is delighted to be sent to Prague on a work trip. Yuri is not a party member. He doesn't usually join in our discussions. Lena laughingly refers to him as her '*pustoya banka*', that is her empty vessel.

Over the two years they give me friendship, numerous meals, presents, and most importantly on one bitter winter's day save me from frost bite. I come home so cold that I go into their room instead of my own. Yuri takes one look at me, and seizes from the bottom of a cupboard what looks like a can of petrol, and I dread will taste like it, but Yuri makes me drink it. Almost pure spirit; nearly knocks me out, but does the trick.

It was very difficult to refuse the many presents given to me, always of their most precious belongings. Among these was the highly valued midnight blue and gold *Gzhel* teapot and tea cup and Lena's Siberian grandfather's bast shoes woven from birch bark. My leaving present was a *Fedoskino* lacquered trinket box engraved with my name.

On one memorable occasion Lena, complete with enamel bucket, took me to forest land on the outskirts of Moscow. Here we joined other mushroom gatherers with many more enamel buckets. Plastic was not evident. I felt secure gathering a range of fungi under Lena's guidance, as Russians are taught how to identify fungi in primary school. Favourites prized for their flavour are Boletus mushrooms associated with silver birch trees and golden chanterelle, known as little foxes ears in Russian. Back in Moscow with our enamel bucket, Lena proceeded to instruct me in the cooking of the precious chanterelle: slightly fried in butter, topped with Smetana – absolutely delicious.

As children both Yuri and Lena had been evacuated to Siberia from Leningrad during the siege. Afterwards they had the choice to return to Leningrad or come to Moscow and chose the latter. My first visit to them really opened my eyes. I knew there was a serious housing problem in Moscow. Now I saw just what that means. The flat has just three rooms, one kitchen and a toilet and a bathroom. Lena, Yuri and Sasha had been allocated one of these rooms. Sasha has never known anything else apart from living and sleeping in that room with his parents. In the second of the three rooms live a kindly faced single mother and her handsome teenage son. The third room is occupied by an elderly woman. On more than one occasion when I accompany Lena in the kitchen, the atmosphere is strained. This third member of the flat is sour faced, I know nothing about her, despite living so cheek by jowl. This is how they live their daily lives for many years. No wonder that Sasha seems older than his years, every day being closeted with his parents. Their room is always tidy and though I often just drop in, I never get a whiff of dissent. They strongly believe a better future awaits them – the government will provide them with a flat for themselves – however long it takes. Lena is saving up to buy desired Baltic furniture –

from 'under the counter' when the day arrives.

I am so lucky to have Lena and her family next door to me. They provide the warmth and friendship I need.

Easter Customs

On March 2nd Easter is marked by the Russian Orthodox Church. But not only by the church. Fortunately I drop in at a friend's house and discover that they still celebrate it but more as a folk custom. Grass had been planted in a tray of earth, now grown thick and high- and nestling among it lay coloured eggs, hard boiled and attractively painted in red and mauve. It seems to be linked to the idea of birth in the manger. However, it probably welcomes new birth in general as it pre-dates Christianity and is practised by non-believers as well. There's a special Easter cake. I'm given a small individual one to take home. It resembles a toadstool and has walnuts inside.

An associated custom is for a boy and girl to take an egg each, knock the ends together, the boy says 'Christ has risen' the girl replies 'Truly' and they kiss. It also seems that coloured Easter eggs were taken to the cemeteries and piled up on the graves supporting the theme of new life, but others I speak to don't seem to know anything about that. The churches are absolutely packed at Easter. Young people go out of interest. I intend to go tomorrow to hear the singing in a cathedral where I'm told the choir is excellent.

The Russian Orthodox Church is crammed with the elderly, mostly standing or moving around to the various icons, which however painfully, the old bend down to kiss, no thought given to hygiene.

Georgia

3-6th May 1967

Georgia. From early childhood a place of imagined wonder thanks to my father's tales of Jason's trials to capture the Golden Fleece from a cave in Colchis. That part of Colchis is now the fertile Caucasian republic of Georgia. Much of the fresh flowers, fruit and vegetables in Moscow's food markets, are flown in daily by Georgians. A group from the Radio are going there for the May Holiday, and I am able to join them. I'm not disappointed. The three days in Tbilisi are packed with vibrant impressions.

The Georgians are ancient peoples and quite different from the Russians: dark, passionate, quick moving and artistic with their delicate metal work and elegant pottery. Fruit and vegetables in all their colours are piled high on the pavements, heady smells of herbs and spices pervade, and the gay wooden shop signs and greenery are a feature of their main street. These shop signs are dominated by one artist, Pirosmanashvili (Pirosmani). He is my introduction to primitivism, supported by an exhibition of his work in the local art gallery. Grape treading and feasting are the subjects of much of his work. I know that Georgian wine is coveted by Russians from the red letter days it arrives in Moscow's shops. In Tbilisi wine can be tasted straight from the barrels in the basements of many of the shops. I try several.[1]

High above on the Sololaki Hill over- looking Tbilisi stands the *Mother of Georgia* statue erected in 1958 to mark the

---

[1] The News images from the 1992 conflict between Abkhazia and Georgia showed the damage to Tbilisi's main street. Painful to see.

city's 1,500 year anniversary. In her left hand is a bowl of wine, the symbol of welcome, in her right the sword to warn would-be enemies. Georgian dances with their passion and elegance, reiterate these symbols. I remember especially those based on military battles of the past with sharply delineated gender roles. The men with swords, a row of bullets on their black streamlined apparel, precise, incisive movements slicing the air as they leap and strut, perched on the toes of their soft boots. Dancing on the first bent joint of their toes in leather boots with no padding confirms their prowess. While the women gracious in long pale blue dresses, glide silently seemingly unmoving peacefully encircling the men,.

Saturday, leaflets scatter in the street advertising a football match. The script is unlike any I've seen, very decorative, a picture in itself.

On Sunday our guides give us a picnic in the mountains. A glorious day. The picnic includes a ram on a spit, yoghurt, and inevitably black grapes and Georgian wine. Food always tastes better outdoors, to this is added the excellence of Georgian food, its freshness and flavour. We sit on the grass not far from a large church, maybe a monastery. The door is open, releasing the beautiful sound of choral singing. After the meal I stand by that open door as the music soars out into the air beyond. The mountains, the song, the picnic, the sun gently above – magical.

On the last of our three days we visit Mtskheta, the old capital and other villages near Gori, Stalin's birth place. I'm surprised to see pictures of him in the windows of several wooden houses and fresh flowers on his mother's grave. Yet another of the stark differences between Georgia and Moscow.

Spring, summer 1967

April: there are actually some birds on a few trees.

Sun in Moscow and the effect is immediate, no doubt the result of the long, hard winters. Come the first sunny weekend and Muscovites are off to the country, me included. Go to any central railway station and you'll find it packed, and not only by people, whether young, old or indeterminate, but also by rugs; pails of smetana (sour cream); camp beds and not to mention rucksacks. Yes, they're off for a day, maybe two. By the luggage you'd think it's at least for a week. But then the Russians do everything in grand style. No picnic consists simply of ham, cheese and cucumber sandwiches, rather loaves of bread, whole chickens, bottles of wine, milk and smetana, and nearly always shashlik – a mutton kebab bought prepared and cooked in the forest.

The nearest British equivalent is probably a bank holiday when crowds gather at a station for a trip to the coast. But apart from the food, and the frequency of trips, and not waiting for a bank holiday, the other noticeable contrasts here in the late 1960s are the frequency of music and health pursuits. Musical instruments accompany most groups: guitars, accordions and balalaikas will be played in the forest. Hiking boots, baseball shoes, tracksuits accompany group after group of young people. Rucksacks are carried by all. I notice girls don't seem afraid of weight.

I spend much of my first summer exploring Moscow and enjoying the contrast with the depressing February of my arrival. Even the uninspiring courtyard below my flat takes on a new identity.

It's a beautiful spring day in April. I'm sitting in the courtyard. There's a slight, warm breeze; the sun is shining; the birds singing; children playing and the first sign of green on the trees. Unfortunately it's all very dusty, but the rest is so good that I'm ignoring the inconvenience.

In this courtyard there are four rows of benches facing a little open air stage where films are projected in the summer for us residents. Apart from the red brick block which houses my flat, there is an ugly red building and a dilapidated plastered 'house' with two large chimneys either side of it. People live in there. On another side of the courtyard is a wooden house and sheds half hidden by old trees. There's also a small one storey work shop. In stark contrast, just peeping behind the wooden house, is the concrete and steel of an office block on the new Kalinin Prospekt.

A group of boys are playing football – their pitch is the whole courtyard, including underneath my feet. There are seven, about 9-10 years old. I like the way they call themselves *"rebryata"* (fellows). Unfortunately I'm now sitting in the shade. I move into the sun and the boys immediately swoop on my abandoned seat and rearrange it for the goal. One of the Dads joins in. There's more noise than movement at the moment. I think the Dad has been relegated to referee.

On this side I see the flats have balconies and French doors, my flat's definitely on the wrong side overlooking the main road.

On some weekends I explore Moscow's outskirts. Today I walk half an hour from the end of a metro line to find what remains of an old area of Moscow, a settlement of wooden houses amongst the fields. A lovely sunny midday has brought out the men, gathered together on the corner and the babushkas sitting on the benches outside the houses and flats.

Now winter has passed, the yards are being cleaned. Hens are clucking. Children are playing a form of hopscotch on the concrete. Most of the houses are in poor condition and have added sheds, and outhouses for animals. Many of the wooden window frames are carved and each house has its own garden with fruit bushes and trees. There is still no running water, just the pumps in front of the houses and privies in the gardens. These remains of a Moscow village with its primitive conditions, is due to be demolished. But how peaceful it appears in the sunlight.

Another Sunday I'm sitting by the edge of a stretch of water. The seat actually stands in the water. For two minutes it's beautifully peaceful, then two stately black swans, beaks of scarlet arrive with three fluffy cygnets. The male attempts to bite the legs of the two people sitting next to me, whilst the cygnets and female feed – no doubt the male has already eaten. Satisfied, they've paddled on further now. But they caused quite a crowd to gather for some time. A few yards out in the lake there's a small hut for the ducks and birds. Further along there's a glass restaurant extending over the water. I'm going to eat there soon. Music is playing over the loud speakers, but not too near. This is all part of the Economic Achievements Exhibition situated on the northern edges of Moscow. Each republic has its own pavilion. Unsurprisingly most of them are closed – *Na remont*[1]. One remains open. As I enter, bird's song fills the air. Inside photos of silver birch forests decorate the walls with stumps and trunks placed around the room: drawing me into an imaginary forest. This a pavilion displaying natural sculptures. Perched on the stumps and amongst the "grass" are shapes selected from trees to display their beauty. Little has been added or carved, so left to the spectator's imagination.

---

1 *Na remont*, for repair. It's a common notice in Moscow and widely believed used also to prevent entry

My first summer found me several times beside the river Moskva, another favourite of Muscovites.

So on 9th July I'm sitting on a steep slope on the Lenin Hills overlooking the Moskva. It's by no means beautiful – and requires effort to prevent sliding down the slope– but it's the only place where no one else is sitting. Below is a road along which bicycles, motor bikes and occasional jeeps pass by. Beyond the road, the Moskva River flows in front of me, with pleasure boats and barges. To my left spanning the river as it bends is a two tier bridge. The top tier is the highway for buses and other vehicles. The lower level houses the metro, its station spanning the river and connecting the Lenin Hills to the main *Luzhniki* Stadium. On my right is a stretch of river where swimming is possible, it's packed with people.

Everywhere people in swim suits are sunbathing or playing games. Stretched out flat on the wall in front of me are several sunning themselves above a non-swimming area, hopefully they won't fall in. One piece bathing costumes are just coming into fashion. Previously unavailable, now they are being imported. Even so most of the women and girls wear a two piece, best described as a one piece cut in two. There's the common addition of middle aged women sitting around in their underwear – even walking along the road. This is a typical Sunday of the Russians remaining in Moscow: swim suits, sun, ball games and if possible, some greenery and water. Woodland surrounds Moscow – but that's also packed with people and this area is conveniently quite near the centre.

A hydrofoil has just gone past with a rowing boat struggling in its wake. Despite my earlier description, it's quite pleasant here. The trains aren't noisy at all. Police launches keep lashing through the water, prow high in the air, but even their loudspeakers warning people swimming not to go out too far, don't jar. I'm told there's not much chance of committing suicide by drowning here. Two groups below me are playing volley ball. A common sight. Anyone can join in – the circle is simply enlarged and both sexes are welcome. It's good that though nearly every young person plays in one game or another, elderly people play as well, shuttlecock especially. Transistors are almost as much in evidence as they are at Southend.

Time to go.

Vera

I'm fortunate to already have a Russian friend who lives in Moscow. Vera and I met in our teens in Gursuf on the Black Sea coast. I was eighteen and enjoying a Challenge Holiday, organised by the British Young Communists. Vera was from Moscow and on holiday with her family. Her smattering of English enabled us to communicate. We got on well. She introduced me to her parents, her older sister Ulya and husband, who were all most welcoming. I remember sitting on the beach for hours doing my best to answer their stream of questions about England. They were keen especially to compare the cost of living. However, just comparing prices is a poor indicator which I realised gives a false impression of reality. Vera and I kept in touch over the years, and both of us are delighted to meet up again. She lives with her family, who make me welcome throughout my time in Moscow.

Vera has been taking gymnastic classes like many young Russians since she was a child. Today she's invited me to watch her participating in a competition at her club. It's impressive to see so many young girls and boys guiding their bodies in the most amazing contortions but mostly with a grace that denies the years of training and effort involved. Vera is now in her twenties, but still performs with such elegant style.

I don't only visit Vera and her family in Moscow. As the weather improves I am also welcome at their dacha[1]. We take the train – the *elektrichka* to the station named *55 Kilometres* (the distance from Moscow) and walk to their dacha along a country path.

---

1 The traditional house in the country. This now a haven for city dwellers, however grand or basic.

Dachas represent a return to the village way of life. For me they evoke the classics, the tales of Chekhov, Turgenev. For weekends and holidays, it doesn't matter that village limitations apply. In Vera's family dacha water for daily use comes from a container in the garden obtained by pulling a string and positioning the samovar, bowl, or face and hands underneath it. I don't think this container is filled by running water in the house, maybe from a well. Vera's father is master of the samovar, I think for my amusement, often placing an old boot on the steam pipe. As the pine cones burn underneath, an evocative aroma arises with its promise of refreshing Russian tea - tea with a slice of lemon, or a spoonful of jam.

The garden is a delight with its birch trees enclosed from the surrounding forest, a table tennis table, flowers and the inevitable vegetable beds. Produce from the dacha, gathered in the summer and autumn, pickled and transferred to Moscow, has been survival food for many, and important to the diet of all.

I'm delighted to discover that by following a stream, their dacha is just a woodland walk from the arts colony *Abramtsevo*. The colony was established in the late 19th Century by some of my favourite Russian artists I've become familiar with in Moscow's Tretyakov Gallery of Russian art. Artists in the 19th Century critical of the Academy's classical approach became known as the *Peredvizhniki*, (The Wanderers). They wandered around Russia to rediscover the art of the people who in turn became their subject matter. The movement was influential across the arts. The artists involved in the Abramtsevo Colony contributed a range of specialisms.

As we emerge from the trees we see several buildings each interesting in their own right. I spy the carved, wooden hut of Baba Yaga, standing threateningly on its chicken's legs.

Baba Yaga is the witch of Russian folk tales used as a threat to control children's behaviour. The hut was designed by Vasnetsov, the artist who was one of the two main illustrators of these tales. Vasnetsov was also responsible for the mediaeval style of the white church which is central to the Colony and used by the local villagers. The artists' studio is wooden with carved folk motives. Inside the church and the main house, is a traditional Russian stove richly decorated by Mikhail Vrubel's painted majolica tiles.

I never tire of visiting Vera's family dacha and Abramtsevo.

Lavra Monastery, Zagorsk

14th August 1967

Lavra Monastery is the religious complex of Zagorsk, a mixture of religious buildings, including a monastery, and of course, cupolas, some gleaming golden, others of royal blue decorated with gold stars. I've arrived here in the north east of Moscow by public transport. Why? I had been surprised to discover that in this religious centre there remains an active religious seminary despite the State's atheism.

Zagorsk remains a centre for pilgrimage whilst also on the tourist trail. Standing outside the office of the Moscow Patriarch, a man in civilian clothes smoothly greets all passers-by, pilgrims and tourists.

A large group of pilgrims cross the central square. They pass a set of *"The Brothers Karamazov"* which is being filmed, its background one of the churches. The costumed actors, the silent pilgrims and the many elderly Russian worshippers, provide a glimpse of pre-revolutionary Russia to offset the tourists milling round this religious site. I join the worshippers and tourists lumbering up the steps of a nearby church. Old women, the *babushkas*[1], who'd been sitting on the ground, push their way into the church establishing their rights. Inside, a section of large rectangular icons is packed with *babushk*as grandchildren and tourists. The kerchiefed women cross themselves, and wherever they can find a space amongst the tourists, kneel on the floor to bend down and kiss the icons. Their faces upturned, godly simplicity, intent

---

1 *Babushkas* refers generally to older women, as well its specific term for *Grandmother*

to catch every word or at least when the priest mentions the appropriate word to require they cross themselves. There's a softness in these faces which have never known lipstick or powder, only suffering and hard work, both of which they can shed here, or at least feel some recompense in this setting. How striking a contrast between these faces and worn out bodies in their sombre prints with their surroundings – the painted walls and ceilings richly ornamented with silver and gold. A tourist pushes through but is ignored by the kneeling women, so intense are they on their devotions. Then they raise themselves as best they can and move towards the inner sanctuary and the altar with the chanting priests. A young clergyman tries again and again to keep a gangway clear for the priests to pass through the congregation with their swinging incense. A little girl, who in the eyes of the pious woman behind her is misbehaving, is pulled out to face the godly men as they wend their way through. Is this to absolve her of her wickedness?

The seminary. A classroom is full of young men studying theology. Here is another world, a centre where religion is alive and well. I'm astounded by the wealth resplendent in this building, a museum of wealth, a stark contrast to the Russian pilgrims crawling up the hill outside.

I'm reminded of sitting next to the pious old man in Red Square, head in hands chanting the Russian orthodox prayer.

Kalinin Prospekt

October 1967

Throughout the street this weekend there is a sense of business, even urgency. Most noticeable are the young people, they are everywhere. Not in the coffee bars – yet to be opened, but pushing wheel barrows, laying paving stones, wielding spades and pick axes, planting trees along the wide pavements. These are young volunteers who along with the regular builders are making an all-out effort to have the street ready

Two retailers are already open, the Bakery and the 'House of Books'.

The Bakery and the 'House of Books', are both magnificent providing a promise of what will follow. The ground floor of the Bread shop offers loaves of all shapes and flours. The floor above has a tea and coffee bar, and counters laden with sweets, cakes and biscuits. Background music is provided.

The 'House of Books' is also over two floors. Accompanying the books, are posters, stamps and stationery. Next emerges the façade of the new cinema – a mosaic of reds and browns, October scenes of 1917. Not surprisingly, it is named *"Kino Oktybr"*. There are two film studios, a buffet, a library, a hall for dancing and listening to music prior to a film, plus an exhibition hall.

Before the transformation, this area was known as Old Arbat, in the 19th century the residences of the nobility. The ground footprint of *Kalinin Prospekt* covers the same area. The extras are gained by height. It will cater for 320,000 daily shoppers.

I look forward to seeing it then.

I'm surprised to see passers-by and photographers, faces upturned, peer at the buildings towering above them.

It is not surprising that members of the public are taking such an interest. Months before the project began, the Moscow press printed the architects' plans. Discussion ensued from readers' suggestions and criticisms. Now they're here to see the results.

50th Anniversary of the Revolution

November 4th, the early hours, I wake up terrified, there's tanks passing below my window. Is it war? No. It's preparation for the 50th anniversary parade in Red Square. For three nights starting around midnight the tanks roll past for a couple of hours. The same route tanks took to defend Moscow in the Second World War. Some of them are so heavy the very flat seems to move. I hate them.

November 7th 1917: the Russian Revolution: a unique day in world history

Morning 7th November 1967: I wake up to see the US flag flying from its Embassy across the road. How ironic, Moscow the capital of the USSR, born only fifty years ago and attacked by these very countries now flying their flags in diplomatic acknowledgement of what has become a world power.

November 7th 1967: a memorable highlight of my stay in Moscow, I've been included in Moscow Radio's delegation to participate in the anniversary and parade through Red Square. We have a clear sky, bitterly cold, but pleasant November day.

November 7th 1967: millions joyfully celebrate their power. Happy people, proud people, pride in themselves, pride in their country; veterans of the revolution, veterans of the civil war, World War 11, mothers, young people, children, all joyfully express this pride. I was to see that for many theirs was another reality, yet at the time it was the impression I had.

I have to leave home at 6am to gather at the Radio by 7.30am by a prescribed roundabout route. Although the Radio is just a ten minute walk from Red Square, and our time for entering the actual parade is not until past noon, we're conducted away from the Square to cater for the many thousands of participants entering before us. Quite an operation.

Already at 6am, the streets are alive with song, banners, posters, flowers, twigs of autumn leaves. The hours until our entrance are such fun. In our Radio group we're dancing and to survive the stinging November cold, we're playing warming games, helped by mulled wine. One of the games designed to combat the cold involves a circle and thumping one another; no wonder Russians wear thick coats. As we pass other contingents the greeting requires making as much noise as possible. Radio people are quite good at this and we have our own band. Revolutionary songs mingle with the popular dance 'Hully Gully'. Young and old participate in both. Total strangers greet one another with *"S'prazdnikom"*, the special holiday greetings. It's all spontaneous and we're having a great time.

What a sight: golden cupolas and flags of all colours lit up by the clear November sun, and a glimpse of the Moskva River gently flowing in the background to a seething mass of chattering, laughing, singing citizens.

Midday, Red Square:
It's our turn. We're in the Square. Heads swivel to the right as we pass the podium of dignitaries above Lenin's mausoleum. We're on the right flank in the Square so have a clear view. I'm thrilled, the first person I spy is Dolores Ibarruri, "La Pasionaria", legend of the Spanish Civil War.

I avoid looking at Brezhnev and the other identical trilby hats. I have no time for these faceless leaders.

As we leave Red Square, glancing back, red predominates strongly against the intensely blue sky, the sun is shining and the bells of St Basil's ringing; unforgettable. Likewise the image of the children running through the lines of sportsmen, flowers in their hands, woolly caps on their heads; running forwards, ever forwards.

The rest of the day I spend with Sally, a Radio Moscow announcer, and her Finnish family. We wander the streets like everyone else. Gorky Street, the central artery of Moscow, throngs with people strolling up and down, arm in arm, greeting friends, pausing at the Central Telegraph Agency to live again Lenin's declaration, " Peace, Land and Bread' as it resounds from the loud speakers. The 'Internationale' fills Gorky Street and the souls of these people[1].

We have lunch and watch the remainder of the parade on TV. Then joined by a couple of Russians, we make our way to the Lenin Hills.

Evening, The Lenin Hills:
I'm continually amazed at the vast numbers of people. Of Moscow's population of 8-9 million, this evening all 8-9 million seem out on the streets. Friends who watched the fireworks from Red Square maintain that the 8 million were there. Apparently afterwards the militia took on an unusual service - delivering shoes: "who takes size 34? 35s over here". My friend came away with a quite different pair than the ones she'd arrived with.

From our fine vantage point high on the Lenin Hills, the city lies in all its glory, illuminated for the celebrations. Muscovites love it. Gleefully they announce: "That's Kalinin Prospekt, our new street. There's the Kremlin. See the TV tower, that's the highest in the world. Look at Lenin high in the sky." The first

---

1 The actual words I wrote at the time.

firework salute resounds deafeningly above us, over the River Moskva, huge clusters of coloured stars burst and scatter. "Hurrahs" spontaneously break from the watchers. Then the finale, 50 firework salutes – predominantly red: the city, the sky engulfed in the red glow – the colour symbolic of the worker's struggle. 50 Salutes, one for each year of struggle. Years which required super human efforts and the loss of millions of lives. These people want peace. Perhaps nowhere else are there so many who know the price of peace so well or value it so highly.

It isn't the end of the celebrations. A few days later my next door neighbours Lena, Yuri and Sasha invite me to a celebratory meal: red salmon, tuna and other sorts of fish consumed with vodka, brandy and wine. Refusals not allowed.

Then to cap it all, I'm asked to interview for Radio Moscow friends of mine who'd come to the Soviet Union for the parade. My first interview,

My introduction: "All of us have just witnessed a tremendous event, the 50th Anniversary of the world's first socialist revolution. We've watched Moscow as the atmosphere sparkled with people enjoying themselves and celebrating what they've achieved. With me in the studio are three young people from Britain, John Durkin and two others.

You've been to Leningrad and Moscow and had the opportunity of seeing, and most importantly, meeting English-speaking young Russians. What has the revolution achieved for them?"

The following year, I'm given a ticket to attend the May Day celebrations in Red Square as a spectator.

Winter sport

When the winter months come around again in my first year, the experience is so much more positive than my arrival in February; much colder with clear blue skies, sun and thick white snow. The main streets are cleared nightly but the snow remains on the side streets, too settled for grey slush. It is so cold that when my friend Ann comes to visit me, her face reacts so badly, she has to spend the week in the flat.

Muscovites take to skiing during the weekends. Now the crowds gather at the stations for the *elektrichka* to whisk them off to the outskirts of Moscow. Their skis are narrow wooden ones for cross country skiing. Not to be outdone and feeling more at home by this time, I also buy a pair of skis and boots. My first venture out is pasted on my memory. I join the throng, destination unknown, but disembark when I see countryside. I stagger up a hill where there is a plantation of baby fir and birch trees. Then fairyland, the trees' bare branches interlaced sparkling in the sunlight with ice and snow flakes.

I discover I can't ski downhill without falling over – but what joy to roll unhurt in the deep snow.

I've actually been skiing three times now, every Sunday for the last three weeks. Last Sunday was great. I went with Tom into the forests outside Moscow. It was so beautiful, trees laden with snow, the ground covered a soft deep white, glittering like jewels in the sunshine. Certainly no photo can do it justice. Then we left the woods for a valley where hundreds are skiing, I'm frozen from inside out and terribly tired - have beautiful bruises on my legs. Still, I will persevere.

Moscow children provide such a contrast to my own feeble efforts and it's entertaining to watch them, even tiny tots, skiing down the Lenin Hills. Many 'skis' are slices of wood tied to the child's feet with string. These makeshift skis frequently come adrift.

But how these children can ski.

Skating is the other winter sport within the town. The rinks, iced over ponds in the parks, look impressive in the sun and I acquire a smart pair of white boots. Saturday I go skating for an hour, terribly difficult though. I can't yet manage on my own. Now, no amount of sun wins me over, the ice is too unforgiving and I am too tentative. The memory of hitting the icy ground hard in my first week in Moscow last February remains too painful. I'll stick to skiing.

Moscow life

With the coming of warmer weather I can walk to the zoo from my flat. Not my favourite place, but I sometimes go to its open air café - it means sharing a table with the sparrows, so hungry from the cold of winter; they have no inhibitions about taking my food. It is here that I'm first hit by the pungent odour of a favourite 'delicacy'- dried fish. Two elderly men sitting on a bench with a version of our fish and chips, complete with newspaper, plus bottles of beer. But, such a smell!

It is on the corner of *Sadovaya Koltso* and the road to the zoo, that I am invited to a flat in a "Wedding Cake" building. Now I see the internal features that make these buildings a stronghold. The internal doors to the flat are of heavy, solid hard wood, the thickest I've ever seen.

Custom and Morality
There's a bus stop conveniently outside my building. One morning whilst I am waiting there it takes on an added significance. I realise that the three women also waiting are discussing me. And clearly disapprovingly, muttering *"Khuliganka, bes stydnaya"* (hooligan, no shame) or words to that effect. "Is she a girl or a boy"?

It's the jeans. I'm proud of them; the latest fashion recently sent me from home. However, they outrage these upstanding citizens. Their country and their culture, not mine. Ashamed, I return to the flat and change.

This is not my only brush with elderly citizens.

It's my first visit to the Pushkin State Museum of Fine Arts. I'm about to enter the first room but am prevented by the *babushka* attendant shouting *"Devochka, shto vy?"* (girl, what are you doing?), and then roundly scolding me. It's impolite (*nekulturnaya*) to enter in outdoor clothes. I come to realise this makes good sense, the extreme cold outside, the warmth inside. However, I discover it is also a custom to be followed in the summer.

These *babushkas* I come to recognise are not to be ignored. They hold the morality of the country in their hands. But I also notice their kindness; they are the first to give up their seats on a bus or tram to a young child, anyone's child. And as fares are passed to the front of the bus, it is they who ensure citizens get their change passed back to them.

On the 7th of April I'm at the Kremlevskii Theatre to see Shostakovich's opera *"Lady Macbeth of the Mtsensk District"* relaunched by him just in 1963 as *"Katerina Izmailova"*, after being banned since the 1930s. So this is quite an event. Tonight it is being performed by an Estonian company. The audience settles down, the performance proceeds. Then I begin to hear a muttering. It gets louder. People start leaving. The protest grows, eventually only about a third of the audience remain. Unfortunately my Russian is too weak to know whether the music, the libretto or both has evoked the protest. It's the only time I witness such behaviour by a Russian audience.

I attend a Russian lesson at the Foreign Languages Institute arranged for me by Bernie. I make little progress. Never mind my mood is raised by a performance of dancers from Dagestan. After that I'm invited by Bernie to watch the figure skating on TV. Zoya, Bernie's wife, was a winter sports champion in her youth and Bernie is of course, a sports correspondent.

Moscow is being dressed for May Day. Red flags and banners are festooned on buildings across the city.

My mother has been sending me copies of "Woman" for the

Pool. But as usual they have arrived opened.

I notice that in the shops, men are as interested as women in what's being sold - presumably a result of the scarcity of consumer goods, or possibly an indication of equality?

Food
Food is a problem. The State shops are dire. It's not long before I realise that the vegetable stores specialise in potatoes, carrots, and tired looking cabbage. This seems to be their staple offering, not much else. The grocery stores sometimes have cheese and always abundant tins of fish. These tins stacked on the shelves are of fish unknown to me; my Russian does not include marine species – apart from caviar. But I do like the varieties of bread, the dairy products and the confectionary – the chocolates from the *Red Oktybr* factory are tasty, quite rightly famous.[1] The bread shops at least contradict the perception that Russian food stores are empty.

Luckily the state food stores are supplemented by items for sale at the place of work. At the Radio I can often buy oranges from the 3rd floor buffet. Apparently men's brief cases contain not papers, but food bought at work. Oranges and other fruit can also be found at the street kiosks. But, even so, I am beginning to tire of these limitations.

The street kiosks are often manned by disabled people. Everywhere the disabled are evident. Presumably the majority are war victims; many squatting on seemingly makeshift trolleys which are hand propelled along the pavement.

Then a red letter day. Bernie and Zoya invite me over for breakfast.

First this entails a visit to the Central Market. What a

---

[1] A prime chocolate maker which has survived all three forms of government, Tsarist, Socialist and now still exists post Soviet.

revelation. Here is every product I could wish for, and many more besides. But the prices. Vendors are allowed to charge up to ten times the price of State shops, so not everyone can afford to shop here, although there are plenty who do. Fresh fruit and flowers flown in daily from Georgia, plentiful milk products including *Ryazkenka* my favourite (fermented baked milk), *Kefir* (a mixture of yeast and bacteria left overnight in milk sometimes described as fermented) producing a slightly sharp taste, *Prostokvasha* (soured milk similar to yoghurt) and of course *Smetana*. Cheeses including *Tvorog* (like cottage cheese) from *kolhozes* (collective farms), often displayed as small offerings including honey and honey comb by individual peasants. I'm welcome to taste their wares. The honeys have such a variety of flavours, the cheeses too. Tomatoes. How I've been pining for a fresh tomato. Laden with fresh vegetables and other delights, we return for breakfast. This is my introduction to fresh raw cauliflower as a morning salad. It tastes good and is much appreciated.

This morning an excellent tenor on the radio is singing rousing songs of the 30s. It's the first time I've heard them broadcast, but this programme is setting the scene for November 7th the 50th anniversary of the revolution. I've now heard three songs – I know them all – "…defending the USSR; then left, right, left – there's a place comrade for you…" my parents sang them in my childhood. It gives me a feeling of home.

I learn about other Russian customs and traditions from my flat. The end of winter, a time to rejoice, is marked by the unsealing and washing of windows. Every one's at it. So must I; mine are filthy.

One evening a friend visiting with a bottle of wine discovers, to his amazement, that I have no opener. No matter. Going wineless is not an option. He knows exactly what to do. He seizes my cushion cum pillow, somewhat to my consternation, which is further increased, when he places it against the wall, the top of the bottle pushed into it and proceeds to hit the base of the bottle hard. I am dreading seeing red wine flowing on pillow and wall. But no, out comes the cork, all else untouched. Apparently this is a fool proof way to get at the wine.

Walking home at night, which I do frequently after seeing so many performances, I realise I feel completely safe. Elsewhere drunks could be a problem, not here. In the winter after drinking indoors, the cold outside hits their legs, they collapse in the snow. But many are still to be seen in a similar position in the warmer weather as well. Russian drunks appear less belligerent than in some other cultures; they are more likely to have reached a state of singing mournful songs or reciting poetry before passing out. Daytime as well, despite roaming around Moscow, I have never experienced that physical feeling of unease that fear can bring. This is despite the fact that serious drinking can start early morning. I now know that if I want to share a bottle of vodka, I queue outside the grocers whilst waiting for it to open, indicate by a three finger tap on the side of my chin that I'll go threes for a bottle, and inevitably acquire drinking companions.

Cost of living
My pay this year is all in roubles. I open a Russian bank account, but without being paid in sterling am unable to purchase any desirable goods available in the foreign currency stores. I mainly spend my money on records, books, and entertainment – all of which there is a rich feast. Travel and household expenses are so stable and so reasonable that I can ignore them. Indeed, one of the attractive aspects I find of life in Moscow is the certainty that the costs of basic living remain stable. My rent is minimal, heating likewise, about 5 roubles per month. The cost of a kilo of oranges in comparison is 2 roubles 50 kopecks and the excellent ice cream – all natural and eaten throughout the year, is 10k -15k,

the favourite vodka, *Stolichnaya* is 3R.62k a bottle. Moscow transport ranges from 5 kopecks (100 kopecks to a rouble) for the metro, 5 for the bus, the trolleybus costs 4K and the tram three. These prices are for any destination within the city, and remain stable, as does the exchange rate 2R to £1.00.

So I understand how this stability in basic living costs gives Muscovites the freedom to splash out when an opportunity presents itself such as I witness in the Pool one day. Someone announces when she arrives for work, that Italian shoes have arrived in GUM, the main department store in Red Square. This is special, not to be missed. All work stops. She makes a list of several pool members' shoe sizes. Off she goes. Money is not a problem. If anyone doesn't have sufficient now, it is lent by colleagues. Next month's pay is secure, rent, heating, travel - all are accounted for and they will have money for the shoes.

Throughout 1967 there have been a variety of events to celebrate the 50th anniversary of the revolution. I am so fortunate to be here at this time. One event stands out above all, apart from November 7th itself. I write home, "Just heard (12th October '67) at the Conservatoire, Oistrakh conducting Rostropovich in a Shostakovich' Cello Concerto. What a cellist, marvellous. They hugged one another on the platform, such warmth, such mastery."

December, and I'm off home for Christmas, a surprise visit to my parents.

1968

Second year in Moscow

The Radio
It feels quite different, I'm bolder, know my way around, and most exciting, I've got a toe into some interesting radio work – at last. I have become the regular announcer for the weekly concerts to the UK and other English-speaking countries: "This is Radio Moscow... ". I even get to write the links myself. Then Doris, doyenne of listener's letters to Radio Moscow, hands this one to me, "Has your country got no pretty girls? All we see is photos of big machines and missiles". I am to answer it on Radio Moscow's programme for young listeners, "This Younger Generation".
And excitingly I get paid for the first piece I write. How's that!

Eventually I not only introduce the Youth and Music Programmes regularly, I do some reporting and write my own material. This is what I had been expecting my work to be. It is far more interesting than the style editing which I was so ill prepared for. In trying to edit the items translated by members of the pool, I have found myself mimicking Russian phrasing in my English. Whereas, when writing my own items and broadcasting them, the English is more natural. Except that humour can present a particular problem in translation – being translated into Russian to receive the ok before it can be transmitted. But though still having to do some style editing, this activity is much more satisfying and I hope of some worth. I do wonder if anyone listens to these broadcasts back in England though - apart from my parents.

I am now in the studios area frequently and so get to know more about the potpourri of announcers: English, American, the English-speaking Russians, the jolly Danish announcer whose Danish sounds as if he's got hot potatoes in his mouth and Sally the friendly Finnish announcer.

Both Doris and Tom tell me more about themselves, although Tom is more forthcoming than Doris.

Doris came to the Soviet Union before the war, and then when having to choose between Soviet citizenship or leave, she chose to stay with her Russian husband. The Cold War meant those like her were unable to visit the UK for many years. I have the impression she has carved out a satisfactory life for herself. She regularly spends the weekends in her dacha with her two dogs.

Tom, like Doris became a Soviet citizen. But unlike Doris, seems dissatisfied with his lot. After participating in the Spanish Civil War, Tom was unable to return home. Something to do with plans finding their way to Russia from the Bristol aircraft factory where Tom had worked prior to Spain. With his Spanish wife, he found refuge in the USSR, but then like Doris, had to take Soviet citizenship. He feels abandoned by the British Communist Party.

I represent the England he so misses so is happy to chat with me. On one occasion he takes me to meet an elderly guy, a sailor who had refused to unload British armaments intended to support the Whites in the Civil War. Hence, he also is unwelcomed back home.

Zena does less broadcasting for the English section, but is friendly and introduces me to her daughters. However, she moves to Mongolia for a year to broadcast from Ulan Bator. She invites me to visit her there. I've always wanted to go to Mongolia. Unfortunately I am unable to buy a ticket in roubles, as a foreigner I have to pay in sterling – which I don't have.

Yuri and I do a number of interviews together for "This Younger Generation".

Bernie is friendly with all the announcers on our floor, particularly with the Americans, so I spend time with them. He does regular sports commentaries and feature programmes as well. Both of the two American women are tall and stately and cut imposing figures. One in particular is known apparently for her stylish hats. On arrival her luggage had been noticed for its number of hat boxes – not a common sight in 1940's Moscow. They came to Moscow as administrative employees of the US embassy and stayed having married Russians. Both women give the appearance of being apart from Soviet politics. Friends of Bernie's from Moscow University's School of Journalism also contribute to the American section; their English is proficient and their journalism professional. Vladimir Posner, like Bernie, at one time a citizen of the US, is urbane with excellent English. In the 1970s he became chief commentator on the North American service of Radio Moscow, Joe Adamov, presents the programme's 'Moscow Mailbag'[1]. When I accompany Bernie to the Journalists and Writers Clubs, we are often joined by one or both of them.

The following items are examples of my broadcasting.

---

[1] Gorbachev's introduction of *glasnost' and perestroika* led to a number of interviews on the BBC with Russians whose voices I recognised: Vladimir Posner and Joe Adamov. There was also a fascinating interview with Bernie's wife, Zoya Zarubina.

Concert – excerpt from one of my first concerts

Announcer: This is Radio Moscow

Our concert today starts in sunny Moldavia, a southern republic famous for its vineyards, fruit orchards, wine and song. We'll begin with the popular *Kalinka*. And we have none less than the Red Army choir to perform it with of course soloist Evgeny Belyaev. Belyaev has become known in France as *Monsieur Kalinka*, his voice is so associated with this song.

Those of you who've seen the choir perform, or even have a picture, will know it consists of almost one hundred men. The choir, the orchestra and the large group of dancers all wear army uniform. Our listeners ask if they are professionals or regular army members. Well, they are now professionals, although the choir originally developed from an amateur group in the army. The choir still draws on army talent when needing to replenish. Furthermore, much of the programme consists of army songs, always popular in Russia……

Kalinka….

Announcer: Next you'll hear the sonorous tones of the organ in the Dom cathedral from Latvia's capital, Riga. This superb cathedral with its outstanding organ is a mecca for all lovers of organ music…..

Announcer: Back to the Red Army choir with *Korobeiniki*, The Pedlar's Tune has become popular, particularly with skaters…..

Announcer: Now the Osipov State Russian Folk Orchestra, which is almost fifty years old, performs with their triangular three string balalaikas. The clack, clack sound comes from the wooden spoons. You'll also hear the shepherds' horn or reed flute....

Announcer: Time to slow down for something quieter and even sentimental here is the Russian Bayan. This is an instrument which resembles the accordion. However, instead of keys, the player presses buttons creating a deeper and richer sound. .....

So here is my first piece for Radio Moscow's youth programme

Announcer: This is Radio Moscow. "This Younger generation"

We've received a letter from a young Irish listener. He asks, "Hasn't your country any pretty girls? All we see of Russia is photos of big machines and missiles."

Well, British holiday makers I've spoken to in Moscow have been pleasantly surprised by the number of good looking young people and their standard of dress. One man had been told by his mates at work that everyone would be sour faced and drably dressed. He ended up using rolls of film in his eagerness to record all the attractive girls in eye catching summer dresses. Anyway I'll tell you about young people in Moscow and their interest in fashion.

On my strolls around the city, I've seen square glass buildings sprouting up almost overnight. These are the new type beauty salons, but not just to look after top knots. You can get yourself over-all serviced as it were; whilst your hair is in rollers you can be having a manicure on the next floor or visit the chiropodist. Then out you emerge with the total look – beautiful toes matching beautiful heads.

As to fashion, often as not with pretty girls go pretty clothes. Sedate, but slowly creeping-up minis can be seen more and more frequently. And Russian girls can certainly wear them. On the whole, I'd say that young women here have excellent figures. This is probably due to all the sport they take part in; even the factories have their own gyms and sports grounds. Popular at present are shift dresses, straight or with a slight flare, particularly when in plain linen inset with a band of traditional Russian embroidery. They are actually going to be on sale in Britain next year. There's also the Russian peasant look - a short shift dress with a wide contrasting band at the hem, neck and sleeves, sometimes worn with matching head square to complete the peasant effect.

Boys are wearing hip-hugging (nothing to do with Hippies), bellbottoms – with a difference. They are high-waisted with a wide waist band plus a pleat at the bottom of the outside leg. In the middle of the pleat is a row of small buttons. All for equality, girls have a similar line of buttons down the centre front of their flared skirts or peeping out from a back pleat.

Incidentally having mentioned equality I reckon an interest in life can influence looks. The opportunities, and hence the actual number of young people having interesting jobs, is far higher than in Britain. And this affects girls. Take technical institutes, around four times as many girls attend them here compared to Britain. I'm impressed that the fairer sex is on an equal footing in making the country tick.

Back to fashion. At present you'll still find better designs in the magazines than in the shops, but most young people either make their own, or have them made by dress makers. The latter surprised me at first, but then young girls don't start with the disadvantage of being under-paid, women get equal pay with men. It's common to take a magazine picture to be used as a pattern for the dressmaker. Designs from the GDR (German Democratic Republic) are popular which are not dissimilar from British designs. It's the cutters who are most sought after. In all the main material shops there's a special section. The customer hands over their chosen material and magazine picture, the cutter takes the customer's measurements, who then sits and waits until the garment is cut ready to sew at home.

I'll return to the letter of our Irish friend. Certainly the Soviet Union has placed its main emphasis on developing heavy industry. It has had to, as would any country building itself to a world power from scratch. But now due to the terrific progress that has been made, it's possible to turn more attention to the production of consumer goods. Light industry, according to this year's statistics, is increasing production at the same rate as heavy industry. For the first time it looks like the Russians are taking a five year fashion leap; judging by the Soviet fashions at the World Fair in Montreal and the international fashion show being held in Moscow. There's a pilot group of designers planning to put Moscow on the fashion map and giving the young look to the with-it worker. The designers will be choosing fashions for mass production from these shows so we will be seeing the new cosmonaut fashions in shiny fabrics with a smooth line effect in the Moscow stores. Yes, the Russians have their feet on the fashion ladder and when the Russians tackle something they go for it in a big way. So watch out London and remember our listener in Ireland, with the export of fashion goes the export of pretty girls.

Thoughts for future Younger Generation programmes

This Younger Generation – Having now begun to broadcast this programme, I made some suggestions to the editors in an aim to enliven the programme. I've Included them here to give a flavour of my thinking at the time. They must have met with some approval, as evident in the programme on the Komsomol which followed. Subsequently I also conducted some outside interviews.

Suggestions for Radio Moscow's youth programme.

What is our aim?
1. To inform young people in Britain about their peers in the Soviet Union.

2. To hold their interest and in doing so counter negative portrayals of socialism.

What is the context?
Our young listeners differ considerably from previous generations. A person of eighteen was born in 1950, after the Second World War. Their political awareness dates from the mid to late 60s. The intense period of cold war in the 1950s is lessening. Despite the basic contradictions between the two systems, this decade has witnessed an outward semblance of contact, even cooperation between the USSR and Britain. Without delving into the political reasons for this, it has meant an increasing awareness of the Soviet Union in the UK. Trade and culture opening up means the name Soviet or of other East European states is no longer unknown. Soviet watches such as *Seconda* are available and affordable, Soviet cameras with Leica lenses from the GDR are respected. Advertising of

such items is quite widespread and the items no longer owned only by communists. Travel, to Bulgaria, unknown when I spoke about its music at school in the 1950s, is now a popular holiday destination, buses display adverts, 'Visit Bulgaria, land of sunshine'. Visitors from the UK are coming to Russia, especially school groups and students learning Russian.

The Soviet Union is acknowledged as one of the two major world powers and so is less ignored in the news. The conspiracy of silence is ending. The attention given to socialism in general and the Soviet Union in particular, has increased considerably. Soviet space achievements are too successful to ignore.

Not all is positive of course but, nor all negative. The BBC film on Novosibirsk and Science City was excellent. It aroused so much interest that there has been a repeat showing. The Sunday magazines now feature aspects of Soviet life. Occasions such as the Moscow Mayor's visit to Britain made an impact when in his interview on TV he detailed plans to introduce free rents by 1970. Such occurrences leave a positive impression even though they in no way lead to mass membership of the British Communist Party.

But the outcome amongst some young people is an interest in socialism and the USSR. And for those questioning the status quo, socialism is considered as one possible alternative.

Who are the young listeners to Radio Moscow?
I would divide them roughly into three groups:

1. The 15-18 age group with a general, healthy interest in the SU, not young communists but youngsters who want to know about young Russians, how they live and think. They may have an interest in the current issues of nuclear weapons, peace and Vietnam.

2. Those who are politically active are involved in peace marches, in debates at school, in youth clubs, attend political classes and regular meetings. Each of the main political parties has an active youth organisations.

3. Students with a special interest especially those studying Russian and wanting to explore its context, the literature and arts - particularly contemporary art.

The interest is there. How to hold it?

Presentation is important. The young person in the west has been brought up on just that, the outside wrappings, all the advertising and selling in which the west excels. A straight translation of a *Pravda* editorial, or even *Komsomolskaya Pravda*, can hardly compete.

Indeed if the content of a programme appears as blatant propaganda they will not listen, unless to laugh. It is no use preaching about the superiority of the socialist system. Information must be given in such a way that the listener draws the desired conclusion. They should feel that they have thought for themselves and not been told what to think. British youth have been brought up on what is termed objectivity, a balanced view. It matters little if this is so, the fact remains that they expect to be shown two sides of the picture. Additionally young people tend to dismiss the status quo and all power politics in general.

I think the most effective form of propaganda is to show the similarities of young people despite the different political systems. Listeners are interested in the day to day life of young Russians and for some, their attitudes to matters of world importance: Vietnam, world hunger, racism, nuclear weapons. From this can stem access to what socialism offers young people.

Teenagers are lively, so should our programmes be. Wherever possible have young Russians themselves talking. There could be more on the spot recordings, harder work but more rewarding and group discussions between young people about the issues of our time. Lively talk is difficult when written in another language and passed through the translator's mill. Why not have Russian students of English sometimes broadcasting.

An example of such an approach could be a programme on the Komsomol:

How about starting with a jazz band from one of the Komsomol cafes? Then posing questions such as, 'What is this – jazz and in Moscow? Where is it from? A youth café, What is a youth café? A café run by the Komsomol? What is that? The Komsomol ……...

I followed up these thoughts with the following suggestions of topics

Programme suggestions:

1. Travel, Central Asia, Siberia, archaeological expeditions, how young Russians spend their holidays (tackle early when young people in UK are thinking about their holidays).

2. Siberia - new towns, young volunteers working there

3. Aid to Vietnam

4. Social problems – what they are , what's being done

5. Young people's opinion on new trends in the arts.

6. Sport, featuring youth participants in coming Olympics

7. Komsomol – its role and activities

8. Pioneer activities and palaces eg space training, children's theatres

9. Opinions of world events by young people who speak English

10. Youth festival in Sofia – news item

11. Leisure – on the spot recordings at youth cafes, clubs, factories

12. Research conducted by young scientists

13. Soviet jazz

14. Attitudes to talks on the Warsaw Pact and NATO

15. Prospects for newly-weds

Writing my own programmes as well as broadcasting them was far more fulfilling. Although not without some frustrations as expressed in this letter to my parents:

"I've just heard a programme that I did with some young Russians. We spent four hours editing the tape and thought we had produced quite a good job. Yesterday it was broadcast after I went home it was further edited. Because they did it without consulting me they cut out (what I considered), the most interesting bits. I'm absolutely furious. The bloke isn't here today, but on Monday I'll inform him that if I do work it is not to be tampered with without consulting me.

What follows are transcripts of some of the programmes I wrote and broadcast.

This Younger Generation:
The Komsomol

Announcer: "This is Radio Moscow. This Younger Generation. (tape of jazz in Youth café)

Not bad. That was a recording of the ….. jazz group playing in a café in central Moscow. It's a youth café entirely run by young people. Who are they? They are young communists known here as Komsomols, members of the Komsomol. And that's just what two of our listeners, John Hunt from Lancashire and Bob Parker from London, want to know about – the activities of the main youth organisations in the Soviet Union. The Komsomol has a membership of 23 million, aged between 14 and 28, and on the increase, so I reckon it can safely be called a main youth organisation by anyone's standards

The café with the jazz band, is just one aspect of Komsomol activity. In their leisure time young people like more or less the same things wherever they live, but they don't always have the same wherewithal. This is where the Komsomol is useful. It provides facilities and organises events – from a local group organising a popular activity like a hike, a skiing weekend, or a national pop festival. The Komsomol has its own cinemas, and runs its own youth clubs. There's a new one currently being built near Moscow University. It promises to be quite something. it will have painting and sculpture studios, as well as scientific laboratories and workshops with up to the minute equipment plus excellent sport facilities including a swimming pool. Not only will it be run by the Komsomol, but members have helped build it.

The Komsomol claims to be a great builder. Its aim is to build communism in the USSR. You might well say that's some lofty aim, but it's set out in concrete terms. In the last few years dozens of new towns have been built by Komsomol members, particularly in under-developed areas of Siberia – where the going is anything but easy. Hundreds of projects like new power stations are also on their slate. The towns they've built are then mainly run by young people: school heads at 22 years of age, factory foremen of eighteen years. Much of the work is done by 'shock teams' supplemented by volunteers after work and during holidays. The Komsomol considers that this initiative is part and parcel of developing a communist culture with its intention that state functions be eventually run by citizens themselves.

I suppose this is really the crux of Komsomol activity – helping the young individual to become a fully developed person. The Komsomol's political education and all round social activity are geared to this aim, whether it is a few people gathering to discuss how to prepare for coming exams, a meeting on the role of the state, or organising voluntary work to raise money for Vietnam. But perhaps I'd better stop here to tell you something about the organisation's structure.

The Komsomol has groups everywhere there are young people. They aim for groups of about twenty, enough to get a good discussion, but small enough for the members to get to know one another.

Each group elects a member to represent them at district level, then at regional level and so on up to the national body. The Komsomol is much involved in the running of the country. I was impressed to learn that Moscow's Mayor attends the meetings of the Moscow City Komsomol. He gives a report of the council's work, takes up suggestions and answers any criticisms made by the Komsomol. It seems the Komsomol ensures that in this country at least, the opinion of young people is not only listened to, but valued as well.

I hope, John and Bob, this answers your question.

Women's Day

Broadcast 5th March 1968, 16.00 hrs.

Today is Women's Day, and we're celebrating our holiday. So this is a recording of me, for Radio Moscow is being manned only by men today, I expect they'll manage.

Women's Day dates back to the beginning of the 20th century, but was not made a public holiday until a couple of years ago. Now it is, and what a holiday. Presents are to be expected from the men folk; chocolates and flowers, mimosa is just out, and presents made by children. Last weekend the shops were crowded with men buying cards, some of them seem to know a lot of women, but it's not only for wives and friends. Every working woman receives at least one card from their male staff, another from the Trade Union and also from management. In the Radio pool each of us had a small pot of flowers on our desks as well. The Trade Union has organised a concert for which we have received personalised invites. Throughout the week there's been a festival of films focussing on women, many showing the great leaps made from illiteracy and backwardness to their legal status of equality. Women were given equal rights to men in 1918, barely a year after the revolution.

Women grumble that they have too much to do, they bear the brunt of running the home whilst working full time, and with still far too few labour saving appliances, but these are factors that they can see are steadily improving[1]. At least women are recognised officially as equal human beings and on Women's Day they shine as such. For some time I've been trying to get a

---

1 1969 decision to give the Komsomol control of domestic services eg laundry, many more now being built

dress made, but the dress makers have been far too busy. Now I know why. It's with new finery for the holiday.

Kindergarten and first grade children have also been busy learning poems which they proudly recite to their mothers and then give the cards and small presents they've made at school. For many mothers that might well be the high point of their holiday. How are women themselves celebrating their day? It seems to me that it might well mean extra work not less. No Russian family can have a holiday without a feast, and who's going to prepare it? Restaurants are one answer. All are fully booked. The same applies to the theatres and concert halls. Leading artists perform for this occasion.

That's why I feel that visitors to the Soviet Union will find women really are appreciated here. That's not only for the heroic part they played in the history of the country, particularly in the Second World War which is still vividly remembered, or just for the difficult subsequent years when the country had to be reconstructed, its loss of over twenty million people put much of the burden on women. Now they play their part in the country's development for the future. The young Soviet women of today are educated, intelligent and healthy. And on that note I'll finish and wish every woman in Britain all the very best

Industrial Folk Crafts school (1968)

Announcer: The following programme was prepared in the studios of Radio Moscow for stations in the United States and Canada

(Music recording of wooden spoons)

The *Khokloma* spoons, a sound familiar in Russian folk music.

In the talk that follows, Genia Browning tells you about her visit to the Moscow Folk Craft School where she found out how these *Khokhloma* spoons are made.

Browning: In this modern age of computers and minimalism in design, tradition has often to take a back seat and this applies to folk art as much as anything else. So it's always encouraging to hear of places where a concerted effort is being made to keep alive the best of the old, and not only that, but to introduce the old into contemporary life, not as something quaint but as part and parcel of the modern environment.

So I'm pleased to be visiting the Industrial Folk Craft School in Moscow. It's a specialist school to develop expertise in traditional folk arts. Its graduates will meet the growing commercial demand for such products. But, and this is an important one, this is no cheap mass production, but the reproduction of traditional forms and techniques and incorporation of this knowledge into contemporary design. The students study a wide range of the country's folk art to become experts in their chosen speciality, and emerge as creative artists arising from their expertise.

This creative process is evident when I visit a class of senior year carpet students. They are designing a child's rug for their diploma project. It has to be presented within a three dimensional model in a room setting, to be viewed in context. These students had previously completed an intensive course in carpet weaving technique and a general course of folk arts. Rug and carpet weaving is taught both on hand looms and industrial machines. I am attracted to the flower patterned floor coverings from Kursk.

Given the vast territory of the USSR there is a great variety of traditional folk art forms. I'm far from exaggerating when I say great variety. In the Russian Federation alone a hundred regions have their own distinctive folk art. Students studying lace for example, can become experts in traditional lace design from a range of areas including Kirov, Vologda or Moscow regions. In other rooms students study wooden, bone or stone sculpture. Wood carving uses Siberian birch as it has done for centuries. Arkhangelsk region traditionally uses bone and the Gorky area soft stone. These specialisms begin in the student's second year.

In their first year all students study a general art course with an emphasis on the traditional techniques of icon painting. Icon painters' traditional use of heated aluminium to produce their gold colour has been adopted by the folk artists for papier-mâché boxes and the *Khokhloma* ware.

The beautiful *Palekh* papier-mâché boxes are well known internationally. Their lids are adorned with fiery galloping steeds in flaming red hues, graceful Russian maidens, and exciting fire birds of folk legend rising from white crested waves. In addition to the icon technique of aluminium, icon influence is also evident in *Palekh's* exquisite miniatures, striking on their black or full colour background.

Whereas *Palekh* boxes use tempera, boxes from *Fedoskino* are oil based. The papier-mâché is saturated with linseed oil, as is the paint, and then baked in the oven after which it can be treated like wood. The first heated layer of paint is black. The design is then painted in white and reheated. The colours are painted on top and heated again. The result is harder and longer lasting than varnish. The layers give depth to the design. The gold of the boxes like those from *Palekh* and other regions comes from the heated aluminium.

Common to all Russian folk art is the flaming brilliance and richness of the reds. Red also predominates on the wooden spoons you heard earlier. They are part of the family known as *Khokhloma* ware. It's found decorating almost every kind of kitchen utensil. The wooden spoons are completely heat resistant, like the boxes they are oven baked. The wood is coated with the layer of aluminium paint providing the gold background when heated. The design traditionally consists of stylised flowers and plants, mostly executed in red and black.

Now would you expect to find a dentist's drill in an art school? Well maybe your imagination is better than mine, but I was truly surprised, although come to think of it, walrus and mammoth tusks aren't really so different from human teeth. And the art students become very expert in handling the drill. Bone combs and caskets of fine spun tracery of birds and flowers and other intricate designs are on show in the school's exhibition room where students' work is displayed on a fortnightly basis. There are also contemporary looking small ornaments depicting an Eskimo or reindeer. Carving animals is traditional. In northern Siberia, hunters used to produce an animal carving as an offering to the gods for a successful hunt.

Old fashioned lace is top fashion for collars and cuffs. Thanks to my visit, I kid myself I know how to make my own. All that's needed is a small hobby horse, countless pins, a detailed design, oh and skill and infinite patience.

Many of the girls in the embroidery room will go into the clothing industry and design the folk embroidery on Russian dresses that is becoming so popular. In the exhibition room are a number of these dresses the girls have made. They not only design the decoration but design and make the whole garment. My eye is caught by the coveralls for nursery school teachers. They have big handy pockets with bright colourful designs that will certainly appeal to the children.

However, not all that looks like embroidery is embroidery. Some of the decorative patterns in red, blues and greens in fine thread on hand towels and table cloths, appear to be embroidery, but are in fact woven. However, as a layman I find it difficult to tell the difference. In the weaving room the looms are antiquated, but this is deliberate. The students learn the old techniques, there is little concession to the computer age.

The course at the school lasts four years. The intake of four hundred students joins from secondary school. The entrance exam is stiff. Competition is high. Entry examinations include Literature, Drawing and Painting.

In their first year students continue their general education as well as the foundation art course. I noticed English words on the blackboard left over from a language lesson in the rug making room. By the fourth year, the students are expected to be aware of the suitability in the contemporary context, the surroundings and the economic potential of their specialism. All these factors must be evident in their final diploma. This informs their work for general production, as evident in the carpet weavers' preparation of the nursery rug.

On graduating, the most advanced students are given places in higher institutions like the Textile Institute. This can lead to post graduate work. A potential outcome is then employment at the Moscow Scientific Research Institute in Folk Art. The majority of students go to work in industry. I wonder if there is sufficient demand for their skill and expertise. After all, though this is the only school of its kind in Moscow, each of the more important folk art regions like *Palekh* has its own workshops to train young specialists. The Principal of the school is adamant though that not only is there sufficient demand, but it is on the increase. This year, the school will double its intake of students. What about the appeal for teenagers to learn old traditions? Well, it appears that's no problem either. The school doesn't advertise, it already has so many applicants. Youngsters apply from all over the Soviet Union.

A fascinating visit made extra enjoyable by my leaving with presents from the students: a wooden painted spoon, embroidery and a small sample of a woven carpet together with a carved animal in bone. Lucky me.

Announcer : That was Genia Browning telling you about her visit to the Moscow Folk Crafts School.

This is Radio Moscow Broadcast 16.00 hours from Radio Moscow to England

Author G. Browning, Editor T. Kitsova, Department Head, V. Levin

Pionerskaya Pravda

"Get me Yuri Gagarin's brother, telephone number, and so on...." obviously, a news man rapping out orders to his secretary.

I'm sitting in the offices of a newspaper alright, but this isn't just any paper, this is *Pionerskaya Pravda,* the three times weekly national paper for the 9–14-year-olds. Its four pages are illustrated in colour with photos and drawings, and it sells for the grand price of one kopeck, that is less than a penny. But I don't think the price is the only reason for its mass circulation of nine million. In fact, it's the top of the Soviet Press hit parade. Why? Well, this is what I intend to find out from the Editor.

I am impressed with the Editor at first sight, a warm and interesting youngish woman. After talking to her for two hours, this first impression is confirmed. She obviously loves her work, loves the children she is working for, she has an intelligent appraisal of their needs and a determination to meet them.

The paper's aim is far reaching, to raise children's interest in study and in life, not simply to instruct and provide information, but to encourage them to think for themselves.

How is this done? The Editor cites a young boy who sent in the question, "Why is man on earth, what for?" This could have been answered in an article by some learned professor says the Editor, "But what value is that to the child?" Instead, the letter was printed in the paper and thrown open to our readers. Thousands, literally twenty-one thousand replies were sent in. A special edition of the paper was devoted to them which then formed the basis of a book. It became a best seller.

One of the most successful ways the paper develops the children's interests is by the *Olympiada* sponsored by the paper three times a year. These are giant competitions in which thousands of children participate. The winners of the latest Olympiad met the head of the Academy of Sciences, Academician Keldish, who maintained it was as useful for him as for the children. Not least it showed him what interested the future generation in the scientific field. In another Olympiad, the winners, a whole class from a school in the Ukraine had cosmonaut Andrian Nikolayev stay with them for three days. Apparently he devoted his time solely to them, despite the city fathers trying to woo him with official events.

It appears that a range of competitions throughout the year are sponsored by the paper. Last year seven million children participated in a football tournament. Currently a chess tournament is being held, the readers competing against Mikhail Tal, Grandmaster and ex-world champion. He plays black, the children white. Whites' moves are determined by the most common suggestion sent in by the paper's readers. Letters, telegrams, telephone calls, they arrive from throughout the Soviet Union.

It seems the most popular of the paper's activities is what could be loosely called "The War Game". Now don't let that worry you. As the Editor reassures me, all youngsters like to play at 'goodies and baddies', cowboys and Indians wherever they are, so why not harness it to something worthwhile. The fifteen million who play this game learn all sorts of useful skills, including radio transmitting, nursing and first aid and compass navigation. The tracking is based on an old Russian game of capturing a fortress and searching for a banner by compass. Every year different competitions are based on this game and held around the country. Last year's was in the farthest north, in Vladivostok. Two fourteen-year-old girls from Moscow who were travelling there for the final, put their knowledge of first aid to good use. A fellow passenger suffered heart failure. I'm told the young girls demanded the crowd disperse, fetched a doctor and then nursed the passenger on the seven-day journey. Apparently on arrival the patient was able to walk off the train as right as rain.

Is the paper political? "To keep the child away from politics is itself political", is the Editor's response. "Children today are subject to so much mass media, particularly TV that it would be wrong to not try and help them understand what it's all about". This is done in a number of ways.

The paper is the Pioneer paper of the Pioneers - the national children's organisation. One of its aims is "Love for your country", so the paper carries regular features on the history of the Soviet Union and on the contemporary life of the republics. There are also international items to develop the children's love and respect for people the world over.

Another area addressed is the difficult one of moral education, much of which is in response to the children's own requests. Many of them are concerned with the eternal boy/girl themes. "Can you be in love in the 8th form?" The Editor emphasises that "The thing is not to laugh, but to treat the problem seriously." Judging by their letters, that approach appeals to our readers. We have a permanent staff of twenty four and further rely on volunteers, just to deal with the letters ".

It seems the Editor and staff of *Pionerskaya Pravda* are doing a good job.

The Komsomol Office

Following my visit to *Pionerskaya Pravda,* I decided to speak to the Soviet youth organisation - the Komsomol.

Yuri Gagarin - cosmonaut, Valery Brumel - many time world high jump champion, what have they in common? Not only are they both Soviet citizens, as such they were reared by the Komsomol. Is the Komsomol just concerned with outstanding personalities? So to find out I've arranged to visit the office of the Komsomol. No, is the answer. I'm informed that the Komsomol aims to bring up every young Soviet person in the spirit of selflessness, courage, love of humanity, hatred of injustice. In keeping with these ideals each member wants to perform some great exploit, hence the role models.

It seems this is backed up by readers' letters to the Komsomol paper, *Komsomolskaya Pravda.* The letters refer to their ideals in life, their aim to follow communist principles of honesty, chivalry, humanism, happiness, living for others, being useful in society. As one letter expresses it, "the society we are building cannot be static, we must keep thinking for it to move ahead".

The letters show these young people have a sober assessment of reality and hate indifference, passivity, and scepticism. They strive towards the new, as expressed in the songs of the young people who go to work in the virgin lands.

The Komsomol claims it is a mass non-party organisation, although I note its main task is to render assistance to the CPSU by raising young people in the spirit of fidelity to communist ideas. Apparently almost all fourteen-year-olds applied to join in 1967. Its national newspaper, *Komsomolskaya Pravda,* has a circulation of five million. Its range of other publications bring the total circulation to fifteen million.

The Komsomol of each Republic organise events specific to their republic. In Georgia this took the form of seminars on young Georgian poets and writers, composers, architects with the added intention of promoting their work. Such activities and support for pioneer camps and pioneer palaces are financed by membership dues and the proceeds from Komsomol publications.

Six years ago at its 1962 14th Congress, the Komsomol adopted a new charter. It specifies the task of youth at the present stage of Soviet socialism.

To add some colour to this dull interview at the Komsomol Office, Yuri Sviridov and I decided to interview the young people themselves. We visited a Pioneer Palace, and attended a Komsomol event to conduct some on-the-spot recording.

Young peoples' Pioneer & Komsomol clubs
Today Yuri and I are visiting a Pioneer Palace to interview members of "The Young Flyers Club". Pioneer and Komsomol clubs exist throughout the Soviet Union. The largest Pioneer Clubs are referred to as Pioneer Palaces. The one we are visiting is near my flat, it's a splendid building.

The members of the Young Pioneer Club attend the College of Aviation's three year course for 14 to 18 year olds. The course covers the technicalities of flying, airplane design, aero dynamics; technicalities of engines, and navigation. Both boys and girls can also have mock cosmonaut training. Additional general courses, including philosophy are taken in their first year. It's pointed out to me that space study involves a complexity of sciences. This course gives them the chance to find out their field of interest. Officially I'm informed that the main aim is not to train future cosmonauts, but develop each young person as an all-round human being, Not surprisingly though, the three young boys I meet all want to be cosmonauts and are taking an intensive course in flying.

Now Yuri and I are at the Komsomol's *Yunost'* (Youth) Hotel to interview young people who have been invited to Moscow to attend a rally as the best representatives of clubs around the Soviet Union.

I'm most impressed by three young women we meet there. Lida 18, Tanya 14 and Ira 16 are from the Komsomol club in Frunze, Kirghizia. Their club has thirty boys and ten girls. There are two and a half hours of school lessons at the club every day. Lida looks about fourteen but has left school and is studying Astronautics and the Planets at university and is an instructor in astronomy and parachute jumping. Ira is in the Physics and Mathematics faculty at the University. She joined the club for mathematics but that led to an interest in astronomy like Lida. Tanya studies Maths at a deeper level. They give me a souvenir from Kirghizia.

Valentina Tereshkova, the first female cosmonaut, is their role model, "When Valentina went into the cosmos, she opened the way for us too."

Other clubs represented at the Rally, include the "Little Academy of Sciences" in Simferopol, Crimea, a Juvenile Drivers School and a club for young writers.

I'm impressed by the Pioneer and Komsomol clubs. Of course, I'm visiting the Pioneer Palace in the centre of Moscow, the capital city, the crème de la crème. At the Rally it's the finest members who have been selected to attend. However, the young people I talk to on both occasions are enthusiastic, engaged and appear to have high expectations of the future. It's no wonder that visiting delegations when shown such places return home impressed.

These few examples are all I have of the transcripts I broadcast. I conducted a number of interviews, but as I only had the initial questions written down, didn't keep them. One in particular was with a couple getting married on New Year's Day. It was most enjoyable.

I remember being chastised in the Editor's Office for indulging in too much laughter.

Helen Goun

Facing me in the pool, her back to the wall, is Helen. A loner in the pool, she rarely engages in conversation. But she has regular escapes into the corridor for a chat and cigarette with Bernie. Out here her deep throated laugh bursts out. A thoughtful, genuine person, Helen sometimes allows a slight cynicism to enter her conversation.

Gradually we become friends. I'm invited to her home, apart from Bernie and Tanya, almost the only person in the pool to do so. The flat has a warm lived in atmosphere. Books cover the walls, the furniture is dark, evoking the atmosphere of an earlier time. Helen lives here with her parents and sister. There is also a young boy, a nephew who seems to be visiting. Helen introduces me to her father. He is sitting in a rocking chair, a rug over his lap. He survived the labour camps but returned home a broken man. The sister's work is something to do with America, which gives Helen access to contemporary literature, she especially likes crime stories. Both sisters are fluent in English.

Helen's own story is like so many, a tragic one. As she is a very private person, the information probably came to me from Bernie rather than herself. From what I remember, her husband had been sent to Siberia. She followed with their baby, who died, as did her husband. She is respected by Bernie. I discover she loves opera but very rarely goes out other than to work. I invite her to join me at the Bolshoi. I remember our first visit was in January 1968 to Tchaikovsky's *Pikovaya Dama*, the Queen of Spades.

On my return to Moscow in the autumn of 1969 for the University course, I brought a number of English books and magazines for the pool. Nothing contentious. I'd arranged to meet Helen in the Radio's foyer for her to bring me the required pass. She was a long time coming. When she eventually came it was with apologies. Uncharacteristically she was visibly upset. The pass had been refused. I was not to be allowed into the place where I had worked for two years[1]. For someone whom I'd always seen calm behind the smoke of her cigarettes, Helen's consternation was heartfelt. I left the books with her to give to the pool.

Years later in 1989 my son Jamie and I went to Moscow for the Christmas and New Year holiday. I phoned Helen and she warmly invited us to the flat. She was delighted to meet Jamie. It was the last time I saw her.

---

1 I didn't find an explanation until sometime after. It was to do with the announcer Yuri. Sviridov

Lenin's Flat in the Kremlin

The 27th February, I visit Lenin's apartment in the Kremlin. This is where he lived and worked when the Government moved from Petrograd to Moscow. The apartment is in the building of the Soviet Council of Ministers. In the early 19th Century it had been a palace.

On entering, all documents have to be checked including my Moscow passport. I'm with a group of thirty from the Radio. All are Russians. I'm impressed by their attitude of respect to the place. We wind up a back staircase to the third floor. My usual critical attitude doesn't work here. I really do feel the atmosphere: this was where the great Lenin sat, governing huge Russia. This is where he lived, as simply as possible, where he refused to accept peasants' gifts of extra food, sending them instead to orphanages. This is the flight of stairs which he climbed after the attempted assassination on his life. We are told that despite being wounded, to avoid worrying his wife and friends, he refused to take the lift or have any help.

We pass through a long corridor lined with bookcases. The first book that catches my eye is Sylvia Pankhurst's "The Suffragette Movement" in English. We enter Lenin's office. A dark rather crowded room, even oppressive. The desk is at the head of a long table covered with red cloth and surrounded by four enormous leather arm chairs. Lenin's is an upright wicker one. On the desk are gifts from various sources; a French/Bulgarian dictionary presented by Georgi Dimitrov, a statue from a firm in the United States and writing equipment from workers in Dagestan. Beside the desk are reference books in revolving bookshelves designed by Lenin himself. Behind the desk, bookcases line the wall; books of many countries, many in their own languages. I am amazed to learn that this truly remarkable man knew nine languages. In a large bookcase on the left hand side are complete volumes of Pushkin, Tolstoy and other Russian classics. Large maps of Russia, Central Asia and Europe hang in any available space together with the plan for Russia's electrification. Candlesticks and candles stand on the desk, a necessity given the frequent power failures.

It was in this office that the famous conversation took place between Lenin and H.G.Wells. When Lenin unfolded the plans for the electrification of this vast country, Wells called him 'The Kremlin Dreamer'. Lenin was not the dreamer.

Hanging on the wall opposite the desk is a portrait of Marx, again a gift from some workers. The large clock standing next to it is stopped at 8.15pm, the time that Lenin last left this room on December 12, 1922. The office opens onto the meeting room since enlarged. Large portraits hang on the walls – Sverdlov, and other first ministers including the first Minister of Food, who was always suffering from hunger and died a few years later from tuberculosis.

The guide tells us a story which he says is true. "A peasant made several attempts to muster up courage to speak to Lenin in his office. At last it came out. 'My grandfather wore *bast* peasant shoes[1]. My father also wore *bast* shoes, and now it's four years since the socialist revolution and I'm still wearing *bast* shoes. Lenin immediately gave him a note stating he was to be provided with a pair of boots. But the peasant was so touched that he didn't know whether to get the boots or keep the note. He decided to keep the note. After Lenin's death when he was lying in the Hall of Columns, the same peasant came to pay his respects. In his hand was the note given to him

---

[1] These are made of woven birch bark and worn over cloth wrapped around the feet.

by Lenin. With tears streaming down his face the peasant said how pleased he was that he had kept the note rather than get the boots".

The kitchen, an unremarkable room, a table for four: Lenin, his wife Nadezhda Krupskaya, his sister Maria Ulyanova and the housekeeper; basic utensils and crockery. Lenin's bedroom: a single bed with iron bedstead, a desk and of course, books and a large portrait of Krupskaya and himself. Krupskaya's room and her bedroom and work room: a desk with portraits of Lenin. Also a small book of newspaper photos of Lenin, a folder with Ilyich (Lenin) on the cover containing letters to the press. On the cabinet more photos of Lenin. I'd read so many times that these two exceptional people lived in all modesty and simplicity that I was on the look out to criticize, but what was there to criticize, they possessed so little that only the words 'simple', 'modest' can be used. Of Lenin's bedroom I'd even use the word 'bare'. Lenin's room opens onto the dining room. Again a very small room, just a table, chairs but a lovely view of a Kremlin tower, the walls lit by the setting sun.

Into Lenin's sister's room. This is a much larger and warmer room. Again a writing table, but here the bed is behind a screen. There are photos and pictures on the wall, among them a striking portrait of their mother, it's beautiful. Here everything is hand embroidered; cushion covers, table cloth, and a Chinese picture hanging on the screen. Both Ulyanova and Krupskaya lived here for many years after Lenin's death.

So, this is my visit to the work place of probably one of the greatest men the world has yet seen.

Well, that is how I wrote to my parents at the time. Whilst I became increasingly critical of the Soviet Union, it has taken me many more years before beginning to re-asses the role of Vladimir Ilyich Lenin.

In 1994 the flat and its contents were removed from the Kremlin to a town outside Moscow.

"The Golden Ring" Souzdal

March 2nd 1968

Thirty churches and five monasteries[1] adorn an area only slightly larger than Moscow University's campus. Souzdal is located in what's referred to as "The Golden Ring", a collection of towns, north east of Moscow, known for their religious buildings. Zagorsk is included for its status, although nearer to Moscow than the Ring. The All-Russian Society for the Protection of Monuments of History and Culture is responsible for restoring the buildings to their former glory. They are now on the tourist trail.

This outing to Souzdal is organised by the radio. We travel past mile after mile of forested land, passing only one town on our 200 kilometers journey – and I remind myself that this is just a tiny puddle in the ocean that is the USSR.

Soviet guides know their subject. Their spiel isn't flannelled with stories of ghosts and abducted maidens. Many guides have an appropriate degree in history or art. Not only do they provide boundless information, but start from the moment of bordering the bus, as ours did in Moscow. Places of interest on the journey are pointed out including the history of the road itself, her opinion of Moscow's new areas and their architectural value, where to find the best mushrooms, all amongst the streams of information which continue unabated on the fifteen hours of our trip. We stop half way, inevitably, for mushroom foraging in the forest.

But on to Souzdal. An impressive gateway announces our

---

1 The Russian word *'monas'tier* includes convents.

arrival. The guide enters an old church re-emerging with our tour *propuska* (permits). We clamber out of the bus and climb up a hill. Facing us is the wall of a monastery and a number of churches. Here we see for real the church most frequently illustrated in the guide books. But the blue of its cupolas is a shadow of the deep shining blues in the coloured photographs. It could actually do with a good wash. But its position is glorious: vivid rolling green hills, the river skirting the town winding its way beneath. In the distance are more cupolas with their gold glistening in the sunlight.

We stand on the high road, overlooking the winding river, the grass cool under our feet. I've introduced the bare foot fashion. Then we sit down on the grass whilst our guide imparts her information on the most exquisite wooden church. The front resembles a house, only the cupola rising toward the sky, reveals that this is a place of worship. The wood is so laid by the craftsmen that the sun catches the beauty of its grain in varying ways; at times it seems that the wood is silver, at times gold. The base composed of whole trunks provides its solidity. The planks of the surrounding wall higher up are laid diagonally to one another. But above all is the cupola. Its shape is formed by interlocking sections of pointed wood. Their light and shade high up in the sky adds to the magic of the workmanship. The craftsman's love for his material is clearly evident. This church has been on a journey, removed from elsewhere to adorn this Golden ring. Kizhi, an island in northern Russia, has a collection of wooden churches of like craftsmanship.

We move on to a white church in stone, yet all the while glancing back to the one in wood. Its grace to marvel at, something that will remain imprinted on my memory.

However, the stonework of the white church is itself interesting. Souzdal's most common embellishment is that of the lion. It's featured in various ways. Around the doorways of one church, small lions guard the entrance to prevent evil spirits entering. Each lion has its own characteristics provided by a few simple lines etched into the stone. In many churches decorative geometric patterns abound, intertwined leaves and flowers are also popular. In the central square, not a very smart one, church walls are dominant; many of them gleaming white, topped by cupolas of slated grey, blue, dull ochre yellow, or gleaming gold.

We now begin a tour of the monasteries, all five of them. One of these we can enter only with a *propusk*. A *remont*[2] is under way. This monastery has been restored only recently from housing a reform school for girls. It's had a chequered history. Whether the monastery was to have a sobering effect on these wild young people, whether they were to be influenced by their ancestors, or by sitting hours after hour uncomplainingly weaving tapestries and embroidering samplers, I cannot say, but anyway the opportunity has gone. The girls have been moved to more modern surroundings.

Before the girls, it served as a reform school for boys. Whether they did not suit the monastery, or whether the monastery did not suit them, is also a debateable point.

Earlier still, the Tzars themselves used the sacred buildings in which to incarcerate their most ferocious enemies. Apparently many bodies lie rotting beneath the holy grounds without their souls having been saved. More than one died from 'loss of reason'.

But let's return to a healthier present. Peace surrounds us as we step away from the past.

---

2 Remont, a much used term, 'Under repair' is used for all situations when limited or no access is sought.

Gagarin

Saturday, March 30th. In the middle of a crowded shop, all movement suddenly stops. The crowd is still.

"This is Radio Moscow. This is Red Square, this is Red Square".

The voice that announced the war, that announced Victory Day, and the start of the 50th anniversary celebrations, the voice that announced the successful launch of the world's first man in space, a Soviet man, this is the voice that every citizen knows, the announcer of each portentous event since 1939. Now in 1968 it announces a funeral, the funeral of Yuri Gagarin.

Slowly, movement resumes. Shop assistants, eyes red, serve customers in silence. People move around the counters at snail's pace, selecting goods with a pre-occupied air.

Just three days ago, on my way to work, a man had come running into the Mayakovskaya Metro, "Listen everybody, Gagarin is dead". Stunned silence. It couldn't be true. But it was. Gagarin, the world's first man in space, a Soviet cosmonaut, had died in a plane crash. It was too hard to believe. Now, hearing the announcement of his funeral, somehow makes it real.

34 year old Yuri Gagarin with his boyish smile, is now reduced to ashes, an urn placed in Red Square's Kremlin Wall. As Red Square stands in the one minute of silence, it seems the whole of Moscow stands; maybe the whole world is still.

Crowds queue up at the newspaper stands. In the buses, in trams, in the metro, papers are read over other passengers shoulders. Strangers talk quietly to strangers.

Gagarin was a symbol of what this socialist country has achieved, recently celebrated; its fifty years of change that "shook the world". The society, where much had been a peasant wilderness, illiterate, uncouth, unemployed, had put the world's first man in space. Gagarin, the cosmonaut who had been acclaimed in Britain as the best diplomat the USSR could send to win friendship and trust between our two countries.

The printed images of Gagarin and his co-pilot lie in front of the Kremlin Wall. Relatives stoop down to kiss the image, as if icons in a church. Only missing are the incense and the golden halo. The Soviet flag is alongside. How far has the culture changed? The evidence of a man in space, had challenged the belief of an omnipotent being. Yet, obeisance continues to this very symbol as generations have done before them. How long does it take to change a culture, to revolutionise a human being? Maybe this is the true test, behaviour at times of great stress.

The past fourteen months have been significant. What have I, a foreigner, witnessed? The celebration of half a century of socialism, the centenary of Maxim Gorky, the first proletarian writer, the 50 years of the Komsomol, the 50 years of the Red Army, and all in such a small passage of time. However, these celebrations, these tragedies are only a marker to what these people may witness in the future, their joys and their future sorrows. This is a country where events are writ large.

Making merry with Lena and Sasha.

Tea with acquaintances across the road.

Vera's parents at the dacha.

Vera in 1967 aged 20yrs. Russian urchin.

The survivor church on Kalinin Prospekt.

To the market...

Young observers.

Uzbek plaits.

Bukhara, my favourite building.

Mausoleum of Ismail Samani.

First Anniversary of the Greek Junta

Situated between the two metro entrances – Old Arbat and New Arbat in central Moscow is Arbat Square. Usually it's a peaceful place, but not today. There's no sign of the elderly natterers and weary shoppers quietly resting on the Square's benches. In their place instead are groups of mostly young people, laughing and chatting, many are young men with dark hair and handsome faces. The babble of voices is not Russian. There's an air of expectancy. Animated faces emerge amongst placards. The occasional passer-by stands and stares, the curious ask 'what's it all about'? "Greece, democracy". It's why Kate[1] and I are here. We've come to join the demonstration to the Greek embassy in protest at the Junta's takeover. The placards tell their story in Russian and Greek and there's a couple in French and English.

From a telephone kiosk, door wide open, we hear an excited English voice:

"This is a five column story, got it?" …..

"Course I know who organised it" ……

"Well no… I don't know the actual name of the organisation, but it's a bunch of Greek emigres they call themselves… and students, mostly students"…..

"Yeah, I'll call you back".

He rushes off, pencil and paper in hand, eagerly snatching at

---

[1] An English friend studying on the one year Language course at Moscow University

this chance of reporting the unusual event of a real live demo in the heart of Moscow. More and more demonstrators arrive, students from Moscow University: Latin Americans, Indians, women from Ceylon. I also hear the tones of American English and among them Kate and myself.

But there's something missing. There are no militia, not a single policeman in sight; a startling omission for those of us familiar with demonstrations in London.

Someone stands up on the wall of a fountain. The groups merge and gather round.

"We are demonstrating on the anniversary of the first year of the Greek Junta's seizure of power…"

Placards held high against the sky. Moving, shuffling into some sort of formation, out of the square, onto the main road. Traffic stops. Still no militia. We move down the middle of the road. Russians eye us curiously from the pavement. Shouts of "Down with the Greek Junta, Democracy" resound in the ears of the shoppers in Gorky Street. We march along the central lane, between the two white lines marking this lane for emergencies, VIPs and tanks.

What are these Soviet citizens thinking? Their faces, almost without exception, are thoughtful, still, silent. There is no move to join us. Do they understand the need to express ourselves in this way even on the streets of Moscow? Do they understand how our very bodies are urging action, yet how helpless we feel just shouting out slogans? Is there sympathy for these young Greeks whose country, the cradle of democracy, is strangled now by a fascist dictatorship? That it's their friends and relations who are now in gaol?

And why are we here, us non Greeks? Is it because we like to shout, or the unique opportunity to march down the centre of Gorky Street, all eyes upon us? No. We feel the necessity to identify ourselves with the world's injustices. Are Russians less concerned? They have experienced the horrors of war to an extent we can't imagine. Russians want peace. But today's demonstration is part of our way of life, no longer theirs. Is it ill-mannered of us to impose our own form of protest on a different culture? What affect will it have on Greek and Soviet relations?

We leave Gorky Street with a sharp turn to the right down a side street named after the great Stanislavsky. This street houses the Greek embassy. A bus positioned sideways bars our way. On either side are the missing militia. One of them approaches demands "Why". A plain clothes official asks the same question. The Greeks continue shouting. Impatience creeps in. "What is happening? Why can't we proceed?" "We were allowed up to the embassy last time". Someone makes a speech. "We've come here to protest against the junta. Long live Greek democracy". But the Greeks do not disperse. The militia give way. "Alright, go. But walk straight past the embassy. No stopping". An initial rush forward, then gradual slowing down and organised shouting. They are not going to pass by the embassy. Here are the representatives of the hated junta. Let them have it. We want them to hear us. Shouts pierce the air.

The militia and plain clothes person try, "Come on, let's move". The Greek guy stewarding the demonstration, races up and down trying to get his compatriots to move. To no avail.

Kate and I leave.

In the taxi on my way back to work, I ask the driver what he thought of the demo. His reply, "It's the anniversary of Lenin's birthday today, the demo shows disrespect." "But this is the anniversary of the vicious Greek Junta." His response, "These things pass. There was Khruschev, now Kosygin. They come and go".

My departing shot, "If Lenin were alive, he'd have joined us".

May Day in Moscow 1968

Past the stalls of apples and sweets, then brandishing my ticket at the police checkpoint – and here I am, in Red Square. Up on the stands. Make sure of a good position. Worm my way in amongst the Japanese and their technical aids: cameras, cine cameras, lenses – seemingly changed after every two shots, and badges. A guy stands next to me, arms akimbo, this is his place. Don't you believe it mate, it's mine. We'll see who wins. Actually we both do, someone else has to move. As far as the Russian spectators are concerned children get priority. They go to the front - everyone makes way for them, and keeps an eye on them, whoever they are. My position is good, with backs to GUM we're facing the podium and mausoleum and hence the back view as the parade makes obeisance to the VIPs across the Square. It's as if we're behind the scene not just witnessing the polished façade.

Participants start entering Red Square from 9am. Parachutists are the first to take their allotted place. Very quiet, very erect. After them are the regular soldiers: noisier, their commanders take some time to settle them. Now I see caps, caps, waves and waves of them: the pink/mauve of the parachutists; green peaks from one soldier's regiment, beige of another. Above me the unbelievable noise of the flags of the 15 republics flapping in the strong breeze. It's a beautiful May Day, the sky is blue, the sun is shining and the breeze is welcome.

10am – they're off. The Marshall stands in an open car. He greets the various army battalions who answer with waves of "Hurrahs". It sounds somewhat uncanny. Then the cannons, *The Internationale* blares out from loud speakers, few are singing. This song should not be so organised. It's a song for people to sing, not sung at them.

The military parade starts. Cameras clicking. I've nothing to say. I've no interest at all in this part. Why should people need a small photo of a tank or rocket? These rockets on show I find repulsive, but for Russians it means a great deal.

They've gone, chased by the roar of motorbikes. The next three sections arrive: Industrial: "300 million tons – We'll fulfil the plan", Agriculture and Science – the latter contingent dressed in lemon and grey.

Athletes in blue and white now stride into the Square. The women carry hoops in groups of five – the Olympic rings. Behind them and right by us, are the children, boys and girls in red, white and blue. They stand in their rehearsed lines. Some are so excited, they can hardly keep still, others deadly serious, are overcome by the importance of the occasion.

The sport contingent drops back, enabling the children clutching flowers and balls to run forward to the podium. They perform some formation moves, but most impressive is the run forward, a regular popular feature of parades. Spectators applaud – the first major unsolicited response, apart from the clicking cameras, of the whole event.

But then, a burst of colour: the arrival of citizens begins. Red blazes against the blue sky. The sun lights up the banners and flags. Huge baskets of flowers appear. Placards promise "Support to the Arab peoples", "Aid for Vietnam", "Down with Imperialism". On they come, in their thousands, organised according to their work place, as we were last November. The television tower is carried aloft. Then the press: a giant sized *Pravda*, followed by *Izvestia*.

What a wonderful colour is red. Other colours inter-weave, but red remains predominant. A full size Lenin moves slowly forward amongst the parade, his image on a frame of gauze. Lenin, Lenin everywhere. And paper flowers, twigs of pink and white spring flowers.

Loudspeakers blare out information. Between parade and spectators is a line of officials, "Keep things in order Citizens". Now it reveals the bands massed at one end. The Army's instrumentalists are certainly enjoying themselves. For them it's a holiday, and they are making the most of it. Many of them buy the boxes of chocolates on sale. But what to do when it's their turn to play? Tie the box to their belts, put them down on the ground, tuck them under their arms, and one is even put in a trombone.

The last of the work contingents are hustled out. At the entrance red flags stretch right across the Square. The flags appear to move forward and then open out to fill the whole Square revealing the young members of the Komsomol. They greet the VIPs on the podium, and then close up together as they make their way out of the Square, once again as a moving mass of red flags.

The Square clears. In come cleaners with water sprinklers and people without a ticket. Many run to catch a glimpse of the cosmonauts as they leave the podium. Children clutching balloons, gather the abandoned flowers.

Later I roam around the Gorky Park of Culture like everyone else, taking advantage of the holiday and the good weather. There's the occasional accordion, numerous guitars. It appears aimless, but it's reminiscent of the villagers stroll on a Sunday evening. Large groups walk arm in arm; as usual girls with girls, boys with boys – adults too. I pause by one of the open air theatres filled to capacity, spectators intently listening to the single artist reciting poetry. Poetry is highly appreciated by Russians, seemingly across the population.

Back home, by Kalinin Prospekt a group of enthusiastic supporters surround a man performing a Russian dance.

The next day it rains.

Weekends
Visit to Kolya's family dacha

Today I'm off to the country with a group of Russian friends. There's a mad fight to get a place on the train. My friends push me on. It's necessary. Bodies are everywhere, including the floor. The train carries us all and totters off to the country, with the proverbial ice cream somehow being sold on the way. Our destination on this occasion is 75 kilometres out of Moscow, about an hour and a half on the train. There are five of us, four Russians and me. We're visiting Kolya's parents' dacha. His father works at GUM, the department store in Red Square. The dacha comes through his work place. GUM pays for the use of a plot of land and lets this out to its workers for the purpose of building and cultivating it. The dachas are built by the people themselves. Kolya's dad started his eleven years ago.

"Never done any of this woodwork before, but well, it's gone well enough".

The whole place was constructed from boxes transported from Moscow. There's a central room with two wings, an arrangement that seems to be a common pattern for dachas. One of the wings is glassed in making a pleasant veranda for meals. A large stove stands in the other and of course, the samovar. What dacha doesn't have its samovar? Eight people can be accommodated quite comfortably. But, like other dachas, it's added to all the time. Even now, eleven years on, Kolya's dad spends the whole weekend sawing wood and doing one thing or another. He's even dug a well in the garden, despite this area being supplied with wells in good shape.

And then there's the garden.

Ten apple trees, currant bushes, peonies the central pride, buds to be watched.

"Come down here almost every weekend; work if you want; rest if you want; take a stroll in the forest".

This time we take that walk. It's a beautiful birch forest. Yellow catkins sway on some sort of low bush. Spring green, wonderful. Silver birches, the sun glimmering on the fresh young leaves, every tree, and each bush seems to have its own particular wonder.

But now a brush with another reality. As we enter a forest clearing, some village lads borrow our ball. But, they have no intention of returning it, as off they go. After a short debate we decide to go after them, why should they get away with it. There's three of them, late teens. Fists up. All they want is a fight. Nasty with it too. Volodya tries to reason with them, but that's not their language. One of the girls defends her boyfriend who's getting the worst of it. A woman shouts telling the lads to "get the hell out of it". She'd let them have a knife earlier and now she's cursing herself for being a fool. Out comes a stream of language from the lads. Socialist values it seems have passed them by: certainly an interlude to set me thinking.

What do these rural villages, often urban overspills, offer to young people? They aren't attached to the land as are the older villagers. Some study in the institutes. Those who are employed, mostly work in factories. But what else is there here for them? It is one and a half hours from Moscow, trains just once an hour at weekends, but Moscow is overcrowded anyway. And here there appears to be nothing, maybe a cinema. Much more fun to get at the trippers from Moscow who tend to look down on the rural folk: differing cultures, contrasting life chances.

Back in the dacha, evening brings the appetising smell of shashlik, not just from our garden, but wafting from all around. It seems all Russians know how to cut the turf, lay the twigs and turn the spit. The meat has been soaking all afternoon in wine seasoned with pepper. Now garlic is added. The samovar sits on pine cones, and is topped with an old rusty funnel. I've yet to see a new one used. And there's time to relax in the warm dusk of the evening breathing in the wonderful fragrance of the pines. Food is ready. Instant activity, a glass of wine and we're all armed with a large skewer, me carefully biting around the pieces of meat, the others taking them off in one fell swoop.

How well I sleep in the country.

Washing from the well in the morning, cold water is no hardship. Sit in the sun until breakfast. Kolya's Dad is up already and sawing wood. We spend the morning sunbathing. Then we take a can to get milk from the next village – in the opposite direction from the hoodlums of yesterday. Every household has its own cow. Fresh milk. What an appetising thought. But we're too late - all sold out. The village consists of two lines of houses constructed of whole birch trunks. They face one another across a wide stretch of green, housing the wells. Young people sit in the sun. There don't seem to be many of them, but they do seem to be well dressed, quite different from their Mums and Dads. Still this is a holiday so there's no judging. The window frames and eaves of the houses are carved in the traditional Russian manner, many refurbished.

Chickens roam, strangely there are few dogs. Concrete bases lie ready for new wells; when do they expect to have running water? Electricity however, has reached this village, thanks to Lenin and his electrification plan.

A woman kicks up a hullabaloo, shouting her head off at an

older woman; something about getting the tractor in. She could be a model for those socialist realism paintings of collective farms: red kerchief, print dress, strong as an ox, in her thirties, bursting with life.

But no milk.

A woman from another village still has some." How far is it"? "Oh, not far just a couple of kilometres." The woman is from Byelorussia. She's an open, friendly character, has a good look at me, a foreigner, yet is willing to talk about her life in the village. Everyone belongs to the kolkhoz, the collective farm. The pensioners get 40 Roubles a month. "Yes, life is hard at times". I wonder what it's like living here in the winter.

We walk and walk – just a couple of kilometres and she does this every day. There is a bus, but some other time, some other place – maybe. The winding road between pine woods and fir trees seems endless. I find it dark and forbidding, so glad my Russian friends are with me. But eventually we pass two pioneer camps in lovely settings, and a plantation of young birch trees, their leaves an unbelievably tender green, it's beautiful. My mood lightens.

Here we are at last. "Come in". Baby chicks in the yard. The house is divided into two sections. The left side houses the cattle stalls and the milking equipment, on the right is the living accommodation. Remarkably the smells also seem to be divided appropriately. Quietness and darkness prevail without being gloomy in this wooden home. Everything is clean and extremely tidy, the scene of people working away from home for long hours each day. Standing in the place of honour is the TV set, a small portable one. Making sure we haven't missed it, the proud owner points it out to us. There's also a radio. The sleeping section is curtained off. Up high in the corner rest two icons, one a small head of Christ surrounded by clusters of brightly coloured paper. There's another one in the kitchen. The lowly hung ultra-modern light fitting jars given that water still comes from the well outside.

At last, tasty, refreshing new milk, still warm. We drink several cupfuls right here on the spot, although initially I do so rather tentatively never having drunk milk straight from the cow before, then make our way back.

This time the pine forest is cool. The trees are planted in lines. The sun casts soft slanting rays through the gloom. Underfoot pine cones lie on the supple earth, and there's a cluster of white wood anemones.

We return to another huge Russian meal. A rest and then we walk through the dusk to the station. The sky, a soft rose, sits on the tree tops, the pines dark, piercing their superiority upwards. The Moscow bound train, is as packed as it was on the way out. We're lucky to find seats. But what's this? Stones shatter our window; the village lads vent their anger at us townies once again. A guard clears up the smashed glass. Frightening, but we're on our way to the bright lights, what do they have? On the train the contrast is marked. It seems no matter what carriage, a guitar accompanies passengers. Rucksacks bundled on the floor, provide a perch for those singing -and then there's the greenery. No one returns from the country without huge bundles of twigs and leaves, up they go on the luggage racks until they reach Moscow, when they are carried aloft down into the Metro, the whole subway a seething mass of green – '…. the woods moved to Dunsinane'.

Muscovites, grubby, tired, but with a general air of contentment, are now ready to work until the next weekend, when they'll be off again.

Multfilm Puppet Theatre

Puppets have such a high status in Moscow thanks to Sergei Obratzov and his puppet theatre, they are commonly used in animated cartoons.

Puppet Film Theatre
We're in one of the quiet corners in Moscow. It has its children's playground and wooden benches for the grandparents who gather for a gossip. A fairy tale white church is carefully guarded by railings and a stout wooden door. Inside though bears no resemblance to a church for puppets of every description peer at the visitors from behind the glass cupboards which line the entrance hall.

This is the home of Multfilm, specialising in cartoons based on puppets. We enter the main rooms, they present a complete shambles. Body parts lie all around - quite ungainly.

But let's start from the beginning. We're taken to a room which is ship shape. This is the mechanics room where the puppet skeletons are constructed – anything from a giraffe's neck to the bent back of an old woman. I'm shown how a neck can move in any direction. The movement is controlled by springs of coiled wire with solid metal joints.

We move with the skeleton pieces to the puppet makers. Most puppets are made of wood, although it can vary dependant on the type of puppet required. The carver works from a scale drawing of the puppet's front and profile views. Faces are carved in fine detail.

The puppets next port of call is the paint room, followed by the dressers. The first section deals with props. No prop is used twice in a performance. The painters work from pictures. This is the tidiest room. Each puppet is given a final facial glow. The work is very delicate. At each stage an overseer checks the standard of the work ensuring it strictly adheres to the original, not to the individuality of the artist. This is because several models of the main characters are required for their different poses, so continuity is paramount. The painters both of props and puppets are generally art school graduates.

Now we climb a winding staircase and enter a film studio. Much mess among which there are miniature sets, each one no more than three square feet. Cameras are trained on miniature stages. Life size beings operate the cameras and the puppets. Backgrounds of the sets all of wool, suggests they are for the same film. Then I see that the props and clothes are knitted wool. The story being filmed is the tale of a little goat. The goat uses his wool to make goods for an old woman to sell. She becomes rich. But she is not grateful. Having no further need of the goat, she throws him out.

But everything the goat made for her to sell unravels. No wonder no props are used twice.

The puppets are amazing. For every frame shot, the animators move the puppets for the next shot. Fingers, eyebrows, eyes, each part is moved as required.

I had always known the Russian children's cartoons are of a high quality, now I appreciate why.

Obraztsov's Puppet Theatre
My initial interest in visiting the home of Multfilm arose from my admiration of Obraztsov's Puppet Theatre.

Sergey Obraztsov's Puppet Theatre is famous. He had been one of the artists to perform in London in the 1950s. With his endearing baby puppet *Tyapa*, he held the audience at the Royal Albert Hall spellbound. So I was eager to visit the theatre whilst in Moscow. Tickets are hard to come by. It's a regular tourist 'must do'. What I hadn't realised previously, is that the use of puppets could be quite subversive. Apart from Obraztsov's signature piece with baby Tyapa, from amongst his sixty one plays he performs, I saw *An Unusual Concert* which is satirical about bad performers and extremely funny. I didn't know what to expect from the play about God making the world in seven days. When god creates the marine creatures he is about to deliver a tin of crab, but he pockets it. The Russian audience are in hoots. Crab is a delicacy hard to get whilst no doubt available to those in power.

Obraztsov is an institution. He produces performances for both children and adults.

Ten Days that Shook the World
Taganka Theatre, 4th July

Ten Days that Shook the World, a theatrical performance of American journalist John Reed's eye witness account of the storming of the Winter Palace.

The production is named as a 'National performance in two Acts with pantomime, circus, buffoonery & shots (shooting) in motifs from the book by John Reed'.

We, the audience are invited to enter the scene.

'The flame of the revolution, the flame of freedom'. The hammer and the anvil, the power thrashes, the light of the flame flutters, flares, dies away.'

Crowds outside the theatre plead for tickets.

Soldiers and sailors in 1917 uniforms, stand guard at the doors, their bayonets ready to pierce our entrance tickets. Programme sellers are in red kerchiefs. "All Power to the Soviets" banners greet us as we enter the foyer where sailors are singing, playing accordions and making speeches. We can choose to wear a red ribbon in support, or not to oppose the revolution as we move from speaker to speaker. Most are wearing a red ribbon, we too are revolutionaries. This is our history, the history of the ordinary man and woman. The singers disappear. Then spot lights, soldiers with their bayonets, workers and peasants march into the auditorium, we follow. Darkness. Shots ring out. The play begins.

I have my ticket, programme, my red ribbon and my leaflet - a facsimile thrown out to us from the stage:

"To the citizens of Russia".

The declaration from the Petrograd Soviet,
25th October, 1917, 10am
"Greetings to the revolutionary workers, soldiers and peasants. Bread to the hungry. Land to the peasantry. Factories to the workers. Peace to the nation".

Moscow parks

Sokolniki

"The Saints" blares out from loud speakers. My feet move to a trad jive. Where am I? A London jazz club, or resting in Hyde Park after a demo? No. This is Moscow in the vast area of Sokolniki Park. In the summer months, Moscow's parks provide an additional venue for performances, replacing the skating rinks of winter. We make our way past the loud speakers, past the kiosks with their array of goods from sausages to *matryoshki,* the nesting Russian dolls, and the tanks of *kvass*[1]. The main paths are all cemented. The seats alongside are taken up by old age pensioners, contentedly scrutinising the passers-by, with an occasional shake of the head and a nudge of a neighbour's elbow at a mini-skirt or other unsuitable apparel. The world passes them by, and on they sit. We take the path on the right.

The Saints is followed by a female Russian voice announcing the programme for the evening: Dancing in the open air to so and so band. At 7pm for the serious minded there is a talk on "Gorky and his early stories" and for the dedicated, "Karl Marx and Scientific Communism" in the Summer Theatre at 7.30pm. I've decided we'll give that one a miss. There's a film show at the Open Air Cinema, then further announcements of concerts, singers, musicians, bands of various musical genre - it seems something for everyone.

A signpost points to the Reading Room. We wander down an inviting side path, restful for our feet after the concrete, leading us to a shady clearing. On three sides are decorative

---

1 Kvass a traditional tasty drink of fermented rye bread sold on the street.in large containers.

open work screens, sheltering desks and seats – a perfect place for students to study for their summer exams, for the old men to read their newspapers. We leave them to their peace. We turn away into the woods with their meandering paths. We catch a glimpse of benches amongst the trees, couples comfortably seated, then another clearing, lighter this time, giving a feeling of being out in the country. Children play over logs and fallen trees; mothers smilingly look on basking in the sun. We return to the undergrowth. Laughter and singing can be heard. Let's follow. A group of teenagers stroll by arm in arm Russian fashion. Shrieks of laughter, they start chasing one another, now playing hide and seek. We next come across them seated on the ground, singing and chatting. They seem quite happy to spend their evening so.

I wonder who does go to the lectures, the concerts, the film shows. Does anyone?

We wend our way back to the main paths following the direction of a lone voice, a man reciting poetry from a small stage. Around him an intent audience: young, old, middle aged, men and women. Once again I see that the Russians love of poetry seems to cross all divisions. We move onto the next performance; resplendent in a long white dress, an opera singer is appreciated by a full audience.

Cafés are plentiful. We try a self-service place. Seats out in the open, some shaded under the trees, well laid out and clean. Unfortunately the same laborious old system of queuing up, first to pay, then another queue for the food, and yet a separate queue for beer. By the time I return to our table, four Russians have joined us bringing the pungent smell of the Russian delicacy, dried fish, recalling a well-preserved "very ancient and fish like smell"[2]. It's reputed to go well with beer –but too much for me.

Gorky Park

Gorky Park, one of the main parks and not far from me, has regular summer performances. In August 1968, I decide to visit a concert at its Summer Theatre. The programme starts with light music and a light dance to match, not particularly impressive, although obviously the artist has had ballet training and is very capable. This is followed by a dramatic dance with a young Red Army man, excellent and much appreciated by the audience. The MC has an interesting opening patter. He uses Opera as his reference point (could this be possible with a similar audience in England?[1]) In one introduction he recites a long poem about a revolutionary programme incorporating farm-yard noises and actions in the telling, much to the delight of the audience. The audience are very attentive throughout the whole show.

Moscow parks give service the year round.

---

2 Shakespeare's *The Tempest*, Trinculo, Act 2, Scene 2
3 Although note since then the popularity of the Proms, and the Three Tenors in parks and football grounds

Uzbekistan

I was eager to see another of the cultures of the Soviet Union so was lucky in the autumn of 1968 to spend a month in Central Asia. I was based in Tashkent, capital of Uzbekistan. Whilst there I worked in the English section of Radio Tashkent. I also visited Samarkand and Bukhara.

Tashkent
Disappointing. Dust everywhere, the trees smothered, the streets thick with it, my lungs full of it: a massive building site since the devastating earthquake just two years earlier in 1966. Cranes pierce the sky. Re-construction is still going on, the speed of re-building is impressive, but not without its problems; 600,000 builders from other republics, many sent under contract for up to two years. There's much after-work drunkenness, conflicts with the Uzbek culture, and pressure caused by the continuing lack of housing. The old buildings are ramshackle. I'm booked into the Hotel Tashkent overlooking the main square, given a vast unwelcoming bedroom, quite rightly charged the higher tourist rate, but will need to write an article for Tashkent radio to meet the cost. I'd hoped to see camels, but no. I hope to get a ride on a donkey.

However, I learned from my February arrival in Moscow last year not to rely on first impressions. The new buildings are a gleaming white, with decorative open brick work and pale blue motifs representing the republics of the builders. Most attractive and a refreshing contrast to the dust. The hotel also improves with a good evening when I wine and dine with members of the UN Forestry Agricultural commission here for a seminar. A UN official from North Devon invites me to join them; members from Jordan, Kuwait, India and Persia. Our table is a focus of attention, not least as it includes me, a rare female in the restaurant.

Contact with Tashkent Radio soon brings change: I am moved to an unnamed hotel belonging to the Communist Party's Central Committee. Small and intimate, roses in the garden and excellent food, caviar and sturgeon in plentiful supply, all at a far cheaper rate. It's situated in one of the old streets, single storey flat roofed houses; tree lined, quiet, a feeling of a country lane. Lovely. Favoured individuals are among the guests such as the popular singer Alla Pugacheva.

An official sightseeing tour has been arranged for me. First stop the bazaar. Here is the exotica, missing from my arrival. The fruit and vegetable market is bountiful: piles of grapes and melons are stacked up on the ground, reminiscent of Georgia. Such an aroma. Old men, squat on their haunches in their traditional dress of gown and boots topped by their distinctive headwear the black, white embroidered tubeteika. Many of the women's skull caps are of velvet and decorated with beads. They sit on their sleek black hair in long plaits, of which the young girls have many. Their brightly coloured dresses are in a fabric of traditional geometric design underneath which they wear trousers.

It's not uncommon to see decorated cradles being carried from the market. Each one has a hole in its base. Why the hole? Apparently this is for convenience, It allows the nappiless infant to remain insitu whilst their mother is working in the fields. I'm told the flat heads of Uzbeks are due to their growth in these cradles, their heads flattened by pressing against the wooden end.

I work at Taskent Radio every day from midday until 7.30pm and mostly spend the evenings in the hotel. On a Sunday evening though, I go to the opera at Tahkent's Navoi[1] Opera and Ballet Theatre. It's a beautiful building, with its Tashkent, Samarkand and Bukhara rooms. Unsuprisingly, the acting fell far short of the Bolshoi and the libretto is banal. The slave girl torn from her lover for the Shah, then discarded in the desert where she dies in the arms of her lover who's escaped from the dungeon. The music though, conducted by the composer himself, is lovely. Unfortunately in the final interval it is spoiled by a transistor blaring out in the foyer.

What a contrast to todays young women that I meet through the Komsomol in my quest to find out about the position of women in Central Asia. The Head of the Tashkent Komsomol is a woman, as is the Tadjikistan First Secretary of the Party. This is seen as positive discrimination in practise. Women are being trained as technical workers: the head driver for the cotton harvesting is female. 50-55% of voluntary workers are women, especially in the country regions, but why not in the paid workforce? In order to bridge this gap in culture, I'm told the Komsomol pay particular attention to school children, organising talks for example by scientists to challenge religion. They also organise lectures and films at collective farms.

As this is 1968 school pioneers and members of the Komsomol organise collections for North Vietnam of both money and goods. Voluntary work on Sundays, Subbotniks, contribute to these funds. Last year a train of eleven carriages took school equipment donated by Pioneers from money raised by collecting paper and scrap iron. In one school I'm proudly informed, the Pioneers collected 25 boxes of school items in one day. On November 11th the World Federation of Democratic Youth (WFDY), held a work day in solidarity with the Vietnamese.

---

1 Alisha Navoi, 15th C Turkic poet adopted as national poet of Uzbeks

Samarkand

It's my second weekend in Tashkent and I'm off to Samarkand. The taxi driver taking me to the airport is a Crimean Tartar. Forcibly removed from his homeland, he's lived in Tashkent since the war - twenty five years. He fought in Berlin and Poland against the fascists. He claims he loves work, has a clean soul, but is not allowed to return to his homeland; "restricted like Negroes". For twenty four years, he'd dreamt of returning home, but was only able to go for holidays. He had no house there, no work, only promises: "in a month", "in a year". Now he believes he never will return. He said the most important thing is for man to be free, then he works twice as well. He's worked as a driver all these years. "Look at my cheeks", they are hollowed, bags under his eyes. "Driving is no life for a man, he wants his vineyards, his garden, his home". Crimean Tartars are a mixed race including Italians and others. He said they are all good folks but many have been treated similarly to him..

The flight over the desert reveals a surprising number of settlements between Samarkand and Tashkent. Most of the route is irrigated, apart from a section on the outskirts of the town.

On arrival a guide takes me to the old tombs and monuments of the Emirs and the Registran. The geometric decoration with its blues and turquoise is stunning, its resplendent glory unhindered by tourists. Restoration work has begun though, no doubt to prepare for future tourism.

The following day I spend hours in the market amidst the donkeys, onions, melons, pomegranates spices and chickens, fascinating place. I wander round the old part of town, no longer the centre, its clay houses and dust lanes now relegated to the outskirts. Here men crouch on the ground making the wooden Uzbek cradles, pipes and metal urns for water and coffee. It takes a whole day to produce a large urn. Sold as new, urns are made out of re-cycled metal. I squat down to watch the process. A used metal object is heated over a fire kept at the required heat by bellows, then dipped in water which turns it a bright bronze colour, it returns to the fire, this time just heated enough for moulding. The final stage is to hammer the metal for an attractive beaten look – a shining urn as good as new.

While I'm watching the craftsman, his wife tells me she got married at sixteen, has six children, the oldest fourteen, she was nursing the youngest while we talked. It's believed that if a woman is still unmarried by twenty, then its already too late; most marry between 15-19 years. Traditional culture generally is still very strong: fetching water by bucket from the street tap, rearing babies, cooking, sewing. Many women still carry the shopping on their heads. Whilst she appeared to accept this life, she had seen progress. Until recently there was no running water in Samarkand. Now in the old town there is a tap in the street. And not only the water situation is changing. In stark contrast to her life, at the airport I meet a smart young woman Intourist guide, she is also Uzbek but a graduate from the English faculty of Samarkand's own university. The university for the town's population of just 300,000.

Bukhara
It's the following weekend and I'm off to Bukhara. The flight itself is an adventure: the small local plane seems like a museum piece. It doesn't help that we take off from a ploughed field; now flying across the desert which seems mountainous in places

The Intourist service however is excellent. I'm met at the airport by the Head of the Local Radio with a car to the hotel; shown to my room and then taken on an excursion around the town.

Bukhara on the old silk route, is over 2,000 years old. We're shown the palaces of the emirs, the Summer Palace of the Emirs is paticularly beautiful and very original. One of the rooms is sparkling white. The white plaster is of exquisite design interspersed by tiny pieces of mirrors. The ceiling is the same. I've never seen anything like it. The craftsmanship is stunning. Moslem religion forbade portrayal of any living creature hence the fantastic richness in geometric design. There's a tower overlooking the pool of an Emir's harem where he used to sit and choose a girl for the night.

However my favourite mausoleum is of plain open brickwork. The Mausoleum of Ismail Samani dating from the ninth to tenth century, is outstanding, deriving its decoration from the brickwork. Fortunately, it was covered with sediment so escaped the notice and subsequently destruction of Ghengis Khan. When unearthed only the dome required restoring, the rest has remained in perfect condition since the 9th century. It used to contain what was considered holy water. The bricks are bound by camel's milk and egg yolk.

The old town consists of tiny lanes, more like passageways between the houses. The houses themselves are made of clay and have no windows onto the street, windows only face the inner courtyards. So from the outside the houses resemble simple squarish bunkers. The rooms however, open onto the riches of the inner courtyard with its vines and other fruits, and most importantly, water. The average family now has 5.5 children. My guide tells me, unbelievably, that he was one of 39, had himself married when 17, and has ten children, many families have up to fifteen.

Donkeys are everywhere. Retaining tradition, the centre of the old town remains the market which is entered by four main throughfares, north, south, east and west, each under its own

cupola. The entrances specialise in a particular type of goods; one is for material and embroidered hangings, another for jewellery. The red dye on the embroidered wall coverings was traditionally obtained from onion and pomegranate juice. I think the one I buy is factory produced and has never seen a pomegranate. Men, women and children selling balloons and other nick knacks, generally squat on their haunches against the side walls. The place buzzes with life, people shopping,walking, cars, buses, donkeys and motor bikes, all pass through the market from any of the four directions, there are no pavements. Movement is accompanied by a bevy of sound; horns honking, donkeys braying, merchants calling out their wares and children shouting, children everywhere.
Here, in Bukhara, the 50th Anniversary of the Revolution was marked by a competition setup at the beginning of the year to find the best farm worker.

Bukhara's new town is built on the outskirts unlike Samarkand with its Soviet buildings dominating the centre. This microregion of Bukhara is very pleasant, much greenery and flats with big balconies. Inevitably there are problems, the authorities are building flats but many people don't want to move out of the old clay houses with their courtyards and fruit. In every one of these old places inhabitants grow their own produce.

Bukhara region is very rich in natural gas which is now being exploited - a gas line to provide the socialist countries is under way. During the last ten years, a number of completely new towns are being built in the desert. They are mostly inhabited by young Russians, average age 30-35 years. I tried to see one of these places, but ran out of time.

Bukhara has just one hotel and I have my meals with the only other westeners: an American from Ohio, Professor of Political

Economy and two Englishmen, Robert Morley the actor and his son Sheridan, actor and critic: an unforgettable experience.

The Morleys had travelled already to Leningrad, Moscow, Tashkent and Samarkand, now Bukhara, and then on the Trans-Siberian railway to Japan. Robert Morley has been commissioned to write a number of articles for Time magazine, his travel paid for, (so this is how these people manage it – it comes with the job). I first met the larger than life Morley at the Hotel reception. The plumbing was primitive; this was not the first class accommodation he had booked. The poor young receptionist had no idea what he was talking about: class divisions in the one and only Bukhara hotel do not yet exist. I explained this, and invited him and his son to join me on my sight seeing drive. We hadn't gone so far, when Morely makes the observation that there are few men in the streets – were they all in prison? Luckily I am able to disabuse him as I have already received an apology from the Radio head that he was unable to accompany me on the excursion as it was cotton picking time, and all hands were needed in the fields. Anyway, very soon Morley demands the car stop to let him out, he'll return to the (inadequate) hotel.

My next encounter is at lunch. Morley had bought a large melon. He needs a knife. A large knife arrives, but not our meal. The dining room is full with a tourist group of East Germans. Waving the carver, Morely loudly announces that we should be served first, "It was us that won the war, not the Germans". The young waitress with little English, not surprisingly looks terrified. Food arrives. I'm not sure she understands our apologies.

When we four departed the following day, Sheridan Morely gave me his copy of the Times, as he felt sorry for me so out of touch with the west. I enjoyed my lively stay in Bukhara enhanced by the Morleys.

I'm back in Tashkent, ear splitting music comes from a group of cars careering through the main streets. Three jeeps their bonnets covered in bright materials, are full of young men playing ancient instruments dating from the 15th century: the long Uzbek horns, the Karnai, and the shorter Surnai, accompanied by the doyra, a framed drum. In accordance with custom an Uzbek wedding is being announced. The bridegroom and his friends will visit the Bride, and eat plov, the ubiquitous rice dish, with the male relatives. After the elders have eaten theirs, more than 200 guests will gather at the table. Plov is strictly made by males, being too important to be trusted to females. The bride remains out of sight at a neighbours. The marriage will take place in the Bridegroom's home.

My last two memorable days in Tashkent.

Firstly I've promised to give a talk to students at Tashkent's Foreign Languages Institute.

John, an English communist, who has lived in the SU for many years, runs the English course. We'd met at the Radio in Moscow and he was most keen that I address the students. Following my talk students' questions range from how to join the YCL[2] to a history of the Beatles and my favourite author, which I answer as best I can.. A packed audience, sitting, standing with an overflow in the corridor both of teachers and students. The students are so pleased that they can understand my English – apart from 'drugs'. I have to explain to the teachers afterwards, but not sure they understand either. I give the Institute my YCL card for their museum.

---

2   See section on YCL in Political Background

The inevitable presentation follows: a Statue of Lenin, postcards, a book of Tashkent, a tubeteika, the Uzbek hat, which is placed on my head – I look ridiculous, flowers and badges. A number of us then visit a restaurant for a huge meal of plov rice with its onion and shredded carrot, meat, quince and garlic.

We stay talking until 6pm when I am due back at the Institute as one of the teachers has arranged to take me for a meal in her old Uzbek home. The large room is filled by the long table piled high with fruit, wine, sweets, and of course plov. Women and men dance. I see a cupboard full of mattresses covered in flowered material and pillows – bed linen for sleeping on the floor. We sit eating and talking all evening. There are yet more questions from the students who want to take me on to their hostel. I'd like to, but John is concerned, I've been talking, answering questions now for hours, he bundles me into a taxi back to the hotel.

The following day women from the Radio take me to the market to buy fruit for my journey, and then to a restaurant for our midday meal – I plead no plov. Our waitress, seeing I'm a foreigner, gives me a little bunch of flowers with her very best wishes. Back to the Radio for a farewell presentation of a rhubab[3]. a traditional string instrument. Most thoughtfully, a gnarled elderly man has been invited to play it for me.

I'd decided to return to Moscow by train to get a feeling of the vastness of the country. Girls from the Institute arrive at the station with huge bunches of flowers and take photos. Three bouquets are also presented to me. Whilst saying my goodbyes, the woman attendant finds vases for the many flowers which now adorn my compartment. People on the platform peer

---

3 The rhubab is now on permanent loan to Horniman's Museum, London

through the window expecting to see a celebrity. Apart from the flowers, I have so much fruit for gifts: two honey dew melons about two foot long, each weighing several kilos, plus a box of fruit with 4 lbs of pomegranites, tomatoes; 6lbs of apples and 8lbs of grapes. And I have my case in which a heavy statue of Lenin now resides. Hopefully, I'll be met at the station.

I leave Tashkent at 4pm Tuesday on "The Uzbekistan" and won't arrive in Moscow until 7pm on Thursday. And this is just the north south distance of this vast country, its length takes far longer. My place number 1 is in a 'soft car' two berth, one of only four on the train. The compartment has a radio and white embroidered covers on the seat backs. The seat opposite is also a table so both occupants, if there was another, could sit by the window. There's a carpet on the floor and a cloth on the table. I'm presented with a teapot and bowl as soon as the train starts. Folding steps enable my case to be put up on the luggage rack. A door opens up to reveal a wash stand and shower with hot and cold water, towels and soap. This adjoins the next compartment, also with just one occupant. Green tea is available whenever I want it. And the carpet is hoovered twice a day by one of the two provodniki who look after the compartment. Very friendly and considerate, these two are husband and wife. Their daughter is learning English at school where they live in Tashkent. They are pleased to be working together, it means they get the same schedule.

Despite welcoming all the comforts and the cleanliness, I do miss the fun of mixing with other travellers. The restaurant is in the adjoining carriage, but the beer drinking men do not attract me.

Steppe, steppe, steppe, scrub interspersed with a few weak, thin trees. Some hills in Kazakhstan, sand and scrub. On

Wednesday, a lone horseman gallops across the steppe, cloak flying. I wonder, Is he taking the news of the 1917 revolution to remote villages, or is he the hero of some film? Flat, short tufted grass, camels wandering, many with covers on them with the two humps sticking out, very funny. Miles upon miles of emptiness apart from jotted occasionally small settlements with low, flat buildings, water towers, and electric pylons all the way; Lenin's promise of electrification. Just imagine what potential there is in such vast emptiness.

Akhtubinsk, the first town of industrial Russia is not reached until afternoon on Wednesday, Moscow Time. The steppe lasts until the Wednesday evening. It is replaced with fields and trees as wind breakers beside the railway line: slender white boughs rising from a bed of gold. Chalk white.

Certainly my visit gave me glimpses of other cultures as I'd hoped. I saw the stark divisions in women's emancipation – at their extremes the high ranking female officials and in contrast the women squatting in the sandy earth bearing child after child. But above all was the warmth I met, the liveliness and interest that the young students showed about other cultures. And most impressive was the kindness and generosity I received.

I did not ride a camel though, nor even a donkey.

Kalinin Prospekt 2

Returned from my month in Uzbekistan I'm eager to check the progress made on Kalinin Prospekt.

It's always interesting to see something develop, and this is no exception. Besides which it's the first new development in the centre of Moscow for some time. I've been watching the buildings grow day by day and behind a screen of floodlights at night. The V shaped office blocks on one side of the street, opposite the flats on the other, have each been rising floor by floor for some weeks. Now they've reached their full height; 26 storeys for the offices and 24 for the five blocks of flats. This, though, is just the basic structure of the street; around them is a whole living complex. For the people about to move in, much is provided. The hoardings come down and reveal the glass shop fronts. Now things are really moving apace.

Vilnuis

November 1st. I'm staying with a family in Vilnius, the capital of Lithuania. The town still has a feel of the middle ages I find it very attractive. The couple are journalists and associated with the arts. They are most welcoming, and I'm being extremely well fed. In return I can help their young daughter who is studying English. The flat is attractive and stylish. And they own a car, not so common. One day we go to the coast which we approach through pine forests and sand dunes. On the way we find ourselves walking through a green burial ground – it isn't enclosed, just simple headstones amongst the undergrowth. Its simplicity and peacefulness impresses me. It's somewhere so pleasant for friends and family to visit and remember.

The children's café in Vilnuis is another imaginative place. Children's café's and theatres are not uncommon in the Soviet Union. This is a particularly attractive one: child size furniture, bright, interesting decoration, a joy to visit.

November 7th and we join the Revolution's anniversary parade. I'm impressed by the spirit, though evidently the emphasis is on Lithuanian nationalism. Lithuanians are 65% of the population. There is much singing and the arts in general are fostered. I'd love to be here in the summer sometime to witness the mass song festivals. It seems each village has its choir. Each Baltic republic has its festival. Then the Republics come together for a combined festival.

The Baltics are also famed for their amber. No wonder, it is beautiful. The illustrative, particularly graphic art, is likewise of a high quality. As a leaving gift, the family insist I take their folder of etchings of Shakespeare's plays. These certainly have nothing in common with socialist realism.

This was a warm and interesting short break.

Moscow Life 2

I arrive back in Moscow for New Year 1968. New Year 3.40am and Moscow is alive with people strolling through the snow. Tanya Kitsova kindly invites me to celebrate at her place. I set out for Tanya's feeling very down in the dumps, lose my way and wander around for one and a half hours by the river – not a good introduction to the New Year. Then find I've upset Lena because I hadn't gone to them.

However, I find I have flu which probably explains the negativity.

Traditional cures
And with the flu comes another Russian tradition - *Banki*[1]. Any illness always produces a range of 'proven' cures not infrequently handed down from a Siberian babushka. One inflicted on me now by Lena, my neighbour is the dreaded *banki*. Glass jars are placed on my back. When removed the air trapped inside supposedly sucks up the impurities in the blood. Lena insists that this will cure my flu. When the jars are removed, I'm left with a back decorated with red rings. A less painful cure is raspberry tea. Pity Lena is made of sterner stuff, I undergo the *banki*.

But Lena is not alone. Unfortunately I need to visit the dentist. Why no injection? "Injections damage your brain cells" I'm assured. Subsequently a friend later informs me, dentists just don't have any injections. I don't repeat my visit.

---

1 Cupping treatment

Another Russia, 18/19 January 1968
Lena invites me to watch a film on TV about young children organising Pioneer detachments during the civil war. My neighbours don't seem to get tired of watching these films, although they know the stories inside out. The effects of war are reflected in many plays as well, such as Bulgakov's, *The White Guard* and the moving *Mothers' Fields* – based on the book by Aitmatov about a mother's life after the loss of her husband and two sons. The war is still so very current to people here and makes their desire for peace so heartfelt and meaningful.

One such TV film I see is about a child raised by a foster parent during the war. Her natural mother finds her after the war, but the child no longer knows her. Such tragedies happened to so many children. In such a vast country this could mean children brought up by nationalities other than their own.

Lena has a friend visiting, also watching television. She lives in a northern village in the region of Arkhangelsk. She's on her way home from a month in a sanatorium. The first time she's ever left her village. She'd decided to have this treat, as her three children she'd brought up alone have now all left home. Her husband was killed in the war. These war films remain personal to so many. There is no TV in her village, only in Arkhangelsk. Winter lasts eight months, snow remains until the end of May. It's hard to imagine such a different life.

It has become apparent to me, that my jeans are not alone in being severely frowned upon. Trousers in general are considered inappropriate wear for women in public – unless trousers for sports. They are unacceptable in restaurants and places of entertainment. Jeans are considered western and also unacceptable. But those young men who have procured a pair from a western visitor, are the envy of other young men, and generally noticed by all. The elderly make their opposition known.

Children, have a special place in the heart of Russians. No matter whose child, everyone pays attention to it, endearingly. There are no inhibitions where children are concerned. "Our children are our flowers". "..children are the hope and expression of our future".

Morality –and the babushkas
The combination of the chronic housing shortage and the babushkas' custodians of Soviet morality can lead to difficult situations. Jeans at the bus stop was an early encounter, but not isolated. However, incidences can always be open to interpretation. The *dezhurnaya* seated by the entrance to our block of flats is for our protection. But it feels also, at least in my case, that any male visitor is noted, and disapproval is apparent if the visitor stays late.

This expression of morality is most marked when I visit a radio technician I know. We have a common interest in jazz so he invites me to spend an evening listening to his collection. As a technician he has access to western music programmes and has copied (pirated) jazz.

His room, actually half a room, is separated by a curtain. On the other side is a middle aged woman, maybe a relation. The jazz is great, but we are interrupted by a militia entering the room. It appears the woman has called him – the issues are many: noise, jazz, lateness, and a woman alone with a man. It is the latter that the militia focusses on. Apparently I am accused of being a whore – my growing Russian vocabulary has not yet encompassed such terms but I am reliably informed by my companion. At this point I draw myself to my full height of 5ft 3ins and announce in my most haughty English, that I will contact the British Embassy. Enough was understood for me to receive an embarrassed apology. But it ended our one and only jazz evening. We hadn't even danced.

The babushkas will not allow feet on seats.

However rights and wrongs are not confined to the babushkas. In December an argument is taking place on the bus between a student and a number of women about the ethics of giving up a seat and of accepting it. These social questions so often are worked out in public with many citizens giving their opinions.

Birth
23rd August 1968. The sun is shining and I'm sitting with Zena's daughters in a beautiful place. It's where they used to have a dacha, adjacent to the Istra River, a tributary of the Moskva. The opposite bank is woodland and we're surrounded by trees. We have also visited two churches, first a 13th century wooden one. Then in the other, we watched three babies being christened. Interestingly, only the grandmothers and father stood with the baby, the mothers were obliged to keep in the background.

Death
I witness the other end of life during one of my wanderings in the countryside. I'm walking through an apparently empty field, when from behind me comes a funeral procession - an open coffin and a group of mourners. The coffin contains both the red flag, and an icon. The mourners include men in suits who seem like minor officials. A few minutes later, a second coffin appears, also open. No red flag, but a picture of the old woman lying in the coffin. The three mourners kiss her picture as if it is an icon. As they disappear ahead, presumably to a church beyond this field, I'm left with a bizarre sense of having witnessed two Russia's: the past remains in the present and the present retains a link with its past.

I am again alone in the vast field.

Street life
What is hard for the English visitor to take although acceptable to the babushkas, is the frequent use of spittoons. They are common on the street and in the metro. Most people spit, women as well as men, and not all into a spittoon. I'm informed it's due to the bronchial trouble resulting from the climate.

As I come to know Moscow, wandering off the wide main thoroughfares, it becomes more homely, even reminding me of London. Higgledy-piggledy, in the side streets are green squares, or the inner courtyards of the blocks of flats. There are of course differences as well, the groups of men playing dominoes or chess in the public gardens. The games don't stop in winter; the boards are balanced on the upturned benches.

In contrast to the remnants of the old wooden houses, and the soviet blocks to house the many, I also discover stunning futurist buildings, a reminder of the exciting experiments across the arts in the early decades of the early 20th century.[2]

April 13th '68. It's Saturday but I'm working. This gives me a day off during the week. I can then visit galleries, exhibitions and museums more comfortably. Russians, both Muscovites and those from out of town, are keen visitors usually in large groups preferably with a guide. The entrance fees don't appear to be a hindrance.

I inform my mother in a letter home that I have an almost impossible task of searching for shoes. I wonder if that's

---

[2] To my dismay, I discovered from an illustrated talk at the Pushkin House in London, that since the demise of the USSR, these buildings having survived the proscribed policies of the Stalin years and the devastation of the war, are now being demolished.

counted as propaganda.

It's the Russian Sino split. The confrontation appears to be coming to a head. We are given a talk at the radio with a video showing Chinese soldiers pricking Soviet border guards with needles. From the window of my flat I can see Russians attacking the US embassy with ink blots. It all seems ridiculous. It's rumoured that the large Chinese restaurant *Pekin* has only rice available.

I've bought a vacuum cleaner having sought out the voltage. It's a conveniently small and comes with six gadgets. I haven't actually tried it yet as there's two small springs with no illustration showing where they should fit in. It cost 40R. If it's any good I'll bring it home with me.

The other evening I met a fine young lad, Volodya, one of the best products of socialist society. So many of the people I've been forced to mix with are negative, I've got heartily sick of it. Volodya reminds me of Joseph, a young scientist I've met a couple of times who works in Akademgorodok Siberia. They're highly educated, fully aware of the problems and mistakes, but they consider as part of society it's up to them to do something about it. They also know what's good here. Really I feel great hope in these people for the future of Russia.

The last time I saw Joseph was 22nd August. He was running to Mayakovsky Station, "I'm so ashamed, so ashamed" he gasped – of the tanks that had entered Prague.

I'm reading Ostrovsky's *How the steel was tempered.*
This depicts a vivid picture of the confusion rampant throughout Russia in the first years after the revolution. It describes how towns and villages passed from one side or faction to another with much of the population completely at sea. (Pasternak's *Dr*

Zhivago paints a similar picture). And this was repeated just over twenty years later in WW2 and we talk about fifty years of socialism and wonder about nationalism.

I've finished Ostrovsky – one of the most moving books I've ever read, I long to read it to others. How many who have read it can feel that their lives have been worthwhile. How many of my days are spent without purpose?

On Sasha's 13th birthday the boys buy one another presents including Ostrovsky's *Heroes of the Civil War*.

1969-1970

1969 Moscow University

For the first quarter of 1969 I remained working at Radio Moscow. I managed to extend my contract by a month or so. In the autumn I returned to Moscow to join a nine month language course until the summer of 1970 at Moscow University.

New Year

As children have a two-week holiday from school, many go to winter camps or to parties and entertainments held at the Pioneer palaces, the Luzhniki Stadium and the Kremlin. If children are seen out with large cartons of sweets, it's a sure indicator that they've been to one of these parties.

Tightly clutching the hand of eight year old Misha, I slither over the frozen ground outside the metro as we wend our way amongst the seemingly continuous stream of Mums and Dads with their penguin like offspring. Tanya has entrusted me with her son to take him to the *Yolka*[1] the children's celebration of New Year at Luzhniki, the Palace of Sports. Excited chatter and laughter fill the air. Loud speakers cut through the babble with instructions, "All wishing to take the bus, this way please".

Misha and I find ourselves in the first section of an open bus. We arrive at the back entrance of the stadium, to be met by clowns and a man on stilts who towers above Misha. Cardboard figures from Russian folk tales indicate our tickets' allotted entrance. We're inside the arena, at this time of year it's an ice rink. A band in fancy dress play children's songs. Meanwhile Mums and Dads queue up with the families' coats, quite an undertaking in itself. As in most venues in Moscow it is unacceptable to keep outdoor garments on inside. Once we're in our seats we can look around. By 4pm it's almost full, that's 10,000 faces alive with anticipation – Mums and Dads as well. A man appears with a microphone - the Compere. His greeting receives an instant response from thousands of young people. This is one audience that doesn't have to be warmed up.

So we begin. First we have a competition, two teams of young boys, armed with rackets and large balloons are said to represent Moscow's most popular sports clubs: Spartak and Dynamo. "Who's for Spartak?" A great roar bursts out. "Who's for Dynamo?" louder still. Misha and I support Spartak. And hooray, our team win. They are awarded a great big bouncy ball. Each boy in the team calls out his name over the mic, probably for them the most thrilling part of all.

A smart young woman now takes the floor. And teaches us the chorus of a new pioneer song. The audience sing with gusto.

Then darkness. An electric silence fills the air. Roving coloured lights sweep over the ice, picking out the skating figures of elves and fairies, singing as they dance. And on comes an old bearded man in a rocket ship - *Ded Moroz*, Grandfather Frost. The show has begun

Vera and Volodya

Time to catch up with Vera and Volodya. Until September '69 they have a short let of a pleasant one roomed flat in a co-operative. Vera wanted them to be on their own for the birth of their first child, due in August, rather than being with her parents. I'm here on the 7th of January 1969 for a late meal to celebrate New Year.

It's a traditional Russian meal. Beer, brown bread, potatoes and sauerkraut, followed by tea, white bread and sausage. And, the piece de la resistance: dried fish from Krasnodar bought on the black market. Which Volodya defends[1].

"Well, what are you to do if it all goes for export. We also like fish".

After six years at college, Volodya will earn 90R a month as a specialist engineer in cosmonaut instruments. The highest pay he can receive after a post-graduate course will be 180R. He contrasts this with the pay of an unskilled labourer doing heavy work who he claims, earns three times as much. I notice that Volodya is efficient and competent about the flat, doing what's necessary without being asked.

Like other young people that I spend time with, I'm impressed by their wide range of interests.

---

1 Volodya is critical but highly defensive of his homeland. In 1989, for example when particular economic difficulties meant a shortage of soap. Volodya was highly indignant of my offerings. He rejected 'hand outs' from the West, "We have soap" showing me a stack in a cupboard.

Baby care

In November 1969, back in Moscow, I'm invited by Vera's parents for Sunday lunch.

The rented flat had to be returned to its owner, so they are now back living with Vera's parents. Most importantly I see baby Anna, who was born in August, and is now three months old. She is lovely. I also meet Volodya's parents. An interesting discussion on child rearing takes up most of the afternoon. It reveals a wide rift between the two generations. And another situation exacerbated by the shortage of housing.

Clothes are an example. Amongst other concerns both grandmothers are sure Anna isn't sufficiently wrapped up. Vera and Volodya disagree. They are far less restrictive. I support the younger generation, but silently.

New Year 1970, with Vera back home, her parents invite me to spend it with them. The flat is full with friends mostly of their generation. The time is spent singing all the old songs. One guest recited poetry.

Such a warm and lovely atmosphere.

An upsetting experience

Visit to offices of the Party Central Committee

Towards the end of my contract, February 1969, I had found a niche for myself at the Radio writing and broadcasting which I was enjoying. Extending my contract became attractive. It seemed that to do so it was necessary to get permission from an official at the Communist Party's Central offices. This entailed visiting an area of Moscow unfamiliar to me.

I was taken aback by the number of supplicants. The queue went winding down the street and round the corner. It was not a pretty sight. Poverty and disability were paramount. Many were invalids wanting pensions, or increase to a liveable pension or help for other desperate needs. Some had travelled long distances to plead at this central office in Moscow. Here were not the one or two amputees seen daily on Moscow's streets, but the overwhelming sight of the many pushing themselves on wooden trolleys low on the ground. War victims a quarter of a century after the war ended. Where else in Europe are there such sights? But then Europe had the Marshall Plan, support for Germany that had been the enemy. Russia who suffered more than any of the allies and had lost more people than all the other European countries combined, had no financial support, but instead outright opposition with the advent of the cold war.

But for me the unsettling question remained, were these factors an adequate explanation for what I witnessed in that queue?

Kalinin Prospekt 3

By 1970 Kalinin Prospekt is displaying its full glory. It has become a shopper's paradise. On one side of the street joining the cinema and bread shop are a grocers, flower shop – set in a courtyard with an ornamental pond, fashion salon with a café where prospective buyers can watch fashion shows, photographic store, a gift shop, ice cream parlour catering for 900 – ice cream[1] is rightly popular all year round, a store for newly-weds, beauty salon and hairdressing with a café and a beauty room for talks on cosmetics.

Adjoining the side of the "House of Books" with its hall for poetry readings and talks, are a jewellers, perfumery and music store, a shop selling synthetic goods, a shop offering pre-cooked food, a restaurant seating 2,000 plus rooms for private parties and a couple of coffee bars. In addition there are services including laundry, shoe repairs, dry cleaning and a hire shop.

However, I'm particularly interested in the far end of the street. For many months a small church nestling against the last block of flats had been wrapped in scaffolding. This in itself was something to celebrate. Originally the planners had intended to remove it, three attempts were made to demolish it with dynamite. Its deliverance was won by a pressure group, the *All-Russian Society for the Protection of Monuments of History and Culture.* The achievements of this and other pressure groups were instrumental in developing my view that the USSR was more complex than often presented. Now the scaffolding is removed to reveal a gem, a glistening white

---

1 Soviet ice cream is made only of natural, fresh ingredients. This was established by State food standards in the 1930s

church with golden cupola, its edges picked out in green. Despite being nestled against the 24 stories of its neighbour, it holds its own, a survival of the Old Arbat but in a re-defined role. It now houses exhibits of natural forms selected from forest growth.

Moscow life 3

Inoculation
January 1969. At work today I am inoculated against the Hong Kong Flu by liquid in my nose. At least it means I escape Leni's *banki*. It's certainly less painful and hopefully more effective. It's in preparation for an expected epidemic. School children are also being vaccinated and shop assistants are wearing muslin masks

Infant custom
Walking past a hospital, I'm reminded of the discussion between Vera and Volodya and their parents; was baby Anna sufficiently wrapped up. The older generation's view is in keeping with hospital practice. Every new born baby is tightly wrapped, restricting their movement, to give them a feeling of security. A common site in Moscow is to see these swaddled parcels held up to hospital windows by the mother inside so the father standing on the street below can have a glimpse of his child. Fathers are not allowed in the hospital on grounds of hygiene. This no doubt was a necessary precaution given the living conditions in the early years of the Soviet Union, but seventy years later it seems unnecessary, and perhaps hinders the father's bonding with their offspring[1].

Suburbs expansion
Come the weekend, time to go skiing again. I take the metro as far as it goes in the North east of Moscow. I was here some months previously and remember a forested area with gentle slopes which I reckon will be just right for me.

---

[1] At a meeting in Ivanovo in 1987 the head of a maternity unit, asked us –a group of 8 British women, whether we thought it advisable that husbands witness their child's birth. A hospital in Leningrad had already introduced this and he was considering doing so.

But emerging from the subway, I get a jolt. All around are blocks of flats, and as for the forest, not a fir tree in sight. Then I remember there had been signs of a building site, a few blocks already built and cranes standing around. But now, in less than a year, people have already moved in. I make my way through courtyards and over builders' rubble until I glimpse a line of trees. There ahead lies the snow for a day of skiing.

The nice thing about it, once I've passed through the building site, I don't have to worry about fences or whether I'm trespassing. This is nationalisation of land. If it belongs to the people in general, who wants to keep who off it? So, no fences. The land is free for all to enjoy – like me when it's covered in snow. Thousands of Muscovites, whole families spend their weekends cross country skiing for free. No one's going to charge you anything.

There is another beneficial aspect of this socialist organisation of land. Russians know that they will always have their forests and green belts. The law ensures that no individual or company can buy the land for their private homes. The Moscow city boundary is fixed by law and is surrounded by 'rest zones', in other words, green belts. As for city development, that too is strictly controlled. New housing is going up, and that's upwards. As I know from my neighbours' communal flat, there is still a desperate housing shortage. As for Moscow's centre, the one thing you won't find is empty office blocks. A number of old houses remain, but future plans, fully discussed in Moscow's local papers between the architects and the public, include schemes to develop the area as a cultural centre serviced by improved transport from the suburbs to the centre.

Professionals' clubs
The Professions have their own clubs. Membership is gained by submission of relevant work. Facilities vary but can include

a restaurant of high quality, bar, lounge, coffee bar, and hall with a stage, and offer performances if appropriate, film shows, discussions. I was taken to a performance of Shostakovich playing his *Preludes and Fugues* at either the Writers or Journalists club. Bernie is a member of both. I remember having strawberries at one of them on my birthday – a real treat.

The system
Another negative experience of the system, although unlike the scene at the Central Offices, this was on an individual scale. I was sitting outside the studio at the Radio when Bernie handed me a large official looking envelope. He silently indicated I should open it.

Inside was revealed:

Your request to accompany the Soviet team to oversee the programme is rejected.

No explanation given.

I was aware that Bernie had been the chief organiser of the Olympic programme for the Soviet team. I also knew how much he'd been looking forward to accompanying the team to Canada. It was a country he knew from a spell in the Canadian army. Bernie was acclaimed internationally as a top sports writer, was trusted with underground rehearsals in case of nuclear war, had been a Soviet translator at the Nuremburg Trials, yet wasn't trusted to visit the West even in support of the Soviet sports teams.

Most upsetting though was his silent acceptance of the official decision; his knowledge that the decision was irreversible. This was another reality of the Soviet Communist party.

Moscow University 1969-1970

My association with the Soviet system did not end on completion of the contract in 1969.

Before I left Moscow I had an interview in the Kremlin with the Deputy Minister of Education about a possible place on the one year preparatory course for teachers of Russian at Moscow State University, the MGU. I'd become friends with Kate who was on the course the previous year. Whoever arranged the interview remained unclear to me, as did its outcome. I returned home to my parents on finishing at Radio Moscow and spent the summer term teaching in a primary school.

Towards the end of the summer, a telegram arrived: the course had started already, and where was I? Apparently, I'd been accepted. My red trunk which had travelled backwards and forwards, was on its way home by sea, but had yet to arrive. On enquiry it appeared it was on a ship bound to Cuba, so had to be stopped midway and re-directed to the UK. We picked it up from Tilbury. I was most indignant when customs insisted opening the bottle of home-made pepper vodka to test its strength. A Russian PhD student had given it to me as a gift. His babushka had made it for him; its strength had not concerned her. Luckily once returned to its original bottle, it was still drinkable.

Most of the contents of my trunk now had to be re-packed for my return to Moscow; my fur coat, my life saving *shapka*, and my hoover. So they travelled with me on the ship the Nadezhda Krupskaya to Leningrad, then train to Moscow. The Nadezhda Krupskaya was on its last sailing of the season. Many of the passengers were cold Africans embarking on studies at Moscow's Patrice Lumumba University. Many of whom said they would have preferred the US. Apparently the ship lacked stabilisers. This explained why most of the passengers were ill as we sailed round the Gulf of Finland. Only nine of us turned up for breakfast – to see our plates sliding off the tables. My assumed superiority of seaworthiness was put in its place, when, on arrival at MGU I was given a Russian test, while I swayed backwards and forwards as if adjusting to the movement of the ship. For months whenever I was tired the sensation reappeared.

So I returned to Moscow, a month late, to attend the language course for teachers of Russian at Moscow State University from autumn 1969 to summer 1970.

On the basis of the oral test, I was allocated to one of the advanced classes which suited me fine – until we had to write. My woeful lack of grammar had me moved down to the class just above the Beginners. Unfortunately the four students in the class were elderly teachers of Russian and concentrated on the niceties of grammar, moreover they were all Indian and I feared my Russian would acquire an Indian accent.

Any progress I made in Russian was due to my time with Tapio, a Finnish student in the Beginners' class with whom I spoke only Russian - freely with no inhibitions as I knew more than him.

Due to my late arrival, there was no accommodation for me with the other course members. I was given a temporary room on the far side of the wedding cake building. It was not only inconvenient, but awaiting me were the dreaded cockroaches. I was promised I'd be moved any day, but the days kept being extended. Not until several weeks later did a room become available with the rest of the course. Luxury, it was one of a pair opening off a small hall way, as did a bathroom for the two of us. Most importantly, we were cockroach free. My neighbour, Annette was French and a fluent Russian speaker.

The delay in a room change was not a good start. As I wrote to my parents at the time….

> *"still not been given another room. I'm promised every day, but no results. The toilet doesn't work now. I've been doing my washing at various people's places and having showers where and when possible. I've also just been changed to another group, a much lower one as my grammar is so poor..... I'm trying to make up what I don't know, but it's difficult as I work in other people's rooms and my books are in different places. In other words I'm back where I was before, but I suppose it will eventually work out alright. Ann, the other English girl on the course and I get on well. And an Indian lady keeps me well fed. I've resorted to Bernie's at times. My room is the coldest place".*

There is an interesting mixture of people on the course; three from Japan and four Indians, a woman from Columbia, a guy from Brazil, a group from Finland, and many from western Europe, Most of us, but not all are in our twenties. We are also on the course for diverse reasons. Tapio is Secretary of the Finnish/Soviet Friendship Society so needs to learn Russian, whereas Italian Jean Carlo Olivetti is learning Russian for trade purposes. I'm not sure why the guy from West Berlin is on the course, the Indians and the Japanese are teachers of Russian. However, it is a great mix helped by the generous stipend provided us, more generous than awarded to soviet postgraduates. Evristo from Brazil spends his grant immediately and invites us all to a feast. We eat bear, reindeer and other exotic ingredients – my vegetarianism is suspended. Then for the rest of the month, Evristo lives off the rest of us. No one minds. He is expecting to be imprisoned when he returns home.

The course doesn't erase my previous Moscow life. Visits to the Bolshoi and other venues continue, just less frequently. I keep in touch with Helen and Tanya, Vera and her family, my old neighbours, and of course Bernie. Trips out of Moscow to Leningrad, Estonia and the churches on the Golden Ring are now organised by MGU.

What follows are some isolated memories of that time.

Culture
Early on I arranged that a couple of dancers from the Bolshoi would run some sessions for us at MGU. I managed to persuade a mixed group from our course to join me. We were not impressive. I think the sessions were short lived.

Tapio and I had a memorable evening at the Bolshoi.

On 20th April we go to see "Evgenii Onegin" at the Bolshoi in a performance to mark 100th anniversary of Lenin's birthday. A most lavish production, wonderful singing and the orchestra was superb. None other than Rostropovich conducted, and his wife, Galina Vishnevskaya sang Tat'yana. We sat up in the gods. In front of us was a kolkhoz delegation from Hungary or Rumania or somewhere that needed translation. This they proceeded to do helping one another – in loud whispers. One of them removed his boots, judging by the odour reaching us. A very large woman sitting in front of me became rather warm and opened her side zip to have a good scratch. For them, and others behind me, the opera only started when the curtain was raised and there was something to look at. I still enjoyed the performance though and was glad we went.

Babushka morality
My friend Tapio invites me to visit a Finnish Communist official who is in Moscow for talks. We spend the evening

in his hotel room. On leaving, the babushka sitting at the end of the corridor accuses me of immorality for spending the evening with two men. We hadn't even been listening to jazz, but discussing politics. In keeping with the times, it is me the female who is blamed. However, hotels in Moscow do have a reputation for prostitutes, especially with foreigners.

Disgrace in Tallinn, Estonia
We have a trip to Estonia. Tallinn the capital is a most attractive town and historic centre. Set up on a hill from where it commands views of the beautiful surrounding countryside it's also on the coast. Our first evening is spent until the early hours watching the sky of the white night. Magical. The weather is perfect, not very bright but a light dusk. I manage a few hours sleep, but then the rest of the day is more eventful than desirable. Tapio has an arrangement to meet with members of the city leadership and invites me to join them. The 'meeting' takes place on a boat, equipped with a bar. We spend hours round a table toasting the normal suspects, peace etc. and trying out various drinks and their combinations. My attempts to desist are ruled out – how can you refuse a toast to peace? Belatedly we arrive at the fortress cum restaurant for lunch - I am unable to eat. We leave for our train to Moscow. Tapio locks the carriage door, ignoring the demand from others to have their place. All I want to do is sleep. The lead teacher berates us, calls me a disgrace, I think it is taken for granted that the Finns get drunk. I stir myself sufficiently to furiously retaliate insisting it is the city fathers who were responsible and not fitting behaviour for leading communists. It is a black mark against me.

End of the course
I somewhat redeem myself with the end of course exams. I achieve the top mark 5 for Russian history and for Literature. And I achieve the Certificate of a Teacher of Russian –

unearned; I am still hazy on grammar. Earlier I make my mark on the hundredth anniversary of Lenin's birth. We were invited to contribute something on Lenin. I choose to speak on Lenin and Youth.

As I described it to my parents:

> *"There's been so many speeches and conferences on the event, including our faculty. Ten of us spoke on Lenin last Saturday. I chose Lenin and youth. I was a success because I didn't read from a script and critically referred to the disenchantment of today's youth. So many of the officials were anything but pleased and my Russian was appalling. My teacher was in despair, says she just doesn't know what to do with me. But the students understood me better than the other speakers, at least the students who know little Russian...'the student from West Germany praised me for a sincere speech - and they all clapped. I was very pleased because he's quite non-progressive (could have been the reason). He said it would have helped to understand English! But still the message got across, which is the important thing. But what I am going to do about the language I just don't know".*

Despite my own limited progress, the course was an excellent and generous gift which most benefitted from.

Journey home

The course ended on the 16th July. Our journey home was an adventure, befitting of my three years in Moscow. Ann and I decided to travel by ship. Then spend a week in Greece, back on ship to Marseilles, train to Paris where we had been invited to stay with Annette's mother before returning home. Our embarkation allowed several hours in Odessa, so different from Moscow. Many of the apartments displayed cards offering tutorials, especially music lessons. The famous steps did not have the same grandeur as depicted in Eisenstein's film. We changed ships in Istanbul. We sat on the floor of the Blue Mosque.

Unfortunately, Ann left me standing with all her luggage and my own before re-boarding, while she chased after a last minute purchase. It was the middle of the day, I couldn't move, she took far longer than intended, when I boarded the ship it was with piercing abdominal pains. Ann called the ship's doctor who declared it was my appendix. He then announced that his instruments were too rusty but insisted I remain in my bunk. When we reached Italy, I had to say my good byes to the Italians through the porthole.

The rest of our travels were fine. I no longer had pains. In Athens we slept under a lemon tree in the garden of a Greek communist recently released from prison. We rented a room and mattresses on the floor in a small village on Aegina for a week, and explored the island. One evening the inhabitants brought out their chairs to the beach to watch the monthly film show against a white painted wall. We followed suit – the films were American with Greek subtitles.

From Greece we took a ship to Marseilles and then spent a week in Paris.

The journey home, in all its variety, seemed a fitting conclusion to my three years in Moscow.

My Friends - afterwards

Lena: my neighbour
Some years after I left Moscow, my neighbours' certainty that they would be provided with a home of their own, was realised. They were allocated a two bedroom flat in one of Moscow's new suburbs. Sasha, by now a student, embarking on his PhD, had his own room for the very first time. Tragically he died a few years later from a blood disorder just on the conclusion of his PhD. Lena and Yuri were devastated. The last time I saw Yuri, he accompanied me to the bus stop. For a man normally of few words, he revealed his feelings, how empty his life now felt. He said after Sasha's death there was nothing to live for. He died just months later.

Lena, once a proud member of the CPSU, now takes comfort from religion. However with the dogged determination for survival common to Russian women, she survives. Now in her eighties, every spring she travels by train far out of Moscow to her simple wooden dacha, returning only in the autumn. There she cultivates fruit and vegetables, much of which she pickles and carries back home for nourishment in the winter.

Student friends of Sasha have retained contact with Lena and at some point came to an arrangement with her, the flat is now in their name on the grounds that Lena remain there, rent free during her lifetime. Lena's generosity to me has continued. Every year, she has sent me presents from the proceeds of the sale.

In 2002 when visiting Lena, to my surprise she told me that the unfriendly woman in the communal flat had threatened to inform the KGB that Lena was friendly with a foreigner. I never felt a whisper of that threat, as Lena and Yuri always welcomed me frequently and warmly .

Vera and Volodya: my friends
Vera and I keep in touch. She and Volodya spend much time out of Moscow in the family dacha, often with their grandchildren. Their son has a good job in IT which has enabled the family including his parents to have foreign holidays. In the early 1990s Vera worked at the Gorbachev Foundation. She found Gorbachev very friendly, but was critical of his readiness to take up each new idea. She left and worked with a woman who, financed by her husband, was producing and selling dolls and teddy bears, for dollars, very expensive. Her private car included an armed driver. For me these two jobs epitomised the contradictory extremes of the Soviet Union at that stage. Vera became an expert in teddy bears writing a book about their history. She insisted on buying a bear for me. She has now retired. I get the impression that Vera and Volodya live their lives unheeded by political issues. Vera frequently sends me photos of holidays and of her grandchildren.

They are all well.

Bernie: my mentor
I continued to see Bernie during my year at the university. When I first returned, we met at the ice cream parlour we used to frequent when I worked at the radio. Unfortunately it seemed for health reasons Bernie was no longer allowed ice cream. He continued to give me the occasional tickets for dance and theatre. Later, when I was accompanying students in Kalinin, I had a couple of days in Moscow and was able to spend an evening at his place. Zoya was out of the country at an international peace conference and had arranged for Bernie's daughter to stay with him. Much later I discovered that was because he had had a stroke. It was not apparent to me at the time, to all appearances he'd recovered. He insisted taking me to the bus stop. It was a long wait and bitterly cold. I tried persuading him to leave and return home, to no avail.

One day, back at my parents, my mother handed me a copy of *Soviet Weekly*. It contained an article regretting the death of the paper's regular sports commentator, Victor Kuprianov - Bernie Cooper.

Helen: my friend from the Pool
When Bernie died, Helen thoughtfully asked his family to let me know. That didn't happen. But when I later visited Moscow, she took me to a cemetery in North Moscow to visit his grave and showed me the death notice in the foyer of the radio which mentioned his underground work[1]. Although Helen said there was much more it didn't say, maybe didn't know about his activities.

When I returned back to the UK, Helen and I kept up a correspondence until she said it had to cease as it was in danger of affecting her sister's work in the US in some way.

In 1989, when I took my son Jamie to Moscow for Christmas and New Year, we had a warm meeting with Helen. We met other members of the family, although her father was no more. Helen and Jamie got on very well. I was so pleased she had met him. It was the last time I saw Helen.

I learnt more about Helen when her cousin Irena, whom I'd not met in Moscow, contacted me in London, Helen had given her my address. In recording Irena's childhood I discovered that in the 1920s Helen and her mother had accompanied Irena's father to England, who worked for the Baltic Steam Company. Helen and Irena went to Broomfield, the oldest private school in Kew. Irena remembers it as opposite Kew Gardens. In the kindergarten they were fairies in a production

---

1 It was the practice to have a photo of employees who died displayed in the foyer.

of "Midsummer Night's Dream". Helen's mother made the green gauze dresses and wreathes of flowers. Irena remembers the time as idyllic, even becoming head girl. But her father was recalled to Moscow when she was 17 years old. What a shock the contrast of Moscow must have been to the privileged life of her childhood. Apparently Helen and her mother didn't remain all those years in London. Maybe that's why Helen never mentioned to me that she'd lived there. Maybe it was connected with her father.

Tom and Yuri: Radio Announcers from the English section
Tom: When I returned to England I made enquiries through the Red Cross on Tom's behalf. A sister was located. Tom informed me that they had since corresponded and was delighted that she had invited him to visit.

At the same time, Tom also informed me that Bernie's role was to keep an eye on Western females. Well, if that were so, he did it very well. At no time did I feel threatened or compromised by him. Maybe he'd decided I wasn't good spy material.

Yuri: When my parents visited Moscow and Leningrad after my return home in '69, I put them in touch with Yuri, Tanya and Helen, all English speakers. Yuri attached himself to their tourist group. He became friends with a young woman whom apparently he decided to marry. It seems the Russian authorities presumed, wrongly, I had arranged this, hence the refusal to allow me into the Radio when I returned to Moscow for the university.

I had no further contact with him.

Apart from my particular friends, it seemed to me in general at that time, that Russians felt they had their backs against the wall. That they didn't really trust foreigners, despite their politeness, such as insisting they went to the front of any queue. However, once a foreigner is accepted, I found Russians' hospitality, their kindness and generosity boundless.

After Moscow
Back in the UK I had to find work. I would have liked to continue radio work in some form, but presumed that would be impossible, so returned to teaching.

However, I was more interested in exploring my experience of the USSR. I took a degree in Sociology with Russian options.at Essex University. In my third year I studied the European reform movements of Yugoslavia, Hungary and Czechoslovakia. My visits to Abramtsevo became the subject of a project. My final long essay was a study of the Agitprop trains.

The degree whetted my appetite. I went on to do a PhD: the position of Soviet women in the political hierarchy, why the glass ceiling for women appeared to stop at *oblast*, district level. This involved research on Women's Councils and political consciousness.[2]

Return visits to Moscow:
In 1975 I joined a group of Russian language students as a deputy leader for a month in Kalinin. I was able to spend time in the library there to research the agitprop movement for my final long essay. We visited Moscow for a couple of days and I was able to see Bernie.

When my son was almost two in 1981, I spent a month in Moscow's Lenin Library researching material for my PhD.

---

[2] Women and Politics in the USSR-consciousness raising and Soviet Women's groups. Genia K Browning Wheatsheaf, 1987,Schuster 1989

In 1989 I was in Moscow twice. The atmosphere was exhilarating, markedly transformed by the Gorbachev reforms of *perestroika and glasnost,* reconstruction and openness. In the autumn I led a group of Labour Party women to meet women's organisations which included a visit to Ivanovo, "The Women's Town". This was followed by a tourist trip with my ten year old son for Xmas then we stayed on for the New Year of 1990 when Jamie met Vera's ten year old son, Vanya and they visited the Moscow Circus.

My last visit in 2002 had none of the excitement of 1989. I arrived in Moscow for just two days on the trans-Siberian railway from Beijing. This was a Moscow I no longer recognised. I took the trolley bus B to Vera's from the notorious jeans bus top outside my old flat on the *Garden Ring* to recapture a sense of the Moscow I'd known.

Thus, I've had a taste of Russia from the 50th anniversary of the revolution to the breakup of the USSR.

My fondest memories of Russia: the countryside, Abramtsevo and Vera's family dacha, the sound of its language and the warmth of its people.

Political Background

I was reared in a 'party family'[1]. The Soviet Union was our hope for the future. My parents were amongst those who stayed in the CP after the shocking revelations of the 20th Congress of the CPSU which first officially unmasked the crimes engendered under Stalin and what was termed 'The cult of the individual'. The effect was cataclysmic. My mother had been defending the USSR since she joined the CP in 1925, the early years of Soviet Russia and the devastation of the Civil War; my father since the mid 1930s. Their lives were organised around the party. To reject all they believed socialism stood for, would have made no sense of their lives. Our cats, three of them, one after the other, were named Joe, after Uncle Joe – Stalin – the man of steel. My father was blind so from an early age I had often accompanied him to meetings and read him party literature including works of Marx and Engels in preparations for his lectures. We were so aware of western countries intent to undermine the 'socialist bloc', from their intervention in the Civil War onwards, that when the uprising occurred in Hungary we assumed it was western interference. Of course, not all party members took this stance. Large numbers left the British party. Within my parent's branch there were irreconcilable divisions, never resolved.

With such a background it was not surprising that I joined the Young Communist League, the (YCL) when I was just 13. The YCL in the 1960s and 70s saw us gradually paving our own path away from the parent party, and especially so in relation to the USSR. We responded to the 60s youth culture, developing a cultural politics and embracing social movements

---

[1] How members commonly referred to the CPGB, the Communist Party of Great Britain

especially the CND. In 1963 the Beatles were given front page coverage in our newspaper "Challenge." Branch meetings were generally weekly, covering a range of topics from Marxism to Jazz. Public activities included selling Challenge (I once had the dogs from a large house sent after me). We campaigned on local, national and international issues.

Internationally from the 1960s our concern was the war in Vietnam. Our support for the North Vietnamese included joining with the Young Liberals in 1965 to hold one of the first national demonstrations against the war[2]. We ran our own agitprop coach, travelling around Britain displaying images of the war, using it as our base for public meetings and collecting money to send motor bikes to the North Vietnamese. The coach raised considerable interest. I remember one of the meetings very early in the morning down at the docks. The dockers responded generously to my appeal for money.

At this same time, the mid 1960s, we had grandiose plans to double the size of the YCL. We launched a campaign, "The Trend is Communism", itself claiming to be trendy. Two of us were financed by the Party to spend three months full time visiting areas where there was little or no YCL activity. I was sent to Walsall in the Midlands, and then in complete contrast to Dorking in Surrey. In the latter I was put up in Redhill with an active member of the 'hard line' division which was associated with support for the Soviet Union. I remember arguing with him and the Surrey secretary. In the YCL we had adopted an anti-Stalinist position. We also opened up the YCL reducing its bureaucracy, no longer annually re-registering members, an activity previously considered sacrosanct. I was on the National Committee of the YCL and welcomed such changes. For a few

---

2 In Grosvenor Square we were met by the strong armed tactics of the police. Our demo was 3 years prior to the 1968 one for which Tariq Ali is famed

months before leaving for Moscow, I became a member of the Executive Committee. This was when I realised that power lies not even in the high committees, but rather in the hands of the full time officers. Such thinking challenged the Party's accepted notion of Democratic Centralism. It sowed the seeds for my later concern about how to democratise power.

In England I had welcomed Dubcek's 'Socialism with a human face'. However, the Prague Spring in August 1968 saw me ensconced in Moscow, wavering about the need for Soviet intervention. The UK Party's paper, "Morning Star", normally available on the street kiosks had disappeared. The 5th floor of the Radio where a wide range of western press was available for those with a pass, was closed. I was cut off from alternative viewpoints. Meanwhile back at home, the YCL strongly condemned the Soviet action; "Challenge" immediately appeared with its front page emblazoned with a photo of the tanks rolling into Prague. The editor of Challenge, together with the YCL's national organiser visited Moscow for talks with the Komsomol. I invited them to hear Bernie expound his theory that West Germany was intent on taking advantage by undermining Czechoslovakia's currency.

They were not impressed.

I came to condemn the invasion, and be ashamed of myself for wavering. I think though this illustrated how deeply the cold war ideologies in my background affected my thinking. But also worryingly, the influence I'd allowed one individual to have.

Reflections in progress

Long ago I rejected the definition of the Soviet Union as a monolith; pressure groups had shown they could be effective, note the restoration of Russian churches. And for some citizens alternative western ideas were both accessible and heeded. I experienced an example of this when researching for my PhD in Moscow. I was asked to give a talk on feminism to a group of professors at the Academy of Social Sciences. We were seated round a long oval table. All were male academics apart from one woman who was the Party secretary. At the head of the table was an elderly man who apparently was writing a book about Leon Trotsky. This in itself was surprising as officially Trotsky remained *persona non grata*. But his announcement that he would do the honours with the samovar was not surprising; it was intended to show commitment to equality.

Just as I began a young woman crept into the room and took a seat behind the others. Afterwards she waited. Her job was to scan western magazines for items of note. She had become interested in the writings on feminism. So although not entitled, she had begged to attend my talk. Her name was Tanya Mamonova. Years later she became one of the leaders in the Soviet Union's emerging feminist movement although unlike many others favoured a reformed socialism. Eventually as a leading Russian feminist she travelled to Britain, the US and many other countries. At a meeting in London she announced that my talk had been instrumental in her becoming a feminist. Gorbachev later consulted feminists on women's issues.

In my PhD study of Soviet women's groups I proposed that change of direction of Soviet society could emerge from within, however unlikely it seemed. This was pre-Gorbachev. Simply dismissal of the USSR as totalitarian explains why most

Sovietologists and Kremlinologists were unprepared for the emergence of Gorbachev and his associates. Their emergence amongst the leadership exposed the diversity, not least the continued interest in the original values of communism. It also exposed the rejection of those values by powerful groups within the leadership and industrialists. After a short spell of *perestroika* and *glasnost*, it was the opponents who won out – again with the help of the US and western powers, which led to the break-up of the Soviet Union, the end of the socialist attempt.

Now Russia stands alone, although with differing relations to its former republics. When I was working in Moscow, Brezhnev was leader of the Union of the Soviet Socialist Republics (USSR); the Soviet Union (SU). He had been since 1964 and remained so until his death in 1982. I gave him little thought, more impressive were the anniversaries marking key dates of the revolution. Accompanying this return to the symbols of the past was always the common desire for peace. Peace was the dominant wish of the First World War, of 1917, of the years of the civil war, and of the Second World War. The loss and suffering incurred has affected almost every family.

However, the Russia I knew might not be a monolith, but could it be called socialist on its way towards a communist society? I suspect not. Even if communism were a viable aim, wasn't its future damned from the earliest days of the revolution? The Bolsheviks (Communists, the CPSU) were successful in establishing control through the Petrograd Soviet. But, at what cost?

In 1917 the demand for change was indeed popular but consisted of a broad range of understanding of what that change should be, ranging from ending the war to a revolution for a communist society and much in between. From the outset there was serious opposition from within Russia and the Russian Empire supported by the swift intervention of the major western powers. A period of civil war, known by the Bolsheviks as "the War of Intervention", devastated the country already suffering from the First World War. Among the groups generally supportive of revolution there was disagreement, opposition and ferment. It was a Socialist Revolutionary who shot Lenin. Many decisions caused dissent amongst the Bolsheviks themselves, not least NEP, the New Economic Policy which re-introduced some private enterprise to ease the devastation.

Intervention did not cease, and among the "victors" there was little coherence of a programme for change. Nor did the expected international support from similar revolutions materialise. To retain their grip and save the revolution, to combat the intrigue and ever continuing attacks, dominant personnel in the Red Army and the Party's security services developed similarly counter methods. This resulted in the systematic loss and murder of old Bolsheviks and other socialists already in the 1920s, who had spent years planning revolutionary change. Suspicion became endemic and self-destructive. This undermined achieving the type of society envisioned.

However, those who remained loyal to the concept of a new communist society worked ceaselessly to bring it about. Self-sacrifice was widespread. Lives were lost when taking literacy to women where religious values opposed it; or constructing the country's infrastructure in primitive conditions and by engendering a controversial, popular culture. Significant progress occurred despite the backwardness, poverty and suspicion of much of the population, and the continuing intrigue of the foreign powers such as the UK and the USA. Not least was the damage self-inflicted by the Communist Party itself. From its inception the actions of some groups of the political leadership and the powerful have undermined the ideals of communism. Evidence however, that the spark remained emerged with the reform movement in the late 1980s, but by then it was too little, too late.

This memoir has described some of my experiences in the Soviet Union. The above thoughts fifty years after my stay owe much to those experiences.

And worldwide people dream and work for a fairer world, for the basic values expressed in 1917.

Culture of my Moscow Years

Throughout my stay I enjoyed a feast of world class culture. Accessibility to ballet, music and theatre was easy. Moscow was rich in cultural events and still benefitted from the relaxation of the Khruschev years.

For my first year at the Radio I was paid solely in roubles. Not until my second year was I able to send part of my salary back home in sterling. The exchange rate was approximately two roubles to the pound. As the cost of my rent, utilities and transport ate little into my salary, I had plenty to spare. For what? Certainly not clothes. Instead, I could indulge in the rich culture of Moscow. Melodya records cost just 1R 70k, (under £2) whether of Cuban jazz, Russian folk, Opera or the great artists of classical music; art books of wooden *luboks*[1] to Art and the Revolution were dearer, but not a problem. Tickets to performances could be as low as the price of a record.

Art really was available for the masses. Indeed, many at the Bolshoi would be kolkhoz or sovkhoz[2] workers up in Moscow for a short visit to buy goods for themselves and their colleagues followed by a visit to the ballet.

Ballet
The main venues for ballet and opera are the Bolshoi, the Stanislavsky Theatre and the Kremlin's Congress of Soviets. Below is a selection of the notes I made on some of the performances.

---

1 Luboks are coloured woodcuts or lithographical prints, of simple images and texts from literature, religious stories and popular tales, sold on the streets from the early 17th century.
2 Kolkhoz collective farms; sovkhoz state farms

The Bolshoi was thriving in the 1960s. Prima ballerina Maya Plisetskaya performed a wide range of leading roles, including the excellent "Carmen Suite" to music by her husband, Rodion Schedrin based on Bizet's score. The premiere was 1967 and I saw her in the role again as part of the Winter Arts Festival. To greet the New Year of 1968, a programme of one act ballets at the Bolshoi included Maya Plisetskaya and Fadeyev in "Bach Preludes." Plisetskaya also performed in Schredrin's music to the tale of "The Humpbacked Horse". Plisetskaya is technologically brilliant, her dancing sparkles, a superb artist, but I find there's something brittle about her.

Natalia Bessmertnova is another ballerina whom I saw in a number of leading roles, not least as Phrygia in "Spartacus" partnered with Lavrovsky and later with Vasiliev. Liepa was outstanding as the Roman General Crassus, as was Vasiliev a powerful and moving Spartacus.

Both Bessmertnova and Liepa danced in "The Legend of Love", first performed in 1965. It's an attractive ballet with an effective male corps de ballet, particularly in the scene of the chase. Costume design in yellows, whites and grey is attractive.

Raissa Struchkova was still dancing leading roles. I had seen her in London during the chink of cultural exchange in the 1950s. Now I saw Struchkova as Kitri in "Don Quixote" at the Bolshoi. I noted this performance as, 'An interesting ballet with some effective dances such as that of the Street Dancers in the 1st Act. Excellent dancing in the café of the 2nd Act. Quixote's dream sequence beautiful on the vast stage of the Palace of Congresses: gauze in soft whites, yellows, grey and pink flowers and love the fairies danced by students. Struchkova for me was a little disappointing. I'd like to see Maximova in the role'. Ekaterina Maximova was trained for leading roles such as "Giselle" by legendary Galina Ulanova. I had had the privilege of seeing Ulanova at the Royal Albert Hall in 1956. Maximova has inherited the same soft lyricism. My favourite artists are the husband and wife partners, Maximova and Vasilii Vasiliev. When I do see them in "Don Quixote", I am not disappointed. Maximova and Vasilev dance with complete abandonment, seemingly utter joy in themselves and the dance.

A number of new productions mark the 50th Anniversary. One of these is "Geologi". I suppose it will be dubbed the 'socialist realism' of dance. Three dancers, two male one female, battle the elements of the Taiga. The choreography is beautiful. It's an expressive and movingly intense piece, a successful combination of contemporary dramatic form with dance. However, there is a mixed reception from the audience, although warmer when repeated in 1968

In January 1968 (premiere 1967), National Artist of the USSR Nina Timofeeva performs Vlasov's "Asel" a ballet based on motifs by the Kyrgyz writer Chinghiz Aitmatov

A second visit to see Khachaturian's "Spartacus", on the 22nd January 1969: (its 33rd performance at the Bolshoi since 1958, and 12th performance since being revised in 1968). Lavrovsky as Spartacus; Akimov as Crassus, Bessmertnova again as Phrigia; Ryabinkina, the erotic Ergina. Lavrovsky was superb. It's a most moving and tremendous ballet, the last act particularly. The final love scene between Spartacus and Phrigia is beautiful. The death of Spartacus and the slaves' bereavement, outstanding. Only the first act seemed not so great, although Spartacus's solo is tremendous. I didn't like the orgy or Ergina's first dance.

Theatre
Chekov's "Seagull" at the Dramatic Arts Theatre was unforgettable, the actor playing Nina so poignant it has

remained my judge for later productions. The Taganka Theatre was exciting and unique under the influence of its director, Yuri Lyubimov[3]. Amongst a number of plays I saw there Brecht's "The Good Person of Szechwan" stands out.

However for me, the production that eclipsed all others, was "Ten Days that Shook the World".

Very different in 1967, was Igor Shverdov's "Rom Baro", a dramatic ballad in three acts at Moscow's Gypsy *Tsyganskiy* Theatre. This is a sanitised version of Gypsy life's improvement with the coming of Socialism. Songs and dances were enlivening and often heart rending

Brecht's "Berliner Ensemble" visit to Moscow in September 1968 provides a powerful experience. I was lucky enough to get a ticket for "Mother". Based on the novel by Maxim Gorky of the same name, it portrays the Mother's growing understanding of the revolutionary actions of her son ending in her own courageous commitment to revolutionary action. As when first performed in 1951, Helena Weigal, Brecht's widow, now in her 80s, plays the leading role of the mother. My programme includes pictures and songs of the production. I also attended an evening of Gisela May performing Brecht's verses.

New theatre to mark the 1917 anniversary included Evgenii Simonov's "John Reed", a historical biography in three parts: America, Mexico, Russia. Performed at the Maly theatre. The portrayal of Bill Hayward, US workers' leader by N. A. Annenkov (National Artist of the USSR) was excellently

---

3 After visiting Britain for the first time, in 1983, and directing a sensational version of Crime and Punishment at the Lyric, Hammersmith, he was stripped of his Soviet citizenship. For most of that decade he worked abroad, in America, and in Europe's opera houses, before being reinstated at the Taganka in 1989 during the period of glasnost'.

performed as a prototype still to be found in the UK amongst open air speakers. The Mexico section was also good. National Artist of the USSR, I. V. Il'insky plays the role of Lenin. He is given pride of place as the first entry in the list of characters despite not appearing until the third section. The audience are opinionated about portrayal of Lenin. Whispering discussion starts with his appearance on stage, but gradually acceptance and then appreciation takes over. It's interesting that this is still a sensitive issue fifty years on. Although the character appears for a short time, the actor takes central place in the final bow. I had the feeling that he was still in character, and sizing up the audience: a most strange feeling.'

Alyoshin's, play "Diplomats" was performed at the Maly theatre in 1968. When the Russian actors perform English characters speaking Russian with an English accent, the audience roar with laughter. Disconcertedly, I could hear it as an echo of my own Russian pronunciation.

Opera

Moscow opened my eyes and my appreciation of opera. The ham acting witnessed on a school visit to Beethoven's "Fidelio" had put me off. I was won over by my first visit to Modest Mussorgsky's "Boris Godunov" at the Bolshoi. I was lucky to hear National Artist of the USSR, Petrov as Boris. The opera is a spectacle, but captured me with its moving depth of feeling, its music and its rich quality of singing; and especially the choral scenes,[4] supported by the expansive stage of the Bolshoi. In addition there is a feast of historical detail; the bell resounds to the exact tones of the Kremlin bell; the sets replicate the rich royal rooms inside the Kremlin.

---

4 Recent versions by both the Maryinsky Theatre and the Royal Opera House which have set the opera in modern times reject the historic set, thus much of the spectacle. A pity, but the issue of consciousness and power central to the opera does lend itself to relevance in other times.

On December 2nd 1967, to mark the 50th anniversary of the revolution, The Bolshoi is staging a new opera, Kholminov's "Optimistic Tragedy" based on the play by Vishnevsky. This tells the story of a female commissar working amongst a group of anarchist sailors. She is betrayed to the White Guards and killed but has achieved much. It's not particularly suitable for operatic form. I'm told the film is better. Nevertheless I was impressed with the male chorus and the design.

Helen and I see Tchaikovsky's *Pikovaya Dama,* "The Queen of Spades" on 3rd of January 1969. The music, so different from Mussorgsky's, is also extremely moving, particularly in the ghost and final scenes.

On November 4th '69, I see my second Mussorgsky opera, "*Khovanschina*". The score is rougher than that for "Boris Godunov"; initially I found it more difficult. However, it grew on me and I came to find it more moving than its companion. The Old Believers mass sacrificial death in the forest by fire, is extremely powerful.

Music
The main venue for classical music is the Conservatoire with its two halls in Herzen Street. Herzen Street retains its old charm, at least from outside. Bernie and Zoya Zarubina , live in one of its flats. The Conservatoire too is steeped in a bygone age, never failing to provide me with a sense of musical location. The pale yellow walls a respectable background to the oval portraits of the classic composers surrounding me as I listen to their music. I wonder what J.S.Bach is thinking as Rostropovich plays his unaccompanied cello sonatas, or David Oistrakh and his son Igor, interpret his Double Violin Concerto? These portraits are ever present. Once again I am well served, the anniversary of the Revolution means many concerts feature the country's most prestigious artists. Thus on November 12, 1967, David

Oistrakh conducts a programme of Brahms first symphony, Shostakovich' "Concerto No. 2 for Cello and Orchestra" and the "Scythian Suite Op. 20" by Prokoviev from *Alla I Lolli 1914-5*. The soloist for the Shostakovich Cello Concerto is Mstislav Rostropovich. Such mastery. The Conservatoire is full, every face intent on this one man and his instrument, himself intent, completely at one with the music. Finale. A storm of applause. Rostropovich kisses Oistrakh. They return to the platform hand in hand. Two great musicians. How modest they are. The slow hand clap of appreciation. Unanimous. They return, each making way for the other.

A month later, December 11, young Soviet musicians perform at the Conservatoire. The standard is most impressive. Elena Obraztsova, a soloist at the Bolshoi, has a most attractive voice, (I'd noted her previously in "Boris Gudonov"), Natalia Sharhovskaya, cellist and already an honoured artist of the Russian Federal Republic, who plays De Falya's "Dance of the Fire", stands out, as does Alexander Slobodyanik, pianist and last year's winner of the Tchaikovsky Competition. Generally the evening presents a feast of talent amongst young musicians.

March 18th 1968 is the 1st performance in Moscow of Mahler's 10th symphony. It's beautiful. This is an exciting event for Moscow concert goers. Schoenburg's "Eye Witness in Warsaw" and David Oistrakh playing Hindemith complete a great programme.

The Maly Hall (Small Hall) of the Conservatoire has none of the mystique of the main hall. It is also uncomfortable, the seats are wooden and the stage is unattractive, with a small, rather ugly backing for the artists.

And much more
This is just a taster of what Moscow had to offer me during my stay. There were also the art galleries, The Pushkin gallery of Fine Arts and the Tretyakov of Russian art and the Andrei Rublyov museum; The Puppet Theatre; the Circus with its tradition of political comment; Variety performances and visiting national groups from the republics and abroad such as Marcel Marceau. The benefits of Khruschev's cultural thaw were still apparent. The Theatre of Satire resurrected Mayakovsky's play "The Bed Bug".

On one occasion in April '68 artists opened their studios to the public. The one I remember visiting was in the artist's basement studio. He received no money from the state as he was considered a dissident painter, his work being mostly of religious images.

Without doubt, I was culturally privileged in those three years.

L - #0084 - 020222 - C0 - 229/152/10 - PB - DID3260985

Options for Influence
Ali Fisher and Aurélie Bröckerhoff

About the authors

Dr Ali Fisher is a director of Mappa Mundi Consultants and a leading international researcher in the fields of cultural relations, public diplomacy and information operations. He has previously worked as Director of Counterpoint, the cultural relations think-tank of the British Council (2006–7), and as Lecturer in International Relations at the University of Exeter. Publications include *Public Diplomacy in the UK* and *Four Seasons in One Day: the Crowded House of UK Public Diplomacy*. He has also written *Changing the Odds: The Influence of the State-Private Network on the Development of American Studies in Europe* and *Open Source Public Diplomacy* (forthcoming). Ali is a regular conference speaker – including at the 'Public Diplomacy in NATO Operations' conference in Copenhagen, on 'Hegemony and Diversity' as a World Cultural Forum panellist alongside Gilberto Gil (Rio de Janeiro), and on 'UK Public Diplomacy' at Real Instituto Elcano in Madrid. Ali received his PhD from the University of Birmingham, where he wrote his thesis on US cultural operations during the early Cold War.

Aurélie Bröckerhoff is a French-German postgraduate student completing a Master's in British Studies the Centre for British Studies, Humboldt University Berlin. Her study interests include cultural policy and management, intercultural dialogue and British Cultural Studies. She is now living in London and working for Counterpoint.

First published in Great Britain in 2008 by Counterpoint – the cultural relations think-tank of the British Council, 10 Spring Gardens, London, SW1A 2BN
counterpoint@britishcouncil.org, www.counterpoint-online.org, www.britishcouncil.org

Printed and bound in Great Britain by Qualitech.

The right of Ali Fisher and Aurélie Bröckerhoff to be identified as the authors of this work has been asserted by them in accordance with the Copyright, Designs and Patents Act, 1988.

This work is licenced under the Creative Commons Attribution-Non-Commercial-ShareAlike 3.0: England and Wales licence. To view a copy of this licence visit http://creativecommons.org/licenses/by-nc-sa/3.0/ or send a letter to Creative Commons, 171 Second Street, Suite 300, San Francisco, California 94105, USA.

A CIP catalogue record for this book is available from the British Library.
ISBN 978-086355-609-8, ISBN 0-86355-609-4.

Cover design by Atelier Works
© **British Council 2008** Design Department/W173/QLT. Some rights reserved

Contents

Acknowledgements	ii
Executive summary	iii
Foreword	v
Introduction	1
1 What is public diplomacy? Whatever you call it, we're in the influence business	3
2 What does your product say about you?	7
2.1 Of communication and selling	7
2.2 Demonstrating the importance of recognising a hierarchy of values	10
2.3 The tension between promoting nations and values	12
2.4 The importance of reception	14
2.5 Negotiation and dialogue	18
3 Where are you located on the spectrum of available approaches?	20
3.1 Alternative approaches	20
3.2 Soft power	21
3.3 Listening	23
3.4 Expressing the way we work: the different approaches on the spectrum	24
3.5 Why consider the spectrum?	31
4 Where in the world(s) is your product targeted?	35
4.1 Global coverage (through physical presence)	35
4.2 Focus outside the region	36
4.3 Local region	38
4.4 Engaging online: the potential of a virtual world	41
4.5 Prioritising countries by issue	45
4.6 Bilateral vs. multilateral	52
5 Conclusion	55

Acknowledgements

We would like to thank Nick Cull, Scott Lucas and Jan Melissen, who have provided much of the understanding on which *Options for Influence* has been developed. Their ideas and insights have been a great asset for us.

From within Counterpoint and the British Council, we are extremely grateful to our colleagues Nick Wadham-Smith, Rachel Stevens and John Worne, without whom this book would never have been completed. We would further like to thank our colleagues at the British Council for their willingness, as ever, to discuss ideas with their think-tank.

And last, but not least, we would like to express gratitude to the public diplomacy practitioners who have been a source of information and inspiration to us.

Executive summary

The concept of public diplomacy was developed in the 1960s. Since then, governments and practitioners alike have debated definitions of public diplomacy and its related fields, such as cultural relations, propaganda and cultural diplomacy. Although definition serves to demarcate territory, technical debates about definition sometimes hinder the understanding of practical implications. In order to allow practitioners to conduct public diplomacy more strategically, it is vital to understand the underlying principles of influence politics. The cultural implications and the choice of building blocks of any strategy significantly influence the success and impact of a programme.

What does your product say about you?
- Consideration needs to be given to the production and reception of the product you are developing. Whether selling or communicating, a product will always reflect more on its origin than anticipated. Organisations and practitioners who are aware of the hierarchies latent in their values and can discriminate between the promotion of a nation and the promotion of values have a relative advantage over their competitors.
- While a contextual understanding is important, international actors should also consider aspects of reception in order to avoid misunderstandings and display willingness to form mutual relationships. 'Culture' can be seen as a framework made up of mainly unconscious components, and as such, the study of the target audience's background becomes important. Building trust through dialogue and negotiation is the key to success for understanding the people an international actor wishes to influence.

Where are you located on the spectrum of available approaches?
- In order for strategies to become more efficient and effective, it is useful to be aware of the different approaches of engaging with foreign publics. These options for influence range from solely listening to purely messaging. On the listening end of the spectrum, facilitation, network-building and cultural exchange feature; moving further down to the telling end, cultural diplomacy and broadcasting lead to direct messaging.

- It is important for practitioners to know where they are located within this spectrum of options, firstly to realise their own preferred approaches and identify alternatives, and secondly to find possible partners positioned in their proximity on the spectrum. Knowing the entire spectrum of approaches also leads international actors to being more creative in the construction of their public diplomacy programmes.

Where in the world is your product targeted?
- Another major aspect when deciding on a strategy is targeting. Targeting offers a convenient way of streamlining public diplomacy engagement without losing impact and reach. Strategic targeting can be along geographical or issue-based lines. It will make a difference whether a public diplomacy programme aims at global engagement or is restricted to the local community. Similarly, a political public diplomacy programme will differ from a programme to increase tourism or trade to a specific area.
- Online engagement opens up new ways of influencing to public diplomacy practitioners. Online platforms can be used in two ways: either to complement existing strategies or to form the basis of new sorts of engagement, such as open source systems. An international actor can also adjust a public diplomacy programme to the needs of bilateral or multilateral engagement.

Options for Influence is not the conclusion of a complex but well-elaborated argument or debate; it represents a practical guide to practitioners in the field of public diplomacy. By considering the different building blocks and their potential presented in this book, practitioners can make more informed decisions about influencing foreign publics and therefore increase the likelihood of success.

Foreword

In a world where ideas, people and cultures mix and move faster than ever before, navigating the complexity of global, international, national and local messages means listening more than ever. Listening, being open to the exchange of ideas and facilitating that exchange are essential to those wanting to exert influence in a complex, interconnected world.

How we manage our relationships with other states, peoples and international institutions – in an environment where virtually anyone has the potential to influence communities almost anywhere in the world – has been an issue of increasing academic and practical importance. A century ago military force and economic power may have shaped the world but persuasion and influence have always played an important role in achieving a nation's goals.

In the 21st century, there are even greater limits to the effectiveness of force. The increasing power of people, the media and the internet to cross borders, change minds and change societies – for better and for worse – mean that engaging people matters more than ever. The barriers are lower too. It no longer takes the resources of a state to change the views and lives of millions in other countries. But the task of engagement is also harder as people can increasingly choose to tune in to debates of their interest and to tune out of what does not speak them.

The British Council has been building trust, influence and engagement for the UK through mutually beneficial relationships with people in other countries for over 70 years. Our work is based on the principle of openness and being prepared to listen as well as speak. The ideas presented in this book have helped shape the way the British Council articulates its work in cultural relations and how it relates and compares to the work of other actors in other countries. The options discussed within it are not intended to set out a British Council position but to help describe, discuss and stimulate thinking about the range of options from which international actors can choose.

We believe effective cultural relations build long-term influence and trust, as well as create shared economic, social and cultural value. The key, however, is not to see cultural relations as simply a more effective way for international actors to get their own way. It is about influencing others by being open to being influenced yourself and building trust by sharing skills, education, language, creativity, innovation, science, arts and culture and sharing the benefits of a more open, interconnected and engaged world.

John Worne
Director Strategy and External Relations
British Council
January 2008

Introduction

Influencing people has a longstanding tradition, although the concept of public diplomacy was developed only in the 1960s. Since then, many interpretations and definitions have been offered, along with the popularised use of terms such as soft power or cultural diplomacy. These and similar labels share a common desire for influence over the target audience.

Communication with populations around the world and the exertion of influence have received increasing attention from academics and governments alike. National organisations in this field have come under pressure, both within the international environment and from domestic demands for financial efficiency and valorisation. This is leading to a shift in the way public diplomacy is seen, namely as a vital profession in the realisation of interests, rather than peripheral to the core activities of international diplomacy. At the same time, the field also needs to be recognised as a whole, rather than merely a sum of scattered attempts at definitions.

Many countries, from the UK to Australia and China to Denmark, have conducted reviews into public diplomacy in recent years as they recognise the increasing importance of engagement with foreign populations. With both NGOs and supranational bodies attempting to exert influence alongside national governments, the competition for attention is increasing. This trend will continue as access to virtual worlds and Web 2.0 provides individuals as well as organisations with the tools to compete more successfully in the field of public diplomacy. Knowing these tools is crucial in such a competitive environment.

The changing nature of the environment of engagement has caused a consideration of the impact of public diplomacy (and its related fields) as one of the core options when trying to influence events overseas. Rather than seeing public diplomacy as an adjunct to the business of policy-making, the field must now be considered a profession. As such, being aware of one's options for influence can provide an organisation, or individual, with an edge over competitors.

Recognition as a specific profession goes hand in hand with a clear transition from merely selling foreign policy to considering public diplomacy as an integral tool for achieving national priorities through changing behaviours within the target audience. Some may argue that to maintain this position practitioners and academics need only to deliver what they have previously promised.

Options for Influence is an introduction to the field of exerting influence through overt international communication. It is neither an attempt to define which methods should be adopted nor an indication that an end to the development of tools has been reached. This is because each international actor has their own priorities, strengths, weaknesses and resources. As such, the options relevant to one actor will not necessarily be appropriate for another. Clarity over one's own aims and objectives and an awareness of the available range of tools and options allow actors to put together the essential building blocks for a successful strategy.

Options for Influence provides an introduction to answering three key questions for an international communication strategy. The first chapter introduces the controversies around definition. The second chapter focuses on the ambiguous nature of products in the field of public diplomacy. When communicating, an international actor will need to consider the conscious as well as unconscious processes involved and look at both the production and reception side needs. The third chapter discusses the variety of approaches an actor can take to conduct a programme, ranging from listening to telling. Chapter 4 looks at the ways in which targeting, either geographically or by issue, can help increase the efficiency and effectiveness, that is the success, of a strategy. This chapter also looks at both bilateral and multilateral programmes as well as online engagement.

Options for Influence introduces the range of possibilities. Each international actor will adopt and adapt the ideas in different ways, but the central tenet that these programmes are about influence remains unchanged. It is merely the way in which the actor seeks to exert influence that varies. When considering the options for influence, the ultimate goal of the programme must not be lost – whatever name you choose, a programme should ultimately attempt to influence the behaviour of the audience.

1 What is public diplomacy? Whatever you call it, we're in the influence business

Since the concept of public diplomacy was developed in the 1960s, many varying interpretations and definitions have been offered. But what does public diplomacy actually mean? And why does this question matter? Rather than focusing on a technical debate about definition, this chapter forms the basis to explore the practical implications and options of being in the influence business.

Many scholars and practitioners have offered definitions of public diplomacy. And there are likely to be many more. For those who are new to the concept, the myriad of definitions can be overwhelming. German labels for public diplomacy include *internationale Öffentlichkeitsarbeit, kulturelle Öffentlichkeitsarbeit* and *öffentliche Diplomatie*, which has led the *Auswärtige Amt* (German Foreign Office) to use the English term in their publications. But in English too, many terms can be used to refer to public diplomacy. Cultural relations and public diplomacy have been used interchangeably as well as in various divergent meanings. The British government, for example, has reiterated the way it understands cultural relations and public diplomacy, and their relationship to each other, in two major reviews over the last six years.

    The concept and practice of public diplomacy are constantly evolving at a rapid rate. As a result, both academics and practitioners frequently put forward their own understanding of public diplomacy, seeking to capture a new perspective on the discipline. Jan Melissen, Director of the Clingendael Diplomatic Studies Programme, defines public diplomacy as 'the relationship between diplomats and the foreign publics with which they work' at the opening of his book *The New Public Diplomacy*.[1]

Although this is a useful place to start, the concept has evolved. It no longer has to be carried out merely by diplomats. Nicholas Cull, Director of the Master of Public Diplomacy Program at the University of Southern California, therefore sees public diplomacy as 'an international actor's attempt to manage the international environment through engagement with a foreign public'.[2] In this context international actors are not just state based. They may be supranational such as NATO or the EU, a multinational corporation, a non-governmental organisation, a terrorist organisation (whether or not they are based in one state) or any other individual or organisation that seeks to exert influence on an international level.

> The Center on Public Diplomacy at the University of South California provides this description which draws on the origins of government-to-government communication and contrasts this standard diplomacy to public diplomacy by expanding out to cover a wider understanding.
>
> 'Unlike standard diplomacy, which might be described as the ways in which government leaders communicate with each other at the highest levels, public diplomacy focuses on the ways in which a country (or multi-lateral organization such as the United Nations), acting deliberately or inadvertently, through both official and private individuals and institutions, communicates with citizens in other societies.
>
> But like standard diplomacy, it starts from the premise that dialogue, rather than a sales pitch, is often central to achieving the goals of foreign policy. To be effective, public diplomacy must be seen as a two-way street. It involves not only shaping the message(s) that a country wishes to present abroad, but also analyzing and understanding the ways that the message is interpreted by diverse societies and developing the tools of listening and conversation as well as the tools of persuasion.'[3]
>
> USC Center on Public Diplomacy

The different definitions already highlight the difficulty of defining public diplomacy in a way that captures the entirety of contemporary thinking in an easy-to-understand way for those being exposed to the concept for the first time. In addition, practitioners regularly use definition to demarcate their territory. Moving beyond academic thought, these definitions entail practical implications for the use of public diplomacy.

Every practitioner either explicitly or implicitly produces their own understanding. In December 2005, the Carter Review updated the definition of public diplomacy for the UK and described it as:

> 'Work aiming to inform and engage individuals and organisations overseas, in order to improve understanding of and influence for the United Kingdom in a manner consistent with governmental medium- and long-term goals.'[4]

This definition reflects the thinking and agenda of the UK government in 2005. It altered the definition provided by the Wilton Review in 2002, which described public diplomacy as:

> 'Work which aims at influencing in a positive way the perceptions of individuals and organisations overseas about the UK, and their engagement with the UK'.[5]

If another debate were to be held within the UK the resulting definition would probably be different again. Definitions are likely to be altered and rephrased over time. As such, to debate definitions is to discuss an ever-evolving concept which is interpreted and reinterpreted by government departments and academics both in the UK and overseas. The energy lost when attempting definition could well be used in the realms of strategy development.

Further complications relating to definition arise when taking into account related activities, with sometimes overlapping and blurred distinctions. The American diplomat Richard Holbrooke wrote: 'Call it public diplomacy, call it public affairs, psychological warfare, if you really want to be blunt, propaganda.'[6] The complex nature of this type of definition can be demonstrated with the NATO Military Public Affairs Policy.

> **Public diplomacy**
> The totality of measures and means to inform, communicate and co-operate with a broad range of target audiences worldwide, with the aim to raise the level of awareness and understanding about NATO, promoting its policies and activities, thereby fostering support for the Alliance and developing trust and confidence in it.
>
> **Propaganda**
> Information, ideas, doctrines, or special appeals disseminated to influence the opinion, emotions, attitudes, or behaviour of any specified group in order to benefit the sponsor either directly or indirectly.
>
> **Psychological operations (Psyops)**
> Planned psychological activities using methods of communication and other means directed to approved audiences in order to influence perceptions, attitudes and behaviour, affecting the achievement of political and military objectives.[7]
>
> NATO Military Public Affairs Policy

These definitions demonstrate that the names for public diplomacy, and related fields, are numerous and have a high degree of overlap. One main aspect in differentiation may be the perception of each term; some are considered positive, while others have a negative bias. Some organisations may choose to label their actions in a certain way depending on how they wish to be understood by their particular constituency. But although the different labels entail specific assumptions or even divergent methodology, the area of engagement is essentially the same.

Trying to define the concept of public diplomacy can thus be compared to trying to nail jelly to a wall. While definitions are useful for bureaucratic demarcation, many practitioners might prefer to adopt the now famous words of Mr Justice Stewart – 'I know it when I see it'.[8]

Whatever label practitioners wish to put on their work, the aim of their activity is not just changing people's perceptions, but rather influencing the way people act. Changing perceptions may be a means to changing action, but, at the end of the day it is changed behaviour that matters. So when addressing the question of how public diplomacy may be defined, the most honest and easily accessible answer might be: 'Call it what you like, we are in the influence business.'[9]

2 What does your product say about you?

Communication with our audiences and partners can entail more than we expect. What we say is not necessarily what we communicate. Being aware of the underlying principles of communication can help increase a strategy's efficiency, effectiveness and impact. This chapter provides an insight into the implications of communicating with audiences, the problems that may arise when engaging in public diplomacy and how these issues may be avoided or minimised.

You can't not communicate. This basic principle of interpersonal communication is vital to the work of anybody considering their options for influence. Whenever an actor chooses to act in public (or not), this will say something about the individual, the organisation and any associated products or programmes. Usually the choices range from selling to communicating. Selling, whether product, programme or political position, is a predominantly conscious act. Communicating, conversely, can be more or less conscious. But whichever approach practitioners are taking, their product will usually say much more about them than they anticipated.

2.1 Of communication and selling

Selling or communicating are not two completely detached options an international actor can choose, but they are likely to be intertwined in any programme. This section presents the inferences of emphasising one or the other.

When seeking to exert influence, organisations need to be certain about the action they are engaging in. Specifically, an actor needs to be clear whether to put emphasis on selling or communicating.

Selling is a strategic action that is undertaken for one's own self-advancement. Consciously communicating aims to reach an understanding that will be beneficial to both sides. This basic distinction has already been made by the pre-eminent social scientist of our time, Jürgen Habermas, who sees strategic action as being in the way of communicative action, that is interaction through honest dialogue aimed at understanding. At the outset for a public diplomacy programme, whether to choose a selling or a communication approach needs to be carefully considered. This section will discuss communication from the perspective of the producer; the latter part will discuss communication from the perspective of the audience and the importance of reception.

> According to Habermas' theory of communicative action, different types of action exist. Strategic actions aim at furthering one's own self-interest, either by self-representation, influencing others or promoting one's own cultural values. These do not require any form of mutuality and do not involve the other. To Habermas, they are limited in their scope and therefore impact. Communicative actions on the other hand aim at reaching a true understanding of the other. While understanding can be the sole purpose of communicative actions, in public diplomacy they can then be the basis for further mutually beneficial actions.[10]
>
> *Habermas* Theorie des kommunikativen Handelns

In attempts to actively sell, products or ideas are usually inscribed with a certain image to increase their attractiveness to a potential audience. For example, budget and luxury airlines both essentially try to sell a product – a journey from one point to another. The budget airline adopts a selling approach in highlighting the movement of people at a low price. A luxury airline, on the other hand, will try to give its product an identity that attracts a different customer base and helps justify the higher price.

The aim of these campaigns is to increase sales by persuading potential customers to buy the advertised product, influencing their behaviour to make them buy the product. Success is then measured in the number of sales that result from advertising, as they are an indication of changed behaviours. The same applies to public diplomacy strategies and programmes. Success can only be effectively measured according to whether or not the programme succeeded in influencing the behaviour of the target audience.

> **The Qantas experience**
> Australian national carrier Qantas, for example, emphasises in its advertising campaign its links to Australia as well as to the experience of flying. In the past years, Qantas commercials have used Peter Allen's song 'I still call Australia home' as a backdrop for images of iconic Australian landmarks interspersed with famous skylines and tourist attractions of potential destinations. A Qantas plane, representing the actual product, features for only a few seconds in the two- to three-minute clips. Many national carriers give their airline a similar identity that communicates particular national characteristics combined with the experience of flying.[11]

Whichever way of engaging an international actor chooses, programmes will be located within this span of communicating and selling. When introducing the spectrum of available approaches in Section 3.4, it will be obvious that approaches vary in the amount of either selling or communicating involved.

The closer to 'telling' on the spectrum, the more the international actor emphasises selling. Conversely, closer to the 'listening' end, the international actor places greater emphasis on developing influence by understanding the priorities of other actors. The shift of focus to communicating rather than selling results from the desire to achieve a genuinely balanced relationship emphasising mutuality and mutual understanding.

Mutual relationships are those that are equally shared by each member of the relationship. In public diplomacy, mutuality provides a way of eschewing one-way communication. In their book *Mutuality, trust and cultural relations*, Nick Wadham-Smith and Martin Rose argue that mutuality is an interconnected set of values that includes respect, trust, openness and a willingness to change one's own mind where appropriate and necessary.

To the authors this relies on open and honest communication which rests on the premise that both sides are aware of their own values.[12] In order for a public diplomacy organisation to be able to communicate and establish mutual relationships, it needs not only to understand its own set of values, but also to recognise a hierarchy of values within.

2.2 Demonstrating the importance of recognising a hierarchy of values

As values are negotiated and renegotiated within different groups of people, international actors will often encounter values diverging from their own. Therefore, when engaging with an audience, it is important to be aware of one's own values and their hierarchy in order to know with which partners and audiences one is willing to engage and also to determine a basis of engagement.

Values are not static, but are negotiated and renegotiated in order to keep validity. Most values evolve as a result of social interaction and are as a result in perpetual flux. Nowadays, with an ever-faster pace of life and change in the world, values need to be renegotiated more regularly. Many areas of the world are facing increased migration and pressure on resources. Consequently, the focus for a number of international actors will be to promote relationships that emphasise often intertwined and overlapping sets of values, such as tolerance, trust, mutuality. Tolerance, for example, whether bound up in the language of freedom, liberty or religious observance, provides space for dissent from a particular belief or practice. It also provides a useful basis for the discussion of the hierarchy of values.

> **One understanding of tolerance**
> Tolerance of other perspectives or actions guarantees the freedom to act as one may wish. As a result, diversity in society is maintained, as numerous 'others' are permitted to exist. Tolerance demonstrates respect for the other and recognises the mutual right to the freedom to act in a manner consistent with the particular cultural, political or religious norms and beliefs of the individual.
>
> Others argue that tolerance is not enough, there must be a movement toward active appreciation and understanding of difference rather than merely putting up with other perspectives.[13]

The discussion surrounding tolerance owes much to the Putney Debates and British philosopher John Locke's work, both of which highlight the tension between different values in society.[14] Rights and values do not exist in splendid isolation; they are maintained in tension with other values recognised by both the individual and society as a whole, and modified through negotiation, in order to reflect the shifting ideals and demands of the present. It is not enough simply to state a value: it must also be acknowledged within a hierarchy of values.

Encouraging a tolerance of difference recognises that there is no single, predetermined way of thinking. Instead, it promotes the freedom of expression. This conceptually not only ensures the existence of difference, but also provides the scope for cultural innovation through open and fearless interaction protected by this freedom of expression.

While an international actor may call for tolerance, this will also require an ongoing discussion about its limits within that particular society. Clearly there are acts which even the most broad-minded would not wish to merely tolerate. Everyone has their limit and it varies from one individual to the next and from one situation to another. However, in establishing a meaning of tolerance beyond concepts of shared values, international actors need to recognise that groups and individuals will construct their own hierarchy of values.

> **A hierarchy of values**
> To demonstrate this, identify three values and then consider a situation which could cause them to conflict. In those incidences when the environment could cause conflict, a choice would be made, creating a hierarchy of values.
>
> In a famous story from the Bible, God commanded Abraham to sacrifice his only son, Isaac. Abraham and Isaac embarked on the journey to Mount Moriah, the chosen place for the offering. On the trip, Isaac asked his father where the sacrificial lamb was, and Abraham replied that God would provide one. Just before killing his son, Abraham was stopped by an angel and God sent a ram which was brought to sacrifice instead of Isaac.[15]
>
> The hierarchy of values represented by Abraham's choice created a situation whereby he placed greater importance on serving his God than on the life of his son.

Many Western audiences identify values such as human rights, democratic elections or the right to worship. However, some Western governments would also argue that an encroachment on human rights is necessary to defend democratic elections or the security of citizens. This creates the hierarchy which has to be negotiated within society, rather than stated as a static list of shared values.

The debate about tolerance dovetails with the need for reciprocity. In effect, many people view tolerance as a reciprocal behaviour of which they need to be a recipient before they will tolerate the behaviour of another. Reciprocity may galvanise the movement toward greater tolerance and create an ongoing feedback loop through which commitment to tolerance can be reinforced. Conversely, tolerance can be undermined in certain situations when there is a perception that it is not reciprocal. In considering their options practitioners must recognise that dialogue about tolerance and values will not just be about what values or ideas people adhere to, but also the limitations and priorities.

> 'I do not want my doors to be walled and my windows stuffed. I want the cultures of all lands to blow freely about my house. But I do not want to be blown off my feet by any.'[16]
>
> *Mahatma Gandhi*

2.3 The tension between promoting nations and values

While many countries and other international actors have protracted internal debates about their identity, many still attempt to project a single external image. But how to represent a nation that consists of so many different values and ideas? This issue is not often acknowledged among practitioners, but a choice between promoting certain values or promoting the international actor may have to be made, as these may require incompatible approaches.

The promotion of a nation can be seen as a means to promoting certain values. However, given the competing hierarchies of values within a society and shifting priorities identified in different situations, promoting nations and promoting values should be considered as two options, rather than two sides of the same coin. While nation promotion and value advocacy may in some instances complement each other, this should be considered and confirmed rather than assumed. A target audience may have had a different experience with a nation in the past which contradicts the ideas and values the nation is now trying to promote.

In demonstrating this potential division between the actions of the nation, or other actors, and the ideas or values which they seek to espouse, the truism that actions speak louder than words springs to mind. To put it another way, the performance of values, rather than the discussion of them, can be important in the transmission of certain ideas.

Values and nations

In the early Cold War, the desire to promote democracy in Europe competed with the desire to promote a positive image of America. The operations intended to promote democracy in Europe included the development of free scholarship, juxtaposed in American eyes to the proscriptive education system in the East. Free scholarship, however, contained certain elements which created tensions for the promotion of a positive image of America. For example at the opening of the Amerika-Institut in Munich, the Director H.F. Peters announced his intention to demonstrate certain 'American realities'.[17]

In the pre-1954 environment, and even after 1954, there were numerous realities, particularly relating to segregation and flagrant racism, which the US Government officials felt were inappropriate for discussion in Europe.[18]

This created tension which placed the promotion of freedom to study into direct conflict with the attempts to promote a positive image of America. The US Government sought to promote the positive image of the nation, through exerting pressure on the Institut, which included for a short time confiscating H.F. Peters's passport.[19]

Contrary to the US Government approach, representatives of the Rockefeller Foundation, which had provided financial support to the Institut, viewed the discussion of 'American realities' a positive demonstration of the values, particularly freedom and democracy, that they sought to encourage in Germany.

In the nearly 60 years since these events, little has changed. The actions of a country, or individuals seen as representative of that country, will at times undermine the values which public diplomacy is intended to promote. In light of the American example, the danger of tension becomes clear. Actions and deeds must be seen to be coherently aligned, but also values and the nation must be seen to be working in harmony. This may be difficult in countries with considerable cultural diversity, whether the result of large minority groups or an influx of immigrants, which alters the realities within a country.

For smaller non-state international actors this may be less of a problem given that they are less exposed to potential target audiences. However, until the nation-state ceases to be part of public diplomacy, the conflict between promoting values and nations will persist. While a negative perception of the international actor may in itself hinder the realisation of other objectives, conducting operations as a model of the values the actor seeks to promote may provide the best means of demonstrating commitment to the ideas or values.[20] A positive perception, on the other hand, may help future public diplomacy activities.

2.4 The importance of reception

Although options for influence are essentially gathered on the producing side, it is important to understand the principles of reception. Often, what is said can be different from what is understood. Cultural frameworks and unconscious ways of creating meaning can lead to an initiative being understood in a completely different way from what was intended. When constructing a programme, international actors should always keep their audience in mind.

The way an actor's actions are received is equally important to the success of a public diplomacy programme as its creation. It is therefore important to understand the mechanism involved when perceiving the world around us. Neither individuals nor the messages they send out exist in a vacuum. They are always part of a wider sociocultural framework.

In human interaction, usually, what you see is not what you get. Every time an individual receives a stimulus from the outside world, their own cultural and personal background, consisting of a complex set of values, beliefs, ideas, etc., helps them make sense of it. The important issues here are the relationship between the physical and those values, assumptions and other contributing myths, habits and beliefs which sit beneath the physical; and a shift from what a person wants to say to how an audience understands what is being said.

The relationship between physical goods and the values or assumptions of a specific culture has on numerous occasions been described as an iceberg. The tip of the iceberg, i.e. the external physical components of culture, represents those things that have been learned explicitly and that can be applied consciously; the things that have been physically created and that can be changed more easily.

They are cultural goods such as music, art or literary works. However, these make up only a tiny fragment of culture. The major part is submerged and can't easily be seen, heard or touched. It consists of values, beliefs, thought patterns and myths. These are usually implicitly learned and operate at the unconscious level. Often, an individual cannot fully explain why situations evoke certain reactions,

For example:

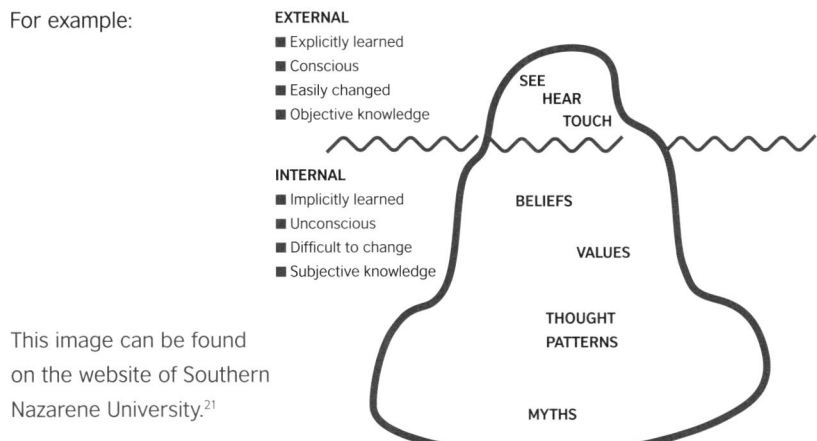

This image can be found on the website of Southern Nazarene University.[21]

because they cannot necessarily see beyond the water surface.

Numerous studies have been conducted to understand and explain what happens underneath the surface. The insights of those studies have been used extensively for marketing purposes. This is why advertisers, in an attempt to increase sales, link their product to certain psychological associations, as with the example of Qantas in Section 2.1.

But while commercial sales are an important area for this type of engagement, changing political and social circumstances can also lead to the desire to change the way an item is referred to, due to the thought patterns associated with the words. Labels for items, as we have already touched upon in Chapter 1, often carry a heavy load of assumptions. In semiotics, the study of sign processes, this is referred to as denotation and connotation. Denotation describes what a word actually refers to, while connotation is the meaning that this word has for a person. Analysing the difference can help in the understanding of how meaning is constructed and understood.

The word 'forest' denotes an accumulation of trees. To a German, this term evokes feelings of serenity, privacy, peace, etc. Thus, for a German, the term has a positive connotation. A French person, on the contrary, usually associates terms like dark, gloomy, or threatening with this word, and therefore the term has negative connotations. These are generalised of course, but recognising this nuance in connotation is an important part of creating strategy. Such connotations can influence the impact of a particular message or programme if the target audience interprets it in a different way from what the producer expected. For example, while to some Uncle Scrooge or Mickey Mouse are merely cartoon characters, to others they may be the embodiment of capitalism.[22]

Understanding the messages that the practitioner is sending by communicating or selling is therefore a precondition for a successful public diplomacy programme. This applies to an awareness of both the message an actor is consciously sending and those underlying unconscious assumptions on which that message is built. Often, changing political, economic or social circumstances results in a change in the connotations of certain words and may cause a society to consider changing the names of the items they refer to.

Changing circumstances, changing names
- French fries became freedom fries in the US at the time of the invasion of Iraq.
- The Frankfurter became the hot dog during the Great War, itself later referred to as the First World War.
- Also during the First World War the British Royal Family changed its name from Saxe-Coburg to Windsor.

The changing of these names within a society demonstrates how changing circumstances causes the connotation of that name to be understood in different ways. In identifying the options for influence, the likelihood of the target audience using their own, different, unconscious cultural assumptions and understandings will influence the way in which they interpret an initiative.

Particular attention has to be paid to the potentially different interpretations when considering broadcasting, cultural diplomacy and messaging. While it is important for all options, those approaches that place greater emphasis on telling than on listening are more likely to run the danger of being misunderstood by the target audience.

Managing alternative interpretations begins with understanding not only what the international actor is attempting to represent to the target audience, by, for example, crafting a message or putting on an exhibition, but also the conscious and unconscious assumptions upon which programmes are based.[23] The international actor will select a particular message or material for that exhibition which is intended to demonstrate certain issues that will represent certain ideas, such as characteristics or values.

An awareness of how messages are encoded with meaning and how these are then read, or decoded, by the audience, has implications for whether a practitioner opts for a communicative or a selling approach. The important part of considering whether an international actor develops a programme either to sell or to communicate is that the nature of either engagement will be dependent on the way the intervention interacts with the pre-existing beliefs, assumptions and understandings of the target audience.

> **Encoding/decoding**
> Stuart Hall's essay 'Encoding and Decoding in the Television Discourse', although mainly concerned with broadcasting productions, offers an insight into the way meaning is produced and received. Hall argues that both production *and* reception are part of the process of production of meaning. From a semiotic starting point, Hall deduces that every signifying element in itself can take on many different meanings. This leads to the fact that nothing has an absolute meaning, but meaning is negotiated on the basis of and within our institutional, cultural, political and social background, which is then arranged in a hierarchical way from dominant to subordinate. Located on the higher end of the scale are the preferred meanings, i.e. the ways in which certain items tend to be understood.
>
> Awareness and knowledge of those can help a producer of a message in bringing across a specific point to his intended audience. In order for a message to influence, instruct or persuade, the recipient must read the message in the same way as the producer has constructed it. No law can ensure that a reader will understand the way the producer intended, he can just make an understanding more likely by relying on the preferred meanings. However, receivers will eventually refer to their own maps of meaning, determined by the codes of personal and sociocultural frames of reference, to make sense of what they see, hear or read.
>
> To minimise misunderstanding, producers must speak through the codes of the receiver. This requires a high degree of symmetry between the position of the producer/encoder and the receiver/decoder.[24]

Understanding is influenced by context. It is group-specific, usually negotiated within certain groupings. Encoding/decoding also argues that individuals, rather than being caught in a static expression of an amalgamated set of beliefs, understandings, myths and assumptions, find themselves in an ongoing process of engagement and negotiation of the world around them.

Homi K. Bhabha, an eminent writer on culture, wrote

'culture is less about expressing a pre-given identity (whether the source is national culture or ethnic culture) and more about the activity of negotiating, regulating and authorising competing, often conflicting, demands for collective self-representation'.[25]

The demands for collective representation, their articulation and interplay are subject to change. Migration and globalisation make exposure to people of different backgrounds increasingly likely. Together with the rising population concentration in urban areas, this 'hybrid cosmopolitanism of contemporary metropolitan life' (Homi K. Bhabha)[26] increases the need of negotiation, regulation and authorisation. With the fast pace at which the world changes and as new concepts of culture and identity (e.g. Britishness) are debated, many individuals, and whole societies, feel a constant need to reposition and rearticulate demands for self-representation.

Attempts to construct influence programmes designed to project a specific identity are particularly subject to the rapid changes both of encoding and decoding. However, they are not limited to direct expressions of national identity. The construction of programmes intended to counter terrorism and climate change also have to consider the impact of encoding/decoding. This is because these programmes cannot exist in splendid isolation from culture and identity.

Although each of the options for influence from the spectrum can be important for an international actor, Homi Bhabha's conception is more about communication than selling, or at least selling alone. Recognising the importance of negotiation and dialogue can be the key to a successful public diplomacy programme.

2.5 Negotiation and dialogue

Dialogue and negotiation are important tools in overcoming the difficulties in international relations. Both help in understanding the people we engage with. Through negotiation and dialogue, international actors open up their viewpoint to others, but are at the same time receptive to other ways of perception.

Negotiation through placing the emphasis on communication rather than selling is an option for persuasion. Negotiation is a vital part of any intercultural work; it can be political but may also be cultural. In political negotiation, treaties and memoranda are negotiated; in cultural negotiation understanding is developed between individuals and communities representing different perspectives.

While in the past most strategies were devised behind closed doors, practitioners are now realising the importance of negotiating strategies openly in order to make the audience part of a process rather than recipient of a finished product. As David Miliband recognised in his recent speech at Chatham House, 'The old diplomacy was defined by a world of limited information. It was a veritable secret garden of negotiations. And secret negotiation still matters.' However, 'the new diplomacy is public as well as private, mass as well as elite, real-time as well as deliberative'.[27]

Engaging in negotiation does not necessarily require giving up on firmly held beliefs, but as Margaret Mead wrote: 'There is no hierarchy of values by which one culture has the right to insist on all its own values and deny those of another.'[28] This statement opens many possible discussions. Some may consider it akin to cultural relativism, believing that there is a superior set of values. Others may read it to suggest that there is neither a recognised system of authority which can demand the total repudiation of all values, nor indeed that there is an agreed hierarchy of values, as discussed in Section 2.2. Still, another alternative may focus on the implication that there is not one ultimate set of shared values, but a number of different understandings which are in a constant state of development and reinterpretation.

Negotiation can be an important part of any public diplomacy work. Negotiation is an obvious element for public diplomacy programmes that focus on listening or facilitation. However, negotiation can inform the full range of options for influence. This will be discussed in further detail in the following chapter.

3 Where are you located on the spectrum of available approaches?

This chapter introduces the spectrum of options which are available to those seeking to exert influence. When viewed as a spectrum that ranges from purely listening to exclusively telling, it has the advantage of demonstrating how different approaches relate to each other and where the emphasis is placed. Using the spectrum, an international actor can assess the range of their options and ensure that their assumptions about the way they will conduct the programme are aligned with the type of programme they have chosen to undertake.

While the previous issues need to be considered by all those seeking to exert influence, each actor will also need to be clear about which specific option from the available approaches they choose to apply. The spectrum of options presents possible ways in which an organisation can influence the way its target audience acts, by providing an overview of the range of approaches available to practitioners. This allows making a more reflected and informed decision when choosing a particular programme, which can, in return, help increase the efficiency of delivery and the subsequent impact of a programme.

3.1 Alternative approaches

Soft power and listening are two approaches to public diplomacy which are located at opposite ends of the spectrum. They are introduced in this section to show the effect of assumptions behind labels.

Soft power is a well-known option for those seeking to exert influence and has become a buzzword in the field of public diplomacy.
    By contrast, listening receives much less attention. The two options achieve influence in very different ways and require the international actor to operate along different sets of assumptions.

3.2 Soft power

The term 'soft power' is very popular in current public diplomacy debate. This section investigates the hidden assumptions and implications behind this concept.

Soft power, much used, but less understood, and public diplomacy are not interchangeable terms. Soft power is not an umbrella term for all cultural activities; it is one of the specific tools that can be used to exert influence. However, although commonly applied, it is inaccurate and potentially damaging to say if something is neither military nor economic activity, then it is soft power. Rather, soft power is an activity that specifically aims at influencing the way people act. Joseph Nye wrote:

> 'Soft power is the ability to get what you want by attracting and persuading others to adopt your goals. It differs from hard power – the ability to use the carrots and sticks of economic and military might to make others follow your will.' [29]

The assumptions of this approach characterise it as neither mutual nor based on a reciprocal relationship. It excludes the development of common goals through dialogue, and does not allow for helping others realise their goals. It is neither compromise nor negotiation. It is a belief in one's own perspective over another. The key to this concept is that people must adopt your position. If enough soft power is exerted, the audience will follow your will because they are led to believe they are actually attracted to your goals more than their own. The logic of soft power lies in using your influence to shape the preferences of others. This facilitates the realisation of your aims and objectives without being overtly authoritarian. 'Soft power rests on the ability to set the political agenda in a way that shapes the preferences of others. [...] If I can get you to *want* to do what I want, then I do not have to force you to do what you do *not* want to do.'[30]

Soft power as one option for exerting influence comes with this specific set of assumptions. While it is tempting to use it interchangeably with other labels or as a catch-all term, it is worth remembering Nye's warning about soft power: it *'is an analytical term, not a political slogan'.*[31]

A common pitfall of using the term 'soft power' can be seen by looking at popular culture. While it is true that a specific cultural entity can be used to support and achieve a public diplomacy goal, this cannot be generalised. Attraction to or consumption of any part of the culture does not necessarily contribute to soft power. Therefore soft power cannot be used in every public diplomacy context.

This partly stems from the fact that a cultural item can be interpreted in different ways by the audience. As Nye put it:

> 'popular culture can be repulsive as well as attractive. It is only soft power where it has a positive effect. The mullahs who run Iran are no doubt horrified at Hollywood movies in which divorced women wear bikinis and go to work every day. But, Iranian teenagers want nothing more than a Hollywood video to watch in the privacy of their home.'[32]

This quote shows that not everyone will react to the consumption of culture in the same way. Public diplomacy organisations need to keep in mind that it is almost impossible to accurately predict how a cultural good will be received and interpreted in other parts of the world.[33] For Nye, 'soft power [...] is the ability to entice and attract. And attraction often leads to acquiescence or imitation.' Nye falls into the trap of assuming that attraction to and consumption of any cultural item contributes to soft power. He believes that because Iranian teenagers are attracted to Hollywood movies, they are subjected to American soft power. However, this is inaccurate. Although they are consuming an American cultural good, they will still apply their own frames of reference when interpreting its meaning and as such may not be attracted to the same messages as the soft power advocate believes represented by that cultural item.

This can be exemplified when looking at an example from popular music. American rock band Green Day released the very popular, award-winning single called 'American Idiot', which left little to the imagination. One of the other songs on the album, 'Holiday', includes the lines 'Sieg Heil to the President Gasman/Bombs away is your punishment/Pulverize the Eiffel Towers [sic] that criticized your government'.[34] They later released CD/DVD *Bullet in a Bible* with a live version of their song 'Holiday'. At the time of release, the song was so controversial that, before performing it live, Green Day front man Billy Joe Armstrong shouts that the song 'is not anti-American, it is anti-war'.[35] He draws a distinction between being anti-American and opposing policy goals.

If the Iranians from Nye's example were watching the Green Day DVD, they might be attracted to consume this part of American culture because it opposes

American policy goals and criticises the American Government. Therefore, Green Day are a part of American culture, but not one which contributes to soft power. Attraction to American culture in this case may result in imitation which opposes rather than supports the soft power aspirations of the US.

> **The power of music**
> Just as recent foreign policy has drawn criticism from within American culture, the Vietnam War also provided the context for music which may have attracted people to oppose rather than support American goals. Examples include the music of bands such as Creedence Clearwater Revival ('Fortunate Son'), Buffalo Springfield ('For What It's Worth') or Jefferson Airplane ('Volunteers'). Crosby, Stills, Nash & Young also produced a number of songs including 'Ohio', which is about the shooting of four students during an anti-Vietnam War protest at Kent State University, Ohio.

Inflated claims about the phrase 'soft power' may overstate its potential. The consumption of any part of the culture will not automatically contribute to soft power. All that soft power can accurately claim is that certain cultural entities have the potential to help in the realisation of a public diplomacy goal.

3.3 Listening

Listening is diametrically opposed to soft power in terms of activity. Listening reflects a genuine interest in the other's perspective and has been increasingly recognised by practitioners and organisations alike. This section shows the opportunities that listening could open up when engaging with foreign audiences.

Consciously and publicly listening to the perspective of others can help in changing the way people act. Listening to another country can therefore be a public diplomacy act in itself. It is more than just polling or using echo chambers, because it demonstrates that different viewpoints are taken seriously and that other perspectives are given consideration. This in itself can already solve an issue, or, alternatively, provide a basis for further negotiation.

Clearly, there is a danger that listening exercises will not be credible if they are perceived as a show act, and a pre-ordained action will be taken regardless of what is said.[36] Crucial for public diplomacy organisations engaged in listening is a willingness to put in the appropriate time, effort, and, most importantly, an openness to the comments they may hear.

Listening can sometimes achieve more in changing people's behaviour than talking to them. This may seem unappealing in a world where getting the message out has become a dominant mentality; a world in which listening does not appear to have a role. However, the message can be transmitted in more ways than the sound bite. Showing a willingness to listen can open up new territory for mutuality. Listening to others shows genuine interest and respect in their matters. This allows relationships to be built on mutual respect and trust. The way an international actor behaves is just as important as the message he sends out.

If a government has a reputation for being arrogant, dogmatic and unwilling to consider other viewpoints, this can create tension. If such a government then merely informs the target audience that they have the wrong perception of this government, the approach is unlikely to be successful. This is because the message mimics and reinforces the very impression it is trying to counter. However, a sustained attempt to listen and understand the reasons behind the bad perception of the government may demonstrate a commitment beyond messaging. A listening approach can do more than just gather information if there is existing tension related to an unbalanced power relationship. A more symmetrical understanding of relationships is entrenched in the listening programme, and could potentially cause the audience to act differently in response.

Listening, however, does have the limitation that it can only demonstrate a commitment to shifting an existing power relationship. It can demonstrate openness and the willingness to engage. However, if there is a particular position which requires advocating, for example, action on climate change, the listening programme can only create a more open platform, but it cannot provide that message.

3.4 Expressing the way we work: the different approaches on the spectrum

This section introduces the spectrum of available approaches to exerting influence. Being aware of the range of options, from listening to telling, can help in the construction of a successful public diplomacy product.

While different definitions and priorities are a reality, it is important to go beyond the arguments about names, to categorise the different forms of activity that may be undertaken. The spectrum of options can be viewed on a scale which ranges from 'listening' to 'telling'. The benefit of recognising this spectrum is that it allows a programme to make the most efficient use of the resources and range of possibilities available. In essence, the spectrum highlights many different approaches which could prevent international actors from turning to the same approaches over and over again.

Nation branding and tourism or trade promotion, which are essentially government-sponsored international advertising campaigns, appear at the 'telling' end of the spectrum and can be generally considered alongside policy advocacy or information correction. Public diplomacy largely based on the facilitation of the aims of the audience, for example programmes associated with development work, resides closer to the 'listening' end of the spectrum.[37]

A full range of these activities can be represented as:

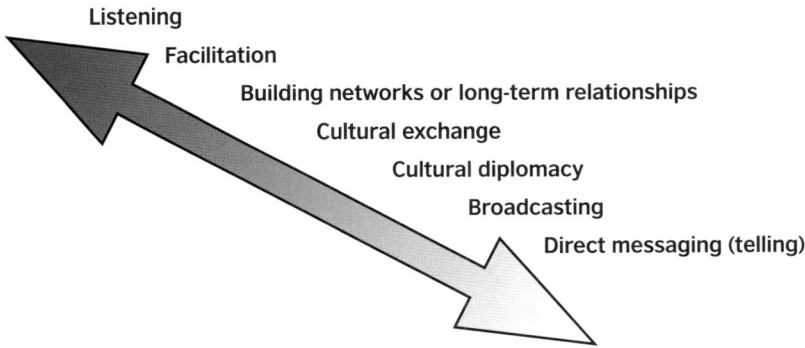

Listening exercise

As has already been described, consciously and publicly listening to the perspective of others can be a public diplomacy act in itself. In the international arena it is often the way you act, rather than what you say, that changes the behaviour of others.

> **Intercultural Dialogue in Africa**
>
> Intercultural Dialogue in Africa (ICDA) is a major project launched by British Council Africa in co-ordination with Counterpoint. It is aiming to develop intercultural dialogue with Muslim communities across sub-Saharan Africa. The project is expected to run for two to three years in 12 selected countries. Research is conducted using reference groups that are set up in every country, consisting of 30 members representing a broad cross-section of each society. Within these groups, established by British Council offices in sub-Saharan Africa, political and social issues relevant to their own communities are discussed. The agenda of these discussions is developed by each community, in partnership with the British Council. Moreover, an advisory group established by Counterpoint in London complements the project with desk research. Counterpoint will then produce three publications annually that reflect African Muslims' views and improve understanding in the United Kingdom. Listening to the views of African Muslims in sub-Saharan Africa in such a manner will help understanding between societies and cultures, which stems from the belief that this will lead to mutual benefit both for the societies themselves as well as for the British Council.

Facilitation

Providing others with the means of achieving their goals can allow an organisation to change the way the target audience acts. Effective facilitation cannot be conducted without genuine listening and entails the provision of projects which are tailored to the needs of the recipient audience. These are determined through negotiation or dialogue. Plans are drawn up in co-operation with the recipient audience to not only meet their requirements, but also to give them a sense of ownership over these plans. This ties the audience to the realisation of goals because they are viewed as being developed in an endogenous rather than exogenous manner. Although, at first glance, this may not seem to be influence in the sense of changing someone's mind, it still provides a platform for influence. Because facilitation can lead to greater mutuality and reciprocity, it makes it more likely that an audience will act in a desired way in the future. Furthermore, it provides the opportunity for the international actor to be seen as central to the process and its resolution, and as such, the actor may also benefit by association.

Niche diplomacy
The power of niche diplomacy – a common way of engaging in a facilitative approach – for Canada and Norway comes from being seen by others as acting as a good citizen. They are providing the utilities which further the well-being of the global community. Preventing injuries to civilians through the banning of landmines or the obvious benefits gained from the reduction in war clearly contribute to the positive image of the facilitating countries. While a positive image in itself is reassuring it does not necessarily translate directly into influence. The positioning of Norway in relation to peace negotiations not only provides it with the opportunity to influence a likely outcome but also the prestige associated with being the host for such negotiations. This shows that the importance of facilitation is not limited to being perceived as a good citizen, it provides an opportunity to shape negotiations from which the actor might otherwise be excluded.[38]

Building networks or long-term relationships
R.S. Zaharna, from the School of Communication at the American University in Washington DC, argues that 'networking has replaced information dominance as the new model of persuasion in the global communication era'.[39] Long-term networks must engage people on the basis of their priorities, because this creates networks of advocates working in the same direction as the public diplomacy organisation. As such, both traditional physical and virtual networks have become increasingly recognised as an important part of public diplomacy. Networking is predominantly based on identifying individuals or groups who will be influential in the future and on taking a long-term view of the relationship with them. Clearly, one tension of acting for the long-term is the increasing pressure to show short-term results. Without clear evidence of what long-term success might look like in the short term, this type of work may become distorted and increasingly myopic.

The effects of networking
The Network Effect, initiated by the British Council in partnership with local organisations, is a series of discussion forums for young people, with the aim of nurturing networks between each other in the future. The forums provide a platform to discuss a diverse range of issues, but every forum tries to answer the question: 'What sort of Europe do we want to live in?' Each forum is attended by around 35 young participants coming from 37 countries in Europe and beyond – from Portugal

> to Russia; Finland to Azerbaijan. The first forum took place in Stockholm in October 2005. Further events include Budapest (March 2008), St Petersburg (June 2008), Tbilisi (October 2008), Barcelona (March 2009) and the final forum in Belfast (June 2009). In the final Network Effect forum in Belfast in June 2009, young people who participated in previous forums will submit proposals of projects the British Council could engage in with the aim of bringing about a positive change to a particular debated issue. The British Council will award funding to the best project proposal.[40]

Cultural exchange
Midway between listening and telling, cultural exchange aims to be a genuine exchange of people, cultural goods or ideas, based on reciprocity and a symmetrical relationship.

This exchange may be physical, but with the increasing use of virtual worlds, online communication and collaboration, traditional travel-based programmes are no longer the sole preserve of cultural exchange. 'Success requires listening to others, recognising the "value of other cultures," showing a desire to learn from them, and conducting programmes as a "two-way street".'[41] Applying the term 'cultural exchange' to one's own operations therefore raises expectations of reciprocity.[42]

> **Leonardo grants**
> The Leonardo da Vinci Programme is part of the European Commission's Lifelong Learning Programme and helps to develop vocational skills and training. Leonardo sends trainees and students on European work placements and aims at building a skilled workforce through European partnerships. Leonardo funds these overseas work placements and promotes the development and exchange of training materials across borders in order to improve training standards.[43]

Cultural diplomacy
As the emphasis shifts away from listening and increasingly towards the promotion of a particular perspective, cultural diplomacy is the act of presenting cultural goods to an audience in an attempt to engage them in the ideas the producer perceives to be represented by them. Some, such as Milton Cummings, attempt to combine cultural diplomacy with the language of cultural exchange by using phrases such as 'mutual understanding'. However, as Milton Cummings notes,

cultural diplomacy 'can also be more of a one-way street than a two-way exchange, as when one nation concentrates its efforts on promoting the national language, explaining its policies and point of view, or "telling its story" to the rest of the world'.[44] Whatever the language used, the main difference between exchange and diplomacy is their respective power dynamics; reciprocity and a symmetrical relationship characterise exchange, presentation and one-way communication play a more significant role in cultural diplomacy.

> **Confucius Institute**
> Confucius Institutes are non-profit organisations aiming at promoting Chinese language and culture, supporting local Chinese teaching, and can enhance cross-cultural and economic exchange on an international level. The headquarters is in Beijing and is under the China National Office of Chinese Language Council International.
>
> Following the establishment of a pilot institute in Tashkent, Uzbekistan, in June 2004, the first Confucius Institute opened in November in 2004 in Seoul and many more have been established in other countries, including the United States, and in Europe and Asia. The Ministry of Education of the People's Republic of China estimates that, by the year 2010, there will be approximately 100 million people worldwide learning Chinese as a foreign language, and it plans to set up 100 Confucius Institutes.[45]
>
> In an alternative approach the Chinese Gardens of Serenity in Malta create an alternative format for the representation of certain aspects of China.

Broadcasting

Distinctions between cultural diplomacy and broadcasting may be small. Media production, mainly news, for mass consumption is also, like cultural diplomacy, essentially one-way communication. It presents a particular perspective of a broadcaster, for example that of Al Jazeera, the *Guardian* or Fox News. In this, it is not limited to cultural phenomena and activities, but can extend to a wider sphere, including social, political and economic topics.

A broadcaster has to balance perspective and content in order to ensure credibility with the target audience. This may be done through classic state-based broadcasting (public service broadcasting), although it may also take a particular regional, political or religious perspective, such as Channel Four Wales.

The movement away from the classic broadcasting techniques has led to an increased emphasis on web-based content.

While clear divisions between 'world' and 'home' services used to be possible, the advent of online 'listen on demand' services have opened up domestic content to audiences overseas.

> **BBC World Service**
> The BBC World Service, launched in 1932, is funded through the Foreign and Commonwealth Office by the British Government. It transmits in 33 languages to many parts of the world, with the English language service running 24 hours a day. The World Service average weekly audience reached 183 million in May 2007. It has been used to broadcast messages and convey ideas to its audience and can be a useful tool for influence because of its widespread reach.[46]

Direct messaging
Direct messaging is constructed to achieve a particular public diplomacy aim and represents the 'telling' end of the spectrum. Direct messaging is not a negotiation, it is not symmetrical. In order to leave as little space as possible for alternative interpretations, this approach usually emphasises the 'need to be simple' as 'the people you're talking to are usually far less interested in you than you are'.[47] It is purely one-way and designed to change the way an audience acts, without a desire for reciprocity.

Should producers become too fixed on purely telling, they run the danger of not bringing across their intended message; either because the audience does not understand what is being said, or because the audience interprets the received information in a totally different way from the original meaning.[48] Approaches associated with soft power focus on a one-way transfer, but they are not the only examples of direct messaging. Nation branding, which has gained influence in recent years, is as much an exercise focused predominantly on a direct messaging approach as it is about transmitting a certain country brand.[49] Concepts of propaganda and psychological operations also exist within telling, although most organisations prefer to keep them at a distance from other methods of engagement, owing to negative connotations which some audiences may attach to these labels.

> **Spain's brand**
> Spain is an excellent example of nation branding. Under the anachronistic fascist rule of Franco, it was an impoverished European backwater. After the death of Franco in 1975, Spain stirred. Armed with an attractive, modernistic sun symbol designed by Joan Miro, it mounted an aggressive marketing campaign to reshape its image, offering 'Everything Under the Sun' to visitors. The 1992 Barcelona Olympics and Seville World's Fair helped propel it into the international spotlight, and today Spain is a major modern European player.
> *Savas Kyriacou and Thomas Cromwell, East West Communications.*[50]

3.5 Why consider the spectrum?

The spectrum of available approaches is an important part of exerting influence because it helps in the positioning of a particular organisation as well as identifying potential partners. This section also shows the application of the spectrum to the area of intercultural dialogue.

The spectrum highlights a number of important elements in an approach to exerting influence. It shows the full set of options for influence, from listening to telling. This helps a public diplomacy organisation to position itself within that spectrum and to recognise its preferred approaches. This not only helps the organisation as such, but also makes it easier to recognise potential partners for certain projects. Awareness of the spectrum helps the practitioner opt for an approach most suited to the specific needs of a particular programme. This increases efficiency and effectiveness and leads to high-impact projects. At the same time, it helps to locate potential partners' tendencies in the choice of public diplomacy programmes and can therefore lead to more productive and successful partnerships.

    The options on the activity spectrum also relate closely to selling or communicating. The closer to 'telling' on the spectrum, the more the international actor emphasises selling. Direct messaging, broadcasting, and cultural diplomacy rely on projecting a particular image rather than engaging in dialogue and developing a two-way communication. The closer to the 'listening' end, the more the international actor places emphasis on developing influence by understanding the priorities of other actors. In this second option, mutual understanding through communication is more important than selling an image to an audience. The shift of focus to communicating rather than selling happens around cultural exchange, which provides a genuinely balanced relationship emphasising mutuality and mutual understanding.

Categorical and blinkered approaches to public diplomacy often stand in the way of success. Viewing public diplomacy programmes as a spectrum whose emphasis continually shifts between listening and telling, acknowledges that the boundaries between the methods are blurred. Rather than being seen as a hindrance, these overlaps should be taken as an opportunity to create flexible programmes that can be adapted and rearranged as required. No international actors can afford to have a restricted view of the available possibilities. As a Jordanian diplomat commented recently, public diplomacy is 'creative diplomacy'; being aware of all their options helps an organisation to be creative.

Clarity over the approach provides an organisation with the ability to make the appropriate selection from the spectrum of options. However, in selecting these options, international actors must not forget about the issues identified in Chapter 2; they must not lose sight of how their product will be understood by the audience.

One tool useful in examining how the issues in Chapter 2 relate to the spectrum of options is the Johari Window created by Luft and Ingham. As a starting point, it identifies the different areas of common understanding; those known to only one side, those shared by both sides and those which are known to neither side.

Robert Gibson, intercultural business trainer, explains:

'Room 1 is where people see eye to eye and share values, attitudes, meanings and behaviour. Room 2 is what they can see but you can't. Room 4 is where you can see and they can't. Room 3 is a mystery for everyone.'[51]

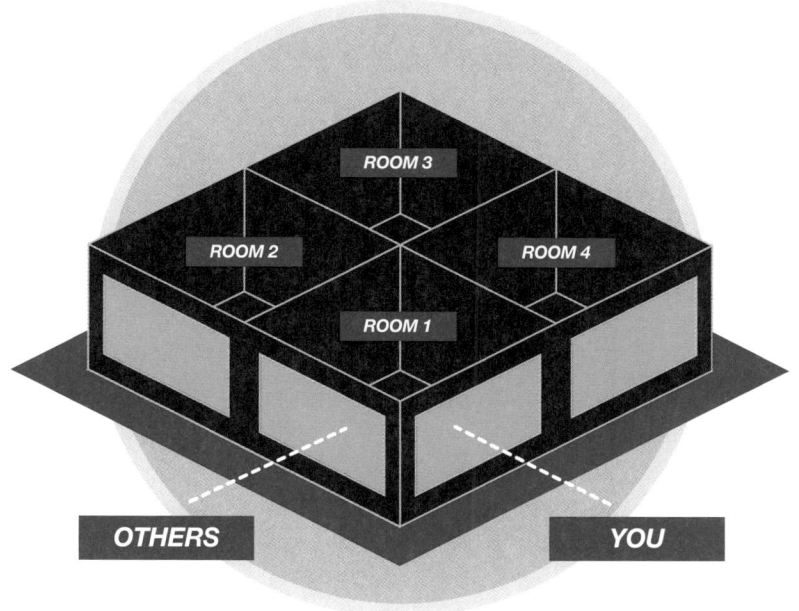

The window can be used to express the various options for engagement. Programmes that emphasise telling, for example direct messaging, broadcasting and, to a lesser extent, cultural diplomacy, attempt to move the perspectives of the international actor, Room 4, into the consciousness of the audience. In effect there is an attempt to sell the understanding of the ideas held in Room 4 to the target audience in the hope that they will become shared in Room 1. International actors do not attempt to take on the values of the audience, but try to convince them to take on theirs.

Listening programmes take the alternative approach. They seek to draw the perspectives of 'the others' from Room 2 into Room 1. This does have benefits for the international actor in altering the way the audience acts, although the emphasis is placed on increasing the understanding of the ideas in Room 2.

Cultural exchange, with the symmetrical relationship and emphasis on sharing, provides two potential options. First, it seeks to extend Room 1 into Rooms 2 and 4. The goal in this iteration is to achieve a situation where all people 'see eye to eye and share values, attitudes, meanings and behaviour'. In effect, the shared understanding must be negotiated, as neither group can insist on all the values being imposed on the other. An alternative goal for such negotiation is for each group to make Rooms 2 and 4 visible to their respective 'others'. However, rather than attempting to expand Room 1, the room of shared values and perspectives, the goal is to understand the reasons behind the alternative perspective. In effect, each group seeks to see the parts of the iceberg which are below the surface, to understand the rationale or encoded assumptions behind certain visible products and actions. This provides the 'mutual understanding' for which many argue, without an emphasis on homogenisation.

A further option which can be identified through the Johari Window is the international actor acting as cultural broker between two groups. In this case the organisation may not only provide the ability to create understanding, as previously identified, but also help the development of new understandings on the basis of the synthesis between different perspectives. This reinforces the importance of two-way communication as more than merely a means of sharing information, values or perspectives.[52] It is a way for international actors to engage in an ongoing development of their own constituency, rather than merely influencing the target audience.

The Johari Window provides one way of demonstrating what is intended to be achieved through the options in this chapter. However, along with a choice of options from the spectrum of activity, there needs to be clarity over how this is to be applied when constructing a strategy. An international actor has to be clear on the difference between an emphasis on selling as a strategic action and being engaged in conscious communication. Furthermore, the actor has to consider the conscious and unconscious parts of the iceberg, along with the impact which encoding and decoding will have on understanding within the target audience. With all these issues in mind, the international actor also has to consider where the programme is to be targeted.

4 Where in the world(s) is your product targeted?

A wide array of options can lead to a specific goal. With unlimited resources, international actors could construct, take up, change and dismiss public diplomacy programmes as they please. But since this is rarely the case, most actors could not bear the costs of trial by error and therefore need to make choices. Targeting, both geographically and strategically, allows a programme to be more focused, which in return leads to success. The right targeting can enhance the effectiveness as well as the reach and impact of any public diplomacy action.

This chapter deals with the question of targeting. As with the first two chapters there is a wide variety of options. Organisational priorities will influence how these options are combined. In addition to geographical targeting in the physical world or online, an organisation must also decide whether projects will be conducted according to certain issues and moreover, whether engagement is bi- or multilateral.

4.1 Global coverage (through physical presence)

It is highly unlikely that an organisation will seek global coverage in the sense of being physically present absolutely everywhere. Instead global can be thought of as presence in a large number of countries, covering all regions of the world. Merely having a website which could be accessed from anywhere does not qualify as global coverage.

Genuine global coverage requires active engagement with the population in the various countries.

> The United Kingdom engages with foreign publics through the Foreign and Commonwealth Office (FCO) and the British Council. The FCO operates 260 diplomatic missions, embassies, consulates and high commissions, and employs 6,000 UK civil servants and 10,000 locally appointed staff. The British Council has 7,900 staff in 110 countries and territories.[53]
>
> *FCO and UK Government*
>
> The US State Department has 260 diplomatic and consular posts in 163 countries.[54]
> *The Department of State and Agency for International Development (USAID)*

The global coverage strategy stems from the decision that a country cannot manage without representation in all regions of the world and that benefits can be gained from having a footprint in most countries and organising initiatives or programmes at the global level. These include economies of scale and an increased interaction between diffuse populations. Any of the various aspects, from the active pursuit of markets, support for foreign policy actions or ideology, can be the reasoning behind a global coverage strategy. It may also be defensive, such as trying to combat an ideology which is seen to threaten certain national interests, such as security and health.

However, despite the possibility to develop projects on a global scale, regional priorities and local nuance will continue to be an important part of any strategy.

Also, this approach includes a high financial cost that might not provide an equally strong return for the practitioner as for the receiving countries. This is why other international actors (and parts of organisations which have adopted a global approach) may prefer to focus specifically on a limited number of countries identified either by geography or other priority.

4.2 Focus outside the region

A focus outside the region can help actors with limited resources by allowing them to carry through programmes with a wider scope in regions where they think it matters, without carrying the associated costs of global engagement.

Usually a limitation of resources will lead international actors to place focus within their own areas. However, to approach the alternative, to focus resources outside one's own region, is also logical. An international actor may consider that they do not have the resources to exert sufficient influence within the region to achieve particular goals. As a result, they may seek to focus a programme outside the region to draw attention to a particular issue which is occurring in the region.

In security terms this may be to ensure that a local dispute will be viewed as having broader importance, or to guarantee that the nations outside the region are sympathetic to a particular side in the dispute. It can be demonstrated through the discussion of military security, though it has many other applications. Singapore, for example, has constructed a part of its strategy based on the need to balance their geopolitical location to ensure Singapore has political and economic space between itself and its neighbours, Malaysia and Indonesia, rather than being perceived as part of their public diplomacy strategies, considering that 'the alternatives are too grim to contemplate'.[55] A central part of this strategy is to look beyond the regional context and 'involve world powers in its well-being'.[56] Singapore runs a relatively small network of embassies, with strong centralised control through its foreign ministry and has economised on its scarce resources through extensive use of 'non-resident ambassadors'. Early examples or developing links and support outside the region include hosting, in 1971, the first Commonwealth Summit held outside London, and extensive engagement with the UN following Vietnam's incursion into Cambodia in 1978.

More recently an initiative by Singaporean Prime Minister Goh with French President Chirac resulted in the ASEAN-EU biennial summit-level dialogue in March 1996.[57]

There is nothing new in this approach. *Selling War*, written by Nicholas Cull, demonstrates the lengths to which the UK went to influence the population of the United States of America to make them more likely to join the Second World War, a war that was, at that time, considered largely limited to other areas of the world.[58] With this, America moved from isolationism to involvement in other regions of the world.

> 'From the eve of the German invasion of Poland to the moment of Japan's attack on Pearl Harbor, the British government mounted a concerted effort to draw the United States into the War.
>
> On February 15, 1942, Winston Churchill broadcast an address to the world. Still flushed with the news of Pearl Harbor and fresh from a visit to Washington, he gloried in the United States' entry into World War II as an event that he had "dreamed of, aimed at and worked for".'
>
> Nicholas J. Cull Selling War[59]

This approach is common for other international actors seeking to promote a specific issue. While regional influence may be useful, being able to engage the countries who have the political, economic, military or other markers of power can be even more beneficial.

Another type of campaign also demonstrates the importance of the focus outside the specific region in question. Live Aid, for example, drew attention to the drought and famine in Sudan and Ethiopia. A local approach focused on action within the region started by these two countries would have achieved little on a global scale. As such, the campaign had to come from outside the region to influence the way populations, particularly in the US and UK, acted towards the region. Equally, the subsequent Live 8 pursued a similar strategy, expanding the target audiences predominantly to the members of the G8.

An emphasis outside the region acknowledges the weak position of the actor in relation to the influence which is required within the region. As such, actors seek support from outside to provide them with the ability to exert influence within.

4.3 Local region

For various reasons, international actors may choose to stay restricted to their geographical region. Prioritising one's locality can help when prioritising local security and trade as public diplomacy goals.

International actors with limited resources may seek to prioritise within the geographic region in which they are based. In the case of a country, this may be part of a strategy to secure borders or resources. Alternatively, there may also be a recognition that the actor's interests are best served by emphasising the regional importance of an issue to provide the message with greater weight within a highly competitive information environment. Two examples are issues of local security and the creation of a regional hub.

The first possibility particularly focuses on regional security, which may face risks in terms of resources, crime, health, etc. Limited resources may be deployed to engage local actors to reduce insecurity. This may be attempted through an operation designed to create understanding, rather than trying to threaten. These programmes may take on any of the options described through the Johari Window in Section 3.5.

Alternatively, there may be an attempt to undermine the ability of an opposing force to create a metaphysical tableau of Good vs. Evil. This can be done through the development of cultural contact between the two populations. Such a move would limit the ability for opposing actors to stereotype and frame the issue as 'with us or against us'.

Security may be considered in military terms but also matters in terms of resources. The options for influence include attempts to change the way a debate about resources might be conducted. For example, is increasing the price of certain resources to a neighbour a reasonable action in a competitive world, shameless exploitation, or evidence of the willingness to renege on previous agreements? The success of a strategy could well have an impact on the cost of certain resources in the future. A successful campaign which reduces the cost of resources can have a benefit which vastly outweighs the cost of running the operation. This narrative may not be as easily recognisable as one which averts or reduces a military threat, yet both options have recognisable security or economic benefits.

In each case the international actor has to target the section of the regional population which appears most likely to be willing and able to influence policy within the target country.

Statistics on resources
Risks for local regions are manifold. The following statistics exemplify the importance of resources for international relations:
- Singapore, which imports around 50 per cent of its water from Malaysia through an agreement which will expire in 60 years.[60]
- European imports of gas from the former Soviet Union, for example Ukraine, where supplies were suspended in a dispute over price. Other countries which could be directly affected include Germany, Hungary and Italy.
- The Japanese steel industry depends entirely on imports of iron ore and coal. The largest supplier in 2005 was Australia, who supplied 61.4 per cent of iron ore and 68.8 per cent of coal imports.[61]

A focus in the region may be for defensive or security purposes, but equally can be used to increase recognition of an actor as a regional influence hub. In nation-state terms this may take the form of a focal point for political leadership, trade, education, technological development or international financial markets. In non-state terms the focus of international actors may be on developing their reputation as a centre of authority on a certain issue.

Dynamic Korea: Hub of Asia
Following the 1997 financial crisis South Korea has used the tag line 'Dynamic Korea: Hub of Asia'. The attempt to create a hub draws on infrastructural development including the opening of Incheon airport, the promotion of e-commerce and availability of high speed internet access. These were designed to create an environment attractive to inward investment, promoted through the hosting of the 2002 World Cup.[62]

An approach to a regional rather than global hub has the potential to balance return on resource commitment with the provision of international influence. The hub approach has commonly been taken to education. The Thai government created a programme to increase the number of international students in the country by making Thailand a regional education hub. This attempt was aided by encouraging universities from China, Egypt and the US to open branch campuses. A similar strategy has been pursued by regions of India, including Punjab, benefiting from the comparatively less expensive education to American, Australian or European competitors.[63]

Other alternatives may include countries, such as Malta, who have the opportunity to become a hub for dialogue through which current international tensions can be mediated. All these options target audiences inside the region that are likely to be able to take advantage of the particular hub.

4.4 Engaging online: the potential of a virtual world

The internet has without doubt heralded a new era of engaging with audiences. The geographical reach, participation and empowerment of the audience have transformed an international actor's work and opened up new opportunities.

The growth of access to the internet provides great potential for communication with audiences around the world. However, the nature of the new technology and the way in which audiences engage with it presents two fundamental questions.

The options available to an international actor require a decision about what the engagement online is for. One option is to allow each part of the organisation (e.g. each country office) to engage online with its physical world audience. An alternative would be to identify a specific part of the organisation responsible for the online engagement. When engaging online, the options for the international actor include using the internet to showcase what an organisation is doing or to consider the internet as another platform, equivalent to the physical world, through which to run programmes.

Most organisations currently take the first option, but there are moves to conceive the internet as another, virtual, area of engagement. Given the length of time which people spend online and the altered power dynamics within these environments, it may become more effective to try to engage an online audience separately from specific physical region programmes.

The argument for the second option rests on the recognition that the markers of power which are used to identify traditional target audiences do not necessarily work online. The website Technorati is 'currently tracking 93.9 million blogs and over 250 million pieces of tagged social media'.[64] It claims to be:

> '... the recognized authority on what's happening on the World Live Web, right now. The Live Web is the dynamic and always-updating portion of the Web. We search, surface, and organize blogs and the other forms of independent,

user-generated content (photos, videos, voting, etc.) increasingly referred to as "citizen media".'[65]

To think of the influence of the most popular of these bloggers in relation to who they are in the physical world would be to miss the point. The blogger might, for example, work in the local supermarket of a country town. But seeing the blogger just as a part-time shop assistant in a rural community would completely underestimate their potential influence as a writer with a possible online readership of thousands.

The question of how an organisation will decide to use the internet will most likely depend on whether the online environment is viewed as a means to showcase projects, communicate messages and provide information, or whether it is a key area for engaging with a target audience. In the near future, it is likely that most organisations will adopt a mixed approach of physical world engagement for information and showcasing activity, while at the same time developing an online engagement programme as an alternative or supplementary means of delivery.

The decision to engage with the target audience online requires the international actor to understand the cultural and social barriers to entry. Most organisations recognise the technological barriers to entry, but in order to be successful at exerting influence online, an international actor must understand how the cultural and social expectations of their audiences online differ from those they engage with in the physical world.

Another aspect of online engagement is the recent spread of open source systems in other areas, such as social networking. Open source engagement is seen as a vital consideration for the future of influence. Its development has enjoyed an increasing influence in the online environment. The original open source system was the Linux core code. Open source means that the creator of a programme releases their source code so that any user can contribute to the development of this programme. Examples include Mozilla Firefox and websites such as Facebook.

Public diplomacy organisations must not simply view the web as a mere tool for dissemination; public diplomacy is also about learning from the online environment. The potential of the open source concept comes from understanding how a community works and how to harness that power to develop different functions, just like the software developers who worked with the Linux core code.

Using open source engagement focuses the mind on the power of a community united around an idea. However, rather than an international actor seeking to own the idea and then make the audience join with it, the ideas are thrown out to see who has similar ideas. This allows people to join, or modify and improve the concepts and the ways of communicating them. This has the power of engaging potential target audiences and partners right at the beginning of and throughout the developmental process. It allows the audience to feel ownership over the ideas and programmes with which they are being confronted, in ways which even the best listening exercises and most advanced echo chambers cannot achieve.

The open source engagement recognises that each community, particularly online, has its own cultural and social expectations. To be able to engage successfully, the international actor has to navigate not just the practical barriers, for example learning how to upload videos, but also these cultural and social barriers. Online communities form around certain ideas and perspectives. Some form around sports, some around celebrity, and others around political issues. Particularly important to understanding open source engagement are those that form around the rejection of corporate messages and emphasising that 'markets are conversations' instead.[66] These communities such as the authors of *The cluetrain manifesto* draw on similar influences to the open source software development.[67]

On the cluetrain

'Most corporations, …only know how to talk in the soothing, humorless monotone of the mission statement, marketing brochure, and your-call-is-important-to-us busy signal. *Same old tone, same old lies.* No wonder networked markets have no respect for companies unable or unwilling to speak as they do.'

Christopher Locke et al. The cluetrain manifesto

'The cluetrain is to marketing and communications what the open-source movement is to software development — anarchic, messy, rude, and vastly more powerful than the doomed bullshit that conventionally passes for wisdom.'

Eric S. Raymond The Cathedral and the Bazaar[68]

Whether the international actor agrees to these perspectives or not, they are a reality, and the communities which follow them have certain cultural and social expectations about the groups they engage with. Perhaps two of the most instructive suggestions from *The cluetrain manifesto* are:

'34. To speak with a human voice, companies must share the concerns of their communities.
35. But first, they must belong to a community.'[69]

This sets out the expectations and to an extent the terms of engagement. The emphasis on human voices highlights the cultural expectations of the community and being part of such a community highlights social expectations. When combined, these perspectives emphasise the need for the international actor to be seen as a peer within the community rather than an 'authority' figure communicating with a subservient network.

To take software development as a metaphor, programmes are either written by companies in a clear hierarchy of managers, employees and customers, or produced by an open source community where each individual is a peer, able to use the code and develop a product as they see fit. To act in this manner, international actors must be able to identify clearly what goal they are pursuing, so that others can also easily recognise whether they can either share or use these goals to achieve their desired outcomes.

Public diplomacy organisations should identify participants on a symmetrical basis, rather than creating a project and then inviting others to become a part of it. Also, they should make the goal of the project an achievable goal for all rather than just aiming for self-promotion. If an organisation acknowledges the fact that a project won't totally conform to pre-determined ideas and that different elements may be run by disparate (and even normally competing groups), this can contribute to achieving the goal.

In an open source approach, practitioners use the platforms already frequented by the target audience, rather than building new ones and trying to persuade people to use them.

This means that the international actor needs to understand the sociocultural expectations of the users. This may appear to be a daunting task, and is one not to be taken lightly. When seeking to engage with online environments and platforms, organisations find each platform to have its own social barriers and expectations. Employing people who can navigate these expectations will be the key to successful engagement through online platforms

Some organisations may debate banning YouTube, Facebook, Friendster, Netvibes, Operator11 or Studiverzeichnis from being accessed at work, considering them a waste of work time. However, the employees using these sites as part of their social life understand the cultural and social expectations of these platforms. As such, they are best placed to engage with these communities in their work life. While these sites should not be used to avoid work, the knowledge of their terms of use can be applied to the development of programmes, allowing an international actor to engage with a human voice and be recognised as a peer. Without this understanding the programme will be seen as intruding on space 'owned' by the community.

4.5 Prioritising countries by issue

Prioritising by issue can be a way of increasing effectiveness and reach while at the same time reducing input of resources and costs. Usually prioritising by issue will still present a certain focus on geographical regions.

Identifying the national interests by issue provides a particular interpretation of priority countries. While each international actor will inevitably identify a different hierarchy of priorities, in many instances these can be broken down into economic, political, environmental, and ideological factors.

Issue targeting may not initially appear to be part of geographic targeting. However, the structure of most organisations will tend toward the identification of 'priority countries' which give issues a geographic representation. This process is likely to continue, as the world is largely still conceived within national units. Even if international actors move beyond the notion of nation into engaging transnational communities, such as Europe or Oceania, these populations will still be geographically concentrated.

The purpose for which a particular strategy is being adopted will dictate the priority countries. This is a truism of any strategy but one which occasionally escapes some public diplomacy planning. The issue-based approach can be illustrated through various factors, particularly economic ones. These include tourism, trade, aid, politics and peace.

Tourism

Tourism is integral in targeting by issue. The attempt to attract the economic benefit which can accrue from tourism is one example of an issue-based strategy. In many instances, this entails a branding approach. Although a programme may also be based on the provision of information, it still, in most cases, falls into a direct messaging approach. Necessarily, this approach will target audiences with sufficient financial resources which are potentially attracted to a specific area. The aim of the programme is the creation of an image of a holiday experience.

Such branding exercises have been carried out in numerous countries seeking to support tourism. However, one should not confuse branding a tourist destination with branding a country. They should be considered distinctly separate activities. Branding a holiday destination, or resort, can hold up a brand which is characterised by its potential to convey the feeling of an experience, especially linked to this particular place. This is because in a resort and many well-organised tourist destinations, the visitors' experience can be influenced or guided through the provision of information and services. Tourist information usually directs visitors along certain routes, landmarks or other points of interest and activities which showcase the country's potential. Information and services can allow tourists to leave the resort to explore without straying away from areas conforming to the image. Consequently, routes to the 'must dos' and 'must sees' are clearly identified, and constructed in a way that tourists do not wander off into areas where the constructed image may be challenged.

If tourists are promised white sand and blue sea, and the services allow them to get from airport to resort without that image being significantly challenged, and the resort is as it was pictured in the catalogues, the branding will be successful. However, if image and reality differ significantly or services are unable to guide tourists away from experiences which challenge that image, branding will fail.

Tourism and World Cup 2006
The 2006 World Cup held in Germany provides a prime example of this approach. With the use of public viewing areas ('Fanparks') and 'The World Cup on the market place' (a programme that was aimed at providing local identification with the World Cup), not only the host cities could realise two areas of interest: firstly, these activities could partly contribute to financing their activities through revenue raised by sponsorship and catering. Furthermore, the cities could transmit a

> specific regional image by branding themselves through the choice of activities and the location of their 'Fan-Fest'. This was designed to ensure a long-term impact on tourists.[70]

The branding of particular experiences, which can be received from resorts, or clearly identified areas ('place branding') must be considered different from nation branding. The 'Fanpark' was successful at channelling fans into certain areas to have certain experiences which allowed each region to present a different emphasis within the confines of the event. However, the reality of an entire nation is a diversity of opportunity and experience, which is problematic when reduced to a slogan or a few key messages.

Trade
Trade features as another important option for targeting. The issue of trade can be approached in various different ways, such as projecting a certain image to attract investment, identifying common trade objectives or the creation of a hub of trade activity.

A projection of a certain image, similar to tourism, can help the pursuit of economic benefit through trade and inward investment. The product image may be efficiency, infrastructure, or skilled labour among others. The narrative of a competitive global environment and the need for a certain country to be recognised has some merit but must be considered within the context of the actual reality within the country, specifically the identification of any unique or specialist traits. The image must reflect this reality, so a specific niche skill may provide a competitive advantage. However, a generic model of good service and welcoming people may struggle to differentiate, for example, Sweden from Malta.

A well-planned, executed and differentiated branding exercise (which accurately reflects the offer) may provide some competitive advantage, but, unlike with tourism, it is significantly harder to control the experience of the potential investor who will usually conduct their own rigorous analysis business. It may therefore merely provide the opportunity to open negotiation.

An alternative approach is to identify common trade objectives and encourage the conceptualisation of shared objectives. The pursuit of a common goal may provide for the creation of a closer identification between the interests of the countries. In this view common endeavour would both transcend and serve national interests.

Such an approach requires a high level of engagement and negotiation to ensure the goals are shared beyond rhetoric. In either sense, the programme will target those countries that have the resources required for trade. This may be the financial resources for inward investment or securing markets, whether major world, regional or local markets for goods.

Yet another alternative is to emphasise the creation of a hub or gateway through which trade in its various forms can flow. In this sense the operation is focused on the population most likely or able to engage in that particular activity. This approach can be exemplified by London as a hub for finance, Malta as an entry point for physical goods into the EU and Ireland or India as providers of outsourced services. These approaches have the following practical implications. London is targeting areas which contain high concentrations of financial institutions, for example the US or countries with large amounts of wealth generated by oil. Malta can target those countries seeking to import a vast amount of European goods, such as China. India or Ireland on the other hand aim to attract those service societies with a high production costs and elevated living expenses. Given the various options the need for clarity is paramount. The programme must have a specific objective. This will determine the target audience.

Aid

A third area of targeting by issues revolves around aid. Influence operations around aid can be divided into two perspectives, namely those by countries seeking to attract aid and those where the donors desire more visibility for their work.

International actors seeking to attract aid or development support can run programmes designed to influence where donors will allocate funds. Aid or development organisations have finite budgets. As a result, an increase in support for one recipient requires cuts elsewhere. However, those same organisations are also subject to political pressures, which create the opportunity to run an influence operation. A successful programme mounted by a prospective aid recipient may be able to leverage political pressure within the constituency of the donor organisation that results in a more favourable settlement for the recipient.

This type of approach will suffer some of the same limitations as tourism and trade; additionally, there will be a twofold limitation of resources. First, an international actor seeking aid or development support is likely to have limited resources to allocate to an influence programme. Second, an expensive campaign designed to attract aid will be undermined if potential donors perceive that the recipient has used its limited resources to mount the campaign.

Targeting is therefore vital to success as resources committed must be low, but impact must be high. While one option would be a direct, well-executed approach to the donor organisation, it is also possible to make an indirect appeal targeted at influential individuals within the constituency of large donor organisations. This focuses attention and pressure on the decision-making process. While not mounted by a country, the Live 8 movement is an example of a programme designed to apply public pressure on politicians in relation to their aid and debt commitments.

> 'Live 8 was and remains a brilliant moment but what is more important is the brilliant movement of which it was a part. This gives the poorest of the poor real political muscle for the first time. [...] It is this movement of church people and trade unionists, soccer moms and student activists, that will carry the spirit of Live 8 on. It is this movement, not rock stars, that will make it untenable in the future to break promises to the most vulnerable people on this planet.'[71]
>
> *Bono*

When providing aid, evaluation often asks for valorisation of a project. Just as potential donors are susceptible to political pressure to provide or control aid to certain programmes or in certain ways, they must also demonstrate the impact of their work. This means mounting programmes to highlight the success of operations. The target will be either within the recipient community, if aid is designed to foster an ongoing relationship with the donor, or within the donor's constituency if the programme is purely for valorisation.

> The Foreign Policy Centre's *European Infopolitik* is a publication dedicated to the development of a European public diplomacy strategy. It outlines various recommendations, among others one that asks for more aid visibility: 'Be more aggressive in promoting EU aid visibility in third world countries:
>
> ... the EU has much to gain from more effective projection and promotion of its activities. This should include the enforcement of visibility clauses of contracts with aid recipients.'[72]
>
> *Philip Fiske de Gouveia* European Infopolitik

Programmes that seek to exert political or ideological influence have a long history which stretches back long before the field of public diplomacy was conceptualised in its current form. However, at the heart of this type of issue-based operation is the exertion of power; success must be measured by action not thought – it is the difference between an opinion poll and an election. Targeting of such campaigns focuses on countries or populations central to the realisation of a particular objective, such as:

- a country about to hold an election, directly attempting to influence the result
- to gain support for policy within priority countries (for example defined by seats on the UN Security Council)
- coalition-building prior to military action
- signing of a particular treaty, e.g. Kyoto.

Clear audience segmentation would be required for these operations so that they have resonance with the group most influential in any given situation. The examples above show that, in effect, the options come down to either trying to change a policy, or trying to change a government.

In the past, there have been many attempts at using influence to change a government. In Hungary in 1956, for example, the National Committee for a Free Europe encouraged Hungarians, through programmes including Radio Free Europe, to rise against Soviet control. These efforts were initially successful in influencing the Hungarian people. The first phases of the revolution were successful, and the Hungarians appealed to the UN for help. The population were hoping for US help when Soviet tanks were deployed in Hungary. But Western societies failed to respond and the Soviet Union invaded Hungary and stopped the revolution. The programme could be considered a success purely in terms of short-term influence but not as part of a co-ordinated strategy, since it led to expectations it could not keep.

> When Soviet tanks re-entered Hungary, the influence campaign backfired. One desperate appeal for help read:
>
> 'In the name of all that is dear to you ... we ask you to help ... Those who have died for liberty ... accuse you who are able to help and have not helped.'[73]
>
> *Quoted in Wise and Ross* The Invisible Government

Similarly, in Iraq in 1991, the encouragement of communities inside Iraq to rise against Saddam Hussein provides an example of a programme which was successful at influencing people. However, it was not part of a fully committed and co-ordinated campaign. The American programmes exposed the communities to the repercussions of challenging Saddam Hussein, but they were lacking military support.

Both Hungary 1956 and Iraq 1991 demonstrate the potential for political programmes and the massive dangers which they pose should an international actor not be willing to fully support the actions they seek to encourage.

Another major aspect of political targeting can be aimed at influencing certain policies or the policy decision-making process. The Stern Review 2006, conducted by Sir Nicholas Stern, Head of the UK Government Economic Service, outlines the economics of climate change. Its aim is to outline the economic challenges caused by changing environmental conditions. The Stern Review also provides the means to promote certain actions in response to climate change.[74] More precisely, these range from environmental taxes to emissions trading or regulation in order for people to face the full social costs of their actions. It also argues for a technology policy that drives the development and deployment of a range of low-carbon and high-efficiency products. Overall, Stern tries to influence the readership, i.e. policy makers, into action to remove barriers to energy efficiency.

> 'There is still time to avoid the worst impacts of climate change, if we act now and act internationally. Governments, businesses and individuals all need to work together to respond to the challenge. Strong, deliberate policy choices by governments are essential to motivate change. But the task is urgent.
>
> Delaying action, even by a decade or two, will take us into dangerous territory. We must not let this window of opportunity close.'
>
> *Sir Nicholas Stern, at the publication of the* Stern Review

The launches of the report, briefings and the subsequent media interest provided a vehicle for the UK Government to influence the debates on the response to climate change. While prioritising the large polluters of the present and future, the report advocated a common global carbon price, thereby expanding the attempt to expand influence to all nations.

As seen, prioritising countries according to certain issues can be an efficient way to exert influence. Programmes developed around a certain issue are more than just representation. They are actively trying to influence the target audience. Thought is followed by action. The success of an issue-based strategy is measured in the way it influenced the behaviour of its recipients.

4.6 Bilateral vs. multilateral

Engaging on either a bilateral or multilateral basis can effectively enhance the objectives of an international actor's strategy. Depending on the stipulated goals, one or the other may present themselves as more useful.

Part of the consideration of how a programme will be targeted is whether it is intended to be bilateral or multilateral. Traditionally, most programmes have been bilateral with the benefit intended to accrue to the instigating international actor. However, multilateral operations will be increasingly common owing to the growth of supranational organisations and the demands on international actors to realise greater impact with fewer resources.

The multilateral operation is clearly ill-suited to a nation brand approach but can conceivably work for other forms of direct messaging from a supranational organisation. Alternatively, if a number of international actors identify a common goal, working in a multilateral manner can create a more efficient use of resources and a higher impact programme.

As an organisation made up of 26 independent member countries, any NATO public diplomacy or information operations must be considered multilateral.

NATO and organisations like it must align the multilateral approach of the organisation with the messages of the individual national governments. The priorities of the individual nations may vary depending on whether messages are intended for international, regional, local or internal audiences. The attempt to align many national concerns, some of which may be contradictory with the priorities of other nations, can lead to slow and labour-intensive communication.

The impact of these multilateral messages can also be undermined by messages from national spokespeople who demur from the NATO line because of their focus on specific bilateral relationships. However, while the multilateral approach has the potential to be hugely difficult to organise, it also has the potential to be more powerful, due to having numerous nations aligned to a single message.[75]

While NATO is a specific entity made up of many nations, EUNIC (European Union National Institutes for Culture) attempts to provide a framework for multilateral co-ordination of the activities of its member organisations.

> **EUNIC**
> The purpose of EUNIC is to create effective partnerships and networks between the participating organisations, to improve and promote cultural diversity and understanding between European societies, and to strengthen international dialogue and co-operation with countries outside Europe.
> EUNIC operates at two complementary levels:
> - Heads or Directors General of the national institutions.
> - clusters of national institutions for culture, based in cities across Europe, co-operating together in common projects. EUNIC Brussels represents both the Heads level and the clusters at the EU institutions.[76]

EUNIC is a partnership of national institutions for culture that engage beyond national borders and usually operate with autonomy from their governments. EUNIC currently counts members from 19 EU countries and its total operating budget is at 2.2 billion euros per annum.[77]

The loose basis of EUNIC membership provides this type of multilateral organisation with both strength and weakness. Unlike NATO it is much easier for EUNIC members to conduct bilateral operations without undermining the multilateral approach. However, this can create a weakness for EUNIC as some organisations will think of themselves as bilateral first and multilateral second. As such, while the EUNIC membership may have a large operational budget, some member organisations may be using much of their share in bilateral rather than multilateral EUNIC operations.

The Hague Project seeks to promote the development of a European strategy for culture. This is multilateral both in its European focus but also through the co-ordination of good practice.

The Hague Recommendations were formulated at the conference 'Diversity Makes the Difference – European Foreign Policy and Culture', which took place at The Hague on 9 March 2007.

> 'Recent research [...] has shown and gatherings of European and national politicians, representatives of cultural institutes (EUNIC), the foundation sector, artists and media representatives have concluded that there is a need to introduce a more coherent cultural component into the emerging EU external relations., [sic] complementing and not substituting the foreign cultural efforts of all the actors concerned. Such an enhanced cultural component would benefit the internal integration of the EU on one side and strengthen its role in the world on the other.'[78]
>
> *Kathinka Dittrich van Weringh*

The Hague Recommendations have practical consequences. On 10 May 2007, the European Commission's Communication on a European agenda for culture in a globalising world outlines the first-ever European strategy for culture. With Sean Doyle as contact partner, it provides for the collection of best practice throughout the EU, which is, at present, still hindered by the inertia of the cultural institutes.

In 2008, EUNIC will organise several events, among others a 'summer camp' and a conference in Slovenia to mark the Year of Intercultural Dialogue. The ability to share good practice, along with co-ordinated resources, provides The Hague Project with potential not only to produce a strong multilateral approach for the EU, but also more effective bilateral operations for the individual members.

These are the available options for targeting. Organisational priorities will influence how these options are combined. However, each international actor will have to make a clear decision about how the programme is to be carried out. In terms of targeting this will require a decision to be made about where the emphasis of the project will be placed: geographically; in the physical world or online; by issue; or bi- or multilateral.

5 Conclusion

Public diplomacy, the politics of influence, has played an important role throughout human history. Yet, new markers of modernity have increasingly affected, changed and transformed this field of work. Shifting power-dynamics, economic advancement and institutional or political changes all strongly influence the nature of public diplomacy.

Trying to find a single approach to sum up the essence of public diplomacy can be a challenge considering the constantly evolving nature of the field. Thus, the three questions from the previous chapters – What does your product say about you? Where are you located on the spectrum of available approaches? Where in the world(s) is your product targeted? – can serve as guidelines with which to navigate the task of creating strategies in these new worlds of public diplomacy.

The questions do not guarantee the creation of a successful programme, as this will also depend on execution, but they offer support along the way. Knowledge is power. Therefore, if international actors have knowledge of the field they work in and are aware of their tools, they can more effectively construct their public diplomacy strategy.

Not every actor will engage in all activities and approaches that were presented in the previous chapters. They will instead use the ones appropriate to their specific purpose. Through understanding the various approaches, the assumptions behind them and the different types of success which they seek to achieve, an actor will be able to construct impact measurement frameworks. These frameworks will conform to the expectations of their constituency. However, whichever combination of options the actor selects from the three chapters, using them as building blocks for their strategy, they will all be about influencing the way the audience acts.

Public diplomacy, the politics of influence, is essential in international relations. It always has been, but, after 9/11, the Madrid and London bombings, the identification of a war on terror and other facets of modern life, it will increasingly play a role in securing a peaceful influence through the international arena. The developments in technology have led to new hierarchies in the dissemination of information. Knowledge and power are not just in the hands of political elites, but rather shared by societies as a whole, or groups within, and distributed via new channels of communication. It is therefore crucial to recognise that it is not just states engaged in exerting influence. Organisations from supranational bodies to small, single-issue NGOs are all engaged and competing for attention in the same field.

This guide is not a conclusion. Continued innovation and the evolution of tools will ensure the future of this important field of work. The guide highlights key aspects which an international actor has to consider and offers guidance along the way. The field of public diplomacy is in continuous transition. No single approach or definition can achieve universal application and stand the test of time. However, knowledge of the field in which they work and sensitivity to the environment can help practitioners in achieving their aims. This is why it is important for an actor to identify the full range of their options for influence.

Endnotes

1. Melissen, Jan. *The New Public Diplomacy: Soft Power in International Relations*, Palgrave Macmillan, 2005

2. Cull, Nicholas. *Public Diplomacy: Lessons from the Past*, LA, 2007, p.6

3. What is Public Diplomacy?, USC Center on Public Diplomacy
http://uscpublicdiplomacy.com/index.php/about/whatis_pd

4. In 2004, Lord Carter of Coles was asked by the government to conduct a review of the current practice of public diplomacy in the UK and analyse its effectiveness and the latest progress and developments.
www.fco.gov.uk/publicdiplomacyreview

5. In 2002, the Wilton Review considered the public diplomacy work of the FCO, the British Council and the BBC World Service in the light of the events of 11 September and the growing role of public diplomacy in communicating the policies, values and achievements of a nation. An Executive Summary of the Wilton Review forms Annex A of the Carter Review.
www.fco.gov.uk/publicdiplomacyreview

6. Holbrooke, Richard, 'Get The Message Out', *Washington Post*, 28 October 2001, quoted in Jan Melissen, 'Wielding Soft Power: The new public diplomacy'. *Clingendael Diplomacy Paper 2*, The Hague, Clingendael Institute, May 2005
www.clingendael.nl/cdsp/publications/diplomacy%2Dpapers/archive.html

7. NATO Military Public Affairs Policy MC 0457/1, September 2007, pp. 28–9

8. US Supreme Court, *Jacobellis v. Ohio*, 378 U.S. 184 (1964)
http://caselaw.lp.findlaw.com/scripts/getcase.pl?court=US&vol=378&invol=184

9. Unattributable answer to the author, Public Diplomacy Conference, March 2007. *The Future of Public Diplomacy*, Wilton Park, 1–3 March 2007

10. Habermas, Jürgen, *Theorie des kommunikativen Handelns* (Bd.1: Handlungsrationalität und gesellschaftliche Rationalisierung, Bd. 2: Zur Kritik der funktionalistischen Vernunft), Frankfurt a.M, 1981, Suhrkamp

11. See Qantas website for more information.
www.qantas.com.au

12. Rose, Martin and Wadham-Smith, Nick. *Mutuality, trust and cultural relations*. Counterpoint, British Council, 2004

13. Kinni, Theodore, 'Exploit What You Do Best,' *Harvard Management Update, Vol. 8, No. 8*, August 2003
http://hbswk.hbs.edu/archive/3684.html

    Proponents of this perspective draw on concepts such as *Appreciative Inquiry*. Cooperrider, David and Whitney, Diana. *Appreciative inquiry: A positive revolution in change*, San Francisco, CA: Berrett-Koehler Publishers, 2005

14. The Putney Debates were a series of discussions between factions of the New Model Army and the Levellers in 1647 which discussed the governance of England following the Civil War. Among other issues the debates considered the relationship between the individual and society demonstrated in part by the extent to which the right to vote should be granted. See: Robertson, Geoffrey, *The Putney Debates,* Verso, 2007

    John Locke, *Second Treatise of Government* and *A Letter Concerning Toleration*, Courier Dover Publications, 2002

15. Genesis 22; 11–21, The Bible

16. Gandhi, quoted in: Bechler, Rosemary (ed.), *Cultural Diversity*, British Council, 2004

17. Translation of Peters, H. F., *Aims and Methods of American Studies*, speech, 7 November 1949, National Archives and Records Administration, US, decimal file, 862.4212/11-1549

18. In 1954 the Supreme Court ruled on the case of *Brown v. Board of Education of Topeka, Kansas*. The court ruled that State-sanctioned segregation of public schools was a violation of the 14th Amendment and was therefore unconstitutional. This marked the end of the 'separate but equal' precedent set by the Supreme Court in *Plessy v. Ferguson* in 1896, although implementation of this decision was not a straightforward process. See: www.archives.gov/education/lessons/brown-v-board/

19. Record of interview, Charles B. Fahs with Oliver Caldwell and Bruce Buttles, 15 March 1950, Rockefeller Foundation Archive, 1.2, series 717R, Box 13, Folder 133

20. For more on this see Lucas, Scott, *Freedom's War: The US Crusade Against the Soviet Union, 1945–56,* Manchester: Manchester University Press, 1999

21. Southern Nazarene University website: http://home.snu.edu/~hculbert/iceberg.htm Modified from Weaver, Gary R., 'Understanding and Coping with Cross-cultural Adjustment Stress' in Gary R. Weaver (ed.), *Culture, Communication and Conflict: Readings in Intercultural Relations*, second edition, Simon & Schuster Publishing, 1998

22. Lambert, Emma, *Don't fight it. You can't whip Mickey Mouse: Disneyland's Cold War,* M.Phil dissertation, University of Birmingham, 1997

23. See, for example: Stewart-Allen, Allyson and Denslow, Lanie, *Working with Americans*, *Financial Times*/Prentice Hall, 2002

    Anholt, Simon, *Another One Bites the Grass: Making Sense of International Advertising: Creating International Ad Campaigns That Make Sense,* Adweek Book, 2000

24. Hall, Stuart, 'Encoding and Decoding in the Television Discourse', Stencilled Paper No 7. Centre for Contemporary Cultural Studies, 1973

25. Bhabha, Homi, 'Re-inventing Britain: A Manifesto', *British Studies Now*, April 1997, pp. 9–10 www.britishcouncil.org/studies/bsn_pdfs/bsn09.pdf

26. Bhabha, Homi, 'Re-inventing Britain: A Manifesto', *British Studies Now*, April 1997, pp. 9–10 www.britishcouncil.org/studies/bsn_pdfs/bsn09.pdf

27. Miliband speaks at Chatham House, 19 July 2007 www.chathamhouse.org.uk/news/view/-/id/392/

28. Mead, Margaret, *And Keep Your Powder Dry: An Anthropologist Looks at America*, Berghahn Books, 2000

29. Nye, Joseph, *The International Herald Tribune*: 'Propaganda Isn't the Way: Soft Power', 10 January, 2003
www.ksg.harvard.edu/news/opeds/2003/nye_soft_power_iht_011003.htm

30. Nye, Joseph, *The paradox of American power. Why the world's only superpower can't go it alone*, Oxford University Press, New York, 1992, p.9

31. Nye, Joseph, 'Our impoverished discourse' *The Huffington Post*, 1 Nov 2006
www.huffingtonpost.com/joseph-nye/our-impoverished-discours_b_33069.html

32. *New Perspectives Quarterly* Special Issue on Public Diplomacy, Summer 2004, Reverse Public Diplomacy: *From Quagmire to Debacle in Iraq*, 'When Hard Power Undermines Soft Power' interview with Joseph Nye
http://ics.leeds.ac.uk/papers/vp01.cfm?outfit=pmt&folder=7&paper=1703

33. The reception and interpretation of a message will be discussed in more detail in Chapter 2.

34. www.youtube.com/watch?v=yRc_9wxniAY, 2:32

35. www.youtube.com/watch?v=neHcGwCfpzo, 0:15

36. See for example, Ozernoy, Ilana, 'Ears Wide Shut', *The Atlantic Monthly*, November 2006

37. The spectrum of options presented here owes much to Nicholas J. Cull, *Public Diplomacy: Lessons from the Past*, Report commissioned by the Public Diplomacy Board, April 2007.

38. Henrikson, Alan, 'Niche Diplomacy in the World Public Arena: the Global 'Corners' of Canada and Norway', in *The New Public Diplomacy*, ed. Jan Melissen, Palgrave Macmillan, New York, 2005

    Rana, Kishan S.,'Singapore's Diplomacy: Vulnerability into Strength' *The Hague Journal of Diplomacy 1* (2006) pp. 81–106

    Also see: Tommy Koh's essay in Arun Mahizhnan and Lee Tsao Yuan (eds.), *Singapore: Re-engineering Success*, Singapore: Singapore Institute of Policy Studies, 1999

    Pardo, Arvid, 'The Origins of the 1967 Malta Initiative', *International Insights*, 9(2) (1993) pp. 65–9

39. Zaharna, R.S. 'The Network Paradigm of Strategic Public Diplomacy,' *Foreign Policy in Focus*, Policy Brief, Vol. 10, No. 1, April 2005
www.fpif.org/briefs/vol10/v10n01pubdip.html

    Also see: Jamie Metzl, 'Network Diplomacy', *Georgetown Journal of International Affairs*, Winter/Spring 2001
www.carnegieendowment.org/publications/index.cfm?fa=view&id=681&prog=zgp

40. www.britishcouncil.org/denmark-projects-network-effect.htm

41. Gregory, Bruce, 'Public Diplomacy and Strategic Communication: Cultures, Firewalls, and Imported Norms'. Presentation at the American Political Science Association Conference on International Communication and Conflict, 31 August 2005 (p.11). Quoting *Cultural Diplomacy: Recommendations and Research*, Report of the Center for Arts and Culture, Washington DC, July 2004, pp. 8–9. While the report is titled *Cultural Diplomacy* this section fits more closely the concept of exchange.

[42] For further discussions of a two-way, non-hierarchical approach see: Melissen, Jan, 'The New Public Diplomacy: Between Theory and Practise' in *The New Public Diplomacy*, ed. Jan Melissen, Palgrave Macmillan, New York, 2005, p.18

Fisher, Ali, 'Public Diplomacy in the United Kingdom: The Future of Public Diplomacy, A European Perspective', Working Paper from the 2006 Madrid Conference on Public Diplomacy (Real Instituto Elcano, Madrid), November 2006
www.realinstitutoelcano.org/documentos/276.asp

Arquilla, John and Ronfeldt, David, *The Emergence of Noopolitik: Toward an American Information Strategy* Santa Monica, CA: RAND, 1999

Zaharna, R.S. 'The Network Paradigm of Strategic Public Diplomacy,' Foreign Policy in Focus, Policy Brief, Vol. 10, No. 1, April 2005
www.fpif.org

Metzl, Jamie, 'Network Diplomacy', *Georgetown Journal of International Affairs*, Winter/Spring 2001
www.carnegieendowment.org/publications/index.cfm? fa=view&id=681

Riordan, Shaun, *The New Diplomacy*, Policy Press, Cambridge, 2003, p.130

Hocking, Brian, 'Rethinking the "New" Public Diplomacy', in *The New Public Diplomacy*, ed. Jan Melissen, Palgrave Macmillan, New York, 2005, p.36

[43] www.leonardo.org.uk

[44] Cummings, Milton, *Cultural Diplomacy and the United States Government: A Survey*, Washington D.C., Center for Arts and Culture, 2003
www.culturalpolicy.org/pdf/MCCpaper.pdf

[45] China National Office of Chinese Language Council International, Community College of Denver and University of Colorado Denver Health Sciences Center

Opening Ceremony, 8 September 2007, Kenneth King Academic and Performing Arts Center at Auraria Campus, Denver, Colorado
www.greatwallchineseacademy.org/CIDProgram.pdf

[46] www.bbc.co.uk/worldservice

[47] Anholt, Simon and Hildreth, Jeremy, *Brand America*, Cyan, London, 2004, p. 29

[48] See Anholt, Simon, *Another One Bites The Grass: making sense of international advertising*, John Wiley & Sons, New York, 2000

[49] Anholt, Simon and Hildreth, Jeremy, *Brand America*, Cyan, London, 2004

Melissen, Jan, 'How Has Place Branding Developed? Opinion Piece', *Place Branding*, Vol 2, No. 1, 2006

Melissen, Jan, 'Wielding Soft Power: The New Public Diplomacy', *Clingendael Diplomacy Papers No.2* May 2005, pp. 22–24

[50] Spain's branding and public diplomacy was considered at Diplomacia Pública, 10 October 2006, Escuela Diplomática, Avda Juan XXIII, Madrid.
www.realinstitutoelcano.org/materiales/docs/ProgramaDiplomaciaPublicavs3octubre_Esp.pdf

This resulted in the working paper: *The Present and Future of Public Diplomacy: a European Perspective. The 2006 Madrid Conference on Public Diplomacy* (ed.) Javier Noya, Real Instituto Elcano, 2006
www.realinstitutoelcano.org/documentos/276.asp

Also see: www.brandsofspain.com/noticia.cfm?idnoticia=11

[51] Gibson, Robert, 'Culture and Business; The Butterfly meets the Wolpertinger', *British Studies Now*, January 1994, pp. 6–7
www.britishcouncil.org/studies/bsn_pdfs/bsn03.pdf

[52] Melissen, Jan, 'The New Public Diplomacy: Between Theory and Practise', *The New Public Diplomacy* ed. Jan Melissen, Palgrave Macmillan, New York, 2005, p. 18

[53] www.fco.gov.uk/servlet/Front?pagename=OpenMarket/Xcelerate/ShowPage&c=Page&cid =1161588728518 (FCO website)

www.direct.gov.uk/en/TravelAndTransport/TravellingAbroad/IfThingsGoWrong/DG_40000 27 (government website)

For information on Foreign and Commonwealth Office see:
www.fco.gov.uk/servlet/Front?pagename=OpenMarket/Xcelerate/ShowPage&c=Page&cid=10070 29394770

For information on British Council see: www.britishcouncil.org/home-contact-worldwide.htm?mtklink=corporate-homepage-contact-us-worldwide and www.britishcouncil.org/annual-report/pdfs/BC-Intoduction.pdf

[54] The Department of State and Agency for International Development (USAID) *Strategic Plan for Fiscal Years 2007 to 2012*, May 2007, p. 4

www.state.gov/documents/organization/86291.pdf
For US embassies see: www.state.gov/documents/organization/86291.pdf; http://usembassy.state.gov/

[55] Koh, Tommy and Chang Li Lin (eds.), *The Little Red Dot: Reflections by Singapore's Diplomats*, Singapore: World Scientific, 2005, p. 105

[56] Leifer, Michael, *Singapore's Foreign Policy: Coping with Vulnerability.* London: Routledge, 2000, p. 35. Also see Rana, Kishan S., 'Singapore's Diplomacy: Vulnerability into Strength', *The Hague Journal of Diplomacy 1*, 2006, pp. 81–106

[57] Rana, Kishan S., 'Singapore's Diplomacy: Vulnerability into Strength', *The Hague Journal of Diplomacy 1*, 2006, pp. 85, 97

[58] Cull, Nicholas, *Selling War: The British Propaganda Campaign against American "Neutrality" in World War II*, Oxford University Press, 1996, p. 3

[59] Cull, Nicholas, *Selling War: The British Propaganda Campaign against American 'Neutrality' in World War II,* Oxford University Press, 1996

[60] Rana, Kishan S., 'Singapore's Diplomacy: Vulnerability into Strength', *The Hague Journal of Diplomacy 1*, 2006, pp. 81–106

[61] Parfitt, Tom, 'Russia turns off supplies to Ukraine in payment row, and EU feels the chill', *Guardian Unlimited* 2 January 2006
www.guardian.co.uk/russia/article/0,2763,1676556,00.html

Figures on Japan see: The Japan Iron and Steel Federation.
www.jisf.or.jp/en/statistics/sij/rawmaterials.html

62. Scofield, David, 'Dynamic Korea: Hub of Asia' – or is it?' *Asia Times Online*, 6 March 2004
www.atimes.com/atimes/Korea/FC06Dg05.html

Jones, Jeffery, 'Dynamic Korea, Hub of Asia', Korea.net
www.korea.net/News/issues/issueDetailView.asp?board_no=336&menu_code=B#top;
Recently this approach has been rebranded as 'Korea, Sparking' which symbolises the lively energy of the Korean people and culture, which you will no doubt experience while travelling in Korea. See Tour2Korea, 'Korea Sparkling! What is it?'
http://english.tour2korea.com/07T2KZone/koreasparkling/sparkling.asp?konum=1&kosm=m7_6#;
Michael Breen, 'Does Korea Sparkle?', The Korea Times, 29 April 2007
www.koreatimes.co.kr/www/news/opinon/2007/11/170_1967.html

63. See for example, The Observatory on Borderless Higher Education
www.obhe.ac.uk/cgi-bin/news/article.pl?id=275&mode=month

64. www.technorati.com/about/

65. www.technorati.com/about/

66. Cluetrain website: www.cluetrain.com/book/95-theses.html

67. 95 theses, The Cluetrain Manifesto, www.cluetrain.com/book/95-theses.html (Emphasis added)

Locke, Christopher, Levine, Rick, Doc Searls and David Weinberger, *The Cluetrain Manifesto: The End of Business as Usual*, Perseus Books Group, 2001

68. Raymond, Eric Steven, *The Cathedral and the Bazaar*. Comments by Eric Steven Raymond, see www.cluetrain.com/book.html, O'Reilly, October 1999

69. 95 theses, The Cluetrain Manifesto, www.cluetrain.com/book/95-theses.html

70. Schulke, Hans-Jürgen, 'Public Viewing bei der WM 2006', Universität Bremen
http://mlecture.uni-bremen.de/intern/ss2006/fb09/vak-09-655/20060522b/folien.pdf

71. www.live8.com

72. Fiske de Gouveia, Philip, *European Infopolitik. Developing EU Public Diplomacy Strategy*, The Foreign Policy Centre, November 2005, Recommendation 12

73. Quoted in Wise, David and Ross, Thomas, *The Invisible Government,* New York, 1964, p. 349 and Lucas, Scott, *Freedom's War: The American crusade against the Soviet Union*, New York University Press, New York, 1999, p. 258

74. Publication of the Stern Review on the Economics of Climate change, 30 October 2006
www.hm-treasury.gov.uk/newsroom_and_speeches/press/2006/press_stern_06.cfm

75. Further information can be found in: NATO Military Public Affairs Policy MC 0457/1, September 2007

76. EUNIC website (Source: www.eunic-europe.eu/EUNIC%20website/index.html)

77. Further information can be found on the EUNIC website: www.eunic-europe.eu

78. E-mail received from Kathinka Dittrich van Weringh, October 2007

Bowel Cancer

By

Carolyn

Copyright © Carolyn Ronald

Table of Contents

Chapter One:
What is Bowel Cancer

Chapter Two:
Bowel Cancer Symptoms

Chapter Three:
Who Is More Likely to Develop Bowel Cancer?

Chapter Four:
Main Tests For Bowel Cancer

Chapter Five:
Food That Can Cure Or Prevent Bowel Cancer

Chapter Six:
Numerous Fruits For Bowel Cancer

Chapter Seven:

How To Reduce The Risk Of Bowel Cancer

Introduction

Conclusion

Introduction

A type of cancer that affects the large intestine (rectum) is called bowel cancer, and it is also known as colorectal cancer. It happens when strange cells in the coating of the colon or rectum develop wildly, shaping a growth. Gut malignant growth is the third most normal disease overall and the subsequent driving reason for malignant growth related passings, with over 1.9 million new cases and 935,000 passings recorded all around the world. The gamble of creating entrail disease increases with age and can be affected by different factors like hereditary qualities, diet, way of life, and

clinical history. Awareness and screening are crucial in the fight against bowel cancer

because early detection and treatment can significantly increase survival rates.

Because bowel cancer can spread slowly over a long period of time and may not initially cause any symptoms, regular screening is advised for people over the age of 50 and those with a family history of the disease. Changes in bowel habits, blood in the stool, abdominal pain, unexplained weight loss, and fatigue are all signs of bowel cancer. In any case, these side effects can likewise be brought about by different circumstances, so counseling a specialist for a legitimate diagnosis is significant. Therapy for gut disease might include a medical procedure, chemotherapy, radiation treatment, or a blend of these methodologies, contingent upon the stage and area of the malignant growth. A colostomy, which involves moving the bowel to an opening in the abdomen to allow for waste removal, may be required in some instances. The prognosis for bowel cancer can be favorable with early detection

and effective treatment, and many people can go on to lead healthy, satisfying lives. Be that as it may, counteraction through sound way of life decisions like a reasonable

eating routine, normal activity, and abstaining from smoking and exorbitant liquor utilization stays vital in lessening the gamble of fostering this sickness.

Chapter One
BOWEL CANCER

A type of cancer that begins in the rectum or colon, it is also known as colorectal cancer. The digestive system includes the rectum and colon, which are the locations where the body absorbs nutrients and breaks down food. A mass or tumor is formed when abnormal cells in the rectum or colon lining grow and divide uncontrollably. Over the long haul, these dangerous cells can attack close by tissues and spread to different pieces of the body, like the liver and lungs, through the circulatory system or lymphatic framework. Adenocarcinoma, the most common type of bowel cancer, and less common types like squamous cell carcinoma, gastrointestinal stromal tumors (GISTs), and neuroendocrine tumors (NETs) are among the different types of bowel cancer. Inside malignant growth is a serious infection that can prompt huge medical conditions and even passing whenever left untreated. However, many people with

bowel cancer can be cured or effectively managed with prompt diagnosis and treatment.

Chapter Two
BOWEL CANCER SYMPTOMS

The most common symptoms of bowel cancer include the following:

1. Changes in your bowel movements, such as having softer bowel movements, diarrhea, or constipation that is not typical for you.
2. The need to urinate more or less frequently than usual.
3. Blood in your bowel movements, which may appear reddish or black.
4. Bleeding from your bottom frequently.
5. The sensation that you need to urinate even if you have just gone to the bathroom.

Chapter Three
WHO IS MORE LIKELY TO DEVELOP BOWEL CANCER?

Although the exact cause of bowel cancer is not always known, it can be brought on by changes in lifestyle, environmental factors, and genetic mutations.

Bowel cancer risk can also be increased by certain health conditions.
Bowel cancer may be more likely to strike you if:

1. You are older than 50;
2. You smoke;
3. You are overweight;
4. You have inflammatory bowel disease, such as Crohn's disease and ulcerative colitis.
5. You have bowel polyps, which are small growths in your bowel.
6. You have Lynch syndrome, also known as familial adenomatous polyposis.

Chapter Four
MAIN TESTS FOR BOWEL CANCER

If a general practitioner thinks you might have bowel cancer and refers you to a specialist, you will have tests to check for cancer.

A colonoscopy is the main test for bowel cancer. A camera and a thin, flexible tube are used here to look inside your bowel.

Although it might be uncomfortable, it shouldn't hurt. To help you feel more at ease, you will be given a sedative and painkillers.

A biopsy, or small sample of your bowel's lining, may be taken for testing during the colonoscopy.

Therapy for entrail malignant growth
Principal therapies for gut disease
The therapy you'll have for entrail malignant growth relies upon:

1. The cancer's size
2. If the cancer is located in your rectum, colon, or both
3. If it has spread to other parts of your body, whether certain genetic changes are present, and your age and general health may be taken into consideration when deciding which treatments to pursue, such as targeted medications, radiotherapy, chemotherapy, and surgery.

Your medical professionals will:
make sense of the medicines, the advantages and secondary effects
work with you to make a treatment arrangement that is best for you
assist you with dealing with the results of treatment
Assuming that you have any inquiries or stresses, you can converse with your expert group.

Medical procedure
Medical procedures might be completed to eliminate disease from the gut. It may also

be necessary to remove some or all of the bowel surrounding the cancer.

You might need a temporary or permanent colostomy or ileostomy to help you recover.

You'll be upheld through medical procedure and recuperation by your expert therapy group

Chemotherapy:
is a treatment that destroys cancer cells.
You might have chemotherapy for inside disease:
after medical procedure to attempt to stop the malignant growth returning
in the event that you can't have a medical procedure
in the event that malignant growth has spread to different pieces of your body

Radiotherapy:
Radiotherapy utilizes radiation to kill malignant growth cells. Radiation beams are directed directly at tumors with the help of a machine.

Targeted Medicines And Immunotherapy:

You have cancer in your rectum, and the cancer has spread to other parts of your body. Cancer cells can be killed with

Medicines that are used in immunotherapy to help your immune system fight cancer. Designated drugs or immunotherapy are some of the time used to treat progress inside malignant growth that has spread to different pieces of the body.

Chapter Five:
FOOD THAT CAN CURE OR PREVENT BOWEL CANCER

While there is no one food that can cure or prevent bowel cancer, a well-balanced diet can help support overall health and lower the risk of developing the disease. An eating routine that is high in fiber, entire grains, organic products, and vegetables has been related with a lower chance of gut disease. These foods can help maintain a healthy digestive system and reduce inflammation, which is thought to be a factor in cancer development. Foods that may be beneficial to people with bowel cancer **include the following:**
Whole grains like brown rice, whole-wheat bread,
and quinoa, which are high in fiber and can help regulate bowel movements.

Chapter Six
NUMEROUS FRUITS FOR BOWEL CANCER

Numerous fruits for bowel cancer have been investigated for their potential to support the treatment of bowel cancer or reduce the risk of developing the disease.

The following are a couple of models:
Berries:
Antioxidants found in berries can help shield cells from damage that can cause cancer. A diet high in berries was linked to a lower risk of developing bowel cancer, according to one study.

Citrus Fruits:
Citrus organic products like oranges, grapefruits, and lemons are high in L-ascorbic acid, which has been connected to a diminished gamble of gut malignant growth. Vitamin C is a potent antioxidant that aids in cell damage prevention and immune system enhancement.

Apples:
Apples contain a lot of fiber, which can help regulate bowel movements and reduce

digestive system inflammation. A study found that consuming an apple every day reduced the risk of bowel cancer.

Kiwi:

The fiber and vitamin C in kiwi can help maintain a healthy digestive system. According to one study, eating kiwi fruit reduced symptoms of bowel cancer like constipation and pain in the abdomen.
It's vital to take note of that while specific organic products might have medical advantages, a reasonable and changed diet is critical to supporting generally speaking wellbeing and lessening the gamble of creating gut disease. For personalized dietary guidance, it's always a good idea to talk to a doctor or registered dietitian.

Chapter Seven
HOW TO REDUCE THE RISK OF BOWEL CANCER

The risk of developing bowel cancer can be reduced by a number of factors, including:

A Nutritious Diet:
An eating routine that is high in fiber, entire grains, organic products, and vegetables has been related with a lower chance of gut disease. A diet high in red and processed meats, saturated fat, and added sugars, on the other hand, has been linked to an increased risk.

Regular Activity:
Bowel cancer risk can be reduced through regular physical activity. Go for the gold 30 minutes of moderate-power practice on most days of the week.

Keeping A Normal Weight: Being overweight or large has been connected to an expanded gamble of inside disease. This

risk can be reduced by eating a
well-balanced diet and exercising regularly.

Keeping Away From Smoking And Drinking Too Much Alcohol: Smoking and over the top liquor utilization have both been connected to an expanded gamble of gut malignant growth. Stopping smoking and restricting liquor admission can assist with decreasing this gamble.

Ordinary evaluating for gut malignant growth can assist with identifying the infection at a beginning phase when it is more treatable. Sigmoidoscopies, colonoscopies, and fecal occult blood tests may be among the screening procedures that are recommended in different countries.

It is essential to keep in mind that although these factors can lower the likelihood of developing bowel cancer, they do not guarantee its avoidance. A healthcare professional is always a good idea to talk to about your individual risk factors and the best screening or prevention methods.

Conclusion:

The serious disease of bowel cancer, also known as colorectal cancer, affects the rectum and colon. If not treated, it can have serious health effects, but many people can be cured or effectively manage their condition with prompt diagnosis and treatment. Regular screening, a healthy diet, regular exercise, maintaining a healthy weight, not smoking or drinking too much alcohol, and all of these things can help lower the risk of developing bowel cancer. A well-balanced and healthy lifestyle can help support overall health and lower the risk of developing bowel cancer, but there is no single food or activity that can prevent or cure the disease. Discuss appropriate screening and preventative measures with your healthcare provider if you are concerned about your risk of bowel cancer.

Bowel cancer is a complicated illness that can affect people of any age, but it is most often found in people over 50. Changes in bowel habits, blood in the stool, abdominal pain or discomfort, unexplained weight loss, fatigue, and other symptoms of bowel cancer can vary depending on the location and stage of the disease. It's important to talk to your doctor if you have any of these symptoms in order to find out what's causing them and how to treat them.

Notwithstanding way of life factors, there are likewise sure hereditary and ailments that can build the gamble of creating gut disease. Inflammatory bowel disease (such as Crohn's disease or ulcerative colitis) and certain genetic mutations (such as Lynch syndrome) are examples of these. Discuss appropriate screening and preventive measures with your

healthcare provider if you have any of these risk factors.

Following surgery to remove the cancerous tissue, bowel cancer treatment typically includes chemotherapy, radiation therapy, or a combination of the two to eradicate any remaining cancer cells. The individual's overall health and preferences, in addition to the location and stage of the disease, will determine the specific treatment plan.

In general, early recognition and therapy are critical to overseeing gut disease and further developing results. By keeping a solid way of life and observing proper screening rules, you can assist with diminishing your gamble of fostering this infection and distinguish it early in the event that it happens. Don't be afraid to talk to your doctor about any concerns

if you have bowel cancer or other health problems.

Printed in Dunstable, United Kingdom

'*Bourdieu: The next generation* is a wonderful, exhilarating read, full of innovative ideas and new ways of thinking about perennial social concerns from social mobility to migration. Its wide-ranging, fascinating insights into how Bourdieu's thinking can be developed for the 21st century breathe fresh life into established social theories. It is a "must-read" not only for those trying to make sense of Bourdieu but for everyone interested in wider philosophical and political issues of inequality, identity and the role of the state.'
—*Diane Reay, Professor of Education, Cambridge University, UK*

'This book is a truly refreshing and accessible account of Bourdieu's work; it breaks with the traditional jargon filled sociological work of the past whilst still managing to discuss highly complex ideas. The authors each strike a delicate balance between discussing research, theory and personal experience. I would recommend this book to all students with an interest in inequality and Bourdieusian sociology.'
—*Annabel Wilson, PhD Student, Cardiff University, UK*

Bourdieu:
The Next Generation

This book will give a unique insight into how a new generation of Bourdieusian researchers apply Bourdieu to contemporary issues. It will provide a discussion of the working mechanisms of thinking through and/or with Bourdieu when analysing data. In each chapter, authors discuss and reflect upon their own research and the ways in which they put Bourdieu to work. The aim of this book is not just to provide examples of the development of Bourdieusian research, but for each author to reflect on the ways in which they came across Bourdieu's work, why it speaks to them (including a reflexive consideration of their own background) and the way in which it is thus useful in their thinking. Many of the authors were introduced to Bourdieu's works after his death. The research problems the individual authors tackle are contextualised in a different time and space to the one Bourdieu occupied when he was developing his conceptual framework. This book will demonstrate how his concepts can be applied as 'thinking tools' to understand contemporary social reality. Throughout Bourdieu's career, he argued that sociologists need to create an epistemological break, to abandon our common sense – or as much as we can – and to formulate findings from our results. In essence, we are putting Bourdieu to work to provide a structural constructivist approach to social reality anchored through empirical reflexivity.

Jenny Thatcher has recently completed her PhD at the University of East London. She is a co-founder and co-convenor of the BSA Bourdieu Study Group.

Nicola Ingram is a Lecturer in Education and Social Justice at Lancaster University. Nicola is also a co-founder and co-convenor of the BSA Bourdieu Study Group and co-convenor of the BSA Education Study Group.

Ciaran Burke is a Lecturer at Plymouth University and author of *Culture, Capitals and Graduate Futures: Degrees of class*. He is a co-founder and co-convenor of the BSA Bourdieu Study Group.

Jessie Abrahams is a PhD student at Cardiff University. Her thesis is focused on the effect of the increased university tuition fees on young peoples' 'aspirations'. She is also a co-convenor of the BSA Bourdieu Study Group.

Sociological Futures
Series Editors: Eileen Green, John Horne,
Caroline Oliver, Louise Ryan

Sociological Futures aims to be a flagship series for new and innovative theories, methods and approaches to sociological issues and debates and 'the social' in the twenty-first century. This series of monographs and edited collections was inspired by the vibrant wealth of British Sociological Association (BSA) symposia on a wide variety of sociological themes. Edited by a team of experienced sociological researchers, and supported by the BSA, it covers a wide range of topics related to sociology and sociological research and will feature contemporary work that is theoretically and methodologically innovative, has local or global reach, as well as work that engages or reengages with classic debates in sociology, bringing new perspectives to important and relevant topics.

The BSA is the professional association for sociologists and sociological research in the United Kingdom, with an extensive network of members, study groups and forums, and a dynamic programme of events. The Association engages with topics ranging from auto/biography to youth, climate change to violence against women, alcohol to sport and Bourdieu to Weber. This book series represents the finest fruits of sociological enquiry, for a global audience, and offers a publication outlet for sociologists at all career and publishing stages, from well-established to emerging sociologists, BSA or non-BSA members, from all parts of the world.

An End to the Crisis in Empirical Sociology?
Edited by Linda McKie and Louise Ryan

Bourdieu: The Next Generation
The development of Bourdieu's intellectual heritage in contemporary UK sociology
Edited by Jenny Thatcher, Nicola Ingram, Ciaran Burke and Jessie Abrahams

Forthcoming:

Drinking Dilemmas
Space, culture and identity
Edited by Thomas Thurnell-Read

Bourdieu: The Next Generation

The development of Bourdieu's intellectual heritage in contemporary UK sociology

Edited by Jenny Thatcher, Nicola Ingram, Ciaran Burke and Jessie Abrahams

LONDON AND NEW YORK

First published 2016
by Routledge
2 Park Square, Milton Park, Abingdon, Oxon OX14 4RN

and by Routledge
711 Third Avenue, New York, NY 10017

First issued in paperback 2018

Routledge is an imprint of the Taylor & Francis Group, an informa business

© 2016 Jenny Thatcher, Nicola Ingram, Ciaran Burke and Jessie Abrahams

The right of the editors to be identified as the authors of the editorial material, and of the authors for their individual chapters, has been asserted in accordance with sections 77 and 78 of the Copyright, Designs and Patents Act 1988.

All rights reserved. No part of this book may be reprinted or reproduced or utilised in any form or by any electronic, mechanical, or other means, now known or hereafter invented, including photocopying and recording, or in any information storage or retrieval system, without permission in writing from the publishers.

Trademark notice: Product or corporate names may be trademarks or registered trademarks, and are used only for identification and explanation without intent to infringe.

British Library Cataloguing-in-Publication Data
A catalogue record for this book is available from the British Library

Library of Congress Cataloging in Publication Data
Bourdieu – the next generation: the development of Bourdieu's intellectual heritage in contemporary UK sociology/edited by Jenny Thatcher, Nicola Ingram, Ciaran Burke and Jessica Abrahams.
pages cm
1. Bourdieu, Pierre, 1930–2002. 2. Sociology – Great Britain. 3. Sociology – Philosophy. I. Thatcher, Jenny.
HM479.B68B676 2015
301.0941 – c23
2015021684

ISBN 13: 978-1-138-59635-1 (pbk)
ISBN 13: 978-1-138-91046-1 (hbk)

Typeset in Times
by Florence Production Ltd, Stoodleigh, Devon, UK

This book is dedicated to our mothers,
Annette Valerie Thatcher, Mary Hughes (nee O'Hara),
Rita Burke and Shelly Abrahams.

Contents

List of tables	xi
Acknowledgements	xii
Notes on contributors	xiv
Foreword	xvi
DEREK ROBBINS	

1 **Introduction: the development of Bourdieu's intellectual heritage in UK sociology**   1
CIARAN BURKE, JENNY THATCHER, NICOLA INGRAM AND JESSIE ABRAHAMS

2 **Bourdieu's theory of practice: maintaining the role of capital**   8
CIARAN BURKE

3 **Narrative, ethnography and class inequality: taking Bourdieu into a British council estate**   25
LISA MCKENZIE

4 **Re-interpreting Bourdieu, belonging and Black identities: exploring 'Black' cultural capital among Black Caribbean youth in London**   37
DERRON O. WALLACE

5 **'It's like if you don't go to Uni you fail in life': the relationship between girls' educational choices and the forms of capital**   55
TAMSIN BOWERS-BROWN

6 **Using Bourdieusian scholarship to understand the body: habitus, hexis and embodied cultural capital**   73
LINDSEY GARRATT

7	Migrating habitus: a comparative case study of Polish and South African migrants in the UK JENNY THATCHER AND KRISTOFFER HALVORSRUD	88
8	The limits of capital gains: using Bourdieu to understand social mobility into elite occupations SAM FRIEDMAN	107
9	Unresolved reflections: Bourdieu, haunting and struggling with ghosts KIRSTY MORRIN	123
10	Stepping outside of oneself: how a cleft-habitus can lead to greater reflexivity through occupying 'the third space' NICOLA INGRAM AND JESSIE ABRAHAMS	140
11	Conclusion: Bourdieu – the next generation JESSIE ABRAHAMS, NICOLA INGRAM, JENNY THATCHER AND CIARAN BURKE	157

Index   165

Tables

8.1	Capitals by origin in elite occupations	111
8.2	Regression of income for all in elite occupations	113
10.1	Habitus interruptions typology	148

Acknowledgements

We would first of all like to thank all our contributors for engaging in debate with us over the years and for putting these discussions into chapters for this book. We appreciate their openness about their own journeys to and with Bourdieu, and look forward to future encounters. On our way to producing this collection we have been very much supported by Derek Robbins and we appreciate his encouragement and advice, not to mention that he is always willing to be called upon to speak at our events. The British Sociological Association supported us in establishing the Bourdieu Study Group, from which this project stems, and we would like to thank them for their ongoing and invaluable assistance. Finally, we want to thank everyone who engages with the Bourdieu Study Group and our lively debates.

Jenny: Thank you to my mother for introducing me to the concept of cultural capital, my father for beginning my journey with social theory through the introduction to the works of Karl Marx, and to Professor Derek Robbins for helping me to continue on this social theory journey through his insights into the origins of Pierre Bourdieu's theoretical framework. I would also like to thank my partner, Kristoffer, and my sister, Shona, for their patience and support.

Nicola: I want to say thank you to Gordon Ingram for introducing me to the ideas of Pierre Bourdieu; my sons, Faolán and Comghall, for making me laugh through their developing sociological imagination; and my parents, Mary Hughes (nee O'Hara) and Philip Hughes, for teaching me to despise injustice and to care about people.

Ciaran: I would like to say thank you to Matt Wood for introducing me to Bourdieu and for encouraging me to engage with the theory, and to my wife, Sydney, for her constant support and keen editorial eye. I would also like to thank my fellow co-convenors; this book is an example of the community of scholars that has developed over the last few years and was made possible by the hard work and commitment you have all shown. Finally, I would like to thank Nathan Emmerich, an early instigator of what was to become the Bourdieu Study Group and a critical friend.

Jessie: Thank you to Dr Will Atkinson for introducing me to the work of Pierre Bourdieu through his Social Class module and nurturing my fascination with the thinker. Thanks to Professor David James for his continual caring and supportive supervision, which is enabling me to take my understanding of Bourdieu to new depths through providing a space for me to *feel*. Thank you to the founding members of the study group: Jenny Thatcher, Nicola Ingram and Ciaran Burke for welcoming me into the community. Finally, I want to acknowledge the support of my mother Shelly Abrahams and my partner Leee Mckenna as they come on this Bourdieusian journey with me.

Notes on contributors

Jessie Abrahams is one of the co-convenors of the Bourdieu Study Group. Jessie is a PhD student at Cardiff University. Her thesis is focused on the effect of the increased university tuition fees on young peoples' 'aspirations'. She has been researching in the area of class and education for a number of years now and is also part of the Paired Peers research team. Paired Peers is a six-year Leverhulme Trust-funded project exploring the impact of class, gender and institution on a cohort of young people as they transition to, through and from university.

Tamsin Bowers-Brown is a Senior Lecturer in Education Studies at Sheffield Hallam University, specialising in the sociology of education. Her main areas of interest are in educational inequalities and in particular the impact of social class on educational experiences and the role of policy in shaping educational practices. Her doctorate explored how girls 'do' education, using concepts from Bourdieu and Foucault to theoretically analyse girls' achievement and hopes for the future.

Ciaran Burke is a Lecturer at Plymouth University and author of *Culture, Capitals and Graduate Futures: Degrees of class*. His research focuses on classed inequalities with a particular interest in graduate employment trajectories. He is a co-convenor of the BSA Bourdieu Study Group.

Sam Friedman is Assistant Professor in Sociology at London School of Economics. He has published widely on class, culture and social mobility, and is the author of *Comedy and Distinction: The cultural currency of a 'good' sense of humour* (Routledge, 2014). He is also a comedy critic and the publisher of *Fest*, the largest magazine covering the Edinburgh Festival Fringe.

Lindsey Garratt is a post-doctoral Research Associate with the Economic and Social Research Council (ESRC) Centre on Dynamics of Ethnicity based at the University of Manchester and University of Glasgow. She previously completed her PhD as part of the Trinity Immigration Initiative in Trinity College, University of Dublin, and was funded by the Department of Children and Youth Affairs, Republic of Ireland.

Kristoffer Halvorsrud is a Researcher for the Knowledge Centre for Education (The Research Council of Norway). He completed his PhD at the University of Nottingham in 2014. His PhD explored South African migrants who have arrived in the UK in the post-apartheid era, with a focus on their sense of belonging. He is also a co-founder and co-convenor of the BSA Citizenship Study Group.

Nicola Ingram is a Lecturer in Education and Social Justice at Lancaster University. She has published widely on classed and gendered inequalities in education. Nicola is co-convenor of the BSA Bourdieu Study Group and the BSA Education Study Group.

Lisa Mckenzie is a Research Fellow at the London School of Economics and author of *Getting By* (Policy Press, 2015). Her primary research interests are around the stigmatisation of working-class neighbourhoods. Through her research and activism Lisa works to challenge negative stereotypes of the poor. She is also the co-founder and co-convenor of the BSA Activism Forum and an elected member of the BSA Trustee Board.

Kirsty Morrin is a PhD student at the University of Manchester. Her doctoral research focuses on UK educational policy reform, more specifically the introduction of academies and the increasing preference of 'entrepreneurship education' in working class communities. In her work she considers intersections of class, aspiration, social mobility, entrepreneurship and inequality.

Jenny Thatcher has recently completed her PhD, applying Bourdieu to a case study of Polish migration and education, at the University of East London. She is a co-founder and co-convenor of the BSA Bourdieu Study Group and member of the Early Career Researcher editorial board for The Sociological Review.

Derron Wallace is a Postdoctoral Fellow at Brandeis University and Teachers College, Columbia University. He recently received his PhD in Sociology of Education at the University of Cambridge, where he was a Marshall and Gates Cambridge Scholar.

Foreword

Derek Robbins

A.H. Halsey and professional sociology

In 2004, A.H. Halsey (1923–2014) published his *A History of Sociology in Britain: Science, Literature and Society* (Halsey, 2004). Chapter 4 offered an account of 'British Post-war Sociologists', a first version of which had been published in the *European Journal of Sociology* in 1982 (Halsey, 1982). Halsey begins by imagining what an American social scientist might have observed in respect of the condition of the social sciences in Britain after the Second World War. At the London School of Economics and Political Science (LSE), the visitor's eye

> might have been caught by about a dozen students of sociology, similar in age but of a style and outlook very different from that of their Oxford contemporaries. They took their degrees, and busied themselves around Houghton Street with a novel aspiration. They wanted to become professional sociologists.
>
> (Halsey, 2004, p.70)

Supposing that this imaginary observation occurred at about 1950, Halsey proceeds to recall his encounter at Nuffield College, Oxford 15 years later (i.e., c.1965) with Raymond Aron, who was visiting from Paris. In an exchange about the condition of British sociology, Halsey reports that Aron commented: 'The trouble is that British sociology is essentially an attempt to make intellectual sense of the political problems of the Labour Party' (Halsey, 2004, p.70). A further 15 years later (i.e. in c.1980), Ernest Gellner suggested that Halsey should write an account of what happened to 'what turned out to be the first group of career sociologists in Britain' (Halsey, 2004, p.70). According to Halsey, the questions that Gellner wanted him to attempt to answer were sociological or socio-historical: 'What had been their political and intellectual concerns? What formed their unprecedented and unlikely occupational ambition? And what happened to them and their intentions?' (Halsey, 2004, p.70).

Halsey knew that Gellner was prompting him to write an account of those who had graduated with him in sociology at '"the School" in the early 1950s' (Halsey, 2004, p.70). Besides himself, Halsey listed 12 graduates between 1950 and 1952 who went on to become professors in departments of sociology in British universities. As he puts it, his article/chapter was about 'an LSE group that became a significant part of the sociological establishment by the mid-1960s' (Halsey, 2004, p.71). Halsey tried to characterise the group. His first comment is that 'most were provincials: provincial in social origin, provincial in political preoccupation, and provincial in their early jobs' (Halsey, 2004, p.72). He proceeded to elaborate, offering a series of rather cryptic assessments: 'The ten natives were born in the slump years between the Wars on the periphery of English society' (Halsey, 2004, p.72); 'Most, if not all, had 'won the scholarship'. There was only one woman (Olive Banks). There were no '"public" school boys among them. They went to their grammar schools' (Halsey, 2004, p.73); 'Few, if any, of them had any notion while at school of going on to a university' (Halsey, 2004, p.73); 'None of the group was active in the student union or LSE Labour club politics' (Halsey, 2004, p.75); and 'They all read Max Weber's two essays on Science and Politics as vocations and chose the former for themselves while in no way abandoning their political enthusiasms' (Halsey, 2004, p.75).

Halsey explained the aspirations of the cohort of students by reference to the influence of David Glass and Edward Shils. The first was committed to the analysis and eradication of social inequality while the second 'presented classical European sociology to his students in an American voice which simply assumed that undergraduates would become graduate students and subsequently professionals' (Halsey, 2004, p.78). Halsey presents this as a dual influence, which combined, for the group, to reconcile political dispositions and professional aspirations. As Halsey summarises: 'Ambition seemed therefore to fit both their political outlook and their personal intellectual abilities' (Halsey, 2004, p.76). In the 1960s, 28 new university departments of sociology were created in the UK. Opportunities matched aspirations for the LSE cohort. Halsey proceeded to make some comments on the correlation between the social backgrounds of his contemporaries and their intellectual affiliations. Some of his generalisations seem rooted in personal autobiography. He contends, for instance, that 'the LSE post-war sociologists were committed to a socialism that had no need for Marxism and no time for communism precisely because it was so deeply rooted in working-class provincialism' (Halsey, 2004, p.84). He concludes that 'the work of the LSE group in the 1950s added significantly to knowledge of the changing social structure of Britain' (Halsey, 2004, p.87). He argues that this work had three main characteristics. It was, first, 'a sociological expression of autobiographical experience – a projection of the country they had learned in their families, schools, work places, and local communities' (Halsey, 2004, p.87). Second, as Aron had suggested, it was 'a sociology of the programme of Labour Party reform' (Halsey, 2004, p.87), and, third, 'it was the assimilation of international sociology and its application to the understanding of British society' (Halsey, 2004, p.87).

Underpinning these three characteristics was one so fundamental that Halsey took it for granted. His account of the LSE group is redolent of a tacit acquiescence in a particular conception of the social function of academics or, especially, professional sociologists, which is never questioned sociologically. Halsey operated throughout his career with a model of society that supposed the function of the professional sociologist is to provide 'knowledge of the changing structure of Britain' generated within academic institutions that are ring-fenced, or themselves protected from the identified symptoms of change. In spite of his 'left-wing' political allegiance, his model of society was conservative. Whether or not it is strictly true, as he claims, that the 'LSE group' had all read Weber's essays on science and politics as vocations, it is certainly the case that he attempted to keep the two spheres distinct in his practice. It was as a professional sociologist that he advised Anthony Crosland, the Labour Secretary of State for Education, on the introduction of comprehensive schools in the 1960s, and that, for many years, he edited Social Trends, which endeavoured to provide social facts for the guidance of policy-makers. The nature of his stance can be illustrated by reference to the analyses of his contemporary, the social historian Harold Perkin (1926–2004). Perkin followed his account of *The Origins of Modern English Society, 1780–1880* (1969) with a sequel, published in 1989 as *The Rise of Professional Society. England since 1880*. This, in turn, was followed in 1996 by *The Third Revolution: Professional Elites in the Modern World*. In *The Rise of Professional Society*, Perkin represented the period between 1880 and 1914 in England as 'the zenith of class society'. Perkin's interpretation of the historical period from 1910 when there were two general elections and 1926, which was the year of the General Strike, is that English society was in the process of choosing between a structure that would sustain the class conflicts of the end of the previous century and one that would reach an accommodation between these class rivalries in generating a new social consensus. He called the new social consensus 'corporatism', which, he claimed, was the 'institutional vehicle' of professional society. The establishment of the Welfare State was, for Perkin, indicative of the emergence in the post-1945 period of both a 'corporate state' and a 'corporate society'. He claimed that 'Between 1945 and the early 1970s professional society reached a plateau of attainment' (Perkin, 1989, p.405), but he also realised that within the same period there were the seeds of decay: 'the professional ideal split into two rival camps which then began to attack each other' (Perkin, 1989, p.437). The split was an opposition between 'private' and 'public' ideals. A key focus of disagreement was in relation to 'equality'. On the one hand, the public sector professionals advocated an equitable distribution of the nation's wealth throughout the population. On the other hand, the private sector managerialists were in favour of equal opportunities for all based on merit. This latter programme would not secure the equal distribution of income promised by the former. Perkin's final chapter was entitled 'The backlash against professional society'. What he perceived was not so much a reaction against professional society but, rather, a domination, which was becoming entrenched, of the private sector over the public sector. He observed the collapse of the 'Keynesian-Beveridgean consensus' (Perkin, 1989, p.474) and identified the growing influence of 'free market ideology' emanating from the Institute of Economic Affairs suggesting economic remedies the Conservatives proceeded to apply 'when they won office, on a minority of the popular vote, in 1979' (Perkin, 1989, p.474)[1].

This was an immanent analysis of the context within which Halsey undertook his social research. Halsey and Martin Trow began in 1963 the study that was to be published in 1971 as *The British Academics*. The Report of the Committee on Higher Education of 1963 (the 'Robbins Report') contained an appendix (III) entitled 'Teachers in higher education', produced by Sir Claus Moser, which provided a statistical analysis of the profession at the time. Halsey and Trow set themselves the task of taking this enquiry further 'in order to provide a sociological portrait of the academic professions, describing and analysing their collective self-conceptions in relation to the programme of institutional expansion in which the Robbins Report would involve them' (Halsey & Trow, 1971, p.26). The Robbins Report inaugurated an expansion in student numbers in UK higher education but, in Perkin's terms, it made its recommendations on the basis of 'private sector' ideals. What has come to be known as the 'Robbins principle' was precisely one of equality of opportunity – that, as Perkin summarises it, 'everyone who was qualified and wished to enter higher education should be provided with a place' (Perkin, 1989, p.452). The question Halsey and Trow asked themselves at the outset of their research was, 'How would academic men in Britain adapt themselves and their institutions to a period of expansion and redefinition of higher education?' (Halsey & Trow, 1971, p.25). In other words, their problematic presupposed the structural functionalist necessity of the existence of a class of academic professionals. The account of their findings in *The British Academics* reinforces this presupposition. They begin with an a priori definition of the British university – 'It could be described as an organisation for community where the community is that of scholars' (Halsey & Trow, 1971, p.28) – and they analyse the characteristics of this predefined group of 'scholars' on the assumption that they share a common social identity as professionals. They introduce their findings on the political attitudes of this professional group in Chapter 15 by summarising the cumulative effect of their previous discussions in the following way: 'We have described the academic professions in Britain as having a distinctive class (Chapter 9) and status (Chapter 10) position which has evolved out of changes in the social and institutional circumstances of intellectual work in the course of modernisation' (Halsey & Trow, 1971, p.399).

Thirty new 'polytechnics' were established in 1969/70. *The British Academics* included an annex that considered the situation of the Colleges of Advanced Technology in the process of receiving university charters, but the emergence of the public sector of higher education escaped the attention of Halsey and Trow. Halsey endeavoured to remedy this deficiency in his *Decline of Donnish Dominion. The British Academic Professionals in the Twentieth Century*, published in 1992. This new book was based on 'three surveys of the British senior common rooms[2] in 1964, 1976, and 1989' (Halsey, 1992, vii). Whereas *The British Academics* examined the attitudes of staff in post towards the proposed increase of student numbers, *Decline of Donnish Dominion* attempted to analyse the views of staff at historical moments during the process of institutional expansion. Writing in 1992, Halsey reported that the total number of students in British higher education approached one million and that 55 per cent of these were in polytechnics and colleges, 9 per cent in the Open University and 36 per cent in the universities (Halsey, 1992, p.3). In 1971, Halsey and Trow had specified that they chose to analyse the academic profession even though they 'could have tackled the problem of the changing role of the intellectual in modern society' (Halsey & Trow, 1971, p.25). They argued that their consideration of the profession would inevitably answer questions raised in respect of the alternative question. In responding to the expanded university system, Halsey, in 1992, fatally persisted in continuing his analysis of the profession, failing to acknowledge the new situation demanded that the alternative question should now become dominant. He was ideologically sympathetic to the move towards mass participation in higher education but, in the end, he was not willing to accept that a democratisation of social knowledge was a necessary corollary of such a movement. In his conclusion, he makes fun of Noel Annan's representation of the 'golden age of the don' (Halsey, 1992, p.267), and he recognises the programme of expansion of the 1960s 'assuaged the guilt of exclusion of the mass of working-class compatriots' (Halsey, 1992, p.267) by giving a select minority of that mass (the 'LSE group') unprecedented access to political influence, but he is unable to offer a creative response to the passing of that historical moment. He offers, instead, a litany of elements in the decline of the academic profession: 'So the prestige of academic people in the eyes of both the politician and the populace has plummeted' (Halsey, 1992, p.268); 'Dons themselves have largely ceased to recommend the academic succession to their own students' (Halsey, 1992, p.269) and 'They [dons] see themselves as an occupational group losing its long-established privileges of tenure and self-government' (Halsey, 1992, p.269). The 'drive towards expansion' undertaken by government action has been at the expense of academic values and institutional autonomy. Halsey implies that expansion without commensurate funding has realised deliberate government intentions to silence independent thought. Halsey still hopes for an alternative development, for 'an enlarged and diverse British system of higher education' (Halsey, 1992, p.270), which would give 'first priority to universal access for 16- to 19-year-olds to a wide range of relevant training for tomorrow's economy' (Halsey, 1992, p.270); would 'make a reality of citizenship through the various forms of *l'education permanente*' (Halsey, 1992, p.270) and would also make 'a place for scholarship and science insulated from the market-place with respect to both worldly rewards and practical curricula' (Halsey, 1992, p.270). In short, Halsey can only contemplate an ideal system of mass higher education, which preserves the rights of a minority to remain in monastic isolation, cultivating science.

We have seen that Halsey reproduced his 1982 article on the 'LSE group' as Chapter 4 of his *A History of Sociology in Britain*, published in 2004. The chapter has a high profile in the historical account of the rise of sociology as a discipline and of professional sociologists. It follows a chapter that, understandably, gives an account of the British 'founding fathers' at the LSE, but the post-1960s narrative is excessively conditioned by the pursuit of the national diffusion of 'the LSE group' and its thinking. In spite of his awareness of the proportionate weighting of polytechnic/new university staff within the British system in the last quarter of the twentieth century, there is a huge blind spot in his analysis of the state of sociology within society in that period. His comments on more than half of the population of British sociologists are based on a letter of November 9, 2000, which he received from Frank Webster as part of his response to Halsey's 2001 survey. Webster was Professor of Sociology at the University of Birmingham from 1999 to 2000, having been a member of staff at Oxford Polytechnic/Oxford Brookes University for the previous 20 years. Halsey devotes five paragraphs to a summary of Webster's letter. He derives from Webster three characteristics of the polytechnic/new university sector – the emphasis of the modular degree structure, the almost exclusive concentration on teaching before 1992 and its subsequent degradation relative to market-oriented research and 'the struggle over feminism' (Halsey, 2004, p.130). Clearly, for Halsey, the rise of the polytechnics/new universities consolidated the 'great betrayal' of the academic profession. Appendix 1 of *A History of Sociology in Britain* lists by name 296 professors who were surveyed in 2001 and on whose responses the book's evaluation of the contemporary situation was based. Of these, by my count, 28 were currently employed in new universities. In his historical survey of the 'Years of Uncertainty 1976–2000' (Chapter 7), Halsey concluded that, paradoxically, tertiary education expanded in the 1990s under the Conservative government. The consequence of this expansion was that 'The number of students of sociology more than doubled and some staff in the ex-polytechnics were awarded the prized title of professor' (Halsey, 2004, p.144). There is no awareness that many of the polytechnics/new universities resisted ideologically the adoption of the career hierarchy practised in the traditional universities. Halsey's survey was skewed precisely because relatively few of the new institutions had, by 2001, chosen to establish a professoriate. Rather than understand the different understanding of professional practice in the new institutions and the consequentially different personnel policies, Halsey chose patronisingly to suppose that a few staff in ex-polytechnics were now measuring up to the stringent standards defined in the dominant institutions of the system. Halsey made no reference to the work of the Council for National Academic Awards, which, in the 1970s, validated sociology degree courses in the polytechnics and, in doing so, scrutinised the credentials of the teaching staff. In short, Halsey tacitly consigned polytechnics to fulfilling a 'further education' role, and the near exclusion of polytechnic staff from his 2001 survey meant he was able to produce evidence for the maintenance of the existing elite system and to write a history of British sociology that eliminated the contributions of at least half of the British sociologists at the end of the twentieth century. Halsey's superstructure of representation, constructed on a prejudiced foundation, continues to legitimise the prevailing hierarchy of social knowledge and institutions in contemporary British society.

Pierre Bourdieu and the craft of the sociologist

Compare and contrast the work of A.H. Halsey with that of Pierre Bourdieu (1930–2002). Let us take the three characteristics of 'the LSE group' identified by Halsey. First, like 'the LSE group' (although not, in this instance, like Halsey himself), Bourdieu was a provincial. His progression from a local, provincial lycée (in Pau, in the Béarn, in South-West France) to the École Normale Supérieure in Paris can be equated with the progression in the same years in England of 'the LSE group' from provincial grammar schools to the London School of Economics. It could also be said that his rootedness in provincial, even peasant, values rendered the influence of Marxist thought as unnecessary for Bourdieu as for the majority of 'the LSE group'. Second, Bourdieu's sociological work always reinforced an ideological position that was 'left of centre', although it was never identified with the platform of a political party. Third, Bourdieu was responsible, particularly in the 1970s when he was editor of the Le Sens commun series for Éditions de Minuit, for commissioning translations of foreign texts such as, for instance, many of the works of Ernst Cassirer.

These similarities, however, are superficial when placed in relation to the dissimilarities in respect of professional aspiration. Although the attitudes of the members of 'the LSE group' were shaped by their social backgrounds, the implication of Halsey's account is that they were all primarily dedicated to establishing the discipline of sociology and of giving it institutional substance. Their prior experiences may have been formative but their aspirations caused them to anonymise their pasts and neutralise their values in the interest of scientific objectivity. By contrast, Bourdieu was not interested in the consolidation of sociology nor of academic position *as such*. In his early article entitled 'Célibat et condition paysanne' [celibacy and the peasant condition] (Bourdieu, 1962), he deliberately attempted to analyse the situations of his contemporaries in his native Béarn so as to test the validity of scientific objectivity in comparison with his recollection of lived experience. His intention was to deploy objectivity to disclose the nature of primary experience rather than to cultivate scientific detachment. Whereas the tradition of British sociology imbibed by 'the LSE group' was empirical, Bourdieu's intellectual formation was in philosophy and, specifically, in epistemology, and, even more specifically, in rationalist epistemology that challenged the assumptions of empiricism. Combined with his interest in phenomenology and ontology, this meant Bourdieu had no inclination to suppress the values of his background in the interest of securing professional achievement but, rather, to carry out research that would constantly juxtapose the perceptions of analysts with those of the subjects of their analyses. Socially and politically, he had no wish to be thought to be a 'transfuge', someone whose education would cause him to betray his origins. Although he was explicit in an interview of 1985 that, in his student days, he 'never really got into the existentialist mood' (Bourdieu, 1990, p.5), he certainly shared Sartre's conviction that 'existence precedes essence' and the corollary of that conviction as famously illustrated by

Sartre through an account of the behaviour of a waiter (Sartre, 1943, p.95) that the adoption of a professional role was an instance of 'mauvaise foi' [bad faith], militating against existential authenticity. Bourdieu disagreed with Sartre in as much as Sartre supposed identity construction is possible in situations of absolute freedom. The fundamental emphasis of Bourdieu's development of the concept of 'habitus' was that identity construction occurs in situations constrained by inter-generationally transmitted characteristics and objective circumstances. Typically, Bourdieu argued against Sartre by suggesting that the emphasis of freedom of the existentialists was a product of the social conditions of Resistance opposition to Nazi occupation. In other words, Bourdieu enacted the differentiation of his position from that of Sartre in a critique that suggested Sartre's constructed philosophical position was historically contingent rather than absolute.[3] Throughout his career, Bourdieu was tenacious in seeking to preserve allegiance to his social origins. There was a constant mistrust of professionalism, which he endeavoured to accommodate by defining his task as a sociologist by reference to those origins rather than to predefined professional requirements.

Bourdieu was a career researcher whose researches were dictated by his social and political commitments rather than by any desire to achieve social and academic 'distinction' *as such*. His earliest research in Algeria was a consequence of his abhorrence of the intervention there of the French army of which he was initially a reluctant, conscripted member. He worked with indigenous Algerians in order to help them to develop a social organisation for a new, independent state, which would correspond with their desires and inclinations. Back in France in the early 1960s, he used his position as secretary to Raymond Aron's research group to direct a series of projects that exposed the extent to which popular culture was educationally and culturally repressed. As Professor of Sociology at the Sorbonne since 1955, Aron had, among many activities, been largely responsible for the establishment of sociology as an undergraduate degree subject, and had also introduced a French translation of Weber's lectures on science and politics as vocations.[4] Bourdieu did not participate in the institutionalisation of sociology and, unlike 'the LSE group', would have opposed the kind of separation of science and politics proposed by Weber and supported by Aron. It was logically consistent that Aron, as we have seen, should have commented adversely that British sociology was too identified with Labour Party politics, and it was also logically consistent that he should endeavour to distinguish his sympathy with the needs of students during the 'May Events' of 1968 from his attempt to analyse scientifically the condition of the higher education system. Aron wanted to encourage government to introduce administrative changes, whereas Bourdieu wanted to give those excluded from higher educational opportunity a voice in shaping its future.[5]

After the 'May Events' of 1968, Bourdieu took control of Aron's research group, as the Centre de Sociologie Européenne (CSE). Bourdieu did not associate himself with the experiment in higher education at Vincennes introduced by the government in response to the student unrest. His collaborator in the research group in the 1960s – Jean-Claude Passeron – became Head of the Department of

Sociology at Vincennes, but Bourdieu remained a Director of Studies at the Ecole des Hautes Études en Sciences Sociales. Bourdieu was committed to the primacy of research determined by a conjunction between social problems and the epistemologically reflexive dispositions of researchers rather than to the consolidation of disciplinary discourses and their institutional embodiments. He attempted to institutionalise a research methodology as a counter-cultural project in opposition to the top-down orientation of the dominant institutions of higher education. The CSE group cohered as a consequence of shared social origins and, under Bourdieu's leadership, as a consequence of a collective articulation of philosophy.[6] Unlike 'the LSE group', the CSE group cohered as one of committed practitioners rather than as one of aspiring professionals. Tom Bottomore recognised this in his fulsome celebration of the activity of the group in his foreword to the English translation of *La reproduction* (Bourdieu & Passeron, 1970) as *Reproduction in Education, Society and Culture* (Bourdieu & Passeron, 1977). There was a sense of regret on Bottomore's part that the impetus of the CSE was not realisable in the context of the new University of Sussex, where he was a professor.

To use one of Bourdieu's concepts, the account given by Halsey of the attitude of 'the LSE group' to foreign traditions of sociology suggested that it turned to these traditions so as to acquire 'cultural capital', to lend respectability or legitimacy to home-grown thought. There may have been an element of this also in the way in which Bourdieu sponsored translations of foreign works for publication in the Le Sens commun collection under his direction. There were at least two essential differences, however. First, Bourdieu supported translations of works in a range of disciplines rather than within an established sociological canon. Second, his editorial strategy involved the revision of some previous works and the creative appropriation of others. His support for editions of the collected works of Durkheim and Mauss (both edited by a member of CSE, Viktor Karady), for instance, was, in the first case, to attempt to retrieve the essentially empirical thrust of Durkheim's work from the distortions effected by his 'post-Durkheimian' disciples (Fauconnet, Davy, Bouglé), and, in the second case, to rescue the work of Mauss from the interpretation offered in an earlier edition produced by Lévi-Strauss. Bourdieu also supported the translation into French of many texts by Ernst Casssirer. This coincided with his own work on a translation of a key text of one of Cassirer's disciples – Erwin Panofsky – (Bourdieu, 1967) and with Bourdieu's shift from a 'structuralist' to a 'post-structuralist' methodology as evidenced by his references to Cassirer in two key articles that register that shift – 'Structuralism and Theory of Sociological Knowledge' (Bourdieu, 1968) and 'Sur le pouvoir symbolique' [on symbolic power] (1977). In short, Bourdieu's attitude towards foreign texts was neither eclectic nor deferential. He turned to them so as to generate the conceptual equipment he thought he needed to consider the social problems that concerned him. Bourdieu incorporated these texts. They were not primarily commodities to be purchased to raise his profile in the market of concepts.

I have said twice that Bourdieu did not court professional position or reputation *as such*. Of course, he was ambitious and had a family to support. My contention, however, is that he retained control of his aspirations, regarding his achievements as means towards the fulfilment of his fundamental aim to reduce inequality and foster socio-political participation. After the publication of *La distinction* in 1979, some of his followers thought the text disparaged working-class culture and anticipated Bourdieu's own acquisition of 'distinction' in his appointment shortly afterwards to the Chair of Sociology at the Collège de France. Almost at the same time, Bourdieu revised his conception of 'cultural capital', now distinguishing between 'incorporated', 'objectivated' and 'instituted' capitals (Bourdieu, 1979). He had come to accept that our social, political and cultural choices are not exclusively the consequences of our personal adjustments of our received habitus but that the objects of our choices contain embodied meanings and values independent of our production. Nevertheless, he remained committed to the view that we have the capacity to deploy these objective systems of meaning to satisfy our personal aims, especially if we subject them to scrutiny. This explains the impetus for the publication, in 1984, of *Homo Academicus* (Bourdieu, 1984). At the moment when Bourdieu was allowing the a priori status of the Collège de France to accrete, as 'instituted' capital to his personal, 'incorporated' capital, he published an article that articulated the relations between forms of capital and also assembled a book that demonstrated the professional power of academic man is not intrinsic but is analysable sociologically in terms of the conversion of accumulated capital from different social contexts. Bourdieu was trying to show that his professional status had nothing to do with maintaining 'donnish dominion' except in so far as it might enable him to contribute to the decline of that dominion and the advancement of the interests of the underprivileged. Bourdieu's turn towards direct socio-political action in the last decade of his life is indicative of this strategy.

The next generation

It has been a pleasure to be associated with the work of the Bourdieu Study Group of the British Sociological Association since before its inception in 2012. It was the self-generated creation of doctoral students and early career researchers in British higher education institutions, and it has remained true to that orientation. From the beginning it set itself a dual task – to provide a forum for the discussion and understanding of Bourdieu's work and also to provide workshops where the relevance of his concepts in relation to ongoing research projects could be considered. The members of the group were drawn together by a common sense of affinity with Bourdieu's integration of theory and practice in responding to social problems. The attachment to Bourdieu's work arose out of a sense of the comparability between his and their lived experiences, social positions and socio-political convictions. There has never been any sense that the work of Bourdieu has casually been taken 'off the peg' simply to legitimise their work.

The work of the Bourdieu Study Group derives from autobiographical origins, has a disposition towards radical politics and, by definition through its responsiveness to the work of Bourdieu, has turned towards a foreign intellectual tradition for guidance. In these respects it shares the same characteristics as 'the LSE group' of the 1950s. However, its attitudes are in sympathy with those of Bourdieu's 'CSE group' in that they are determined their work should have an impact within society. They want to earn a living wage and they have their personal ambitions, but they are not driven by the pursuit of academic distinction. To date they have exploited social media to communicate their ideas and discussions widely. They are well aware that their desire for political engagement necessitates a questioning of the validity of the status of the tradition of sociological knowledge as transmitted traditionally in liberal institutions of higher education. One of their early workshops was dedicated to consideration of 'Bourdieu and Public Sociology'. The group was aware that new technologies enable the existing relationship between academics and the public to be revolutionised. They help to actualise Bourdieu's conviction that sociologists need to situate themselves reflexively within society rather than suppose they inhabit a sphere within which to generate detached analyses.

This collection of essays written by members of the group is welcome because it will facilitate discussion of the *form* of sociological work as well as its content. It is an exercise in the practice of the 'trade' of the sociologist, to adopt the title of the handbook for researchers Bourdieu published with collaborators in 1968 (Bourdieu, Chamboredon & Passeron, 1968). Bourdieu would have welcomed this extension of his legacy. He concluded his posthumous self-analysis with the following words about his own work:

> Nothing would make me more happy than to have succeeded in enabling some of my readers, both men and women, to recognize their own experiences, difficulties, problems, sufferings, etc in mine, and that they should derive from this realist identification, which is completely different from an exalted imagination, the means to act and live a little bit better what they live and do.
>
> (Bourdieu, 2004, p.142)

These essays suggest that he would have been gratified by the responses of the authors. In turn, the work of the group should have the same effect on its readers.

Notes

1 For further discussion of Perkin, see my 'Business and Management Education and the Rise of Entrepreneurial Society in England, 1945–1992', which was written in 1992 and subsequently collected as Part II, Chapter 12 of Robbins, 2006, pp.297–322.
2 As a member of staff of a polytechnic/new university since 1970, I have never encountered a senior common room.
3 See Bourdieu and Passeron, 1967.

4   See Aron, 1959.
5   For further discussion, see my 'Social Theory and Politics: Aron, Bourdieu and Passeron, and the Events of May 1968' in Susen and Turner, eds, 2011, pp.301–327.
6   I have discussed this further in my contribution to Susen and Turner, 2014, pp.265–91.

References

Bourdieu, P. 1962. Célibat et condition paysanne. *Etudes rurales.* 5–6, April–September, pp.32–136.
Bourdieu, P. 1967. Postface to E. Panofsky. *Architecture gothique et pensée scolastique* (tr. P. Bourdieu). Paris: Éd. de Minuit.
Bourdieu, P. 1968. Structuralism and theory of sociological knowledge. *Social Research.* XXXV, 4.
Bourdieu, P. 1979. *La Distinction: Critique Sociale du Jugement.* Paris: Les Éditions de Minuit.
Bourdieu, P. 1977. Sur le pouvoir symbolique. *Annales.* 3, pp.405–411.
Bourdieu, P. 1984. *Homo academicus.* Paris: Minuit.
Bourdieu, P. 1990. *In other words. Essays towards a reflexive sociology.* Oxford: Polity Press.
Bourdieu, P. 2004. *Esquisse pour une auto-analyse.* Paris: Raisons d'Agir.
Bourdieu, P. & Passeron, J.-C. 1967. Sociology and philosophy in France since 1945: death and resurrection of a philosophy without subject. *Social Research.* XXXIV, **1**, pp.162–212.
Bourdieu, P. & Passeron, J.-C. 1970. *La reproduction. Eléments pour une théorie du système d'enseignement.* Paris: Ed de Minuit.
Bourdieu, P. & Passeron, J.-C. 1977. *Reproduction in education, society and culture.* London-Beverley Hills: Sage.
Bourdieu, P., Chamboredon, J.-C. & Passeron, J.-C. 1968. *Le métier de sociologue.* Paris: Mouton-Bordas.
Halsey, A.H. 1982. Provincials and professionals: the British post-war sociologists. *European Journal of Sociology.* **23**, pp.150–75.
Halsey, A.H. 1992. *Decline of donnish dominion. The British academic professionals in the twentieth century.* Oxford: Clarendon Press.
Halsey, A.H. 2004. *A history of sociology in Britain. Science, literature, and society.* Oxford: Oxford University Press.
Halsey, A.H. & Trow, M. 1971. *The British academics.* London: Faber & Faber.
Perkin, H. 1989. *The rise of professional society. England since 1880.* London & New York: Routledge.
Robbins, D.M. 2006. *On Bourdieu, education and society.* Oxford: Bardwell Press.
Sartre, J.-P. 1943. *L'être et le néant. Essai d'ontologie phénoménologique.* Paris: Gallimard.
Susen, S. & Turner, B. 2011. *The legacy of Pierre Bourdieu. Critical essays.* London/Delhi/New York: Anthem Press.
Susen, S. & Turner, B. 2014. *The spirit of Luc Boltanski. Essays on the 'pragmatic sociology of critique'.* London/New York: Anthem Press.

Chapter 1

Introduction
The development of Bourdieu's intellectual heritage in UK sociology

Ciaran Burke, Jenny Thatcher, Nicola Ingram, and Jessie Abrahams

This book serves as recognition of a growing and diverse range of scholars brought together through the British Sociological Association's (BSA) Bourdieu Study Group. From its establishment in 2012, the group's central aim has been to critically extend and consider the application of Bourdieusian social theory into contemporary research. This is achieved through bringing together researchers from different areas of inquiry and stages of career to foster an academic community. The contributors to this book have been active in the establishment of this network and the facilitation of critical discussion.

Our central aim as editors is to consider and demonstrate the ways in which Bourdieu's intellectual heritage is being developed in UK sociology through the work of a new generation of Bourdieusian scholars. It reflects on the use of Bourdieusian theory in interrogating social realities in a contemporary context. It is clear that there has been a disruption in the sociological imagination of a new generation of researchers, whose engagement with Bourdieu's thinking may not be embedded within a historical context when utilising his concepts. Indeed, the contributors to this book are not initiated in the same philosophical orientations that previous generations of scholars, including Bourdieu, would have been. Many will have been initiated into understanding and working with Bourdieu second hand through the work of established UK scholars such as Diane Reay and Derek Robbins. We show that this disruption can mean his concepts are taken forward and re-appropriated in creative ways, allowing us to move beyond the habitual use of habitus as previously discussed by Diane Reay (2004). Heeding Nash's advice that 'borrowing the emperor's clothes can leave one looking very naked' (1999, p.172), this book is not concerned with reifying the man but rather putting Bourdieu to work. In this spirit, we unashamedly celebrate the use of Bourdieu's thinking tools in ways in which he, himself, did not use, including migration, 'race'/ethnicity and gender. In addition, we address the practical and theoretical limitations within Bourdieusian social theory and demonstrate ways forward through revisiting concepts and applying them in a different formation, such as the directive features of capital, and the benefits of thinking with Bourdieu alongside other theories and theorists including Foucault, Hall, Fanon, Archer,

Butler, Burawoy, Bhabha, De Beauvoir, Derrida, Goldthorpe, Gilroy, Lahire, Puwar, Reay, Robbins, Savage, Skeggs, as well as many more.

Theory of practice

A central theme of the research within this book and indeed a guiding principle of critical sociology, a lot of which is Bourdieusian, is one of social justice and equality. In order to meet this charge we feel it would be beneficial to some of our audience to provide a brief summation of Bourdieu's central thinking tools, discussing how and why they were used in practice. Bourdieu's work was formed in the context of the competing perspectives of Structuralism, advocated by theorists such as Claude Levi-Strauss, and Phenomenology with Maurice Merleau-Ponty as one of its central figures. Each of these perspectives afforded a great deal of power to either structure or agency, respectively, and therefore could not adequately account for social change nor social reproduction. This can be understood as the starting point for Bourdieu's theoretical project and the problem that was to be addressed: the interpenetrative relationship between structure and agency.

While it is not our intention to provide an inventory of the various concepts Bourdieu developed and used, it is beneficial to consider the central thinking tools, which for many of the contributors served as the point of departure for their own work, namely habitus, capital and field. The habitus can be understood as norms, values and dispositions inculcated via the family, education and to a lesser extent the environment. The habitus is perhaps the most contested and critiqued concept within Bourdieu's toolbox, often being charged with removing the element of choice from the human experience and returning us to the iron cage (Archer, 2007; Jenkins, 2002). In part, this is a justified critique as a common reference from Bourdieu when describing habitus is 'systems of durable, transposable *dispositions*' (1977, p.72, emphasis in original). Indeed, dispositions formed in an early period of an individual's life that are seen as both durable and transposable do not provide a great deal of room for agency. However, for Bourdieu it is not so much that the habitus is void of choice but rather the range of choices and attitudes will be influenced by social structures leading him to also define the habitus as 'a socialized subjectivity' (1992, p.126).

In addition to habitus, the concept of capital is central to Bourdieu's project. Capital can be understood as particular resources that individuals have access to, which can be invested or exchanged for goods – tangible and otherwise. These resources largely fall into one of three forms of capital; economic, social and cultural. Alongside capitals being seen as resources for investment and exchange, levels of particular capitals are used to locate an individual's position within a social hierarchy or a social space. The position within social space an individual occupies will affect objective issues such as life chances and experiences but position will also affect levels of aspirations and expectations, what Bourdieu refers to as the 'field of the possibles' (1984, p.110). The final concept we wish to focus on is field. The concept of field can be read as an active and dynamic site in which habitus and capital interact. Thompson (2008) points out that the term Bourdieu used in French for field was *le champ*, meaning battlefield, rather than *le pre*, which, on the other hand, offered images of a calm and conciliatory environment. As such, field should be understood as a site of competition and aggression in which an individual or group is required to negotiate, and their ability to manoeuvre within a particular field will be influenced by habitus and capital. Bourdieu's theory of practice, based on an attempt to bridge structure and agency, operates through an interpenetrative relationship between these three concepts. In schematic form this has been expressed [(habitus) (capital)] + field = practice (1984, p.101). It is this theory of practice that has been assimilated into a significant amount of British sociology through the constant translation of Bourdieu's work and the steady application from what we see as first generation anglophile researchers.

Structure of the book

Rather than this book being demarcated by stringent themes, in conflict with the bridging principles of Bourdieu's thinking tools, the chapters explore individual researchers' application of elements of Bourdieu's theoretical framework and concepts to diverse empirical studies. The various studies investigate many issues Bourdieu himself directly addressed, such as social mobility, social class and political transformations. However, although there are some similarities with the original issues Bourdieu chose to study, many of the empirical investigations in this book have been conducted in a different economic and political context to that of the 1960s when Bourdieu was first developing his concepts. As such, each researcher in their own way shows the enduring and continuing relevance of Bourdieu's theoretical concepts and the possibilities of adapting them to recently occurring conditions as well as newly-arising concerns. This has required that each researcher adopts Bourdieu's reflexive approach to Sociology. This was not only so the researcher reflects on why they chose the particular topic they did, but must also consider what it was that initially drew them towards the work of Pierre Bourdieu. These reflective accounts help to illustrate one of the book's central purposes – that of a whole new generation of researchers' attraction to the work of Bourdieu. This, in some way, has meant that each author has exposed themselves by recounting childhood memories and structural conditions that led them to Bourdieu. Sam Friedman in Chapter 8 perhaps sums up what many new scholars think when they first encounter Bourdieu: 'My mental tussles with the ideas of Pierre Bourdieu began long before I actually knew who he was.' Throughout the years of hosting Bourdieu-related events, the collective narrative – from particularly postgraduate students – is the sense of euphoria when first encountering the work of Bourdieu and being able to make sense of the world through theory often when students have felt a sense of frustration with the persisting gaps in explanations of the social world in the work of other grand theorists.

This book consists of nine chapters based on empirical case studies covering many research interests. Although each chapter was written by individual researchers drawing on their own research data, there is a unique flow between the chapters. We see how Bourdieu's concepts are put into practice in diverse studies, yet each of these studies complements the others. We see often-similar results in which Bourdieu's theoretical concepts produce explanations across the various case studies.

In Chapter 2, Ciaran Burke reflects on the tendency for the concept of habitus to be the primary focus of research, relegating capital and field to secondary conceptual tools. In his chapter, he demonstrates the directive influence capitals have over individual and group trajectories. In a further unpacking of empirical findings on the role of class on graduate employment trajectories, Burke charts the socially mobilising effect access to particular capitals can provide. In addition, Burke illustrates the consequences when particular forms of capital are spent and the implications for future trajectories, now that a level of mobility has been experienced.

Lisa Mckenzie in Chapter 3 acknowledges the difficulty of reading original Bourdieusian texts, particularly for students. Yet despite this, Bourdieu's conceptualisations of different capitals, and especially the relational aspect of economic and cultural capital when it came to understanding social class, made Mckenzie pursue Bourdieu's work further and apply it to her own research. Mckenzie uses Bourdieu in ethnographically mapping the economic disadvantage on a British council estate. She reveals the symbolic violence that residents undergo as they are de-valued and stigmatised in wider society due to their 'lack' of the accumulation of particular forms of capital. However, she shows how these residents re-define their own value system by acquiring different forms of capitals that are highly valued on their estate.

In Chapter 4, Derron Wallace provides a critical discussion on 'Black' cultural capital. Wallace demonstrates the multi-faceted forms of 'Black' cultural capital that Black Caribbean youth in London draw upon to counter social stigma and formulate their own definitions of 'success'. Wallace uses Bourdieu to go beyond intersectionality and considers the relationship between 'Black' cultural capital and gender to demonstrate the fluid and relational character of 'Black' cultural capitals in the formation of social hierarchies between Black ethnic groups.

Tamsin Bowers-Brown highlights the importance of putting theory into practice in Chapter 5. One of Bourdieu's main emphases on his theoretical framework was that it was not simply reified, but that researchers should demonstrate the relevance of his concepts through empirical inquiry. Bowers-Brown does just this through her exploration of constructions of 'achievement' within secondary education and the choices girls make about the educational pathways they pursue. Bowers-Brown also draws on another of Bourdieu's central positions – that of researchers' reflexivity. She reflects on her own politics and feminism as influencing the decision she made to study gender and education by looking specifically at girls' educational choices.

Lindsey Garratt in Chapter 6 discusses the opportunities and benefits of using Bourdieusian social theory when researching the body, in particular habitus, hexis and embodied cultural capital. Garratt reflects on the limitations of previous approaches to the body, post-modernism and post-structuralism – arguing that these approaches largely produce a Cartesian dualism, which favours mind over body. Through embodied cultural capital, Garratt demonstrates the effectiveness of adopting Bourdieu's structural constructivist approach when thinking about the body.

Jenny Thatcher and Kristoffer Halvorsrud, in Chapter 7, trace the early developments of Bourdieu's concept of habitus back to the empirical work he did in Algeria when he looked at how the Kabyle adapted to the political and social transformations occurring in their society. Emphasising the origins of the conceptual developments, they apply Bourdieu's concepts of habitus and capitals to a comparative case study of South African and Polish migrants in the UK. They argue the relevance of the comparison is that both sets of migrants also experienced large structural political transformations with the fall of apartheid and communism, respectively. By doing this, Thatcher and Halvorsrud show the continuing relevance of Bourdieu's concepts by applying them to the study of individuals migrating from two societies that have been in transition in the last 25 years.

In Chapter 8, Sam Friedman's reflexivity offers insight into why a whole new generation of scholars are attracted to the work of Pierre Bourdieu. Friedman's recollections of childhood confusion and bewilderment about why some people were accepted into a middle-class social circle, while others were not despite their economic capital, gets to the very heart of the importance of cultural capital to the middle classes in British society. It also reveals another element of Bourdieu's attraction – that of 'discovering' his work for the first time and experiencing a sense of excitement when things that had once confused him about society suddenly all started to make sense. Friedman's chapter draws on the results from the BBC Great British Class Survey (GBCS) as well as qualitative interviews to illustrate intra-occupational disadvantage and how those from working-class backgrounds experience a 'class ceiling' despite relative social mobility.

Kirsty Morrin in Chapter 9 reflects on her working-class upbringing and the industrial past of the Northern town where she was raised. Morrin speaks about how she immediately felt some biographical affinity with Bourdieu and that through Bourdieusian insights of habitus-field disjuncture she has been able to understand why she did not quite 'fit-in' during her first year at an elite university. Upon returning home after her degree, Morrin's sociological training meant that when she heard about an Academy opening in her town and being the first high school to become one that specialised in 'entrepreneurship', she instantly wanted to research what was happening to her home town. Through a Bourdieusian framework, she contests the so-called 'lack of aspiration' or 'poverty as a cultural facet' discourse that was used to establish the school.

Finally, Nicola Ingram and Jessie Abrahams in Chapter 10 draw on Bourdieu's concept of 'cleft habitus', discussing the painful yet creative experience of living life within multiple yet incommensurate social fields. Similar to earlier chapters, Ingram and Abrahams emphasise the negotiation processes an agent has to undergo in order to adapt or resist the transformation of their habitus when they feel the pull of different field structures at once. They chart the range of possibilities of habitus interruptions in which the outcome in some cases may be production of a 'third space'. In turn, Ingram and Abrahams argue that the occupation of this 'third space' by the working class student can lead to greater reflexivity.

Conclusion

As this edited collection brings together a new generation of Bourdieusians in the early stages of their careers, it is perhaps important to give a few thoughts on why Bourdieu's theoretical framework has become so popular with a new generation of sociologists. Bourdieu's work explored sociologically fundamental philosophical and political issues – such as the nature of personal identity and the nature of the State. This may be attractive to a new generation that wants to think sociologically but is not committed to organising a career within the circumscribed field of professional sociology as currently practised.

Many of the authors of this book have come from non-'traditional' educational pathways. Furthermore, all of the authors are concerned with inequalities and social justice. This will mean that many may be critical of the way academic sociology is currently practised. In *The Coming Crisis of Western Sociology*, Gouldner (1970) argued that universities were becoming increasingly bureaucratised and individuals were being subordinated and pressured to conform to the status quo of their established authority. He said that sociology was going to become more reflexive in the future and that being a reflexive sociologist necessitated not surrendering to those who control the distribution of knowledge. A sociologist's job was to assist people in their struggles to understand the society and culture of which they are a part. Academic sociology must not simply be for those who wish to escape the world that will inevitably penetrate the university (Gouldner, 1970). This philosophy is very much at the heart of Bourdieu's own thinking on academia and sociology. In the last years of Bourdieu's life, he was committed to reflexivity. As Robbins states:

> The coherence of Bourdieu's work derived from the fact that he never allowed himself to think that his own practices were formally anything other than those he observed. Bourdieu's anthropological, sociological or cultural analyses became increasingly inseparable from his analyses of the social or institutional contexts in which they were generated. To ignore this is to expose Bourdieu's work to a slow death by academic exploitation.
>
> (2007, p.91)

The attraction of Bourdieu is that his concepts demand sociologists to be reflexive not only in the issues they are analysing, but also on their own situations. This is a central theme running through every chapter in this book.

To end with, it is important to acknowledge the problematic ways in which Bourdieu's theoretical framework has been applied due to his increasing popularity. Anyone employing Bourdieu's concepts must have an understanding of the origins and early developments of these concepts in order not to reify them. Bourdieu asserted that his concepts must be employed reflexively and also recognised the socio-historical contingency of his concepts (Robbins, 2005). By a new generation of researchers applying these past conceptualisations reflexively to present situations, we have shown how Bourdieu's theory is still relevant to contemporary issues.

References

Archer, M.S. 2007. *Making our way through the world*. Cambridge: Cambridge University Press.
Bourdieu, P. 1977. *Outline of a theory of practice*. Cambridge: Cambridge University Press.
Bourdieu, P. 1984. *Distinction: a social critique of the judgement of taste*. London: Routledge and Kegan & Paul.
Bourdieu, P. 1992. The purpose of reflexive sociology (The Chicago Workshop). In: Bourdieu, P. and Wacquant, L. (eds) *An invitation to reflexive sociology*. Cambridge: Polity Press, pp.61–217.
Gouldner, A. 1970. *The coming crisis of Western sociology*. New York: Basic Books.
Jenkins, R. 2002. *Pierre Bourdieu: revised edition*. London: Routledge.
Nash, R. 1999. Bourdieu, 'habitus', and educational research: is it all worth the candle? *British Journal of Sociology of Education*. **20**(2), pp.175–187.
Reay, D. 2004. It's all becoming a habitus: beyond the habitual use of habitus in educational research. *British Journal of Sociology of Education*. **25**(4), pp.431–444.
Robbins, D. 2005. The origins, early development and status of Bourdieu's concepts of 'cultural capital'. *The British Journal of Sociology*. **56**(1), pp.13–30.
Robbins, D. 2007. Sociology as reflexive science: on Bourdieu's project. *Theory, Culture and Society*. **24**(5), pp.77–98.
Thompson, P. 2008. Field. In: Grenfell, M. (ed.) *Pierre Bourdieu: Key Concepts*. Durham, UK: Acumen, pp.67–81.

Chapter 2

Bourdieu's theory of practice
Maintaining the role of capital

Ciaran Burke

Bourdieu, in a rare moment of clarity, provided a schematic for his logic of practice: '[(habitus) (capital)] + field = practice' (1984, p.101). This formula has been the foundation for the application of Bourdieusian social theory in the years since; however, within the schematic and from Bourdieu's extensive 'tool box', capital and field appear to have taken a back seat to habitus. Diane Reay (2004) argues that there is a habitual use of habitus, and this overuse is certainly to the detriment of the latter concepts. Within this chapter, the case for the application of capital will be made.

There are two objectives within this chapter: first, it will demonstrate the malleability of Bourdieu's thinking tools, a feature that both led me to Bourdieusian sociology and has allowed me to continue applying it to different and new empirical settings by discussing the different forms of capital and the manifestations these capitals may take within a research project. Capital is not fixed nor determined but relational; drawing from processes within an empirical research project concerned with the role of class on graduate employment trajectories, I will discuss how I operationalised and measured capital in an empirical study based in Northern Ireland. Second, through considering how capitals are 'invested' and the consequences of the 'devaluation' of some forms of capital, I will demonstrate how the application of capital allowed me to chart an individual's employment trajectory and offered both a more thorough and a dynamic understanding of their life history.

Theory of practice: concepts

Bourdieu's theory of practice can be read as part reaction and part compromise to the rigid determinism of Structuralism, most notably attributed to Levi-Strauss at that time, and the firmament agency advocated by Phenomenology, particularly Merleau-Ponty. Indeed, it has been Bourdieu's structural constructivist position that has allowed me and fellow young researchers to apply a pragmatic position to the relationship between structure and agency in the face of late modernity's growing influence in the academy and wider understandings concerning the malleable nature of social space. Bourdieu's attempt to occupy the middle ground and present an interpenetrative account of structure and agency was aided by a number of 'thinking tools'. Bourdieu's particular toolbox included both multi-function and single purpose items and the occasional extension; however, the three central tools were habitus, capital and field.

Habitus, at its most fundamental definition, can be understood as norms, values and dispositions. They are formed and directed by a number of different influences; however, according to Bourdieu (1977), the family and the education system are the two most influential forces, followed by environment and peer groups. The habitus is seen to direct pre-reflexive actions, often referred to as the 'feel for the game' (1990, p.66). While the habitus is unique to each individual, in order to assist empirical research, a group habitus is a permissible term (Nash, 1999). The extrapolation of habitus is further legitimised through the argument that individuals from similar backgrounds/locations will have been exposed to a similar environment, leading to an increased chance that their habitus will be similar (Bourdieu, 2002). Thatcher and Halvorsrud, in Chapter 7, make an interesting argument that habitus is also nationally, historically and politically bounded in their comparative case study of South African and Polish migrants. Capital, as a partner to habitus, is understood to also direct certain pre-reflexive actions, namely aspirations and expectation – or what Bourdieu refers to as 'the *field of the possibles*' (1984, p.110, emphasis in original). Bourdieu (2004) was anxious for his readers to move beyond a literal economic understanding of capital, so his three main forms of (relational) capital are economic, social and cultural. The nuance and relational outcome of capitals' interaction with each other has been demonstrated by Sam Friedman's (Chapter 8) discussion on the disparity between those occupying the same economic position and the likelihood of social mobility based on their accumulation of cultural capital.

Pinpointing levels/forms of capital allow us to plot individuals' positions in social space. Through creating a map of social space, we can begin to see patterns and demarcate areas in which large numbers of individuals share a similar position, leading to the formation of social groups based on similar levels of capital and attitudes. Crossley (2008) reminds us that similar positions in social space do not necessarily lead to individuals sharing experiences and attitudes; however, as is the case with habitus, a similar position within social space is more likely to foster complementary life chances and attitudes between individuals. As capital influences attitudes, we can then assume certain class attitudes. Sam Friedman, in Chapter 8, draws on the Great British Class Survey and shows the disparity between those occupying the same economic position and their chances of social mobility based on their accumulation of cultural capital. For Bourdieu (2004), it was capital that removed the element of chance from the games we play; it 'decides' the path not taken. In addition to being used as a descriptive tool, indicating position within social space and directing the field of the possible, capital should also be read as a tangible entity, one that can quite literally be exchanged for goods and services.

The final concept within Bourdieu's triad is field. Field is often seen as merely the context or setting in which habitus and capital interact. While field provides an environment for both habitus and capital, it is not reliant on their patronage for legitimisation. Rather, field progresses along its own trajectory, often requiring groups and individuals to reconfigure their own actions in light of an altered field. This is captured nicely in Chapter 10 of this book as Ingram and Abrahams discuss the way in which a cleft-habitus can be reconciled during the process of social mobility despite individuals occupying multiple and incommensurate fields.

Bourdieu provides an – albeit misleadingly – simplistic but concise account of how these three conceptual tools operate: '[(habitus) (capital)] + field = practice' (1984, p.101). Habitus and capital interact together within a dynamic context, engendering practice or strategic agency. Bourdieu's theory of practice has enjoyed both a sustained and wide application within UK sociology, including (higher) educational research (Reay *et al.*, 2005; Ingram, 2009; Bradley *et al.*, 2013), sociocultural identity (Savage, 2000; Crompton & Scott, 2005), labour experiences (Hebson, 2009; Atkinson, 2010;) and many more paths of research. While the academy has certainly benefited from the inclusion of Bourdieusian theory into so many areas of enquiry, there are issues related to the frequency in its use, often leading to the concept being referenced rather than applied. Reay (2004) discusses the habitual use of habitus within British Sociology. The key problem is that, as Bourdieu is increasingly the 'go to' theorist, his concepts are used without the necessary theoretical consideration or empirical reflection required for a rich and nuanced conceptual tool such as habitus, resulting in an under-theorised position.

An additional issue connected to the habitual use of habitus is that the other key thinking tools within Bourdieu's triad are ignored or considered secondary to the habitus. Bourdieu's schematic presents a model of practice where habitus and capital have an equal role in directing practice; however, the majority of research focuses on habitus rather than on the directive role of capital. The preoccupation with habitus can be demonstrated through the critical reception Bourdieusian social theory has received. The common charge against Bourdieu and, therefore, against advocates of Bourdieusian social theory is one of structural determinism. The march back towards the iron cage is articulated through the concept of structured and pre-reflexive dispositions, reproduced and directed via the habitus (DiMaggio, 1979; Jenkins, 2002; Archer, 2007). The central barrier to an appreciation of agency and acceptance of reflexivity is understood to come from the habitus.

In reaction to such criticism, a number of Bourdieusian 'modernisers' (Sayer, 2005; Adams, 2006; Elder-Vass, 2007; Atkinson, 2010) have attempted to provide a clearer agentic element within Bourdieu's theory of practice; however, my point is further demonstrated as these various attempts still primarily focus on the habitus. According to Bourdieu (1992), in times of crisis and significant change, the habitus can become rational. Adams takes this idea as his starting position, suggesting that, as society becomes more liquid, characterised by the constant disembedding of the familiar, 'crises' will become a feature of everyday life. As the environment becomes more rational and reflexive, it will inform the habitus, leading to a stronger reflexive element. Similarly, Sayer advocates for a model of practice in which mundane reflexivity works alongside habitus, operationalised through the 'recognition of the close relationships between dispositions and conscious deliberation' (2005, p.50–51).

This durable fixation on a re-modelled habitus again begs the question about Bourdieu's remaining conceptual tools – especially capital, due to where it sits within Bourdieu's schematic. For Bourdieu, both habitus and capital are predisposed to reproduce themselves; they direct individuals to occupy certain positions within social space and carry particular attitudes, and, in turn, these individuals form the environment influencing the next generation's habitus and capital. Changing or breaking the habitus is possible; Bourdieu (1992, p.133) comments that a significant change in environment can alter the habitus, but he immediately tempers his argument suggesting that entering such an environment is highly unlikely due to the habitus itself. A similar position towards capital can be argued. As capital directs our 'field of the possibles', it limits individuals' ability to venture into new terrain, and, due to the durable nature of doxa – a set of values shared among the dominant groups, which are often see as legitimate – and the reproductive apparatus employed by the dominant group to secure their position, the buying power of most capital will remain fixed. However, the multi-faceted and relational character of capital combined with its contextual currency suggests that capital may provide a more likely defence against some of the charges of structural determinism and, therefore, requires as close an inspection and appreciation as has been primarily given to habitus.

Empirical introduction

The empirical research that forms a portion of this chapter (Burke, 2015) used capital(s) both as a descriptive device, to plot respondents' position within social space, and a generative concept of practice, considering the directive influence of capital alongside/with habitus. The emergence and development of post-industrialisation (Bell, 1973) is characterised by a knowledge economy; the new leaders within this economy are the technical elite – typically university educated. The previous form of social stratification, based on peerage and nepotism, is replaced by one demarcated allegedly by effort and merit, ushering in large-scale opportunities for social mobility via education. As a result of the meritocratic narrative within post-industrialisation, perpetuated by successive government policies (DfES, 2003; Cabinet Office, 2011), there has been a significant rise in participation in higher education. Heath *et al.* (2013) report that 47 per cent of 18–30-year-olds are registered in university, which has necessarily led to an increase in the level of graduates; the ONS (2013) reports that 38 per cent of the UK population are graduates. In contrast to the dominant meritocratic discourse, as the level of graduates in the UK has steadily risen, so too has the level of graduate underemployment (Purcell *et al.*, 2013). In the context of increased participation driven by the desire to become socially mobile, this research – based on qualitative interviews with 27 university graduates stratified by gender, class and institution attended (pre-1992 institution [Southern] and post-1992 institution [Northern]) – examined which graduates enter the graduate labour market and what variables are required to make this transition. In particular, the research examined the role of class on graduate employment trajectories.

Measuring capital

An immediate requirement for this research was to categorise respondents into classed groups. Coming from a Bourdieusian position and extending previous research examining higher educational trajectories toward graduate employment pathways (Brown & Scase, 1994; Brown & Hesketh, 2004), this research adopted a binary classed model of dominant and dominated – or working and middle class. Stemming from heuristic necessity, respondents' class position was initially measured using the NS-SEC self-classification questionnaire, a quantitative measurement of class based on employment offering a class hierarchy divided into three groups; higher managerial/professional occupations, intermediate occupations and routine/manual occupations. This form of class measurement is not particularly Bourdieusian; however, as Archer (2003) has previously argued, a crude model or base-line of socio-economic status is a legitimate starting point when measuring social class. In addition to the NS-SEC, Bourdieu's capitals were employed to provide a fuller picture of respondents' position within social space based on relational capitals rather than solely economic status.

Economic capital

Economic capital, access to financial resources, is perhaps the most straightforward type to discuss and measure. Among the respondents, a spectrum of economic capital appeared. It was quite clear that a number of the respondents had access to a considerable amount of money. This financial fluidity was apparent of John (middle class); John had commented in his first interview that his family were comparatively 'broke'. When I more fully investigated this matter, it transpired that he meant this statement in relation to the upper-class families with whom his parents socialised. He explained that, in effect, they were quite comfortable:

> Well, I guess, you're not really poor, like, but you earn lower middle class money, really.

In contrast, there were a number of respondents who displayed signs of not being as well off, possessing quite low levels of economic capital. This factor was evident within Nikki's (working class) biography. She commented on the factions within her grammar school year and where she understood herself to be:

> The rich girls would be over here [. . .] That whole money thing in [grammar school], that did my head in [. . .] I hadn't really experienced that before. I kinda realised that I wasn't in that league.

She discussed the 'rich girls' who were in her grammar school, which points to a low level of economic capital on her part, as she did not belong to their group. It was these comments and others like them that led me to label respondents as having lower or higher levels of economic capital, a level of economic capital that can be used to further an individual's position or reproduce a position of power.

Social capital

The second form of capital I considered was social capital. The central concept concerning social capital is a network of social contacts – who you know and how you use your contacts to your advantage. There were respondents such as Katie (middle class) who displayed high levels of social capital, seen through her having sustained social contact with influential individuals and her ability to utilise these contacts to her advantage. Katie explained that her father's close friend is the head of the firm where she now works; he gave her advice and explained how to manoeuvre successfully within this particular market:

> I've always been told by the likes of my Dad, who was in the [firm] until recently, and his friends – he has a lot of friends who went higher than him. His best friend is [General Manager] – he said, 'Listen, get your degree under you. If you can do it now, get it under you and have it there. It helps to have a degree so you can promote whilst [working].' He always said, 'If you want to promote and go places, get the degree under you now, and, you know, see how – keep it there. You'll have it. It'll save you later on.'

Katie appeared to use this advice, as this path is loosely how both her educational and subsequent employment trajectory progressed. It is not enough to have contacts; high social capital is based on being able to use them. In a sense, social capital was operationalised as being 'high' when individuals were able to use that capital to progress in a particular field and increase or reproduce their life chances. This same understanding is also how I defined low social capital. There were a number of respondents such as Fergal (working class) who had a large number of social contacts; however, his social contacts only aided him in his lateral progression, accessing other low status jobs. On graduating from university, Fergal was a cleaner. He explained how he found that job:

> I knew someone who knew the boss. They told me that I should go and ask. I was hired on the spot. It was a family-run business.

Later in his biography, Fergal discusses being made redundant from his position in a bookshop. After unsuccessfully looking for other forms of employment and spending some time on benefits, he returned to the same bookshop. Again, this movement was through social contacts, as he explained:

> [I] ended up getting my old one back at [bookshop] through sheer nepotism.

Again we see how the measurement of social capital goes beyond simply having social contacts; it is how they can be used. Fergal had a number of different social contacts upon whom he could call to find employment; however, each of these positions were low status, non-graduate jobs, which suggests quite a low level of social capital. It was through observing not just the level of contacts but how they were used that allowed me to understand whether a respondent had high or low levels of social capital measured on the transferable character or 'buying potential' of this form of social capital.

Cultural capital

The final form of capital that concerned my research was cultural capital. This capital is perhaps the most difficult form to appreciate, as it is a sense of understanding and belonging to situations connected to a social class group; it is the most challenging to measure. The manner in which cultural capital is understood seems to be that individuals either possess cultural capital or they do not. The danger is in how a researcher defines or decides what is high culture and what is low culture. Bradley (2014) has recently charged the Great British Class Survey (Savage *et al.*, 2013) of relying on highly selective cultural class markers. When attempting to measure or appreciate levels of cultural capital, I considered within what form of environment – linked to a particular level of social class – a respondent is comfortable. Does the respondent display qualities that would be typically linked to a level of social class? Can these qualities be effectively used to advance their position? Crucially, I would temper or reassess the displays of comfort and qualities presented by respondents through a sense of where they do not belong. As opposed to me deciding what was of cultural worth and what was not, I was interested in observing and measuring the level of absence of cultural capital – not fitting in to a certain environment and seeing a socio-economic group as 'other'. This approach was influenced by Scott's (2002) comments suggesting that, within a classed society such as the United Kingdom, while individuals may find it difficult to present their own class identity, they will be aware of class differences. Essentially, an individual's strongest grasp on class is created through difference and where they feel they belong. In Chapter 3, Lisa Mckenzie talks about the alienation working-class women living on a council estate experienced from the outside community and how their working-class culture was mocked and stigmatised as possessing lesser value by wider society. Yet, the council estate became a site of belonging for these women, who ascribed value to working class practices and culture.

In terms of my own respondents who possess high cultural capital, this level was understood through displays of being comfortable in a middle-class environment, demonstrating qualities akin to a middle-class identity, displaying cultural artefacts and seeing 'lower' or working-class environments as 'other'. As with social capital, these qualities needed to be utilised in a successful manner. Hannah (middle class) demonstrated a number of these qualities. She was quite comfortable within middle-class environments such as grammar school and university. She commented:

> When I started going to my grammar school, I knew I was in the right place.

and:

> I met so many people when I was in university [. . .] we were so similar and so friendly, and we went through so much together.

Equally, Hannah recognised herself as being quite cultured – often more cultured than others. She felt 'out of place' within a working-class environment, as she explained:

> When I worked at the [local cinema] box office, it was a sort of call centre-y type thing. I didn't fit in there.

The only position in which she felt uncomfortable was a typical working-class job. It was this feeling of 'being a fish out of water' that pointed to some respondents' high level of cultural capital. Similarly, respondents who displayed lower levels of cultural capital within a hierarchy of capital were understood through displays of being comfortable within a working-class environment, demonstrating a sense of understanding middle class as 'other' and being uncomfortable and unable to successfully move within a middle-class environment. Catherine (working class) displayed a number of these qualities. Throughout her life history, she would present herself as being with elite or middle class individuals, but, at the same time, she was never one of them. She recalled her time at school:

> [I] hung out with the very top fliers. My best friend – she was a deputy head girl and captain of the hockey team.

The way this comment is phrased suggests that she was not one of the 'top fliers'. Similarly, when discussing her extended family, she says:

> They're the ones who went to university in Oxford and live all around the world and, you know, are cultured.

Catherine also constantly displayed a sense of understanding the middle classes as 'other'; it almost appeared to be a novelty to her. Catherine is a junior solicitor. She describes her colleagues as simply 'La de da' and the various law formals and socials she attends as 'Highfalutin' la de da'.

It is through understanding middle-class individuals and middle-class activities as being something else – something removed from her identity – that Catherine comments on it in such a fashion, suggesting another form of cultural capital. Catherine also commented that she feels more at ease or comfortable within what could be understood as a working-class environment. She explained that she has, essentially, two social groups: one of childhood friends and people she met through working part-time in bars and restaurants during her degree, and the other of individuals she met during her time studying for the LPC and through working at a solicitor's office. She explained that there was a difference in how she felt when she was socialising within each group:

> [Older friends] don't care as much. They do things for shits and giggles, while professional people – it is trying to get ahead.

I pushed her more on this idea in our final interview. I asked her in which group she felt more at ease, and she explained she felt more comfortable within the working-class social group:

> I wouldn't go as far as saying it's a stress, but you're always a wee bit worried about saying something wrong. Whenever you're with the bar friends, if someone takes offence, it's like, "wise up to yourself" and it's fine, so – not that I would say it's more stressful, but I'm definitely more myself around my bar friends.

It was through these sorts of comments and displays of comfort and ease provided that allowed me to identify respondents as having lower or higher levels of cultural capital.

For the purposes of my research, each individual's social class was appreciated and classified through the composite of preliminary NS-SEC classifications, family background, self-classification and a thematic/theoretical interpretation of their life histories. In an effort to appreciate Bourdieu's (2004) three forms of capital, it was necessary to go beyond the simple NS-SEC classification. For example, through the NS-SEC, Catherine was defined as being middle class; however, through appreciating family background, social capital and, as discussed, cultural capital, I was able to create a fuller understanding of her social class and, subsequently, define her as being a working-class respondent.

Using capital to understand trajectories

The findings of this study have been discussed at length elsewhere (Burke, 2015). In general, a binary class model was observed; middle-class graduates equipped with a habitus complementary to the tacit relations of the graduate labour market and high levels of capital were able to successfully negotiate the graduate labour market. In contrast, their working-class counterparts were largely unable to make the transition from higher education to graduate employment, often settling longterm for non-graduate jobs – again, directed by habitus and capital. This study reflected an extension of patterns previously presented concerning the role of habitus and capital on higher educational trajectories (Reay *et al.*, 2005), youth transitions to work (Hodkinson, 1998) and the general labour market (Atkinson, 2010). In addition, it provided a closer Bourdieusian analysis of findings that mirrored previous graduate employment research (Brown & Scase, 1994; Brown & Hesketh, 2004; Smetherham, 2006).

While the research findings presented a general binary classed system of privilege and reproduction, there were a number of conceptual groups that existed, to various degrees, outside of the larger binary model. One such group was the converted working class; this group was categorised as working class but had also successfully made the transition from higher education to graduate employment. For the majority of their life histories, the converted working class fitted quite neatly into the general working-class model. Members of this conceptual group presented weak levels of strategy, practical mastery and low levels of aspiration and expectation, leading to a socially reproduced dominated position within social space.

A number of themes present within the group can be demonstrated through Catherine's life history. Catherine, who is now a junior solicitor, presented a durable level of weak strategies. During the educational phase of her life history, she displayed quite a poor and limited understanding of the educational market, which can be seen through the difficulty she experienced in 'choosing' a university at which to read for her degree:

> I think there are about 20 colleges in England that you can do the LPC in, so, even then, it was which one do you choose. I can't even be bothered going through which one is the best, which one looks good on the C.V. There's one in Northern Ireland, go to the Northern Ireland. [Southern] was probably just laziness, sheer laziness. That's why I went there.

Understanding the rules of the game is a central component of successfully navigating the field. Catherine did not know how to properly choose a university; she opted for the 'easy' choice. Following her into employment, her weak level of employment strategy could be placed through her linear understanding of the exchange between education and employment, arguing, for example, that History graduates can only teach History. Catherine provided quite superficial and unreflective accounts of her employment trajectory. Even when pushed, her only account for becoming a lawyer was based on a television programme she watched as an adolescent. In addition, Catherine, through her superficial knowledge, displayed an inability to understand the market. She would often talk about Law and Medicine but offered no specifics; she could present no in-depth knowledge, even in her own field. Catherine's educational strategies often failed; when at university, she opted into a work experience programme offered by her university – Southern. It was eventually seen to be a moot point, as no Northern Irish employers recognise it as a qualification of any merit. She explained:

> [Southern] did a, uh, Work Experience Award. I ended up doing that, which I thought was going to look good on the C.V., but no one really understands it because it's only a new thing [. . .] Trying to explain it to employers, it's like, right okay.

Catherine equally displayed weak employment strategies when discussing what she would do if she was not successful in applying for the Legal Institute. Catherine was not successful in her first attempt to get into the Legal Institute, and, until it was time to apply again, she worked in the hospitality industry:

> [N]o, I worked in a hotel restaurant for a summer season. I did the Institute exam and I was like 97th on the waiting list, and it was like another year to re-sit it [. . .] If I had not got in after the third time, I would have given up and just done hospitality, but I wouldn't have wanted to.

Catherine's position points to a weak level of employment strategy. If she was unable to get into the Legal Institute, she would simply stay in a low status industry that she did not enjoy. It suggests that she did not know how to use her degree in the employment market other than traditional applications; therefore, she was willing to settle for a low status position.

As was the case with the other members of the converted working class group, Catherine was able to use a one-time exchange of a specific form of capital in order to find a graduate position (Burke, 2015). While the particular form of capital differed between members of this group, Catherine's specific capital was social/familial. When Law graduates enter the Legal Institute, they must find both a firm to take them on as an apprentice and what is known as a 'Master'. Catherine explained that her sister was solely responsible for finding her a firm that would take her. She commented:

> Where I'm working now is just the solicitors in the town. To be honest, I'm only there because my sister works in the local bank. She would be their contact there.

Catherine further discussed the interview she sat for her job:

> It was like, 'Ack, [Catherine], how're you doing?' It was like we were old friends just because he knew my sister. That's why I got the job, but it wasn't really an interview because the decision had already been made before I came in that I was getting it because who I was.

This experience is a one-time use of capital – the social capital she enjoys from the relationship with her sister can only be exchanged with this one firm, as they use her sister's bank and her sister, by chance, is their contact. The capital cannot be used for promotion or to move to another firm. Catherine did not suggest that she could use her sister's connection again. The importance of her sister is shown in the phrase, 'I'm only there because my sister'; unless she had her sister's contacts, she would not be where she is now.

Catherine's entry into a graduate profession, via her limited capital, encouraged an equally limited form of employment strategy. Catherine explained that, now she is in the firm, she is trying to make herself as useful as possible in the hope of being kept on after she qualifies:

> I'm trying to make myself indispensable to [the law firm], so they'll know what they're missing or whatever.

By the time of the follow-up interview, Catherine had successfully sat her qualifying exams. She explained that she intends to stay in the firm where she worked during her time in the Legal Institute. This continuation suggests a return to her previous low levels of expectation, as she commented in relation to her classmate who wants to eventually become a judge:

> I'd rather – this is going to sound awful – but I'd rather be a mediocre average solicitor [laughs] than waste, in my opinion, two years of your life. She seems happy enough. That's her plan. She wants to be a judge one day. She's going places [. . .] I'm not – if they offered it to me I wouldn't say no, but I'm quite happy just being a solicitor for the rest of my life.

Similarly, Catherine displayed a weak understanding of the employment market; she explained that she did not fully understand the extent of professional opportunities afforded to her:

> [I]t's only after I started to get into it, I realised that there's so much more you can do after being a solicitor.

Catherine's working-class habitus and levels of capital, essentially low or ineffective, have reproduced her position within social space. Influenced by the family, school and the general environment, Catherine's educational and employment trajectories have demonstrated a durable level of weak strategy. She, like other members of her conceptual group, displayed a low level of practical mastery or feel for the game. Additionally, while she aspired to be a solicitor, she has no alternative plan, or strategy, other than a linear progression from university to the professional institute to a solicitor's office. While her field of the possibles had been extended to include the legal profession, if this could not be realised, they reverted back to their previous form as indicated by her willingness to settle for working in hospitality in the eventuality of not being admitted to the Institute. What changed, however, was her capital – or, more specifically, the buying power of capital she already owned.

I have suggested members of the converted working class were able to take advantage of a one-time exchange of specific capital within a specific context to secure a graduate job. Capital is understood to influence or offer 'the field of the possibles' (Bourdieu, 1984), but capital is also, in a sense, tangible and can be overtly exchanged. With Catherine, we can see that she possesses – in contrast to her relatively low and under-resourced forms of capital – a level of social capital that is 'context rich'.

Subsequent to their 'transaction', members of the converted working class began to demonstrate higher levels of aspirations and expectations and also relatively stronger strategies. Once Catherine had successfully gained a position in the solicitor's office, she set about making herself indispensable to the running of the office, often performing tasks that were not necessarily her responsibility. Similarly, Atkinson (2010) discusses what he terms 'social space travellers' – the upwardly mobile working-class respondents from his study. One of the influences, he suggests, behind this particular cohort of students becoming upwardly mobile is their higher levels of capital in relation to his working class/dominated cohort. Quite unlike Atkinson's social space travellers, however, members of the converted working class appeared to revert or return to their previous low levels of aspiration and expectation and demonstrate weak or poor employment strategies. This reversion can be appreciated through Catherine's comments that she would prefer to remain 'just a solicitor' and that – even now, having been employed full time in a law firm and having graduated with her professional qualification – she does not fully understand the various avenues the legal profession covers.

This issue could be understood as a 'Pygmalion Dilemma'. In George Bernard Shaw's (1912/2003) classic play, Pygmalion, a young lower-class woman, Eliza Doolittle, is brought into high society and 'educated' on areas such as the 'proper' manner to address a person, 'correct' pronunciation and 'good' posture. There is, however, a particular 'flaw' or self-destruct button within her 'new' identity. When Miss Doolittle is reunited with her father, a lower-class individual with whom she shares a background, she reverts back to her previous tone, meter and stance; she is brought back into her habitus' previous form. In a sense, this return is what has happened – or stands to happen – with this cohort of graduates. The context-specific form of capital allowed them to break or alter their position in social space and their habitus' previous character. The context-specific capital created a new environment that provided a degree of mobility within the social space and, as such, the strategies and aspirations demonstrated were synonymous with an individual who resides within a higher position in the social space than the converted working class previously had. The context-specific capital was also time sensitive; it could normally only be used on one occasion and, once it was exchanged, it no longer stood out from the respondents' general low levels of capital.

It was clear that Catherine did not generally enjoy high levels of social capital, and this job was the only occurrence where she was able to use social capital in a successful way. Similar to Eliza Doolittle, when met with their previous levels of capital – one could say 'normal' levels of capital – this group reverted back to previous dispositions and aspirations. Once the capital 'left' or stopped being influential, the attitudes presented and the actions carried out were not enough to reproduce or secure their apparently socially mobile trajectory. Catherine is currently in graduate employment; however, she demonstrates a sense of discomfort within this field and, with regard to promotion or climbing the ladder, many of the converted working class do not know how to achieve. In contrast to the general middle-class group, they appear unable to continue to be socially mobile.

The concept of the 'Pygmalion Dilemma' shares a number of features with Atkinson's (2012) 'Icarus effect'. Here, Atkinson discusses the effects of the meritocratic discourses within the knowledge economy and the push (via media, politics and specific individuals) for people to work harder in order to achieve increased life chances. The direct result for Atkinson's sample was two respondents with low levels of self-confidence, who had both left education after GCSEs, entering higher education as mature students. These respondents demonstrated an increased level of aspirations; however, relatively early in their university careers, both respondents withdrew from university due to lack of fit with the institutional ethos or pressures from outside life becoming increasingly incongruent with the demands of higher education. Atkinson's main point is that, while the respondents presented increased self-confidence and a desire to enter higher education, contrary to the attitudes required for social reproduction, they soon, due to lack of necessary dispositions and capitals, return or fall back to their previous dominated position within social space.

It is clear that the Icarus effect and Pygmalion Dilemma are complementary; however, in addition to providing an account of an individual's trajectories, the Pygmalion Dilemma shows the generative effect of capital and provides a closer account of the genesis of respondents' return to their previous position. In the spirit of this book and in the guise to ensure the durability of a Bourdieusian school of thought within UK sociology, these concepts are not mutually exclusive. The context specificity of the Pygmalion Dilemma could lend itself to being one approach to accounting for a more general Icarus Effect.

Conclusion

This chapter points to the importance or influence of capital. The purpose of Bourdieu's schematic for practice was to highlight the function or presence of each of these conceptual tools; habitus, capital and field. In my research, capital was used to provide an accurate and relational picture of respondents' positions within social space. For the converted working class, the role of capital accounts for the – albeit transitory – change in trajectory. The longevity or durability of the habitus within this group is quite clear from my findings; once the capital is spent, it is their durable habitus that returns their practice to its previous form, but an understanding of their life history requires an examination of both concepts. Without this limited exchange of capital, members of the converted working class would most likely still be in non-graduate employment and further reinforce the 'traditional' picture of social reproduction. The over-use of habitus is much more than a sinistrodextral leaning from the presentation of Bourdieu's schema of practice but is, rather, from a durable focus on the concept both from Bourdieu's supports and critics. It is safe to say that the contributors to the present book celebrate and welcome the continued application of Bourdieusian social theory within expanding research areas; however, as this chapter has demonstrated, capital can be generative and needs to be fully considered when examining trajectories and not seen as something that merely adds to the influence of habitus.

References

Adams, M. 2006. Hybridising habitus and reflexivity. *Sociology.* **40**(3), pp.511–528.
Archer, L. 2003. Social class and higher education. In: Archer, L., Hutchings, M. and Ross, A. (eds) *Higher Education and Social Class: Issues of Exclusion and Inclusion.* London: Routledge Falmer. pp.5–21.
Archer, M.S. 2007. *Making our Way through the World.* Cambridge: Cambridge University Press.
Atkinson, W. 2010. *Class, Individualisation and Late Modernity: In Search of the Reflexive Worker.* Basingstoke, UK: Palgrave Macmillan.
Atkinson, W. 2012. Reproduction revisited: comprehending complex educational trajectories. *The Sociological Review.* **60**(4), pp.734–752.
Bell, D. 1973. *The Coming of Post-industrial Society: A Venture in Social Forecasting.* New York: Basic Books.
Bourdieu, P. 1977. *Outline of a Theory of Practice.* Cambridge: Cambridge University Press
Bourdieu, P. 1984. *Distinction: A Social Critique of the Judgement of Taste.* London: Routledge and Kegan & Paul.
Bourdieu, P. 1990. *The Logic of Practice.* Cambridge: Cambridge University Press.
Bourdieu, P. 1992. The purpose of reflexive sociology (The Chicago Workshop) In: Bourdieu, P. and Wacquant, L. (eds) *An Invitation to Reflexive Sociology.* Cambridge: Polity Press. pp.61–217.
Bourdieu, P. 2002. Habitus. In: Hiller, J. and Rooksby, E. (eds) *Habitus: A Sense of Place.* Farnham, UK: Ashgate. pp.27–34.
Bourdieu, P. 2004. The forms of capital. In: Ball, S.J. (ed.) *The RoutledgeFalmer Reader in Sociology of Education.* London: Routledge Falmer. pp.15–29.
Bradley, H. 2014. Class descriptors or class relations? Thoughts towards a critique of Savage et al. *Sociology.* **48**(3), pp.429–436.
Bradley, H., Abrahams, J., Bathmaker, A-M., Beedell, P., Hoare, T., Ingram, N., Melor, J. and Waller, R. 2013. The Paired Peers Project Year 3 Report (online). Available at: www.bristol.ac.uk/spais/research/paired-peers/report [accessed 16 August 2015].
Brown, P. and Hesketh, A. 2004. *The Mismanagement of Talent: Employability and Jobs in the Knowledge Economy.* Oxford: Oxford University Press.

Brown, P. and Scase, R. 1994. *Higher Education and Corporate Realities: Class, Culture and the Decline of Graduates Careers*. London: UCL Press.
Burke, C. 2015. *Culture, Capitals and Graduate Futures: Degrees of Class*. London: Routledge.
Cabinet Office. 2011. Opening Doors, Breaking Barriers: A Strategy for Social Mobility (online). Available at: www.gov.uk/government/publications/opening-doors-breaking-barriers-a-strategy-for-social-mobility [accessed 14 May 2015].
Crompton, R. and Scott, J. 2005. Class analysis: beyond the cultural turn. In: Devine, F., Savage, M., Scott, J. and Crompton, R. (eds) *Rethinking Social Class: Culture, Identities and Lifestyle*. Basingstoke, UK: Palgrave Macmillan. pp.186–203.
Crossley, N. 2008. Social class. In: Grenfell, M. (ed.) *Pierre Bourdieu: Key Concepts*. Durham: Acumen. pp.87–99.
Department for Education and Skills (DFES). 2003. The Future of Higher Education (White Paper). Cm5735, London: HMSO.
DiMaggio, P. 1979. Review: on Pierre Bourdieu. *American Journal of Sociology*. **84**(6), pp.1460–1474.
Elder-Vass, D. 2007. Reconciling Archer and Bourdieu in an emergentist theory of action. *Sociological Theory*. **25**(4), pp.325–346.
Heath, A., Sullivan, A., Boliver, V. and Zimdars, A. 2013. Education under New Labour 1997–2010. *Oxford Review of Economic Policy*. **29**(1), pp.227–247.
Hebson, G. 2009. Renewing class analysis in studies of the workplace: a comparison of working-class and middle-class women's aspirations and identities. *Sociology* **43**(1), pp.27–44.
Hodkinson, P. 1998. Career decision making and the transition from school to work. In: Grenfell, M. and James, D. (eds) *Bourdieu and Education: Acts of Practical Theory*. Routledge: London, pp.89–104.
Ingram, N. 2009. Working-class boys, educational success and the misrecognition of working-class culture. *British Journal of Sociology of Education*. **30**(4), pp.421–434.
Jenkins, R. 2002. *Pierre Bourdieu: Revised Edition*. London: Routledge.
Nash, R. 1999. Bourdieu, 'Habitus', and educational research: is it all worth the candle? *British Journal of Sociology of Education*. **20**(2), pp.175–187.
ONS. 2013. Full Report – Graduates in the UK Labour Market 2013, Office for National Statistics.
Purcell, K., Elias, P., Atfield, G., Behle, H., Ellison, R. and Luchinskaya, D. 2013. Transitions into Employment, Further Study and Other Outcomes: The Futuretrack Stage 4 Report. Manchester, UK: The Higher Education Careers Service Unit (HECSU).
Reay, D. 2004. It's all becoming a habitus: beyond the habitual use of habitus in educational research. *British Journal of Sociology of Education*. **25**(4), pp.431–444.
Reay, D., David, M.E. and Ball, S. 2005. *Degrees of Choice: Social Class, Race and Gender in Higher Education*. Stoke-on-Trent, UK: Trentham Books.
Savage, M. 2000. *Class Analysis and Social Transformation*. Buckingham, UK: Open University Press.
Savage, M., Devine, F., Cunningham, N., Taylor, M., Li, Y., Hjellbrekke, J., Le Roux, B., Friedman, S. and Miles, A. 2013. A new model of social class? Findings from the BBC's Great British Class Survey experiment. *Sociology*. **47**(2), pp.219–250.
Sayer, A. 2005. *The Moral Significance of Class*. Cambridge: Cambridge University Press.
Scott, J. 2002. Social Class and Stratification in Late Modernity. *Acta Sociologica*. **45**(1), pp.23–35.

Shaw, G.B. 1912/2003. *Pygmalion: A Romance in 5 Acts.* London: Penguin Books.
Smetherham, C. 2006. Firsts among equals? Evidence on the contemporary relationship between educational credentials and the occupational structure. *Journal of Education and Work.* **19**(1), pp.29–45.

Chapter 3

Narrative, ethnography and class inequality

Taking Bourdieu into a British council estate

Lisa Mckenzie

The work of Pierre Bourdieu is not easy; in actual fact, that may be an understatement. It can appear to be near impossible to read and make sense of if you are an undergraduate student, or even a postgraduate student, lecturer in sociology or anyone else. I came across Bourdieu's seminal work *Distinction: A Social Critique of the Judgment of Taste* for the first time as an undergraduate student, and was confronted by the first line:

> Sociology is rarely more akin to psychoanalysis than when it confronts an object like taste, one of the most vital stakes in the struggles fought in the field of the dominant class and the field of cultural production.
> (1986, p.11)

I was simultaneously both terrified and intrigued, reading this after a third-year lecture in contemporary social theory, and became interested in this 'French guy' who thought that inequality is both cultural and economic. I was fascinated by his critique of how people were viewed and known through their activities, what they wore, the music they enjoyed, the food they liked to eat and the programmes they watched on television. It seemed to me this 'French guy' was arguing that these cultural practices, tastes and likes were not arbitrary; they had meaning, but they were also judged. What I took from that early reading of Bourdieu was social class and cultural pursuits had values attached to them, and it was the tastes of the middle and upper classes that were always valued above those of the working class. I understood how class could be easy to read on the body, the way you walked, talked and the clothes you wore, but also through practice; what a person does, where they go and what they enjoy in life. This made sense to me; I was a mature undergraduate student, a mother, living on a council estate and working class. I instantly recognised what this meant, and how it was directly connected to my life and to those who lived in my community. Until that point the main focus through the sociology lectures in understanding and critiquing social class had been linked to employment and earnings, a very traditional way of thinking about class. I was instantly inspired, and I understood what it was like to be judged on my accent, where I lived and the clothes I wore.

I delved into *Distinction* further and realised I was entering a strange world, with language I was struggling to understand.

When confronted with this very difficult language, and a turn of phrase that initially appeared illegible to me, I was annoyed. This was yet another high academic piece of work, written by an academic locked in his ivory tower and had no relationship to the world that every day people, like me, lived in. My initial reaction was that it made me feel inadequate and angry (and actually still does when I read academic work similar to this); especially when that work is supposedly speaking to matters of inequality, unfairness, poverty and the dangers of elitism. This type of writing still has the ability to make me want to tear out my red hair, and to be honest it is not the way I would want to write and get my research, the work that I do, out into the public. However, as I negotiated my way around the work of Bourdieu and because I was inspired by it, I began to understand more about the man behind the difficult prose and became inspired by his work and by Bourdieu himself.

Pierre Bourdieu wanted his work to be used; he understood his theoretical philosophy as tools, and worked with them through social examination of the world. In the previous chapter, Ciaran Burke outlined how Bourdieu's concepts can act as a tool box for sociologists conducting empirical research. That is exactly how I have used his work; the theories laid out in the many books and articles I have read have all been drawn upon and applied. Furthermore, I have read the work of many others who also apply Bourdieu's theoretical framework in similar ways to mine. This is why I advocate the work of a French sociologist who writes in such a way that it makes me angry! It is applicable because I make the theory work for me and it helps me to explain the subtleties, the complexities and the painful experiences of class inequality. Consequently, from the beginning of my relationship with Bourdieu, I vehemently believed and subscribed to his idea that

> The task of sociology . . . is to uncover the most profoundly buried structures of the various social worlds [and the] relations of power and the relations of meanings between groups and classes.
> (Bourdieu & Wacquant, 1992, p.7)

This was my first understanding of Bourdieu and this is how I put him to work in my own research in a council estate in Nottingham. How far away from each other do those things seem; the upper echelons of French academia, philosophy and society, to a council estate in a very dreary and brutal inner-city place in the East Midlands of the United Kingdom.

Bev Skeggs and respectability

I cannot take full credit for understanding and working with Bourdieu's theories, which relate to taste, culture and value. To be truthful I was struggling with the raw theory in Bourdieu's books. It wasn't until I came across Bev Skeggs' (1997) work, *Formations of Class and Gender* – an ethnographic study set in the North West of England during the 1990s – that things became clearer. It was Skeggs' work that brought to life the tools, the theories and the meanings behind the work of Bourdieu for me. Her work illustrates the type of injustice I was struggling to make sense of in my own life, and then in the research with working-class women on a Nottingham council estate.

What Skeggs did with this work was nothing short of genius to me. *Formations of Class and Gender* became my bible throughout my PhD, and since. Skeggs showed through her research with working-class women in the north west of England that these women were never 'good enough'; they felt 'deficit'. Consequently, some of the women in Skeggs' study placed importance in trying to accumulate middle-class cultural capital. They felt this was their only means of improving their working-class positions – to be different from whom they were. Similar findings are discussed in Chapter 5 by Tamsin Bowers-Brown, in her research on teenage girls' academic trajectories in the East Midlands region of England. Skeggs' study put the concept of 'respectability' at the heart of working-class women's lives, and she demonstrated that being and doing working-class culture was never 'good enough'. What Skeggs' work presented to us in the 1990s, and has been showing us ever since, is that this type of distinction in taste, practice and class is central to injustice within the politics of aspiration.

Using Bourdieu shows class is a lived experience – what we 'do' and 'like' is judged with harshness, and often without rationality. Consequently, sections of society are being forced to dis-identify with their working classness, their culture, in order to 'self improve'. The women in Skeggs' study try to adopt middle-class culture through ways of dressing and speaking. However, they are always aware that they can never 'do middle class right' (Skeggs, 1997, p.82). They are aware that they get it 'wrong' and they feel shame about their social position (ibid., p.88). This concept of distinction taken from Bourdieu and the process of 'de-valuing' people through culture is central to Skeggs' work. I used it, and continue to put this at the heart of my own work exploring working-class communities and council estates in the United Kingdom.

A conceptual framework of Bourdieu's symbolic economy

Bourdieu's theory of practice has been extremely important in academic work that critiques social class hierarchies, as have critiques produced by academics from working-class backgrounds. This work resonates with those of us who understand and have felt first hand the pain of snobbery, and being in a place where we feel uncomfortable because of our class position. Bourdieu's theory of practice, place and identity has allowed us to contextualise and examine new ways of investigating identity, social space and behaviour. Using this theory in my own work on St Ann's council estate in Nottingham, I show how working-class people have been de-valued over time because of their class position, the place where they live, but also because of what has been called (in policy terms) 'welfare sub-culture' (Skeggs, 2004). The New Labour Government introduced this phrase through the social exclusion discourse during their first term in government in 1997. However, the 'righting' of the 'bad culture' of the working class supposedly leading to 'bad behaviour', has been the objective of successive governments and institutions for many decades (Welshman, 2007). Consecutive governments, at least since the 1970s, have used the rhetoric of the 'deficit' model of working-class people. For example, Thatcher's Conservative government during the 1980s introduced the term 'underclass'. Tony Blair, the former prime minister, and his New Labour government employed the rhetoric of 'social exclusion' through their introduction of 'social exclusion' units. Recently, Prime Minister David Cameron has applied the discourse of 'Broken Britain'. These are all attempts to justify and implement harsh prescriptive solutions, with a particular focus upon all that is 'lacking' in the people of 'poor' neighbourhoods. Bourdieu's theory of practice can provide a way of thinking about the rich complexity of poor working-class life in the UK, as opposed to the discourse of 'lack' coming from mainstream, government and media dialogue. It allows us to engage in arguments that traditionally academics and lobbyists on the left of the political spectrum have found difficult to participate in. Through this theory, we can understand behaviour and ways of being, and recognise cultures within council estates and other poor communities. The theory of practice enables us to engage and debate seemingly 'problematic' behaviours, which have often developed as ways of being and dealing with the harshness of daily lives on council estates, as well as the wider discourses of taste, legitimacy and 'acceptable' citizenship. Bourdieu's theory of practice helps us untangle how poor neighbourhoods are often experienced and enacted through local practices, both positively and negatively. By doing this, I expose the realities of stigma and stereotype.

Using Bourdieu's theoretical tools to explain injustice, which is based on capital movements through social space, provides a bridge for the dialectical relationship of culture and the economy. Bourdieu (1977) argues that space is structured by the distribution of the various forms of capital. These capitals are capable of giving strength, power and profit to their owners. Bourdieu (1977) then uses the concept of habitus, which is the internal organising mechanism that intertwines social relations with the possession, accumulation and exchange of the different capitals. From this framework we can see how power and 'value' are distributed within an abstract structure. It is also possible to use this framework to understand the agency of those whose positions are not valued because they 'lack' access to the various forms of capital that Bourdieu suggests are required within and across a social field.

This framework also shows that class formation can be dynamic, as different capitals are acquired, negotiated and exchanged in different fields, but also within different 'games' (Bourdieu, 1986, pp.213–219). Within a social field there may be many different 'games' being played, and therefore capital has different values within these various situations. I argue, based on my own research, that a council estate or poor neighbourhood is a 'game' within a field, and therefore the values of the resources within that 'game' cannot be known unless the value system at work is decoded (1986, pp.211–214).

Bourdieu the ethnographer

Bourdieu understood that in order to decode 'the game', in-depth study was required. Pierre Bourdieu was a philosopher, a social theorist, but also a hands-on researcher. During the early years of his academic career, Bourdieu spent many years as an ethnographer, living with and researching the Kabyle community in Algeria (Bourdieu, 1962). Consequently, his theoretical model of value, practice, space, symbolic violence and the accumulation and movement of capital, was grounded in ethnographic mapping and critical theory. Bourdieu used the example of the economic field within traditional Kabyle societies, arguing that there are two different 'games' being played within this one particular field. Women were allowed to tell the economic truth, while men were held at a point of honour. A man could not ask for a price or date when goods might be paid for; however, women among each other could ask the price of something, as well as ask when she would be paid for her work or services (1998, pp.99–100). Bourdieu's key argument was that this value system is based on a symbolic exchange of honour, which excludes women as they cannot become a person of honour, and thus allows them to act differently within the economic field (1998, p.99). Bourdieu's understanding of how practices translate into meanings initially may seem confusing. However, through his outline of the Kabyles' economic practices, we are able to analyse how different groups enact different practices within the same field. This analysis and critique has been central in my own work relating to class, belonging and community. What Bourdieu's theory of practice helps us to understand is how practice grows within communities organically, while identifying what resources are 'valued' and work within their systems of exchange. It also shows what is not attainable for a particular group, and the ways in which they may act differently in order to compensate for what they do not have. Consequently, this critique lends itself to how power works in social space and who is 'valued' in society. I argue that Bourdieu's theoretical framework has become central in understanding social class divisions and inequalities in contemporary British society.

The importance of value and value systems

Value, who is valued, and who is de-valued is at the centre of my research. This extends to the physical space that working class people inhabit and I have investigated the consequences of de-valuing people, but also the spaces where they live. This is where the social exclusion discourse might be useful, showing how social capital is being undervalued and destroyed through the actions of the market, rather than the actions of the residents.

Networks and engagement located in neighbourhood culture was often practiced through representation, how people who lived on the estates represented themselves within. When I asked people on the estate 'to tell me about themselves', they often replied with 'I'm typical St Ann's'. This identification of who you are and the neighbourhood you live in was common, and I consequently called this identification 'being St Ann's'. 'Being St Ann's' is a term that explains how the residents recognised themselves and each other through ways of dressing, speaking and acting; this is part of a local culture and code showing you belong. Most of the women wore a lot of gold jewellery. Big Creole earrings, and expensive branded sports wear and trainers are important. The women on the estate spoke in local dialect, a mixture of local Nottingham and a Jamaican patois; these were the symbolic resources of value within the neighbourhood, and were sought after. The women felt a real sense of injustice that they were constantly 'disrespected' by those on the outside. However, it seemed that conformity – not wearing the big gold earrings, not wearing their hair in particular ways and not speaking in a locally-influenced Jamaican patois – was never considered in order to 'not stand out', and 'be respectable'. Sam Friedman in Chapter 8 writes about how working-class people experiencing social mobility symbolically retain their working classness by not conforming to middle-class established norms, such as ways of dressing and speaking – even though this would make them 'fit' into the new fields they inhabit.

One of my participants, Tanya, told me one day that she could not understand why 'on the telly' when someone was supposed to be 'common' they were represented by wearing big, gold hooped earrings. The women I spoke to in St Ann's told me they wore big, gold hooped earrings, and liked them. One of the young mothers in St Ann's told me she knew that some people would call her a 'chav' because of the amount of gold she wore. She also spoke about how she had been followed around shops being mistaken for a shoplifter. She thought this was because of the way she looked and dressed: 'too much gold, tracksuit and trainers, black baby in the pram.'

The way the women appeared, dressed, acted, how they spoke and how they decorated their homes, was often referred to by them as 'their taste'. They liked the way they dressed, particularly wearing a lot of gold jewellery, and did not seem to care whether 'others thought they were common'. However they also knew that these cultural markers had two values, one on the inside of St Ann's, and one on the outside. Therefore, 'being St Ann's' was a way that the women could feel 'of value' in and around the estate. Other people also valued them and their taste; it gave them respite from 'being looked down on' from the outside.

The resources that are valued within a council estate are only of use-value to those who live there, and therefore can never be legitimated or capitalised upon because they have no exchange value outside of that specific location. It is the resources that become legitimate capital through their exchange value that can be traded within the wider social field, and it is those resources the poor communities do not have access to. They are restricted from appropriating them, which also restricts their social mobility and disadvantages them. Therefore, Bourdieu's model of capital exchange can expose the mechanisms of how power works to advantage some groups, while disadvantaging others. However, a more flexible approach to capital accumulation is needed so that we can recognise a resource as legitimate, not because it has profit through exchange, but because it has use to the holder. What Bourdieu's symbolic economy also shows us is that, by examining value systems on the outside of the dominant value system, as Bourdieu did in Algeria, we can understand how and what is of value within those communities, and also what actions are necessary by individuals to become a person of value within that system.

Taking Bourdieu into the council estate: capital legitimation and accumulation

The concepts regarding capital and capital accumulation have been key in my work of council estates, and in understanding how value works. In 'Distinction' (1986, pp.53–54, 99–101), Bourdieu identifies four different types of capital, and it is the accumulation of these capitals that determines the inclusion or exclusion from society: cultural, economic, social and symbolic. Economic capital includes income, wealth, financial inheritance and monetary assets. Cultural capital can exist in three forms: in an embodied state that is in the form of long-lasting dispositions of the mind and body, for example 'masculinity' and 'femininity'; in the objectified state in the form of cultural goods; and in the institutionalised state such as educational qualifications. Bourdieu defines cultural capital as high culture: that is, culture that has been legitimated through a middle-class acknowledgment (1986, p.51). Bourdieu also recognises symbolic capital, which is a value that is not recognised as such. Prestige and positive recognition, for example, operate as symbolic capital because they mean nothing in themselves, but depend upon people believing that someone possesses these qualities and values them. Finally there is social capital: resources based on connections and group membership; this is capital with value through relationships (1986, pp.10–12).

Bourdieu *et al.* (1999) explain the process of the negative naming of the places where the poor live through his concept of reified social space. Bourdieu argues that reified social space has been attributed different values, defined by the 'distribution of agents and the distribution of goods in social space' (1999, p.125). The result of this reification of physical space means there becomes a concentration of the 'rarest goods and their owners in certain sites of physical space' (ibid., p.125), while in other physical spaces there becomes an over-representation of the poorest and disadvantaged groups, as in St Ann's. This physical space becomes a reified social space; it has meanings for those who live in it and for those who do not. Bourdieu argues that both spaces, wealthy and poor, have positive or negative stigmatising properties, which attach themselves to the people who live in, work in and occupy them. What this means, according to Bourdieu *et al.*

(1999), is that there becomes 'a silent call to order' through which the 'appropriated or reified physical space' is one of the mediations in which social structures gradually convert into mental structures, and into systems of preference and meaning (ibid., p.126).

This is where Bourdieu's concept of habitus can work in a way to explain how an individual becomes part of a recognised group, as in a class distinction, but also bridges the conceptual gap between what actions take place and the importance of the context in which a social group may find itself, while also allowing for diversity within that social group. Bourdieu alerts us to the space of everyday life in all its complexity and how it is lived. This space is full of bodies, experiences and social relations. It is dynamic and moves from one possibility to another, adapting as it moves (Bourdieu, 1986, pp.170–178). The habitus is a system of dispositions, a system we might describe as a person's character, or even their temperament. This framework also has the ability to produce or originate a relational disposition; it is dynamic and it aligns embodied actions with social locations. However, Bourdieu warns us that life is not only about possibilities; it is also about predictability (1977, pp.110–111). Therefore, the system of habitus is also constrained, normalised and has a pattern. Bourdieu suggests the habitus is the internal organising mechanism entwined within social relations and expressed through the possession, accumulation and exchange of the different capitals, giving varying amounts of value to those in whom it is embodied (1986, p.171). Therefore, social differences and inequalities become observable, as the habitus is the product of those divisions as well as the space that reproduces those social divisions through power and the accumulation and exchange of the mechanism of the capitals. In order to understand class, and cultural relations of the many groups within society, the concept of habitus allows us to consider language, ideas and practices, in addition to power relations and resources (Bourdieu, 1977, p.112).

Bourdieu's concept of habitus is important in his analysis of social identity and also the process by which individuals and groups identify themselves. It has been important to my research in understanding how class is a lived and embodied experience. In order to understand the ways in which the social can be incorporated into the self through the habitus, we need to consider a number of theoretical effects. Chris Haylett (2003) argued that the most important of these is to say 'that class cannot be reified as an actor but is a matter of the embodied social practice' as this varies, changes and unfolds as a cultural space (p.62). This, argues Haylett, is a very different understanding of class to the empiricist, aggregate-position approaches and the economic capitalist system approaches, she argues tend to diminish consequences for working-class people. These are important arguments when trying to understand the difficulties of measuring working-class social or collective action. As capitalism takes on different forms, it also changes class practices. Consequently, Bourdieu's concept of habitus allows us to examine the ways identities, cultures, practices and classes are constructed through wider and relational space. Bourdieu's aim is primarily to show the deep entrenchment of arbitrary social hierarchies upon the body, but praxis orientation does not necessarily rule out ideas of agency and change. It seems what is at stake then is not so much the idea that habitus forecloses a dynamic account of agency, but rather how agency and change are conceptualised. This is an important argument because, when individuals and groups – and especially those from poor neighbourhoods and low social class positions such as the people who were part of my research in Nottingham – engage in social practices, social networks, cultural practices and ideas that are not recognised and therefore misunderstood by the wider population, these practices are either invisible, or of no value, or are deemed as having negative connotations for those involved. Their agency is not recognised because their capital is misrecognised.

Does symbolic and cultural capital equal value?

Bourdieu is inclined to understand the valued capital within a society as inherently belonging to the middle class, legitimated through middle-class values and the economic sphere (1986, p.50). This is the process that happens when capitals can be exchanged and traded up into the open market. Bourdieu always uses education and, in particular, higher education as ways of demonstrating this (1986, p.55). For Bourdieu, it is only the cultural capital of the middle classes that is legitimised this way. Bourdieu is accurate in his assessment of this process, in particular when considering the economic field; it tends to always resign those who cannot take part in this process as of little or no 'value'. Not to possess symbolic capital from your cultural and economic capital, as Lawler (2008) argues, is to fail in 'the games' of judgement, aesthetics, knowledge and cultural competence (p.128). However, there is value within poor communities. Poor communities, in the absence of the legitimated capital and value system, create their own value systems, as Bourdieu acknowledges in his work *Outline of a Theory of Practice* (1977) and *Practical Reason* (1998). Alternative value systems can run alongside the legitimate system, or in opposition, turning the social 'norms' of wider society on their head, but are often a hybrid version of all. Although alternative value systems are recognised by Bourdieu, he has been accused of leaving little room in his conceptual framework to consider the scope for recognising working-class identities and cultures that exist as positive in spite of economic inequality (Lawler, 2005, p.120). Bourdieu argues this point in *Distinction* (1986), through a discussion of 'taste' and class. He argues that 'taste' belongs to the middle class, as they are further away from necessity and therefore have choices. This doubles freedom, because the middle class use 'taste' to 'exhibit their objective distance from necessity' (1986, p.55). He goes on to argue that, as distance from necessity grows, lifestyle becomes the product of what Weber calls a 'stylization of life' (Bourdieu, 1986, p.55). Bourdieu then turns his attention to the legitimation of certain lifestyles and 'taste', which then become the inevitable difference of a practical affirmation (1986, p.56).

However, what Bourdieu is most concerned with is how those who regard themselves as the 'possessors of legitimate capital' fear above all else 'the sacrilegious reuniting of tastes which taste dictates shall be separated' (1986, p.56). It is not that Bourdieu believes poor people have no or little value, but instead he demonstrates how the symbolic economy works against granting recognition and value to the poor. This is an important argument, especially to Bourdieu's critics, who often accuse him of having 'a theory of reproduction' rather than practice; these accusations usually centre on determinism, and restriction (Giroux, 1983, p.95). However, Bourdieu's concern is to uncover the logic of practices that perpetuate power relations and inequalities.

A way of demonstrating this is to show that working-class and middle-class cultural capitals are not equal but different. The difference working-class people display is 'made into inequality' through symbolic violence. For example, in order to examine a particular cultural capital, it needs to be analysed in relation to other capitals within that field, but also within 'the game'. Skeggs (1997) also demonstrates how Bourdieu's theory of practice can be used to analyse femininity, which can be seen as a legitimate form of cultural capital. However, this is only so when it is analysed through a version of middle-class femininity, which is associated with 'morality', and only then in comparison to working-class femininity and masculinity in general. What Skeggs (1997) is demonstrating is exactly what Bourdieu (1998) argues: that symbolic violence is bestowed on those who do not have access to legitimate capital. They then struggle for legitimate capital. However, Bourdieu also argues that

> people are not fools; they are much less bizarre or deluded than we would spontaneously believe precisely because they have internalised, through a protracted and multisided process of conditioning, the objective choices they face.
> (Bourdieu & Wacquant, 1992, p.130)

If working-class people in the UK have had their social positions denigrated, and their access to legitimate capital has been restricted, it is suggested here that there has been a 'resistance' to this positioning, even though it may not be understood or recognised.

The work of Pierre Bourdieu has been extremely important in my journey from an access course in a further education college to a researcher in the London School of Economics. His work has helped me to understand my own class position, but also some of the snobbery and stigmatisation I have experienced during this journey. However, Bourdieu's theoretical tools have also guided me through my own research process and continue to be central in my work, which I like to think is exposing inequality, unfairness and injustice. Through the use of Bourdieu's theory of capital accumulation we can understand how the poorest sections of our society are often named and known as people of little 'value', and the neighbourhoods they live in have come to represent the 'chaos' and 'lawlessness' of Britain's 'underclass' through a de-valuing process that is connected to practice, and predominantly through the legitimation of cultural resources connected to middle-class lifestyles. My ethnographic research unravels the complexity of the inequalities, particularly within poor inner-city neighbourhoods in the UK, by examining closely the relationships between the class system, cultural capital and the valuing and de-valuing processes of institutional legitimation. I have argued that, over time, working-class people have become devalued not just within political discourse, but also within their own communities. They have been positioned as people of little 'value'. Their communities are often referred to as 'sink estates', their 'deficient' culture being passed on from one 'deficient' generation to another. Morrin in Chapter 9 also speaks about the rhetoric of working-class 'deficiency' as produced through policy discourse, while Wallace in Chapter 4 critiques the extension of the 'deficiency' model to Black communities. I have shown that the devaluing process has led to shifts in how working-class people want to represent themselves in order to protect their own profiles from further devaluing. Working classes do not only understand their class identity or social position through their economic position, but also by the way they are viewed, represented and understood by those on the outside of their communities. Within this chapter, I have used Bourdieu's theory of practice in my analysis of social identity and in the process in which individuals and groups identify themselves. The concept of habitus allows us to examine the way that identities, cultures, practices and classes are constructed through wider and relational space.

Bourdieu's metaphor of symbolic economy helps us to understand the behaviour of those who live in poor neighbourhoods through recognition of the context. It is through the symbolic economy that we can understand how power works within social structures. It is Bourdieu's metaphor of capital that can provide not only a framework for understanding power, but also exchange in the reproduction of inequality. The metaphor of space has a similar explanatory value for understanding movement through social space and restrictions on it. The metaphors that Bourdieu provides us with of spaces and places enable an understanding of the distribution and allocation of resources and, as Skeggs has argued, for 'people to be framed' (1997, p.12). There is a real complexity around working-class identity in contemporary Britain, with little understanding shown in mainstream discourse. Specifically, there are misunderstandings of working-class ways of life that may be simultaneously positive and negative for those who embody them.

Therefore, what this chapter has done is to explain how important it is to contextualise practices within poor working-class communities. By doing this, we can see what the community values are, and we are able to examine that particular value system against that of the dominant value system. Through this we can see not only what the community considers valuable, but also what is not available within that community and, therefore, how the individuals within the neighbourhood, but also the neighbourhood as a collective, might compensate for what they have no access to.

References

Bourdieu, P. 1962. *The Algerians*. Boston, MA: Beacon Press.
Bourdieu, P. 1977. *Outline of a theory of practice*. Cambridge: Cambridge University Press.
Bourdieu, P. 1984. *Distinction: a critique of the social judgement of taste*. London: Routledge.
Bourdieu, P. 1998. *Practical reason*. Cambridge: Polity.
Bourdieu, P. et al. 1999. *The weight of the world: social suffering in contemporary society*. Cambridge: Polity Press.
Bourdieu, P. and Wacquant, L. 1992. *An invitation to reflexive sociology*. Cambridge: Polity.
Haylett, C. 2003. Culture, class and urban policy: reconsidering equality. *Antipode*. **35**(1), pp.55–73.
Giroux, H. 1983. Rationality, reproduction, and resistance: toward a critical theory of schooling." In: McNall, S. (ed.) *Current Perspectives in Social Theory*, vol. 4. Greenwich, CT: JAI Press, pp.85–118.
Lawler, S. 2005. Disgusted subjects: the making of middle-class identities. *The Sociological Review*. **53**(3), pp.429–446.
Lawler, S. 2008. *Identity: sociological perspectives*. Cambridge: Polity.
Skeggs, B. 1997. *Formations of class and gender*. London: Sage.
Skeggs, B. 2004. *Class, self, culture*. London: Routledge.
Welshman, J. 2007. *Underclass: a history of the excluded*. London: Continuum International.

Chapter 4

Re-interpreting Bourdieu, belonging and Black identities
Exploring 'Black' cultural capital among Black Caribbean youth in London

Derron O. Wallace

Introduction

It has been a vivid pleasure, though at times unsettling, to think about the relevance of 'race' and ethnicity in Bourdieu's scholarship. For much of the last five years, I have pondered questions such as: was 'race' simply understated or entirely unacknowledged by Bourdieu? Was Bourdieu at all concerned with racial domination? To what extent was 'race' a mappable coordinate on Bourdieu's theoretical radar? How can critical conceptions of 'race' enrich understandings of Bourdieu's work? Is the study of 'race' an imposition on Bourdieu's scholarship, an invitation to innovation or an important extension? Rummaging through Bourdieu's translated works, I have searched for hints to a class-rich set of analytics on 'race' and racialisation – or an antidote to rigid 'race'-or-class binaries in sociological scholarship. My entree into the study of 'race' and Bourdieu, however, was never a quest to undo the analytical primacy of class. Instead, I envisaged it as an attempt to discern how class is 'raced', or to question whether experiences of the working and middle classes differ according to 'race'.

Questions about the unequal, 'raced' experiences of social class surfaced during my first year in university. My roommate and I were second-generation working-class teens raised in politically conscious families in different parts of New York. For both of us, social class was not a vapoury abstraction – it was an influential rubric that constrained the choices in our lives, particularly in wealthy, elite institutions. Within the confines of our dorm room, we often derided our middle- and upper-class peers, particularly the ones who 'wore' their class privileges daily – girls who wore long-sleeved Ralph Lauren shirts with popped collars, necklaces with two scores of 10-millimetre freshwater pearls and suede Ugg boots with sheepskin to warm their feet; boys who donned Birkenstock clogs, Ray Ban sunglasses and two Abercrombie and Fitch shirts at a time with all collars raised. Nothing incited rage in us quite like classmates who declined support from the university's 'free' writing tutors because their parents or paid tutors at home could 'do better'.

The overwhelming class angst that united my roommate and me initially divided us eventually, as we realised that we often encountered our class positionality in contrasting ways. By the end of our first term it became clear that despite our shared class heritage, whiteness functioned as a resource for him, and blackness often served as a liability for me. Truth be told, it was my roommate who first brought these racialised class distinctions to my attention. It occurred to him, and eventually to me, that at our predominantly white institution, where the majority of our peers were upper class and middle class, 'race' influenced the expression and reception of our working class identities.

I wish I could say that I had the theoretical clarity as a first-year university student to name the race and class conundrums I encountered. However, Bourdieu's penetrating scrutiny of contemporary class arrangements afforded me the relevant language to think about racialised taste and style distinctions across and within class groups. The quest to understand 'race' and its relationship to Bourdieu's conceptual toolkit became a key feature of my doctoral training. Throughout that time, I have found that analyses of 'race' and ethnicity in Bourdieu's work are sparse (Rollock, 2012; Rollock *et al.*, 2011; Reay *et al.*, 2005; Reay, 2004b). In fact, analytical treatments of 'race' and ethnicity in Bourdieu's theory of practice are likely to be economical. While classic pieces such as *Distinction* (1993) represented France as ethnically undifferentiated (Bennett *et al.*, 2009), works such as *The Algerians* (1962) and *Weight of the World* (2003) shed some light on Bourdieu's sensitivity to ethnicity, migration and displacement as social factors that complicate class hierarchies. Yet even within the above mentioned works, Bourdieu's class consciousness is 'race light' at best.

Bourdieu's building blocks for a 'raced' class analysis

Despite the fact that Bourdieu's work has not consistently addressed 'race' and ethnicity, his theoretical concepts have long been used to interpret the experiences and outcomes of racial, ethnic and class minorities (Rollock, 2007; Reay *et al.*, 2005; Reay, 2004a; Carter, 2003). One such concept is cultural capital, which Bourdieu defines as 'instruments for the appropriation of symbolic wealth socially designated as worthy of being sought and possessed' (Bourdieu, 1977, p.488). The 'instruments' or resources Bourdieu refers to include cultural cues, social styles, schemes of expression, acquired bodies of knowledge, (re)presentation styles, manners of speaking, consumption practices and patterns (van de Werfhorst, 2010; Moore, 2008; Silva, 2005; Yosso, 2005; Reay, 2004b).

Despite Bourdieu's specific definition and clarifying commentary, cultural capital is at times deployed in ways that promote deficit views of racial and class minorities. To be clear, deficit perspectives frame racial and class minorities based on what they 'lack'. A more balanced reading in keeping with Bourdieu's proposition focuses not only on the fact that the skills, tastes and styles of racial and class minorities are often not legitimated, but how the limited symbolic recognition accorded them in the white middle-class mainstream is based on asymmetrical power relations – ones that are often racialised. In this chapter, I offer what I deem an asset-based reading of cultural capital: 'Black' cultural capital. 'Black' cultural capital is a generative interpretation that considers the resources that matter in dominant and non-dominant settings. It sees power arrangements as producing structures of suffering that can limit the conversion of 'Black' cultural capital into economic capital, depending on the national context and social fields within it (Lizardo, 2010; Bourdieu, 1999).

Bourdieu's key notion of cultural capital has been expanded to mitigate his failure to more thoroughly account for 'race' and ethnicity in the classed experiences of disadvantaged groups. Stanford sociologist Prudence Carter, for example, extends Bourdieu's notion of cultural capital by examining the varied cultural practices and valid resources low-income African American youth draw upon in schools and social organisations in her much celebrated ethnography, *Keepin' It Real* (2005). Based on a 10-month-long community-based ethnographic study of 62 low-income African American and Latino youth, ages 13 to 20, in Yonkers, New York, Carter (2003) argues that valuable, desired resources abound among low-income, minority youth as well, not only among a mainly white, middle-class majority. Conventional perspectives, Carter explains, suggest that cultural capital abounds among some communities, but is absent, or at the very least deficient, among others (Yosso, 2005). Carter (2005) therefore argues that conventional interpretations of cultural capital ignore non-dominant forms of cultural capital, and in so doing promote deficit perspectives of what the poor and working classes lack in their negotiation of inter-group class relations. She suggests that the appreciations, tastes, styles and coded expressions of urban African American youth – which she refers to as 'Black' cultural capital – afford cache, recognition and ultimately power, within their local, social contexts. In a similar way with class as reference point, Lisa Mckenzie in the previous chapter, as well as Kirsty Morrin in Chapter 9, both critique the 'deficit' view of working-class people as supposedly 'lacking' in cultural capital and/or aspirations. Mckenzie argues that the working-class community she studied in Nottingham inverts their so-called 'lack' by ascribing value to their own working-class culture within and across their own communities.

Building on the scholarship of Pierre Bourdieu, this chapter further develops Prudence Carter's (2003) notion of 'Black' cultural capital and highlights the social status hierarchies among Black ethnics in a London state school as understood by Black Caribbean youth. I wish to make the case here that there is no singular, clearly delineated 'Black' cultural capital to which all Black ethnics subscribe universally. Each Black ethnic group (be they African, African American, Black Caribbean or Black British) possesses distinct cultural capital sets, rendering 'Black' cultural capital dynamic and diverse. I offer empirical attention to the 'Black' cultural capital assortments among Black Caribbean youth in order to underscore the view that Black cultural capital is, in fact, a set of fluid, stratified resources that vary according to social fields.

Defining 'Black' in Black cultural capital: finding value in variability and the vernacular

Carter (2005) contends that there are two core forms of cultural capital at play in the lives of her participants: dominant *and* non-dominant cultural capital. She defines dominant cultural capital in keeping with Bourdieu's original rendition of cultural capital – that is cultural knowledge, specialised skills and distinct practices inherited and invoked by privileged classes to maintain high status and reproduce power in mainstream society. 'Non-dominant' cultural capital, on the other hand, refers to the cultural resources lower status groups convert to capital to manage their social status within their local communities (Carter, 2003). Those who operationalise dominant cultural capital in home and social contexts experience cumulative advantage in schools (Lareau, 2011; 2000), whereas those who draw on non-dominant cultural capital greatly or exclusively develop and experience an oppositional culture in schools (Ogbu, 1988; 1978; 1974).

Giving particular credence to the non-dominant forms of capital, Carter (2003) explores the ways in which 'speech codes, dress styles, musical preferences and other attributes framed as 'black'' (Carter, 2003, p.139) are used as symbolic forms of recognition for individual cultural status positioning and group cohesion. 'Black' cultural capital, she maintains, is but one form in a range of non-dominant cultural capitals based on the performances, preferences and ultimately, power that local youth label and legitimise as 'Black'. She argues that African American youth in urban contexts possess tastes, styles, knowledge and ways of being (capital, in essence) that are valuable in local networks and desirable by their minority peers and, increasingly, by the white majority as well (Warikoo, 2011; Thomas, 2007).

The Black in 'Black' cultural capital is based on entrenched racialised worldviews youth possess, and is mediated by ethnicity, nationality and locality. As originally conceived, 'Black' cultural capital is a porous construct that influences the position and power of Black youth in peer group hierarchies. The concept speaks to the fluid and ambiguous ways in which some racial, cultural or economic minorities produce and perform Black identities. In a racialised class order, 'Black' cultural capitals are the resources with which youth in stigmatised positions or stigmatised settings procure power to alter perceptions of self and society. As will be empirically illustrated throughout this chapter, 'Black' cultural capital requires moving beyond ethno-national identification schemes to performative scripts popularly recognised as 'Black'. 'Black' cultural capital is therefore part of the everyday 'social curriculum' necessary for offsetting, at least in imagination, the hidden injuries – material, social, psychological – of inner-city schooling (Anyon, 1997).

The 'Black' cultural capital to which Carter (2003) refers is arguably, within the confines of her research, African American cultural capital as noted through the specific linguistic currency, musical preferences and coded expressions her research participants employ. But what about the function of 'Black' cultural capital among Black Caribbeans – particularly those outside the US? This chapter illustrates that 'Black' cultural capital is not exclusive to African Americans. Furthermore, 'Black' cultural capital as expressed by African Americans is not exactly the same for Black Caribbeans. The participants in this study shed light on the locally developed, Caribbean inflections of non-legitimised cultural capital and its prominence in dominant non-dominant places. 'Black' cultural capital does not necessarily inspire an oppositional stance to white, middle-class authority and academic achievement. Instead, 'Black' cultural capital spotlights the relational and ethnic resources used to celebrate an authentic 'Black identity'. To this end, 'Black' cultural capital is a contextual heuristic for non-dominant cultural capital based on salient, local meanings.

To her credit, Carter concedes that '[c]onceivably, other ethnic groups racially identified as "Black" possess their own cultural capital portfolio' (Carter, 2003, p.151). Yet, to date there are no clear empirical examples of this beyond the African American community, particularly for Black Caribbeans. More empirical evidence is needed to show how 'Black' cultural capital applies to other Black ethnics, such as Black Caribbeans and Black Africans and how it is performed differently across local geographies. Such studies may suggest that not all types of 'Black' cultural capital are valued and desired equally among Black ethnics and even the white majority. The ethnographic research showcased in this chapter reveals that some forms of 'Black' cultural capital are more dominant than others, given their global reputation and rising popularity (Thomas, 2007; Hall, 1997; 1996). 'Black' cultural capital is therefore neither singular nor static, but instead, its character is multidimensional and its value, contextual.

It is also worth noting at this juncture that 'Black' cultural capital is not limited to a particular social class. Put plainly, 'Black' cultural capital is not solely the preserve of poor and working-class Blacks; Black middle-class youth also invoke multiple, complex iterations of 'Black' cultural capital – a perspective altogether missing from the existing literature. Whereas Carter (2005) focuses on low-income African American youths' expressions of 'Black' cultural capital, my research indicates that working-class and middle-class Caribbean youth also draw on 'Black' cultural capital in an attempt to legitimise their status as racial 'others' in an inner-city context. It is arguably a response to the historically marginal position of Blacks in British society – a weight often shouldered by Blacks in Britain irrespective of middle-class privilege (Vincent *et al.*, 2012). 'Black' cultural capital is therefore a set of resources working class and middle class Black Caribbean youth deploy to make meaning of Black identities, forge networks of belonging and counter their marginal status, given Britain's racialised power relations.

In the remaining sections, I showcase the validity of 'Black' cultural capital among second-generation Black Caribbean teenagers. After outlining the sample and methods of the study, I make two core arguments: first, local contexts matter – they shape dynamic expressions of 'Black' cultural capital even across ethnic groups; and second, in academic and social spheres, 'Black' cultural capital is crucial for proving authenticity. The chapter empirically illustrates that while the specific expressions of 'Black' cultural capital among Black Caribbeans in London are not exactly the same as African Americans in New York (as described by Carter), the instrumental aims of 'Black' cultural capital are often the same: to garner higher status and social recognition.

Sample and methods: contextualising the study on Black identities and migration

This chapter focuses on data from in-depth interviews with second-generation Black Caribbean boys and girls from a state secondary school in South London. Findings showcased in this chapter come from a larger 14-month ethnographic study investigating the national, political and cultural factors that position Black Caribbean youth as 'high achievers' in New York relative to African Americans, and 'underachievers' in London compared to Black Africans. The focal participants discussed in this chapter include 15 boys and 15 girls between the ages of 14 and 16. Students were initially recruited for this study through letters sent to the parents of children in years 10 and 11 who were registered as Black Caribbean on their school records. In an attempt to develop a more fine-grained understanding of second-generation Black Caribbean youth in London, participants were identified using screening questionnaires, which solicited preliminary information about their class background and generational status. Of the 382 students who completed the survey, the 115 second-generation Black Caribbean students were invited to participate in focus group interviews. Thirty of those second-generation Black Caribbean young people who completed focus group interviews completed one-on-one interviews. Pseudonyms are used throughout this chapter to ensure the protection and anonymity of the study's participants.

An analysis of the interview sample examined in this chapter indicates that 13 participants were from Black middle-class families (as determined by parents' university completion and professional ranking), and 17 were from working-class families. Semi-structured, open-ended interviews were conducted over a seven-month period from 2012 to 2013 in homes, classrooms and social venues across South London. The duration of interviews varied between 55 minutes and 85 minutes, though on average interviews lasted for 65 minutes. These individual interviews explored participants' educational experiences in state schools, perceptions of racial and ethnic relations in school and society and constructions of social and learner identities, among other factors. Given the scope and required length of this chapter, I use the remaining sections to focus on students' beliefs about their aspirations, authenticity, and 'appropriate' behaviours as Black Caribbean youth.

The participants discussed in this chapter are year 10 and 11 students at Newton Secondary School in South London, a large, historically white state comprehensive. Though Newton Secondary and the surrounding area have traditionally served the white working classes, there has been a marked increase in the number of Black Caribbeans and Black Africans living in the area over the past 20 years. The school remains predominantly white (50.5 per cent), but is diversifying at a fast rate, as noted by greater enrolment of minority ethnic students in the last five years. Racial and minority ethnic groups constitute 46.2 per cent of the student body, with students of Caribbean origin forming the largest subset of this population. The recent shift in the demographics in the school and community makes Newton an intriguing site for cultural analysis because in many respects it is reflective of the mixed racial make-up of most inner-city schools in London (Reynolds, 2013; Warikoo, 2011; Reay *et al.*, 2007).

'Black' cultural capital among Caribbean youth in local settings

The data provided suggest that 'Black' cultural capital is a locally determined resource that affects relational and affective bonds among Black Caribbean young people. In a context where some second-generation Black Caribbean youth may locate themselves as being in the nation but not of it, the locality can become the centre in which belonging is negotiated and Black identities, real and imagined, are celebrated. It is within local milieus that counter-discourses emerge that challenge historic structures of exclusion. To this end, the local deployment of 'Black' cultural capital is not merely a theoretical extension, but represents the economies of value in which historically non-legitimised practices and styles are promoted and preferred in social settings. 'Black' cultural capital arguably serves to re-value participants' de-valued Black identities among their peers based on locally understood styles and expressions. Findings suggest that it is within the locality that some Black Caribbean young people redeem the power of 'Black' cultural capital undermined in the nation. Odain, a working-class year 10 pupil of Jamaican descent whose mother works as a cleaner, explained on several occasions what being Black meant to him and how such definitions are locally formulated. The following is his most gripping description:

> Being Black is about having power, respect, you get me? . . . yeah, it means having power, may be not with the teachers, but definitely with friends. So many people want to be Black or to be like us, especially on the social scene. With my mates in school or on the street, it's the best thing to be, unless the FEDs (police) are around. Black Caribbean people have a lot of culture – we set the trend 'round here, you feel me fam? I can talk like a Jamaican, know some Marcus Garvey, listen to Stylo-G and grime [Britain's fusion of hip hop and reggae] . . . that's what young people value . . . being for real . . . that's money on the street . . . [But] in school, in the cafeteria, on the football field, it is important. Being Caribbean makes me proud of who I am . . . I am Black and I might not be British, but at least I know where I come from.

Odain's claim that the linguistic expressions, musical tastes along with related styles often labelled 'Black' are prized symbols of differentiation in local settings and peer networks is not at all uncommon among the findings. Complementing Odain's point of view, Keith, a middle-class year 10 pupil also of Jamaican heritage, contends that the value attributed to the styles and tastes of Black youth are high in his local community because of the number of Black Caribbean and Black African young people in his school and neighbourhood. He maintained:

> I'm proud to be Black and to have roots inside and outside this country . . . When you're in a school or a place where you have a good number of Black people, I think it makes it a bit easier for people to understand how and why I talk the way I talk, with slang or patois or the kind of music I listen to sometimes . . . or even the type of dancing that I like . . . while teachers and older people in general may not like it, you get a lot of respect from people, especially young people. They know they can't mess about – that you have culture. Some people think their culture and background is boring, but nobody thinks being Black Caribbean or Black African is boring. You get me?

Another working-class year 10 student, Cashmere, whose parents hail from Guyana and now work as carers in London, also explained that in some instances being Black accords her considerable power in her local multi-ethnic peer groups at Newton, which is not easily transferred to all settings. She argued:

> It's a funny thing because the way I talk, the kind of music I listen to, and even what I know about the latest about what's going on in Guyana and about Black people here, my friends know that I'm a real Black person, know what I mean? I don't have to beg it . . . they know I am not fake. British society still looks down on Black people, but our school, and in our community, Black people have a lot of power. It's kind of a weird contradiction, but it makes sense. I'm Black and my Indian friends and white friends from Newton try to talk like me sometimes or listen to my music. None of us ever try to talk like Indians or geezars, unless we're busting joke . . . When I go visit family in Liverpool or my father's friend in Glasgow, slangs and dress codes don't mean the same as they do in London . . . they don't have the same power . . .

For Odain, Keith and Cashmere, the power and value of 'Black' cultural capital is bound to context and the actors in it. It is about forging paths of belonging in local geographies, even if constrained to do so in the nation writ large. Among their peers in London, the musical, interactional and communication styles of Black Caribbean young people is of high significance, while in some settings they may be subordinated or pathologised as simply being ethnic or youth expressions. As Odain suggests, the cultural resources he draws upon are not about highbrow aesthetic culture, but are instead based on a set of symbolic codes imbued with meaning and value by Black youth (even in multi-racial coalitions) in local settings. 'Black' cultural capital is arguably the resource set Black Caribbean youth such as Odain, Keith and Cashmere deploy to move beyond cultural identification to 'authentic' racial representations. It is based on locally situated performances of Black identities as 'real' representations of blackness. To this end, the practices associated with 'Black' cultural capital, as understood by participants such as Odain and Cashmere, represent an accomplishment that reflects personal and projected identities (Alexander, 1996).

Not surprisingly, Odain, Keith and Cashmere are not alone in representing 'authentic' 'Black' expressions as valued resources. During a one-on-one interview with Cory, a year 10 middle-class male of Jamaican descent, he suggested that being Black was about 'acting Black', about performance, not simply phenotype. The extract that follows sheds light on the complex interplay of 'race', ethnicity and performativity to negotiate Black identities and iterations of 'Black' cultural capital.

DERRON: What do you mean by 'act[ing] Black'?
CORY: Oh (He chuckled, then paused), you know, I can just be myself, use my culture, just talk normal. I don't need to sound posh or talk about British things. You see what I mean? No need to be on my ps-and-qs. I can just be a Caribbean lad from South London.
DERRON: I understand but if someone else is not a Caribbean lad from South London, does it mean they can't 'act Black'?
CORY: Oh no. It's about knowing where you come from, you know? It's about showing respect for a Black culture – Caribbean, African, or whatever. If you're Nigerian, or can act or talk like a Nigerian, people will know you're a Black person with a strong culture. If you're Black American and you listen to hip hop or whatever, that can get you attention too. Even white people can act black, you know [what I] mean. It's hard to do, but I guess it can happen if they really learn how we talk and relate to one another . . . what gets you real recognition is based on how popular and cool that culture is. It all depends on where you are, or as my mother would say, 'which part yuh deh.'
DERRON: Tell me more. What do you mean by it's about where you are?
CORY: Well, you can't be Jamaican acting like a Black American in South London. People will laugh at you 'cause they know you're beggin' it. That won't get you any credit. That's what happens to white British [people] when they try to act Black . . . You get more credit if you connect with your own black culture and [if] it's popular or expected in the places where you are. Jamaica and Nigeria are popular. If you're the only one from, I don't know, Botswana or Djibouti, even though you're African, you won't get much cred for those cultures.

Cory, Odain and a host of their peers suggest there is a set of resources that enables camaraderie among their peers in inner-city social contexts. These include, but are not limited to, musical tastes, communication codes and knowledge of cultural history. These resources enable them to relate to their peers, improve their social status and promote senses of belonging. For Black Caribbean youth in a South London context, these are the expressions of 'Black' cultural capital. What is peculiar about Cory's claims are the ways in which his perceptions of what constitutes 'acting Black' is not contingent on a single, universally understood Black identity, but instead his perceptions of what 'Black' means gives heed to the particularities of locality, ethnicity, nationality and performativity (Thomas, 2007; Butler, 1993; Hall, 1993). To this end, Black identities, and the value attributed to them, is dynamically articulated and richly understood. Cory emphasises that although the communication and interaction styles among Black ethnics at Newton Secondary may differ according to ethnicity, such expressions of 'Black' cultural capital are creative, racialised cultural responses that can counter the on-going symbolic violence marginalised young people experience in schools and society. In essence, while illustrations of 'Black' cultural capital vary across Black ethnic groups, Cory points out that they are all locally understood as necessarily generative 'Black' expressions.

Cory further suggests that while there are multiple Black identities and cultural capital collections, 'Black' cultural capital assortments are differentially valued. This arguably creates hierarchies of popularity or economies of value that influence the recognition and volume of 'Black' cultural capital(s) deployed in local contexts. Displaying the tastes, linguistic currencies, and cultural knowledge of Djibouti and Botswana, he reasons, may verify one's cultural authenticity as an African, but may not earn power and prestige among peers in a local South London context, where there are not as many immigrants from these two countries as there are from Ghana and Nigeria. Deploying the musical tastes, language and cultural ways of being of Nigeria or Jamaica, however, by virtue of the size of their immigrant populations and international reputations can constitute more legitimate forms of 'Black' cultural capital (Thomas, 2007). This suggests that among Black ethnics, and even among Black Africans, social status stratification persists. 'Black' cultural capital becomes the resource for scaling hierarchies of legitimacy and securing high social status positions.

Cory argues that 'Black' cultural capital can be acquired by white British youth. For low-status whites in London such as white working-class youth, many of whom are stigmatised and stereotyped (Stahl, 2012; Ingram, 2011; Reay, 2004b; Willis, 1977), they *can* learn to recognise and utilise 'Black' cultural capital, especially through their friendship networks with Black Caribbeans and Black Africans. Cory's claim is in keeping with scholarship on black–white peer relations in London. Based on his ethnographic study of Black and white youth in South London estates, Back (1996) argues that given rates of intermarriage and residential mixing black–white friendships are commonplace and in some instance result in improved racial and cultural literacy (Winddance Twine, 1999; 1996). In this context, 'Black' cultural capital is recognisable and desired by the white majority, whether working classes or those with 'white' middle-class cultural markers (Winddance Twine, 2004; Carter, 2003). White working-class youth could conceivably draw on the musical preferences, linguistic codes and interactional modes (handshakes and other salutation gestures) recognised as 'Black' as an expression of cross-racial and cultural competence.

Cory and Odain's responses suggest that 'Black' cultural capital is, at its core, a relational resource recognised in local communities that is useful for altering lower-status position or maintaining high status in peer groups. 'Black' cultural capital, as expressed by Cory, Odain and scores of other Black Caribbean youth in South London, shapes relational dynamics and changes the power structures of peer networks. Participants suggest that much of the social recognition and peer power that 'Black' cultural capital has garnered is based on local geographies and groups. To this end, local context matters for the consideration and interpretation of 'Black' cultural capital.

Begging it or being it: acts, art and the pursuit of Black authenticity?

Although it is conceivable that 'Black' cultural capital may be acquired by and ascribed to Blacks and non-Blacks, proving authenticity in peer networks is a much more challenging exercise. The discursive construction of authenticity constitutes an attempt to police performances and practices classified as 'Black'. Approval of racial or ethnic authenticity is often based on a set of desired cultural markers (aesthetics, accent, attitude, behaviours, etc.), although the terms and conditions of authenticity shift according to social groups. Authenticity is necessary for the classification of in-groups and out-groups and the establishment of permanent or stable group affiliations.

Claire Alexander considers the politics of authenticity in her ethnography, *The Art of Being Black* (1996). She suggests that Black ethnics draw upon 'signs and symbols of belongingness' to defend their racial and ethnic authenticity (Alexander, 1996, p.2). She argues that in some instances 'being black' is as much a discursive accomplishment as it is a locally situated performance for cultural production and social positioning. Based on in depth interviews and close observations of 15 second-generation Afro-Caribbean and Black African men in East London, Alexander (1996) suggests that the 'art of being black' is based on the valuable cultural production of inner-city Black youth: speech styles, dress codes and the political 'know-how' needed to navigate inner-city spaces. They become examples of, but not sole representations of, 'blackness' as a broad interpretative resource. These everyday expressive 'art forms' underscore the importance of racial authenticity and cultural exclusivity that are messy but meaningful. The locally contingent expressions to which Alexander (1996) refers are arguably 'Black' cultural capital.

As in Carter's (2005) study, Alexander (1996) claims that acknowledgement of 'cultural authenticity' is dependent upon appropriate representation of 'Black' identity, as marked by phenotype and locally recognised cultural practices. She reasons:

> Any perceived inappropriacy was immediately cast as an aspersion on the individual's 'racial' (or, indeed, gender or class) identity. 'Being black' was, then, at once fluid and transiently rigid.
>
> (Alexander, 1996, p.194)

Young black men, she points, draw on speech styles, dress codes, and other popular 'Black' expressions, as locally determined, to verify their racial identities. These are some of the resources with which they justify their position in local social spaces, build bonds with peer networks and create counter-narratives of affirmation, given the dominant pejorative perspectives on Black masculinities in British society (Wright et al., 1998; Sewell 1997). Furthermore, in academic contexts where Black Caribbean pupils experience negative perceptions, speech styles, dress codes and related expressions of 'Black' cultural capital arguably provides them a sense of belonging and esteem needed to re-position their status in schools. In this section, I unpack notions of 'belonging' and 'begging' blackness, to shed light on the complexities and contradictions of 'race', class and ethnicity in urban schools.

For Black Caribbean adolescents at Newton, 'Black' cultural capital functioned to celebrate and verify Black authenticity across racial boundaries. Akilah, a year 11 middle-class student-athlete explained the distinction between an occasional use of cultural markers popularly recognised as 'Black' and the consistent usage of these symbolic markers as a way of life. Consider the following extract from her interview.

AKILAH: ... 'acting Black' is a funny thing because some people can turn it on or turn it off, pick it up and put it down. When you turn off the accent or slang you learned at school in order to be cool, that's one thing, which is what my white and Indian friends do a lot. But when you have to turn off the way you normally are at home – your accent, your music, your being, it is hurtful ... it's just wrong. It's like you're being told that how you operate doesn't belong in some places. That's why when I'm outside of class, I have to check some people because they want the benefits of acting Black' but none of the responsibility.

DERRON: Who do you check and how do you check them?

AKILAH: I check any of my friends or people I see around who try to 'act Black'. I'm like, you can act Black, yeah, but you can't be real. They [are] begging it, but they can't really be it, you know what I mean?

DERRON: Tell me more about how you check your peers.

AKILAH: I mean, that's easy. You simply tell them what you think. A lot of my friends will say: 'Yo, why you beggin' it for?' Or, if you think someone has gone too far, you can say, 'You takin' the mic. fam.' And sometimes you have to say that to Black people, but a lot of times I have to say that to my white and Indian friends ... they can come close to the line, but they really shouldn't cross it.

Efforts across racial boundaries to invoke the signs and symbols recognised as 'Black' are not at all new (Gilroy, 2013; Hall, 1996; Fanon, 1986). As Akilah mentioned, pupils from a variety of backgrounds deploy 'Black' tastes, styles and expressions to make sense of their social location – and more importantly to develop power within them. The extracts from Akilah's interview speak to the ways in which Black expressions are portable in ways that Black identities sometimes are not. Black cultural capital is then understood as both an essence and a positioning (Hall, 1990). Akilah suggests that the development of racial and ethnic boundaries is necessary for the demarcation of in-groups and out-groups, for drawing distinctions between ascribed versus acquired identities. Other participants reinforce the significance of establishing symbolic limitations to the use of 'Black' cultural capital, and point to the ways in which such power resources, as Carter (2003) considers them, are policed during day-to-day lived experiences, particularly in social settings. Kayla, another Black middle-class student-leader in year 10 suggested:

> I mean, everyone can speak with a Jamaican-type British accent with a South London slang ... everyone wants to show that they not racists and have friends beyond their race, but it's important for people to know their place. Not because I listen to One Direction [an all-male British band] or rock music or sometimes call my white friends geezer, or do anything else that people would associate with white British culture, doesn't mean that I am white. Likewise, not because whites listen to Stylo-G [a Jamaican reggae artist] and can say things like 'dem ting' and zeen', doesn't mean they should think they're down [use her index and middle fingers to mimic quotation marks]. We are all different.

Jamie, a year 10 working-class student of Antiguan heritage explained:

> If everyone gets to 'act Black', then who's really Black? You have to have a way to separate the real from the fake, and if you're real like me, it's your job to make sure people who are just acting just to get in, know that they are fake, really fake ...

Such contestations about the meanings and authenticity of practices frequently signalled as 'Black' are salient for some Black Caribbean youth. It is important to note, however, that the tensions around black authenticity are not solely about the arbitrary maintenance of distinctions between Black and non-Black youth in social settings, but about the preservation of the resources Black youth have for recognition and affirmation. Gregory, a year 10 football player of Jamaican and Trinidadian background argued:

> When I talk street in class, or talk like I do at home with English and Caribbean slang, I automatically get looked down on ... I can't really be

> myself. When I am on the street or heading home, I realise that who I am and how I speak is valuable. You just can't be too posh outside when you are talking to young people. A lot of older teachers don't know how to do this, but I do. I can connect with other Caribbean and African boys quick . . . and that's cause of how I speak.

Joseph, another year 11 student who was born in Britain but identifies as Jamaican, explained:

> A lot of time, I feel down in class. It's like me and my Caribbean mates don't do so well, and it's obvious. I crack jokes and fool around, but I really want to do well . . . It's hard not to look down on yourself when you think other people are looking down on you . . . Outside of school, I can be the man in charge. How I talk, how I dress, make[s] me feel better about myself because that matters outside of school . . . I wish it mattered inside school too.

To Gregory and Joseph, 'Black' cultural capital arguably represents counter-cultural forms of reaffirmation enacted in non-dominant spaces that stand in opposition to the micro-aggressions experienced in dominant spaces. It is perhaps an attempt to un-do and re-do domination – to reposition Black cultural expressions as locally dominant even in a political context that deems them marginal to the nation. The recognised value of 'Black' cultural capital speaks to the formidable influence of Britain's black communities to shape networks of power to which even non-Black pupils seek to subscribe. The need to take 'Black' expressions, practices and tastes ('Black' cultural capital) seriously is underscored by Gilroy (1992) in *There Ain't No Black in the Union Jack*, in which he reasons:

> The culture and politics of black America and the Caribbean have become the raw materials for creative processes which redefine what it means to be black, adapting it to distinctly British experiences and meanings.
> (Gilroy, 1992, p.154)

Gregory, Joseph, Akilah and other Black Caribbean participants suggest that such rich understandings of 'race' generally, and Black identities specifically, can prove profitable for identifying more complex iterations of non-dominant cultural capital.

Conclusion

'Black' cultural capital, as defined by Prudence Carter (2003), is an important extension of Bourdieu's notion of cultural capital. It is a contemporary species of non-dominant cultural capital that stands as profound criticism to the subjugation of 'race' in twenty-first-century analyses of social class. In this chapter, I offer a brief empirical analysis of the nuanced and complicated ways in which Black Caribbean young people's practices, preferences and performances that are typically labelled as 'Black' function as valid and valuable resources in social settings. I offer two core arguments about 'Black' cultural capital. First, in local economies of value, Black cultural capital bears formative influence that results in recognition or, in cases of demonstrated authenticity, respect. Second, Black Caribbean pupils establish symbolic boundaries to police and preserve 'Black' cultural capital – distinguishing between efforts to 'act Black' versus being Black. Although the scope of this chapter does not permit the divulgence of as much details as would be preferred, I close by highlighting important points to consider for further extension of 'Black' cultural capital.

I am mindful that 'Black' cultural capital, as framed in this chapter, can serve both as symbolic constraint and symbolic resource. It can be simultaneously empowering and disempowering. Arguably, the definitions and forms of blackness youth celebrate in local urban contexts are problematic because they often represent 'Black' identity and expressions as informal and colloquial. However, such definitions and representations of blackness are not fixed; they are locally determined and specific to the South London context within which the participants reside. It is nonetheless conceivable that a range of other expressions and experiences may be defined as Black in suburban and rural settings. More empirical studies are needed that consider the changing meanings of 'Black' cultural capital across different regional and national contexts – particularly in nation-states where there are multiple competing definitions of Blackness such as in South Africa and Brazil. In a later chapter, Thatcher and Halvorsrud illustrate the intersection between 'race' and class for white Polish and South African migrants living in the UK, and this provides an interesting contrast to consideration of 'Black' cultural capital. They argue that both sets of migrants in their study are reflexive about the 'racial' hierarchies that exist in Western societies and, in turn, attempt to draw on their 'whiteness' as a way to facilitate their 'acceptance' into a new, predominantly 'white', host society. Yet, their migrant status and differing social class backgrounds come into play as some of them are seen as 'not white enough' as they do not possess 'white middle class' cultural capital, which is highly valued in British society. This offers possibilities for the extension of the notion of racialised forms of capital and also highlights the complexity of multiple intersections of definition categories.

Despite efforts made in this chapter to attend to the intersection of 'race', ethnicity and class, other categories of identification should also be carefully considered. In the lived experiences of Black Caribbean young people, 'race', ethnicity and class are not discrete factors that operate in isolation from gender, generational background and sexuality. An intersectional analysis can yield richer understandings of Black cultural capital, especially their gendered and generational dimensions. For one, the ways in which Black boys display 'Black' cultural capital can differ from the ways in which girls do. What is more, the degrees to which second-generation Black middle-class girls utilise 'Black' cultural capital can perhaps vary from first or second-generation working-class girls. Future research should infuse an intersectional approach in order to explore the relevance of

'Black' cultural capital to different constituencies, including non-Black groups as well (e.g. white working-class boys).

Although there are communities of scholars for whom the extension of cultural capital to consider 'race' and ethnicity more significantly may be an unbearable stretch of Bourdieu's theory of social practice, the impact of globalisation and the influence of immigrant communities on the UK require that twenty-first-century exegeses of Bourdieu's oeuvre examine 'race' and ethnicity more closely (Gilroy, 2012; Pears, 2012) if its relevance is to endure and expand. Furthermore, because interpretations of Bourdieu's scholarship have been used to promote perspectives of Black youth as lacking cultural capital, more scholarship is needed that show Black youth are not deficient of cultural capital; they often possess different cultural capital sets that prove meaningful for navigating their local social settings. Whether their use of 'Black' cultural capital is valuable in mainstream society and privileged fields of power suggests much more about the unequal social structures Black Caribbean youth negotiate than it says about the youth themselves.

References

Alexander, C. 1996. *The Art of Being Black: The Creation of Black British Youth Identities*. Oxford: Oxford University Press.
Bennett, T., Savage, M., Silva, E., Warde, A., Gayo-Cal, M. and Wright, D. 2009. *Culture, Class, Distinction*. New York and London: Routledge.
Bourdieu, P. 1993. *Distinction: A Social Critique of the Judgement of Taste*. London: Routledge.
Bourdieu, P. 1962. *The Algerians*. Boston, MA: Beacon Press.
Bourdieu, P. 1999. *Weight of the World: Social Suffering in Contemporary Society*. Cambridge: Polity Press
Butler, J. 1993. *Bodies That Matter: On the Discursive Limits of Sex*. London: Routledge.
Carter, P. 2003. 'Black' Cultural Capital, Status Positioning and Schooling Conflicts for Low-Income African American Youth. *Social Problems*, **50**(1), pp.136–155.
Fanon, F. 1986. *Black Skins, White Masks*. London: Pluto Press.
Gilroy, P. 1992. *There Ain't No Black in the Union Jack* (2nd edn). London: Routledge.
Gilroy, P. 2012. 'My Britain Is Fuck All': Zombie Multiculturalism and the Race Politics of Citizenship. *Identities: Global Studies in Culture and Power*, **19**(4), pp.380–397.
Gilroy, P. 2013. 'We Got To Get Over Before We Go Under': Fragments for a History of Black Vernacular Neoliberalism. *New Formations*, **80–81** (Winter 2013), pp.23–38.
Hall, S. 1990. Cultural Identity and Diaspora. In: Rutherford, J. (ed.) *Identity, Community, Culture, Difference*. London: Lawrence & Wishart, pp.222–237.
Hall, S. 1993. *Negotiating Caribbean Identities*. Coventry, UK: Warwick University Centre for Caribbean Studies.
Hall, S. 1996. The After-life of Franz Fanon: Why Fanon? Why Now? In: *The Fact of Blackness*. London: ICA, pp.12–37.
Hall, S. 1997. The Local and the Global: Globalisation and Ethnicity. In: McClintock, A. Mufti, A. And Shohat, E. (eds) *Dangerous Liaisons: Gender, Nation & Postcolonial Perspectives*. Minneapolis, MN: University of Minnesota Press, pp.173–187.
Hall, S. And Jefferson, T. 1993. *Resistance through Rituals: Youth Subcultures in Post-war Britain* (2nd edn). London: Routledge.

Ingram, N. 2011. Reconciling working-class identity and Educational Success: A Study of Successful Teenage Boys, Locality and Schooling. Ph.D thesis, Queen's University Belfast.

Lareau, A. 2000. *Home Advantage: Social Class & Parental Involvement in Elementary Education*. Maryland, MD: Rowman & Littlefield.

Lareau, A. 2011. *Unequal Childhoods: Race, Class, and Family Life. A Decade Later*. Berkeley, CA: University of California Press.

Lizardo, O. 2010. Pierre Bourdieu as a Post-cultural Theorist. *Cultural Sociology*, **5**(1), pp.1–22.

Moore, R. 2008. Capital. In: Grenfell, M. (ed.) *Pierre Bourdieu: Key Concepts*. Durham, UK: Acumen, pp.101–116.

Ogbu, J.F. 1974. *The Next Generation: An Ethnography of Education in an Urban Neighborhood*. New York: Academic Press.

Ogbu, J.F. 1978. *Minority Education and Caste*. New York: Academic Press.

Ogbu, J.F. 1988. Class Stratification, Racial Stratification and Schooling. In: Weis, L. (ed.) Class, *Race and Gender in American Education*. Albany, NY: SUNY Press, pp.163–182.

Pears, E. 2012. 2011 Census: British Africans Now Dominant Black Group. *The Voice*. [Online] 12 December. [Accessed 12 May 2015] Available from: www.voice-online.co.uk/article/2011-census-british-africans-now-dominant-black-group

Reay, D. 2004a. Education and Cultural Capital: The Implications of Changing Trends in Education Policies. *Cultural Trends*, **13**(50), pp.73–86.

Reay, D. 2004b. 'Mostly Roughs and Toughs': Social Class, Race and Representation in Inner City Schooling. *Sociology*, **38**(5), pp.1005–1023.

Reay, D., David, M. and Ball, S. 2005. *Degrees of Choice: Social Class, Race and Gender in Higher Education*. Stoke-on-Trent, UK: Trentham Press.

Reay, D., Hollingworth, S., Williams, K., Crozier, G., Jamieson, F., James, D. and Beedell, P. 2007. 'A Darker Shade of Pale?' Whiteness, the Middle Classes and Multi-Ethnic Inner City Schooling. *Sociology*, **41**(6), pp.1041–1060.

Reynolds, T. 2013. Them and Us: 'Black Neighbourhoods' as a Social Capital Resource among Black Youths Living in Inner-City London, UK *Journal of Urban Studies*, **50**(3), pp.484–498.

Rollock, N. 2007. Legitimizing Black Academic Failure: Deconstructing Staff Discourses on Academic Success, Appearance and Behaviour. *International Studies in Sociology of Education*, **17**(3), pp.275–287.

Rollock, N. 2012. The Invisibility of Race: Intersectional Reflections on the Liminal Space Of Alterity. *Race, Ethnicity and Education*, **15**(1), pp.65–84.

Rollock, N., Gillborn, D., Ball, S. and Vincent, C. 2011. The Public Identities of the Black Middle Classes: Managing Race in Public Spaces. *Sociology*, **45**(6), pp.1078–1093.

Sewell, T. 1997. *Black Masculinities & Schooling: How Black Boys Survive Modern Schooling*. Stoke-on-Trent, UK: Trentham Press.

Stahl, G. 2012. *White Working-Class Boys' Negotiations of School Experience and Engagement*. Cambridge: University of Cambridge.

Thomas, D.A. 2007. Blackness Across Borders: Jamaican Diasporas and New Politics of Citizenship. *Identities: Global Studies in Culture and Power*, **14**(1–2), pp.37–41.

Vincent, C., Rollock, N., Ball, S., Gillborn, D. 2012. Intersectional Work and Precarious Positionings: Black Middle-Class Parents and Their Encounters with Schools in England. *International Studies in Sociology of Education,* **22**(3), pp.259–276.

Warikoo, N. 2011. *Balancing Acts: Youth Culture in the Global City*. Berkeley, CA: University of California Press.

Willis, P. 1977. *Learning to Labor: How Working Class Kids Get Working Class Jobs*. New York: Columbia University Press.

Winddance Twine, F. 1996. Brown Skinned White Girls: Class, Culture and the Construction of White Identity in Suburban Communities. *Gender, Place and Culture*, **3**(2), pp.205–224.

Winddance Twine, F. 1999. Bearing Blackness in Britain: The Meaning of Racial Difference for White Birth Mothers of African-Descent Children. *Social Identities: Journal for the Study of Race, Nation and Culture*, **5**(2), pp.185–210.

Winddance Twine, F. 2004. A White Side of Black Britain: The Concept of Racial Literacy. *Ethnic and Racial Studies*, **27**(6), pp.878–907.

Wright, C., Weekes, D., McGlaughlin, A. and Webb, D. 1998. Masculinised Discourses within Education and the Construction of Black Male Identities amongst African Caribbean Youth. *British Journal of Sociology of Education*, **19**(1), pp.75–87.

Yosso, T. 2005. Whose Culture Has Capital? A Critical Race Theory Discussion of Community Cultural Wealth. *Race Ethnicity and Education*, **8**(1), pp.69–91.

Chapter 5

'It's like if you don't go to Uni you fail in life'

The relationship between girls' educational choices, habitus and the forms of capital

Tamsin Bowers-Brown

Introduction

I first encountered the work of Pierre Bourdieu at night school where I was undertaking an A-level in Sociology. The classroom was an escape from the tedium of working for an agency on temporary contracts. I was already heavily influenced by politics and in particular the politics of social class and I had fortuitously ended up in a Sociology class as there were insufficient enrolments to the Politics class I had intended to take. Learning about educational inequality on this course was where I first heard the name Pierre Bourdieu. Bourdieu's concepts, in particular the forms of capital and later habitus and field spoke to many of the feelings of unrest I had about my own class position, but they also helped me to think more deeply about the social class inequalities about which I was already so passionate about highlighting and tackling.

My early career as a research associate involved writing research reports for government agencies that were not expected to be theorised. When I came to undertake research for my doctoral study, theory was something that I initially found daunting despite understanding its importance. Although I was aware of Bourdieu's concepts I had never read any of his original work, rather I had used introductory texts and had found journal articles written by Diane Reay to be interesting and accessible. With Reay's work in mind, I was concerned about inaccurately aligning my research with theoretical perspectives that seemed appropriate merely because they have traditionally been linked with the subject of educational choice-making. Reay (2004, p.432) argues that habitus has been used as an 'intellectual hairspray, bestowing gravitas without doing any theoretical work'. Ciaran Burke, in Chapter 2, argues that the overuse of habitus has sometimes meant the neglect of Bourdieu's other concepts such as capital and field. It is also important to remember that Bourdieu's concepts are relational and cannot be isolated from each other. Furthermore, Butin argues: 'we have embraced theory (for theory's sake) to the detriment of actually engaging with theory as lived practice' (Butin, 2006, p.372). This occurs particularly when theory is not used beyond description; for example, Reay argues that Bourdieu seeks to implement 'habitus as a conceptual tool' (2004, p.439); in this sense she argues that the misuse of habitus manifests itself when 'habitus is assumed or appropriated rather than put into practice in research accounts' (Reay, 2004, p.440). Operationalising the concepts would involve showing how the empirical research could be understood through these concepts. The theory-practice relationship for sociologists is one of Mckenzie's main arguments in Chapter 3. May argues that social researchers understand the social world and give it meaning by admitting 'the inevitability of the relationship between theory and data' (2011, p.44). In fact, as I began to read Bourdieu's original texts alongside the introductory texts analysing his work, I became unable to see anything without thinking about the relationship between theory and everyday practices. I found that Bourdieu's concepts were extremely relevant in helping to elucidate how the girls in my study made their educational choices and how they experienced secondary education, the core foci of my research.

Background to the study

In this chapter I present some of the findings from the case study secondary school where I conducted my doctoral research (to ensure anonymity it will be known by the pseudonym Greenlea Comprehensive). The research participants were girls in year groups 8–13 as well as staff from the senior leadership team. The focus of the study was how girls 'do' education, their perspectives on achievement and the choices they make about their educational pathways.

It was a political decision to focus my research on girls rather than all pupils within the case study school. There has been an emphasis in policy on the 'underachieving boy' in recent years, which has led to a binary positioning of girls as the success of the UK education system. Girls' overarching success has resulted in a justification of the individualisation of the curriculum that feeds into a larger defence of a market-driven education system. For example, in the UK, 'feminist research has highlighted how girls, because of their apparent educational success and their propensity for hard work, are instrumentalised as "ideal" neoliberal subjects' (Shain, 2013, np). Girls are seen to be fulfilling their role as 'good pupils' who through hard work are able to achieve what the education system requires of them; this generalisation raises several concerns both in relation to expectation and a lack of understanding about the intersectional inequalities that lie beneath the overarching headlines proclaiming girls' success. In addition to educational success, McRobbie emphasises the requirement placed on girls to have a 'lifeplan', something she argues is a 'modality of constraint' that results in individuals being 'compelled to be the kind of subject who can make the right choices' and, thus, 'new lines and demarcations are drawn between those subjects who are judged responsive to the regime of personal responsibility, and those who fail miserably' (2009, p.19). The focus of my research, in looking at how girls 'do' education, involved asking my participants about their educational choices and hopes for the future. Admittedly, this could be perceived as fuelling the 'life-plan discourse', although this was not my intention. I had concerns that my questions would reflect an assumption that successful girls should be 'the embodiment of neoliberal values: adept at change, engaged in a discourse of choice, and highly versatile' (Pomerantz *et al.*, 2013, p.190). In reassuring the girls that they were not expected to 'know' the answers, I hoped to diminish the neo-liberal expectations identified by Allen (2013, np), who warns of the dangers of an emphasis on personal aspiration, labelling it a 'powerful rhetoric'. Allen's (2013, np) concern is that this rhetoric is 'increasingly understood through the lens of individual pathologies and deficits'; where certain decisions are judged against others as 'worthy', or alternatively of lacking value. The progression of the 'deficit' model in the public narrative is discussed later by Kirsty Morrin (Chapter 9) in the context of her study into an entrepreneurial academy. I was concerned about using Bourdieu's forms of capital to a study of working-class girls supposedly 'lacking' the accumulation of specific capitals. Although I could see how the issues my participants discussed were associated with the possession of capitals, I had no desire to judge the choices that my participants had made and did not want to place certain choices in a 'deficit position'. After talking this through with other academics I began to understand that Bourdieu's ideas would help me to demonstrate the dominant norms indicating a pre-existing hierarchy that positions some choices as 'worthy' or symbolically powerful while others are undervalued. A similar approach can be seen through Burke's attempt (Chapter 2) to 'measure' his respondents' forms of capital in a relational sense in the context of their place/influence within a pre-existing hierarchy. As Bourdieu (1990) argues, the universalism of symbolic power is achieved by making people believe or accept its legitimacy; the education system plays a part in this process. The perpetuation or reproduction of symbolic power is compounded by those with greater levels of economic and cultural capital who are ultimately in possession of a symbolic capital that enables them to 'reinforce the power relations which constitute the structure of the social space' (1990, p.135). In highlighting that these hierarchies exist rather than taking them for granted, I was beginning to take a Bourdieusian approach to my research, which would help me to 'make explicit the forms of misrecognised symbolic power that underpin the implicit logic of practice, expectations and relations of those operating in these fields' (Deer, 2008, p.122).

My discussion of girls' choices is explored using a Bourdieusian framework (Bourdieu, 2006; 2000; 1984; 1977), operationalising the ideas of habitus, field and the forms of capital. These concepts were useful to this study because they consider both the individual (through habitus) and the educational institution (through the concept of field), alongside the values that are placed on different knowledge (capitals and symbolic violence) both strategically in relation to government policy as well as at a micro level within the school. I undertook my research in a state-funded English comprehensive secondary school for pupils aged 11–18. The academically oriented curriculum was most valued as it provided a clear pathway into the school's sixth-form for post-compulsory education (age 16–18). There was an expectation that progression to higher education would follow. The research methods I used were predominantly qualitative and incorporated: focus groups (with 42 pupils), open-ended survey questions (160 respondents), Facebook messages with nine pupils, eight semi-structured interviews with staff, observation of 16 interviews and guidance sessions for post-16 careers and education and three workshops with sixth-form pupils. In this chapter I demonstrate the utility of habitus and the forms of capital to understanding my research. Specifically, how the forms of capital the girls possessed contributed to how they 'play the game' and how they negotiated entry to the post-16 opportunities that they perceived to be within their grasp.

Educational value

As Burke has previously noted in Chapter 2, through the emergence and development of post-industrialisation the UK economy has moved from one based on hard skills and labour to soft skills and knowledge. As a result, the academic trajectory is that which carries the most prestige in the English education system; schools are judged accordingly on their GCSE pass rate. The governmental Department for Education places particular emphasis on the importance of pupils achieving GCSE grades A*–C in the subjects of Maths and English. The academic trajectory is associated with particular forms of knowledge that are historically located and favour those with corresponding capitals that can be converted into academic success: 'To a given volume of inherited capital there corresponds a band of more or less equally probable trajectories leading to more or less equivalent positions' (Bourdieu, 1984, p.110). The capitals Bourdieu identifies as corresponding with academic success are economic, cultural and social. Bourdieu (1977, p.87) argues the 'habitus acquired in the family underlies the structuring of school experiences'; consequently, those pupils whose habitus is congruent with the educational field and who have inculcated the valued forms of capitals through the home environment are recognised and rewarded by the education system. As Webb *et al.* clarify, 'schools are really disposed to serving the interests of children who have already had access to the kind of values and environment which the school system promotes, at least partly through the discourses that it employs' (2002, p.122). The discourse employed at Greenlea Comprehensive was one that emphasised measurement of attainment in relation to Ofsted's [1] expected levels of pupil progress. Progress is calculated by predicting what a pupil is thought to be capable of on the basis of their test results in Year 6 (age 10/11). These predictions are then presented to pupils in the form of target grades. At an individual level, pupils are monitored to ensure that their progression does not deviate from the linear and upward progression associated with their predicted attainment. The participation in this attainment discourse both by the teachers and pupils alike ensures its perpetuation. It is important to recognise that Bourdieu sees this participation as linked to an 'effect of power' rather than an act of 'voluntary servitude' (Bourdieu, 1996). He argues that the durable effects of the social order have established these dominating processes and therefore the complicity is not a 'conscious, deliberate act'. For the teaching staff and pupils at Greenlea Comprehensive School, the adherence to 'the rules of the game' was not disputed. For Bourdieu, this management of the field is achieved through what can be seen as a 'compromise formation', that is:

> One can equally say that agents take advantage of the possibilities offered by a field to express and satisfy their drives and their desires, in some cases their neurosis, or that fields use the agents' drives by forcing them to subject or sublimate themselves in order to adapt to their structures and to the ends that are immanent within them.
>
> (2000, p.165)

Indeed, the ordering of the social world through such processes is maintained by the dominant groups for whom the validation of the system is demonstrated through its reciprocity. For those who are 'vertically partitioned' and sit within the upper echelons of the 'individualising pyramid', its maintenance requires nothing more than a group of people who benefit from the 'legitimation of social hierarchies' (Foucault, 1977, p.152). Bourdieu asserts that this is because the 'cognitive and political symbolic struggles over knowledge and recognition' are inseparable and therefore people will accept the 'principles of social reality most favourable to his or her social being' (2000, p.87). In a school where girls' overarching achievement is above the national average, the complicity in maintaining the hierarchy would seem logical.

Habitus and the forms of capital

Bourdieu explains that 'academic capital' is the 'guaranteed product of the combined effects of cultural transmission by the family and cultural transmission by the school (the efficiency of which depends on the amount of cultural capital directly inherited from the family)' (1984, p.23). Therefore, those whose cultural capital has been appropriated through their home environment are in an advantageous educational position. The validation of inherited cultural capital by the education system is a contributory factor to the reproduction of social positions. As Bathmaker *et al.* affirm, the knowledge of how to 'play the game' forms part of the habitus, which means some students 'appear to have a more internalised or taken-for-granted orientation to the mobilisation of capitals' (2013, p.730). The difference in possession of capitals, Bourdieu argues, is what distinguishes the 'conditions of existence' between the different social classes:

> The primary differences, those which distinguish the major classes of conditions of existence, derive from the overall volume of capital, understood as the set of actually usable resources and powers-economic capital, cultural capital and also social capital.
>
> (1984, p.114)

Implementing a curriculum that has been created through a top-down approach is likely therefore to exacerbate rather than reduce inequalities as the curriculum reflects the values of the capitals inherent in ensuring the perpetuation of the existing order. Indeed, this is evidenced in the failure of different administrations to close the attainment gap at each key stage between children in receipt of free school meals and those who are not (DfE, 2013).

The projected attainment for each pupil in the case study school was determined in part by their prior attainment at Key Stage two (their test results on leaving primary education at the age of 11). This was nuanced by the school through judgements about the types of qualifications for which pupils were seen to be most suited; although the school offered vocational alternatives, these were not seen to be for all pupils. Staff at the school stated that they were trying to move away from the idea that vocational courses were the route for those pupils who were not as academically capable. However, it was evident this was a deeply ingrained perspective that would be difficult to change. Parental and teacher complicity in ensuring the 'appropriate route' was pursued appeared to be classed and gendered. This is where Bourdieu's concepts began to elucidate my findings as the social capital networks that the pupils discussed highlighted how aware the pupils were of their options and which were most favourable to their 'ways of being'.

Decision-making processes, habitus and the power of capitals

Although staff at the school played a key role in determining which study routes pupils considered, pupils also expressed their preferences for the options they thought would be most appropriate. Consistent with other research findings, my research indicated that decision-making influences were never isolated. For example, Winterton and Irwin (2012, p.859) note 'the significance of family educational backgrounds, parents' expectations, academic identity, school and institutional influences and friends and peer influences in the shaping of young people's expectations'. Furthermore, Greenbank and Hepworth demonstrate that pupils are knowledgeable about the advice available and use it as appropriate to them: 'Students make decisions about careers within a complex set of relationships or "networks" made up of parents, relatives, friends, professionals (i.e. teachers, lecturers and careers advisers) and other people they come into contact with' (2008, p.34). These networks represent forms of social capital that may be utilised in the career decision-making process. For instance, networks may be used to obtain information and advice; or they may provide access to job opportunities. The pupils at Greenlea Comprehensive demonstrated localised social capital networks were used to gather information that would help them make their choices:

> 'I have based my options on the career choice I have made. I have a family member who has experienced this career, therefore they have influenced me the most.'

'My brother is working in a garage and I'm interested in the job.'

'I listened to someone in the family that does a job in the area that I am interested in.'

(Survey responses)

The responses reflect what Ball and Vincent term 'hot-knowledge', that is, information gathered from '"the grapevine", a particular manifestation of social networks, and one which clearly arises from the private realm in order to address the public arena' (2005, p.378). Hot-knowledge comes from personal experience and local networks whereas 'cold-knowledge' is 'official' and 'constructed specifically for public dissemination' (2005, p.380). Meszaros *et al.* argue that young people, despite becoming more independent, 'continue to depend heavily on parents in the area of career development' (2009, p.392). This can be problematic when parents rely on their localised or 'hot-knowledge' to support their children. As Raty *et al.* (2006, p.5) noted, the advice parents give can indeed be stratified, their research indicated that: 'parental evaluation of school subjects contains elements of social distinctions in terms of social position and gender'. This was reflected by a member of the senior leadership team, who recognised that parental guidance was sometimes ill-informed:

> Some are very aware what's out there and maybe they're involved in it or other options or some who don't realise what the school offers or don't take an active part so they're very . . . not narrow-minded, that's the wrong term, but very . . . only see one direction. Or you see other parents that they left school at 16 and they're doing alright for themselves, so there's not that much importance on education.
>
> (Mr Brownlee, Head of Year)

The accepting of the familiar, or making choices because of their familiarity, is linked with Bourdieu's concept of habitus and field. Bourdieu believes that the habitus is what reproduces social positions: 'it adjusts itself to a probable future which it anticipates and helps to bring about because it reads it directly in the present of the presumed world' (1990b, p.64). This then leads choices to be made that incline 'agents to cut their coats according to their cloth, and so to become the accomplices of the processes that tend to make the probable a reality' (1990b, p.65). The influence of family friends or siblings demonstrated that social capital networks or a reliance on hot-knowledge can restrict choices to careers that are easily accessible or understood; this may result in positive outcomes for the pupils but it may also mean that certain choices are not considered. As Jenkins simplifies:

> Pupils whose familial socialisation bestows upon them the appropriate level of cultural capital – both more of it and the and the "right kind" – will necessarily achieve more academically than those whose relationship to the

cultural arbitrary is more distant. The habitus of the subordinated class(es) will, in generating an acceptance of the system's legitimacy, reinforce their disadvantage by inhibiting their demands for access to the higher reaches of education by defining it as not for the likes of us.

(2002, p.112)

Although there was impetus within the school to encourage pupils to consider progressing to university, it was also clear that decisions about pupil suitability to pursue certain courses were made by teaching staff. Indeed, the limitation placed on pupils' expected trajectories occurs on entry to the school in the form of their prior achievement. As there is a notable difference in attainment levels based on stratification, social-class differences can be perpetuated by the cap that limits pupils' learning on the basis of what is expected of them.

The responses from the pupils demonstrated the importance of capitals and reinforced the value of what it is to have ownership of them. This possession of capitals and its localised nature complies with Archer's work. In using Bourdieu's conceptual framework, Archer et al. (2007, p.167) demonstrate that 'social and educational inequalities are understood as contextually produced (within and across social fields) through interactions between the "habitus" and forms of resource or "capital" (economic, social, cultural and symbolic),' that is '[(habitus) (capital)] + field = practice' (Bourdieu,1984, p.101). Whereas the participants in Archer et al.'s research had capitals that were seen to be deficient in relation to what constituted educational value, the pupils who participated in my focus groups demonstrated that they had the 'the capital that is associated with scholarliness and academic achievement' (Archer et al., 2007, p.167).

Despite identifying several sources of information available to them in decision-making, the key person the girls turned to for guidance in the choices they made was their mother. One of the survey respondents indicated her trust in her mother's judgement of her ability:

> My mum influences me as I am very close to her and she helps me make decisions like this. She knows my ability so she gives me advice on what she thinks would be the best for me. She leads me in the right direction.

This clearly demonstrates how Bourdieu and Passeron's (1977) concept of social reproduction can ensue; particularly where inaccurate judgements are made about a pupil's capability. For example, Raty et al. state that 'parents' education relates to the trust they place on their child's educational potential' (2006, p.5). Social reproduction could be further compounded when a pupil has limited access to other sources of advice. Reay writes that 'the skills and competencies developed both inside and outside of the labour market generate powerful reproductive tendencies that shape the relationship between class groupings and education' (2005, p.112). This relationship between the reproductive nature of familial advice for future opportunities was reflected in my research findings:

Because I've got like family that have maybe done some of the things that I'd quite like to do, so they can help me. So if I pick a subject I know that I've got help for that subject from my family. I've picked the subject because I like it, but I know that like I've got family that can help me.

(Year 9 respondent, focus group)

Family was also discussed as a motivating factor with girls making reference to 'making my parents proud', which sometimes was associated with competition in relation to other family members. Where siblings or cousins had been to university or taken a certain subject, some pupils felt it was their responsibility to 'keep up' with their relatives. This supports the notion of a 'familial habitus', which Reay *et al.* refer to as 'the deeply ingrained systems of perspectives, experiences and predispositions family members share' (2005, p.61). Zara, a Year 13 pupil, indicated that this desire to do well educationally was linked to a family expectation that children should do better than their parents had. These comments seemed to reflect Bourdieu's belief that habitus can indeed be practically transformed: 'a fraction of the class will deviate from the trajectory most common for the class as a whole and follow the (higher or lower) trajectory which was most probable for members of another class' (1984, p.111). For Zara this was achieved in part by a change in circumstances and associated capital accumulation:

I think because those two (my parents), because we were in quite a lot of poverty when I was younger, I mean serious poverty, that I think they don't want me to go through that, the same and now we've climbed up the ladder a bit, they don't want me to start off like they did basically.

(Zara, Year 13)

Zara's story demonstrated that her parents valued education, studying at night school to improve their own prospects and in order to move to what Zara identified as a 'better area'. Family was also an indirect influence in that they motivated pupils 'not to be like them'; there was also discussion about 'going to university' as an achievement to make family members proud. These discussions were linked with social class background; for example, Penelope, a Year 13 student when I first interviewed her, sent me a Facebook message having completed her first year at university. She explained:

Without sounding like a sob story, I have been aware of the struggles involved with raising a family and paying bills since I can remember and I have hope that I can change the course of my life. This is what makes me do things I might be wary of, such as, taking the step to go to university and move into halls.

(Penelope, sent as first year undergraduate).

A number of the pupils fell into the 'first generation HE applicant' category (a target group identified by the Sutton Trust). Rather than feeling 'disadvantaged' at being the first in the family to go to higher education, the pupils in the focus group discussed how it took the pressure off them in relation to their hopes for the future as they did not feel a burden of expectation from their family. These girls were independent and knowledgeable; they had already shown a commitment to their learning by opting to attend what they thought was a prestigious sixth-form rather than progressing to a local 'college that was less academic'. Were they not as knowledgeable about the potential routes that they could pursue, the girls could have been inclined to pursue options that were known to them in their immediate sphere of influence. The expanded higher education system, although still stratified, may have contributed to what Bourdieu (1977, p.78) terms a 'different mode of generation'. The girls' expectations demonstrate the change in the 'conditions of existence' between generations in relation to educational opportunity and in particular what is deemed to be 'impossible, possible and probable'. Nonetheless, higher education is not an opportunity that can be deemed as 'probable', and the structural factors the girls discuss indicate it is a possibility that requires planning and careful consideration.

Within our discussion, university application was something the girls casually mentioned, although it was clearly a topic with which they were preoccupied. The girls' discussion indicated that they understood there was a need to demonstrate more than academic success in order to gain a place at university. They felt that they had the academic capital required to progress to higher education but they were acutely aware that they would need to fabricate the cultural capital the UCAS application form would require them to demonstrate. Although the girls understood educational capital was not enough for them to 'play the game', their ideas about what could enable them to secure a place demonstrated that they were not entirely aware of what was valued. Knowing how to 'play the game', or understanding the illusio, is important when the other forms of capital could be considered as deficient in relation to the dominant academic discourse; however, this too requires an understanding of what is valued. The girls stated that they had no 'noteworthy' credentials, and they were clearly aware that this was something required and therefore were attempting to 'play the game'. This supports Bathmaker *et al.*'s findings, which suggest that 'some middle-class students have an internalised understanding of the game and play it well without actively considering the mechanisms of their own operations while others operate in a more intentional way' (2013, p.730). The girls within my focus group knew the system was flawed in that it only viewed certain activities as 'noteworthy', but they were prepared to 'imitate' what was required for the purposes of the UCAS personal statement in an 'intentional' way, because they maintained a 'belief in the absolute value of the stake (a university place) and therefore concealed a collusion which reproduced the illusio' (Bourdieu, 1984, p.250):

CHARLOTTE: And personal statements, three weeks today our first draft has ... got to be in.
NATALIE: What?

CHARLOTTE: That's what Mrs Kay says.
KATIE: Oh gosh.
NATALIE: I don't know what I want to do. I've got no hobbies, I've got no life.
CHARLOTTE: Yeah, you need to have a load of extracurricular activities, I don't do anything. I've got no hobbies.
KATIE: I'm going to say I do volleyball, badminton and ice-skating.
NATALIE: I might just like start a canoeing club and just go canoeing for a day and then I can say I've done it.
CHARLOTTE: Once I've finished school I don't want to go home and have to learn some other skill, I just want to go and watch telly and let my brain just go numb.
NATALIE: Could you imagine though if you had all these like extra-curriculums after sixth form, I think I'd like drive myself into a grave.
KATIE: I put on my CV that I do ice-skating lessons and it's still not got me a job! . . . a pro or something and I do all this and I write my own articles and they're still not accepting me.
CHARLOTTE: I've got no credit worthy like background really.
KATIE: I don't think I've even got time for a job at the moment.
NATALIE: I have, I'm hoping that might wangle me into uni having a job now, I've got nowt (*sic*) else to write on my personal statement.

The discussion demonstrated that there was a superficial understanding of what a university application should include and also that they knew they did not possess the experiences that would be looked upon favourably. The girls clearly understood there was a game to be played and they joked about fabricating experiences or extra-curricular activities they felt would be viewed in a positive light. Even were they to do so, these fabricated experiences would not necessarily reflect the internalised understandings highlighted by Bathmaker *et al.* (2014), in part because their view of what would be valued was not necessarily congruent with the requirements of a university. Charlotte wrote a personal statement and although she claimed to have no 'credit worthy' background she began a BA in Politics and Sociology at a Russell Group University the following September. Charlotte's academic success and her ability to 'play the game' in an intentional way enabled her to achieve what was required. However, the application process is an example of how the judgement of capitals can be used to 'reinforce the power relations which constitute the structure of the social space' (Bourdieu,1990a, p.135). The acceptance of this process as a legitimate way to determine who will be capable of achieving educational success misrecognises those who do not possess the required capitals or who do not understand how to play the game.

University as the only valued option

Of particular concern to the participants was the feeling that even if they had made a choice it may not be viewed as 'the right choice', or indeed that it would be viewed as inferior by society as well as by teachers. Byrom and Lightfoot discuss how the massification of higher education has resulted in those who choose not to progress to university as being 'othered' or 'discursively constructed as abnormal' (2013, p.817). The discussions about applications to university highlighted these factors further; inevitably more so by sixth-formers who demonstrated some anger at the situation. There were a number of discussions that indicated students were planning to go to university because they did not feel there was a viable or respected alternative; or at least not one that had been discussed with them. Simultaneously, the emphasis on A-levels and higher education as the esteemed option reinforced the lack of parity between vocational and academic qualifications; the distinction and hierarchies of knowledge was an issue that emerged in the focus group findings frequently. At Greenlea Comprehensive, the girls in the study felt that the over-emphasis on progression to university placed all other choices in a deficit position, and indeed if they did not go to university they would feel regret:

> I think you put pressure on yourself more than like anywhere else, because you get told about it all the time that you end up, part of you, that you think, "Oh I've got to go to university," and if I don't then I'm not doing well and I don't know, it's like I feel like I'm missing out if I don't go to uni.
> (Year 11, Focus Group respondent)

Pupil responses demonstrated that there is a perceived status attached to A-levels as being appropriate for those pupils who are 'clever'. Therefore the emphasis to continue in education may have been targeted at those who were seen as 'likely candidates' for A-level and then university. A discussion of these routes with a member of the senior leadership team demonstrated that the school valued the partnership with a local college that gave pupils the option of studying vocational courses one day per week but that once pupils were on their 'pathway', be it vocational or academic, their future was then seen to continue along either of these routes. One teacher discussed this as a pupil responsibility, that they often maintained this route because it felt familiar and comfortable. This reflects Bourdieu's concept of social reproduction, which is in part related to the habitus whereby 'conditions of existence which, in imposing different definitions of the impossible, the possible and the probable, cause one group to experience as natural or reasonable practices or aspirations which another group finds unthinkable or scandalous, and vice versa' (1977, p.78). The links with familial advice on career routes reflected both social reproduction and the associated use of social capital networks.

As with the undergraduates in the Paired Peers research, pupils at Greenlea Comprehensive school showed similar knowledge of 'how to play the game': 'certain students ensure their advantage through the development of capitals and put themselves in the best position to win the game' (Bathmaker et al., 2013, p.730). Advice had been sought from a variety of sources, but one pupil demonstrated the importance to her in personally seeking out how she could meet the requirements of the institution to which she intended to apply:

> University prospectuses will provide the most information for subjects to choose for our course! School try . . . but with so many students sometimes you're better being independent and finding out for yourself. I want to do Law at (local pre-1992 institution) and currently have a conditional offer. For my choices I looked at what the universities look for subject wise and what will help me at uni. That's the best advice I could give anyone!
> (Year 13, survey respondent)

Where pupils did not have the information they required, they were advised by the school to seek out this information from other sources. The lack of capitals that some students have in relation to knowing about the career options and associated routes to get there means that they rely on their academic capital acquired through the school to research their options independently. Byrom and Lightfoot (2013, p.817) describe this as the 'emerging secondary habitus' that has been inculcated through their school rather than home experiences.

> I don't know anyone else who's done the course that I'm doing or anything similar and in class they're not really focussing on helping you with the decisions of uni, they're focussing on getting you to pass A-Level, so no one really talks about it, except for them to say, 'Go and look at uni, go and see what courses they do,' so I just did that. Just went on websites and things, because it was sort of left up to you to read about things and decide whether you'd like it and could do it. It took me a long time to find a course that I thought would be suitable to me, tried to find one with no exams, which I did.
> (Penelope Cash, Year 13, interview)

The school perspective on advice was that all Year 11 pupils undertake an interview to discuss their post-16 options, and the intention was to start guidance earlier. However, the influence of the family in educational choices demonstrated how pupils were able to use different forms of capital in order to gather an understanding about the subject area or the career options associated with those choices. The combination of advice available to young people whether about university or other post-16 options, from informed sources or anecdotal conversations, appears always to be partial. The idea then that pupils can make rational decisions is flawed from the outset because the premise of the decision may be based on inaccurate or prejudiced advice. The pupils recognise this and some seek solutions by undertaking the research they feel is required to inform their decisions. However, for others there is an apparent frustration in being guided into routes they feel duty bound to pursue regardless of whether or not it will help them achieve the future to which they aspire.

Economic capital

Three of the participants in the sixth-form focus group, who had identified themselves as working class, discussed the importance of having paid employment as they did not have the economic capital to go to university without this reassurance. Katie indicated that she was thinking strategically about undertaking work that would enable her to progress through university that would allow her an alternative career if she did not reach her educational goals. Although this showed thoughtfulness, it also demonstrated the lack of confidence and uncertainties about university, perhaps reflecting her unfamiliarity with the 'field' of higher education and her fear of debt. The fear of debt was something Charlotte felt could be compounded if the wrong decision was made:

> I don't know whether to go to university, I want to go, but I don't know what I want to do, because I don't know what I want to be when I'm older. So I don't know if I want to get the debt.
>
> (Charlotte, Year 12)

Although Charlotte discussed taking a year out to work, she completed her A-levels and was successful in her application to a Russell Group university. Katie's solution was to have a 'back-up' in case she was unsuccessful in her academic studies; she stated:

> I want to get trained in something else if all else fails, like nails or something it's a one day course that I can do it. I just want to earn because I just feel like if, going to uni with no money, I just feel like I can't go.

In the same way that Davies' research found girls' talk demonstrated that 'girls' discussions tended to prioritise rapport and a sense of group solidarity'(2005, p.214), Katie's peers did not question her 'back-up'; rather, they demonstrated that they too would need to earn before or alongside studying at university. The issue of financial security also arose in the survey responses where pupils stated that this is what they hoped for in the future:

> Secure job being able to pay off any debt. Family life. No worries financially. In a stable, well earning career.

The concern with financial issues perhaps reflected the age of austerity in which these pupils were considering their futures and therefore practical matters were of as much importance as specific aspirations. For some pupils, particularly those who had identified themselves as working class, there was a measured discussion of the potential benefits and problems of progressing to university. However, for other pupils there was no choice other than university worth considering. Baker found that for some young women, university was an 'inevitable path' that was a 'natural progression for them, unquestioned and normalised' (2010, p.7).

This is supported by Bradley *et al.*, whose typologies of decision making include the 'taken for granted pathway: going to university is seen as normal, majority in family has a degree, siblings are already at university, most people at school are going' (2013, p.3). Although progression to university for some pupils was seen to be 'taken for granted', it was not always associated with having prior familial experience of higher education. There were several pupils who wanted to create a 'better future' for themselves; this was positioned by what they felt their parents had achieved:

> I think I've got a couple of friends that are only going because of their parents, but I've also got a lot of friends that are going just because, I think it's a trend, I don't know, I think it's becoming a trend anyway, more than, 'Oh I'll go because I want this sort of job,' whereas I'm going because I definitely want a better future than what my parents had.'
>
> (Zara, Year 13)

This desire for upward social mobility, 'Where I want to be, and hopefully higher up' (survey respondent), was seen to be achievable through education.

The findings concur with other research that suggests a multitude of influences contribute to pupils making a choice about their progression to university. As concluded by Bornholt *et al.*, a better understanding of choice behaviour illuminates that a 'general model of personal and social factors explains diverse pathways to higher education' (2004, p.226). This supports the socio-ecological approach to choice behaviours that integrates these decisions in circumstances, not necessarily of the students' choosing, which support and constrain realisation of student aspirations. This too is relatable to Bourdieu's assertion that demonstrates the constraints of self-expectation that can be associated with socio-economic circumstances.

Conclusion

Bourdieu's concepts helped me to think about how the research participants' expectations and experiences were intertwined. Their social capital networks or who they knew was a crucial part in information gathering about the choices they perceived to be possible. The success many of the girls achieved at Greenlea Comprehensive can be associated with their understanding of how to 'play the game'. They understood that they needed to develop themselves in relation to their studies as well as their extra-curricular activities or cultural capital. This transcended the academic and vocational pathways and the participants on both routes saw the value of undertaking related activities that would enhance their understanding of their intended post-16 pathways. I was concerned that there was evidence that the reliance on social capital networks meant there was a disparity in the quality and types of information advice and guidance (IAG) the girls received. The reliance on the mother as a source of advice clearly demonstrated the potential for social reproduction. The social capital networks the pupils had meant that for some pupils considerations about their future career paths were limited to 'what was known' by those within their immediate social networks; these networks were often localised to family and family friends. The influence of the school was seen to be of secondary importance to pupils who valued maternal advice above all other sources of information. These findings reflect Ball and Vincent's (2005) concept of 'hot-knowledge' accrued from informal networks and the less-valued 'cold-knowledge' that comes from official sources. The links therefore between habitus and field and in particular the social, cultural and economic capitals that the girls possess played an important role both in how they perceived their futures and the choices that they made – yet they did not always determine their futures. As Hodkinson found, there is a 'reflexive relationship between positions, dispositions, practices and relations' (1998, p.102). The pupils in my research study demonstrated that there was likelihood towards social reproduction associated with social capital networks in choice making and the levels of cultural capital they possessed, but that there was also a counter argument whereby the research participants demonstrated reflexivity and an understanding of the rules of the game and therefore used this knowledge to deliberately work against what may have been predicted for them.

My research has demonstrated that the 'successful girl' label needs to be understood in relation to the socio-economic context of the school. Where the field of the local community reflects the aspirations of the educational institution the school is able to employ techniques that mould the 'docile bodies' of its pupils and inculcate a scholarly habitus. The school accepts its responsibility through doing what it feels is necessary for pupils to achieve the levels of progress as defined by Ofsted; this in turn ensures that the school maintains its pedagogic authority. In a school where many pupils perceive their futures involving application to university, it appeared that specific individual advice needed to be tailored more carefully. Individual guidance was seen to be provided at too late a stage and some pupils felt they lacked the advice they needed. This is of concern particularly in relation to the likelihood of social reproduction given that the pupils' main source of advice was their mother.

Educational success requires an acceptance of the rules of the game and therefore pupils can perpetuate the symbolically violent practices without realising their complicity or because they do not perceive an alternative. The sixth-form girls at Greenlea Comprehensive acknowledged the need to construct a UCAS personal statement that reflected more than academic success and they colluded in this process so they could stay in the game. This ultimately 'reproduced the illusio' (Bourdieu, 1984, p.250).

As Bourdieu (1998, p.21) argues, 'familiarity prevents us from seeing everything that is concealed in the apparently purely technical acts achieved by the school institution'. The familiarity with tests, target grades and expected achievement formed part of the girls' scholarly habitus, which enabled them to participate in the practice of occupying a 'good pupil' subject position.

Using Bourdieu's concepts enabled me to question the practices of the school and education policy more broadly. They helped me to think about the wider societal issues that mean education alone cannot negate inequality. The value of the stake needs to be seen by the pupils as either possible or probable in order for them to want to play the game, otherwise its practices are experienced as symbolically violent.

Note

1 Ofsted is the government's education inspectorate.

References

Allen, K. 2013. Aspiration as a cruel attachment? Young people's futures and vocabularies of inequality in an age of austerity. 5 November. *Troubling Youth Transitions*. [Online] [Accessed 26 April 2014] Available from: http://troublingyouthtransitions.word press.com/2013/11/05/aspiration-as-a-cruel-attachment-young-peoples-futures-and-vocabularies-of-inequality-in-an-age-of-austerity.
Archer, L., Hollingworth, S. and Halsall, A. 2007. 'University's not for me – I'm a Nike person': urban, working-class young people's negotiations of 'style', identity and educational engagement. *Sociology*. **41**(2), pp.219–237.
Baker, J. 2010. Great expectations and Post-feminist accountability: young women living up to the 'successful girls' discourse. *Gender and Education*. **22**(1), pp.1–15.
Ball, S. J. and Vincent, C. 1998. 'I heard it on the grapevine': 'hot' knowledge and school choice. *British Journal of Sociology of Education*. **19**(3), pp.377–400.
Bathmaker, A-M., Ingram, N. and Waller, R. 2013. Higher education, social class and the mobilisation of capitals: recognising and playing the game. *British Journal of Sociology of Education*. **34**(5–6), pp.723–743.
Bornholt. L., Gientzotis, J. and Cooney, G. 2004. Understanding choice behaviours: pathways from school to university with changing aspirations and opportunities. *Social Psychology of Education*. **7**(2), pp.211–228.
Bourdieu, P. 1977. *Outline of a Theory of Practice*. Cambridge: Cambridge University Press.
Bourdieu, P. 1984. *Distinction: A Social Critique of the Judgement of Taste*. London: Routledge.
Bourdieu, P. 1986. The forms of capital. In: Richardson, J. (ed.) *Handbook of Theory and Research for the Sociology of Education*. New York: Greenwood, pp.241–261.
Bourdieu, P. 1990a. *In Other Words: Essays toward a Reflective Sociology*. Stanford, CA: Stanford University Press.
Bourdieu, P. 1990b. *The Logic of Practice*. Cambridge: Polity Press.
Bourdieu, P. 1998. *Practical Reason: On the Theory of Action*. Cambridge: Polity.
Bourdieu P. 2000. *Pascalian Meditations*. Stanford, CA: Stanford University Press
Bourdieu, P. and Passeron, J-C. 1977. *Social Reproduction in Education, Society and Culture*. London: Sage.
Bourdieu, P. and Wacquant, L. 1992. *An Invitation to Reflexive Sociology*. Oxford: Polity.
Bradley, H., Abrahams, J., Bathmaker, A.-M., Beedell, P., Hoare, T., Ingram, N., Mellor, J. and Waller, R. 2013. A degree generation? The Paired Peers Project year 3 report.

[Online] [Accessed 26 April 2014] Available from: www.bristol.ac.uk/spais/research/paired-peer//s/report/spais/research/paired-peers/documents/report.pdf

Butin, D,W. 2006. Putting Foucault to work in educational research. *Journal of Philosophy of Education.* **40**(3), pp.371–380.

Byrom, T. and Lightfoot, N. 2013. Interrupted trajectories: the impact of academic failures on the student mobility of working-class students. *British Journal of Sociology of Education*, **34**(5), pp.812–828.

Davies, J. 2005. 'We know what we're talking about, don't we?' An examination of girls' classroom-based learning allegiances. *Linguistics and Education.* **15**(3), pp.199–216.

Deer, C. 2008. Doxa. In: Grenfell, M. *Bourdieu: key concepts.* London: Acumen, pp.119–130.

DfE (Department for Education) 2013. *First Statistical Release GCSE and Equivalent Results in England 2012/13 (provisional).* [Online] [Accessed on 25 May 2015] Available from https://www.gov.uk/government/uploads/system/uploads/attachment_data/file/251184/SFR40_2013_FINALv2.pdf

Foucault, M. 1977. (English Translation) *Discipline and Punish: the Birth of the Prison.* New York: Random House.

Hodkinson, P. 1998. Career Decision Making. In: Grenfell, M. and James, D. (eds) *Bourdieu and Education: Acts of Practical Theory.* London: Falmer Press, pp.89–103.

Greenbank, P. and Hepworth, S. 2008. *Working Class Students and the Career Decision Making Process: A Qualitative Study.* Manchester, HECSU.

Jenkins, R. 2002. *Pierre Bourdieu: Key Sociologists.* Abingdon, UK: Routledge.

McRobbie, A. 2009. *The Aftermath of Feminism: Gender, Culture and Social Change.* London: Sage.

May, T 2011. *Issues in Social Research* (4th edn). Buckingham, UK: Open University Press.

Meszaros, P.S., Creamer, E. and Lee, S. 2009. Understanding the role of parental support for it career decision making using the theory of self-authorship. *International Journal of Consumer Studies.* **33**, pp.392–395.

Pomerantz, S., Raby, R. and Stefanik, A. 2013. Girls run the world? Caught between sexism and post feminism in school. *Gender and Society.* **27**, pp.777–798.

Raty, H., Kasanen, K. and Karkkainen, R. 2006. School subjects as social categorisations. *Social Psychology of Education.* **9**, pp.5–25.

Reay, D. 1998. *Class Work: Mothers' Involvement in Children's Schooling.* London: University College Press.

Reay, D. 2004. 'It's all becoming a habitus': beyond the habitual use of Pierre Bourdieu's concept of habitus in educational research. *Special Issue of British Journal of Sociology of Education on Pierre Bourdieu.* **25**(4), pp.431–444.

Reay, D. 2005. Doing the dirty work of social class? Mothers' work in support of their children's schooling. In: Glucksmann, M., Pettinger, L. and West, J. (eds) *A New Sociology of Work.* Oxford: Blackwells, pp.104–116.

Reay, D., David, M.E. and Ball, S.J. 2005. *Degrees of Choice.* Stoke-on-Trent, UK: Trentham Books.

Shain, F. 2013. 'The girl effect': exploring narratives of gendered impacts and opportunities in neoliberal development. *Sociological Research Online.* **18**(2).

Winterton, M.T. and Irwin, S. 2012. Teenage expectations of going to university: the ebb and flow of influences from 14 to 18. *Journal of Youth Studies.* **15**(7), pp.858–874.

Chapter 6

Using Bourdieusian scholarship to understand the body

Habitus, hexis and embodied cultural capital

Lindsey Garratt

In 2008 I walked into my first fieldwork site. I had begun my doctoral work two months previously as part of a larger project called the Trinity Immigration Initiative [TII], whose remit was to examine immigration to the Republic of Ireland [hereafter Ireland]. TII had six work package streams and my work came under the project focusing on children, youth and community relations, the aim of which was to gain a child-centred perspective of how children, aged seven to 12 years, experienced diversity. We chose to examine these dynamics within seven primary schools in Dublin's North inner city, as this locality is historically the poorest part of the city and of the state and had seen a sharp rise in immigration in the previous 10 years (Curry *et al.*, 2011). Taking a grounded research approach (Glaser & Strauss, 2008 [1967]) we gathered data from seven schools over a six-month period interviewing 343 children, 10 teachers and gathering hundreds of hours of observation. From this dataset I focused on the experiences of the youngest boys from seven to nine years of age and completed a second round of fieldwork with one class group a year after the initial data collection period.

The beginning of fieldwork is always a nervous but exciting time, and this feeling was compounded by conducting fieldwork in primary schools. One's first encounter with a school playground, as a fieldwork site, is an intense sensory experience. Beyond being exposed to the January elements the collective voice of hundreds of children shouting, laughing, crying, calling, praising and chastising each other is at once a collection of individual voices but also a singular roar. Immersed on all sides by sound the researcher must also watch their step or risk wandering into a game of football, block a chaser as they tear after their target and when trying to retreat to a quiet corner disturb a small group who have gathered to be in each other's confidence. At this point it is easy to fall into the trap that this collective is the perfect example of how the adult world should follow the example of children and leave divisions behind. But one is not yet sensitised to the invisible boundaries at play *in* play. Far from an equitable paradise this is a world of status, reputation, speculation and fluctuating friendship circles, where racism is woven within encounters and peer interactions (Curry *et al.*, 2011).

These initial sensory impressions have some value though, as they emphasise how physical and embodied children's worlds are. The body soon came to be central to my study of racism and masculinities. I contend elsewhere that the body is both an object of value, which is assessed and denigrated, but also the site of habitual processes of misrecognition and apperception, which sustains but also disguises racism (Garratt, 2012; forthcoming – a). In my analysis, young boys' evaluation of each other was rooted within habitual schemas of perception based on racist and gendered conceptions of whom can be said to 'authentically' enact locally-validated notions of hegemonic masculinity (Garratt, forthcoming – b). To make this argument I have drawn on the work of Pierre Bourdieu, specifically the concepts of habitus, the bodily hexis of habitus and Bourdieu's philosophical influences within phenomenology. Bourdieu (1990a) pays considerable attention to how the body is moulded by society and read as a sign within symbolic systems. In a Bourdieusian approach the body plays a significant role in signifying one's status and belonging within fields; it is therefore a form of capital and especially a form of cultural capital, as one's deportment, demeanour, accent and tastes in adornment are linked to one's social origins and experiences. I focus specifically on the body as a site of value but this connects with the arguments made by Wallace in his Chapter (4) on Black cultural capital, which is arguably a form of cultural capital that is founded on embodiment. For Bourdieu (1990a) these schemas of the body are the hexis of habitus; one's accumulated matrix of perceptions and dispositions. In my research, the way in which young boys' bodies were shaped through hexis and the appearance of their phenomenological bodies had considerable symbolic exchange value within their field of play (Garratt, 2012). Moreover, the way in which peers judged each other was rooted within somatic schemas of perception inculcated in their habitus. Hence, Bourdieu's (1990a) work gave me the framework to understand the role of the body as both an object that is perceived but also as the medium of this perception. I will consider the concepts of hexis, embodied cultural capital and the body as the medium of perception in the second half of this chapter, but the path to conceptualising my findings in this manner and engaging with these concepts was not a direct one.

While I had some previous exposure to Bourdieu's work, due to the grounded method of this project, I opted to review the vast immigration and racism literature after the first round of data collection, as this work initially appeared to have analysed the body in depth. However, within the review process I soon came up against a central problem; namely, the body seemed to be brought back into theorisation simply to eradicate it further. Action did not happen through the body, but rather in spite of it as something to be overcome rather than the seat of practice. When comparing this literature to the data, it did not chime with my observations. In light of this, the aim of this chapter is to lead the reader through some of the main perspectives of the body in the racialisation and gender theories to argue these perspectives are underpinned by existentialism and Cartesian dualism that thwarts the researcher's ability to meaningfully analyse the body. I will finish this chapter by contending that Bourdieu's work and his influences within phenomenology provide a more fruitful way to recast the body as central to practice by providing the tools to unpick the tight interweaving of racism from perception.

Hence this chapter is designed, not as an exhaustive account of how Bourdieu theorises the body,[1] but rather to argue for the greater analytic ability of a Bourdieusian approach in contrast to the dominant discursive perspective that prevails within the fields of racial and ethnic studies, especially in relation to gender.

Racialisation

Contemporary biology no longer uses the concept of 'race' and within the social sciences a significant corpus of work argues human characteristics or phenotypes are only given meaning through a process of racialisation. While there is tension in the consistency of meaning and use of the term 'racialization' (Barot & Bird, 2001), Murji and Solomos argue it has become 'a core concept in the analysis of racial phenomena, particularly to signal the processes by which ideas about "race" are constructed, come to be regarded as meaningful, and are acted upon' (2005, p.1). Back and Solomos argue the concept has been fundamental in moving the debate beyond the ontological certainty of 'race' to perhaps the more important question of 'why certain racialised subjectivities become a feature of social relations at particular points in time and in particular geographical spaces?' (2000, p.20). To engage with this question, many authors have drawn on the work of Foucault (1975), especially his concepts of governmentality and bio-power. Foucault argues that once discursive categories of normality are developed, its antonym is created; the deviant, pervert, hysteric and psychotic are formed. State racism in this context is understood as the elimination of the so-called 'deviant', whether 'deviant' people or behaviour, as a threat to the vitality of the nation. It is a 'racism that a society will practice on itself, against its own elements, against its own products: it is an internal racism ... that of constant purification ... one of the fundamental dimensions of social normalisation' (1978, p.55). 'Rationality'[2] in this context is analysed not as a way to undermine racism but as a causal factor in its development and protraction. A number of theorists have analysed the connection between modernity and racism. Goldberg (1994) argues modernity shifted the conceptual order to regard people as 'rational individuals' rather than the subjects of God, and where there is a rational agent there is an irrational one, a rational society an irrational one, both of which have generally been understood as pre-modern and largely non-Western (Said, 1995 [1978]). Indeed, Hall (1997) contends the classification of people in this way has generally lead to the reduction of the cultures of 'black' peoples to nature, through essentialising seemingly 'natural' characteristics, such as irrationality, idleness and immaturity. In this context a rational state must protect itself from the 'irrational' both internally and externally through immigration.

There is little doubt this is a powerful theoretical position linked to a framework with strong explanatory power. Indeed, in my data, countries other than Ireland were often categorised as pre-modern and inferior. The bodies of migrant origin boys, especially those of African and South Asian origin, were also victims of debasing rumours and jokes that served to position the majority group as superior in comparison (Garratt, 2012). However, while the racialisation literature has importantly highlighted how the linguistic semiotic convention creates deviance and designates 'others', this argument is made purely through an abstracted discussion of language and labelling. Here the analytic value of the body is simply through its discursive categorisation. *Why* the body is judged is addressed, but not *how*; how is judgement operationalised and what do categorises mean for the individuals in practice? From a Bourdieusian perspective, our practice is rooted within our habitus, which is the inherited, embodied, predisposed but also adaptable ways individuals have of reading, understanding and interpreting the fields and societies in which they live (see the introductory chapter of this book for further elaboration of Bourdieu's theory of practice). While Bourdieu (2000) also puts considerable importance on how people are judged for their bodies, in his analysis this is linked to the wider system of capital accumulation in which a person's habitus is enacted through somatisation. The concept of bodily hexis focuses on how the body is not a fixed entity but is partially constructed by the medium of the habitus. Within a discursive approach this analysis is precluded, as a distinction is made between the self and one's body, which is a legacy of the existential philosophical tradition in which it is rooted (Sartre, 1969).

Philosophy and the body

For existentialism the body is understood as a natural and conservative force, which must be risen above in order to achieve enlightenment (De Beauvoir, 1972 [1946]). In this tradition the body is subordinated to the mind and reduced to a vessel to contain the self or, as many critics argue, it is treated as a machine to house the ghost of the mind or spirit (Ryle, 1949). This metaphor is commonly used to describe the Cartesian perspective, the generally accepted root of mind/body duality. In *Mediations*, first published in 1641, Descartes searches for a point of certainty on which scholarship can build from. After doubting everything in the external world including the existence of his body, he decides he cannot doubt that he is always thinking, thus his famous dictum 'cogito ergo sum', 'I think therefore I am' (Sorell, 2000). If the body can be doubted but not the mind, and still be, the essence of who he is must be located in a disembodied mind. Recent empirical literature within whiteness studies and some work within masculinities questions if disembodiment in a pure sense is possible. A growing body of work has argued structurally dominant groups gain much of their status through being defined as disembodied, but this is in fact an embodied identity, as 'rationality' is only maintained as long as one can embody certain, often classed, demeanours (Hughey, 2010; Vincent, 2006), or in Bourdieu's (1990a) terms, have an appropriate bodily hexis with a high exchange value within fields. A disembodied identity, then, is not due to anyone rising above their body; rather, it is facilitated by somatisation but remains hidden from public consciousness. The impact of this finding, that 'disembodiment' is only facilitated through embodiment, has had very little impact within the wider canon of literature in comparison to the legacy of Cartesian thought, especially within gender studies.

Gender and the body

In my work I contend racism and hegemonic masculinities mutually construct each other, but the former is obscured by the latter through habitual schemas of perception that prevents racist behaviour being labelled as such by both perpetrator and victim (Garratt, 2012). Marginalisation of minority boys tended to be dismissed with the platitude that 'boys will be boys', an assumption that all bullying was somehow equal opportunities even though migrant origin boys were persistently picked on for their appearance and for how they used their bodies in sports and games over and above those from the majority group. This ridicule was particularly painful for them, as has been observed by many commentators; to be overtly linked to the body is to be feminised, as in many respects the flesh in contemporary society is female and an identity associated with the body feminine (Grosz, 1994).

Within the wider gender studies literature, the attempt to understand the body has created considerable tension, which has been fundamental to the field's development. Early work focused on detaching the idea of 'sex roles' from nature and the body. To achieve this, early theorists accepted a duality between mind and body. For instance, De Beauvoir (1972) argued that biological bodily differences exist but have no relevance, as they derive their meaning from larger society and the cultures men and women live in. However, this neat sex/gender division began to be revised largely through the work of three distinct areas of feminism; materialist, ethnomethodological and poststructuralist, who argued from divergent perspectives that the sex/gender distinction had not gone far enough, as biological 'sex' had largely been ignored and existed simply as a 'natural base' onto which gender is painted (Kessler & McKenna, 1978). The body came back into the debate, but as a target for further deconstruction and as a foil for analysis of agency and structure.

It is on this point of agency that Butler (1990) based her work *Gender Trouble*. Butler argues that bodies 'cannot be said to have a significant existence prior to the mark of their gender' (1990, p.8). For her, sex, sexuality and gender are brought into existence through action and she uses Derrida's concept of iteration as evidence that social norms are inherently unstable and repetition a sign of 'constitutive instability' (Stoller, 2009). However, her reiterative performative agency can only succeed if an ontological core to gender located in the body can be dismantled. To do this she focuses her analysis on heterosexual hegemony and draws on Foucault's (1978) work on sexuality to contend that gender is not created by sex but is discursive and constructed through gender. For Chambers (2007), however, Butler's heavy reliance on Foucault ultimately undoes her argument. He highlights that Butler misreads Foucault's work as he does not argue 'sex does not exist' but rather contends that 'sex in itself' does not exist; causality reasoning cannot be established, as if sex in itself cannot exist neither can desire nor gender. Therefore, one cannot be the spark point of another, but all must exist together.

Ultimately then this thesis is inconsistent in its theorisation of the body, as its narrow focus on sexuality relies on a causality argument that cannot be sustained. Furthermore, this limited focus on sexuality in relation to the body reveals a paradox in this work and the wider empirical research, as there is an attempt to deconstruct the body through biological sex and sexuality but this is done through a subordination of the body to linguistic abstraction (Tyler, 1991; Benhabib, 1995a; 1995b; Fraser, 1995; Rottenberg, 2003). Hence, while this corpus of work is successful in showing structural indeterminacy, instead of bringing the body back into analysis this literature appears to have subjugated it more. These approaches critique the use of embodiment to 'other' certain populations; however, they implicitly support a rationalised perspective of the world as they only see embodiment as inhibiting. Hence, rationality, which elsewhere has been heavily critiqued as the origin of racism, is implicitly reproduced by the very tools of this dissection. Indeed, what if we see the body not as an impediment to who we are, something to be transcended in order to achieve enlightenment or to achieve equality, but rather a fundamental aspect of ourselves?

My observation of the school playground and what I have termed the 'child world'[3] of the school made it clear that identity was firmly rooted within the body. Not only was the body used by children to designate insiders from outsiders, friends from strangers, it imbued all aspects of their exchanges. Young boys described in detail the physicality required to interact with their peers; they compared the growth, shape and skill of their bodies to each other to determine their 'boyishness'. Moreover, I found the ease with which they could move within the field, feel comfortable playing sports, games and move through their local area (or where perceived by their peers as comfortable) had a big impact on their status within their class group (Garratt, 2012). When I did my initial review of the literature I found the work detailed could not take into account these practices. So I went in search of an approach through which it was possible to consider agency, not through the transcendence of the body, but as a capacity of it.

Beyond dualism: habit and habitus

While the theoretical perspectives of gender studies and racialisation are largely underpinned by an existentialist perspective, Bourdieu's work is rooted in phenomenology, which seeks to analyse how the subjective consciousness is structured by its relationship to phenomena and the conceptualisation of knowledge (Elliot, 2004). One of the crucial differences in this philosophical tradition is in the role of the body. Phenomenologists such as Ryle (1949) have set out to break down dualism by contending Descartes takes for granted the separateness of the mind from the body without a full examination. For instance, he takes the convention of using different languages to explain 'mental' and 'matter' as evidence for their discrete existences but he does not doubt everything as he neglects to question the convention of these languages. Indeed, Cartesian thought begins by predetermining that intelligence cannot be embodied but must exist separately to the body, 'when they witness intelligent behaviour they believe that they are seeing two things: intelligence and behaviour' (Crossley, 2001, p.40). Ryle (1949) argues that the same thing is counted twice and therefore the very essence of Cartesian thought; that intelligence, emotions, consciousness and perception are located within an inner theatre of the mind is based on a categorical error. In contrast he contends this process is far from discrete but fundamentally linked to our perception of the outside world understood through our bodies. For instance, the bodily processes experienced in emotions are fairly similar for many positive and negative states, but it is the nature of the outside event that triggered them that gives them meaning; emotions are not purely introspective in a Cartesian sense but are intimately connected to the social. Ryle (1949) extends this argument to contend that if emotions are partially constructed by experience and outside forces, so are the very structures of thought, consciousness and perception as these states can only be experienced indirectly. For instance, we can perceive objects and subjects but we cannot perceive perception or be conscious of consciousness without using some construct from our relationship with the outside world such as language, images or emotions to represent them. Consciousness and perception then are a 'sensuous relationship to the external world' (Crossley, 2001, p.47) where an inward inspection always takes an outward turn. From this perspective, Descartes would never have been able to think intelligently without a connection to the outside world experienced through the body.

Meaningful action and intelligence then do not exist in a separate realm of the mind and Merleau-Ponty (1965; 1962) reiterates many of the same points Ryle makes in his deconstruction of the immaterial mind, but also examines and critiques the mechanistic view of the body. He does this through a detailed critique of behaviourism. For Merleau-Ponty (1965; 1962) the human organism is both material and simultaneously more than the sum of its parts. Our relationship with any environment then cannot be simply understood as an objective factor impinging upon a person, as any effect of the environment derives its meaning through the way a person perceives it:

> It is as false to place ourselves in society as an object amongst objects, as it is to place society in ourselves as an object of thought, and in both cases the mistake lies in treating the social as an object. We must return to the social with which we are in contact by the mere fact of existing, and which we carry about inseparably with us before any objectification.
> (Merleau-Ponty, 1962, p.362)

Indeed, the phenomenological tradition endeavours to decentre the subject/object divide and show the way objects are perceived and our development as perceptual subjects is rooted in our 'being-in-the-world', fundamentally developed from the interaction our body has with the environment, described as 'body-subject'

(Crossley, 2001, p.89). For Merleau-Ponty (1965) intelligence is an embodied 'know how'; it is the ability to move within an environment and simply fit without conscious effort. This does not mean there is anything natural or pre-social about this; it is a learned ability but it has been incorporated within the logic of the body as a habit to such an extent that it seems natural. Bourdieu's development of the concept of habitus is therefore foreshadowed by Merleau-Ponty, but Bourdieu moves this perspective beyond simply an outline of habit by linking it to forms of power and the wider structures of society.

If Bourdieu's corpus of work could be naively distilled, perhaps a succinct description would be that nothing in the social world is fundamental and inevitable but our habitus makes them so. In *Pascalian Meditations* he defines habitus as 'a system of lasting, transposable dispositions which, integrating past experiences, functions at every moment as a matrix of perceptions, appreciations, and actions' (Bourdieu, 2000, p.86–87). It serves as a somatised lens from which a person's knowledge and experiences are understood through, developed by, but not restricted to one's family, class position, gender, religion and ethnicity. However, objective factors do not produce actors uniformly, but the possibilities presented are combined to produce one's own unique yet predisposed habitus. Therefore, while people from similar backgrounds do not act in accordance with a set of rules, they may have general similarities and strategic behaviours at the level of the habitus, as the structures of society influence the possibilities presented for them to combine. In the context of the charges of structural determinism Bourdieu received, as discussed by Burke in Chapter 2, the concept of habitus is at pains to offer a third way between the objective and the subjective. Bourdieu contends this is a false dichotomy, which thwarts the researcher's ability to adequately understand the social world and produce knowledge with epistemological authority. Here the concept of habitus is woven within the wider system of distribution; it describes not only how individuals meaningfully engage with society as the concept of habit describes, but links this form of action with structures of inequality – this is best exemplified in his analysis of field.

For Bourdieu (1990), structures are a combination of social fields and institutions. Social fields are specific contexts in which people act, for instance one acts differently in the educational field than one would in a sporting field, as each has its own particular habitus or logic. This is expressed through the ability of individuals to act appropriately without propositional thought, but instead through the embodiment of a logic specific to the field. Burkitt argues Bourdieu 'seeks to emphasize how this type of learning, which affects men and women's perception of their bodies and selves, does not occur at the cognitive level but at the bodily level' (Burkitt, 1999, p.88). To demonstrate this, in his 1978 essay *Sport and Social Class*, Bourdieu draws on the heightened example of sport to argue that one's embodied feel for the game links the structure of the field to the specific behaviours or practices of the individuals within them. In this approach the central concepts of field and habitus are bound together in the body, as an individual or groups' 'practical belief' in the game is a state of the body, 'instilled by the childhood learning that treats the body as a living memory pad' (Bourdieu, 1990, p.68). Yet for an individual to participate and be interested in a field one's habitus must be developed in relation to the resources and rewards within it; otherwise they would not be recognised or valued as capitals (see Mckenzie's Chapter 3 for more on the recognition of capitals within fields). To be committed to a field, then, the learned must be conflated with the natural, what is constructed disappears into 'anamnesis', a 'familiarity gained by the reappropriation of a knowledge (connaissance) that is both possessed and lost from the beginning' (Bourdieu, 2001, p.55). The constructed nature of the field, habitus and capitals disappear and are understood as inevitable and inherently valuable instead of arbitrary. For Bourdieu, then, the illusio of the field gives capitals their meaning. The illusio is defined as

> [t]he fact of being in the game, of being invested in the game, of taking the game seriously. Illusio is the fact of being caught up in and by the game ... That is what I meant in speaking of interest: games which matter to you are important and interesting because they have been imposed and introduced in your mind, in your body, in a form called the feel for the game.
> (Bourdieu, 1998, p.76–77)

The body here is at the centre of action; it is one's filter for perception in the phenomenological tradition but also connects us to fields, making what could be considered arbitrary phenomena important for our self-worth. If action is recast as a combination of mindful action and embodied intelligence (Crossley, 2001) with meaningful practice not reliant on an abstracted propositional view of intelligence before it is undertaken,[4] mindful behaviour can be recast as 'a feel for the game', something that is learned but forgotten, which feels natural, inevitable and obvious. This reconfiguration has real consequences for how we understand racism.

If we reconsider what can be termed as racist, as not necessarily reliant on a conscious rational intention to be racist (Song, 2014), but rather as a form of practice and habitual perception, the insidiousness and pervasiveness of racism is more easily revealed. Within my work the marginalisation of migrant origin boys was rarely understood as racist by either perpetrator or victim, but instead recast as something that everyone just knew, something that felt natural and obvious; where minority boys were simply not really 'Irish' nor could they be considered as tough and masculine as those from the local area (Garratt, 2012). Racist ideas of who could be perceived as authentically Irish and masculine also affected those with phenotypical bodily differences more readily than those from other migrant groups. Indeed, Bourdieu (2001) argues symbolic domination is particularly dangerous when there are phenotypical bodily differences to hook onto. In *Masculine Domination* he contends the body is viewed through a 'social programme of perception', which highlights certain features of the body and denies others, which in turn shapes the legitimate expression, habits and hexis of the body (Krais, 2006). Here presumed difference is linked to the body as an object, but perception embedded in the habitus to view difference even when it may not be present. Hence, this is the most insidious form of social construction, as arbitrariness is completely hidden through the use of material body difference to justify and naturalise it. While all social structures gain power through being defined as inevitable or the way things must be (Gramsci, 1995), by using a Bourdieusian approach racism and sexism can be seen as the epitome of this, as they link to conceptions of 'naturalness' more successfully than other structures especially in their intersection, leading to their production and reproduction through the habitus (Fowler, 2003). Racism, like gender, can be thought of as the embodiment of doxa, the 'somatization of the social relations of domination' (Bourdieu, 2001, p.23) manifested and maintained in day-to-day interactions, or what Bourdieu refers to as a circular causality of observation, somatisation and naturalisation:

> Because the social principle of vision constructs anatomical difference and because this anatomical difference becomes the basis and apparently natural justification of the social vision which founds it, there is thus a relationship of circular causality which confines thought within the self-evidence of relations of domination.
>
> (1984, p.11)

Hence, while racism may exist as the evaluation of another as 'inferior', this evaluation is also embodied; therefore, what is perceived is circularly constructed to expect difference even when no material differential exists. In my data this was the evaluation of minority boys as not as good at football or tough as other boys. Indeed in his more direct dealings with the physical body, Bourdieu also provides a way to understand how the body is evaluated as an object in the field in his concept of embodied cultural capital or bodily hexis.

Embodied cultural capital

For Bourdieu (1984), illusio allows capitals to be misrecognised as innately valuable. Bourdieu (1984) identifies five inter-related capitals specific to each field; the first four, economic, political, social and cultural capital, are said to be accumulated and exchanged within specific fields in order to achieve the fifth, symbolic capital, i.e. prestige, honour and social worth. Conversely, though, the possession of symbolic capital legitimates actors' possession of other forms of capital, giving them a cylindrical or dialectic relationship. For Bourdieu and Wacquant (1992) the attainment and maintenance of capital is the primary concern for those within fields as the amount of capital one has determines one's place within it and therefore the power one has. The possession of capitals though is not open to everyone as they are controlled and limited by organisations and those who are already rich in capital; therefore, the richer in capital you are, the more ability you have to regulate the field for your benefit. Thus, Bourdieu (1984) argues those in positions of power within a field have an interest in maintaining an orthodoxy that justifies and naturalises the dominant groups' claim of symbolic capital. However, the possession and exchange of capital does not take place from a position of rational choice but is somatised and expressed through the body. The concept of cultural capital most obviously illuminates this. Bourdieu (1984) contends cultural capital is manifested in three specific forms; embodied, objectified and institutionalised. Embodied cultural capital is the bodily hexis of a person's habitus, which is strongly related to one's origins; for instance it is the accent one develops, the manners one employs in social situations, the way one presents oneself to the world through dress, deportment and the tastes one develops and exploits. The body is therefore not a fixed entity but is partially constructed by the medium of the habitus:

> It follows that the body is the most indisputable materialization of class taste, which manifests itself in several ways. It does this first in the seemingly most natural features of the body, the dimensions (volume, height, weight) and shapes (round or square, stiff or supple, straight or curved) of its visible forms, which express in countless ways a whole relation to the body, i.e., a way of treating it, caring for it, feeding it, maintaining it, which reveals the deepest dispositions of the habitus.
> (Bourdieu, 1984, p.190)

Moreover, fields have appearance and disposition norms that reflect the interests of the dominant group richest in capital within that field. The bodily hexis of habitus then can either facilitate or constrain actors as they interact within social fields, as capital accumulation is enabled by one's ability to be 'a fish in water', as the apparent ease with which one moves through it will designate you as someone who belongs, understands the field and does not question its values (Bourdieu, 1977). If one's body is too big, small, weak, strong, or if one dresses inappropriately or does not control the movements of one's body to fit with accepted demeanours, it will be more difficult to blend in and be accepted in the field or even gain access to it in the first place. Chris Shilling (2003) has used Bourdieu's concept of embodied cultural capital to conceptualise the body as a bearer of value in contemporary society; he does this by pushing the notion of embodied cultural capital beyond the cultural realm and conceptualising it as 'physical capital'. He uses this concept to describe the ways in which the body can be constructed and moulded to signify power, status and value within social fields. Shilling (2005) explicitly states what Bourdieu alludes to, which is that the body has an important bearing on one's life chances within certain fields and for one's accumulation of resources. Moreover, he contends dominant groups have a greater ability to define their bodies and lifestyle norms as superior and worthy of reward, while the bodies of 'others' are devalued and have a lower exchange value within fields controlled by the dominant group. Indeed, for Bourdieu (2001), norms in interactions and tastes within social fields reflect those associated with the dominant group and become naturalised as the 'rational' way of doing things. The implication of this is that those already powerful are more easily able to integrate these standards within their bodies and have more incentive to do so as they value the capitals on offer. In consequence, the bodies they craft and the attributes they validate become misrecognised as one's natural talents and dispositions, and it is this misrecognition that allows them to justify their position and legitimise their power, as their bodies signal their 'moral' superiority to others. Hence, Bourdieu's (1984) famous claim that the symbolic does not stand outside of hierarchy but is woven within it, as the symbolic justifies certain groups' claim that they are worthy of power and have the natural right to dominate.

Conclusion

While at a surface level Bourdieu's analysis of embodied cultural capital can be accused of similarities to other notions of how the body is denigrated, it fundamentally differs as he deals with what it is to both *have* a body that is judged, and simultaneously somatises this judgement in our being in the world. Bourdieu's work helps us locate where racism resides in habitual perception and how this is constructed, perpetuated and linked to resources and rewards. Embodiment then is not simply something that demeans 'other' groups; but it is our state of existence in the world and the means by which we come to know what the world is. When the body is the target for debasement, then, the impact of this goes further in a Bourdieusian approach, as the body is not a peripheral aspect of ourselves, it is who we are. It also helps us to differentiate the impact of racism. In my research the body was always the target of debasement, however differences in skin colour added another layer of domination to this process, as phenotypical differences where used to further justify marginalisation as something evident and inevitable. While this is not to say that racism can only be perpetrated on 'black' peoples by 'white' peoples, it is to argue that not all racial practices are equivalent in their impact[5] (Song, 2014). The impact of racism goes further in a Bourdieusian account, as debasing one's body does not aim at the surface of ourselves but penetrates to our core (also see Fanon, 1982 [1952]). While the literature in racialisation and gender studies has usefully analysed the body as an object of value and deconstructed rationality, the solution offered in these approaches seems to be to transcend the body; which is impossible. In light of this an anti-racism strategy that shows how we are all embodied but highlights how structures of power problematise embodiment for some people more than others seems a better approach to take.[6] Through Bourdieu, we gain the tools to directly deal with the body in ethnic and racial studies, without slipping into essentialising notions of the body or of racism. Perhaps with a nuanced use of the concepts of habit, habitus and hexis we can finally exorcise the ghost from the machine.

Notes

1 For a thorough review please see the work of Nick Crossley and Chris Shilling.
2 As defined by the enlightenment tradition.
3 Spaces in which children's attention was primarily on their peers in lieu of adult supervision and control.
4 Which presupposes that any act or perception is only intelligent if it is thought about or reflected upon propositionally. If this were true, however, any thought would be infinitely regressional, as not only would the act have to be reflected on, but the reflection itself and then that reflection and so forth.
5 Racism of course must also be understood in the wider global history of power relations between 'black' and 'white' peoples.
6 Indeed this also brings into question how racism can be tackled and whether consciousness raising strategies are effective if they do not tap into the habitual root of prejudice.

References

Back, L. and Solomos, J. 2000. *Theories of Race and Racism*. London: Routledge.
Barot, R. and Bird, J. 2001. Racialization: The Genealogy and Critique of a Concept. *Ethnic and Racial Studies*. **21**(4), pp.601–618.
Benhabib, S. 1995a. *Feminism and Postmodernism: An Uneasy Alliance*. London: Routledge.
Benhabib, S. 1995b. Subjectivity, Historiography, and Politics. In Benhabib, S., Butler, J., Cornell, D and Fraser, N. (eds) *Feminist Contentions: A Philosophical Exchange*. London: Routledge, pp.107–126.
Bourdieu, P. 1977. *Outline of a Theory of Practice*. Cambridge: Cambridge University Press.
Bourdieu, P. 1978. Sport and Social Class. *Social Science Information*. **17**, pp.819–840.
Bourdieu, P. 1984. *Distinction: A Social Critique of the Judgement of Taste*. London: Routledge.
Bourdieu, P. 1990a *In Other Words*. Cambridge: Polity Press.
Bourdieu, P. 1990b *The Logic of Practice*. Cambridge: Polity Press.
Bourdieu, P. 1998. *Practical Reason: On the Theory of Action*. Stanford, CA: Stanford.
Bourdieu, P. 2000. *Pascalian Meditations*. Cambridge: Polity Press.
Bourdieu, P. 2001. *Masculine Domination*. Cambridge: Polity Press.
Burkitt, I. 1999. *Bodies of Thought: Embodiment, Identity and Modernity*. London: Sage.
Butler, J. 1990. *Gender Trouble: Feminism and the Subversion of Identity*. New York: Routledge.
Chambers, S.A. 2007. 'Sex' and the Problem of the Body: Reconstructing Judith Butler's Theory of Sex/Gender. *Body & Society* **13**, pp.47–75.
Crossley, N. 2001. *The Social Body, Habit, Identity and Desire*. London: Sage.
Curry, P., Gilligan, R., Garratt, L. and Scholtz, J. 2011. *Where To From Here? Inter-ethnic Relations among Children in Ireland*. Dublin, Ireland: Liffey Press.
De Beauvoir, S. 1972 [1946]. *The Second Sex*. London: Penguin.
Derrida, J. 1976. *Of Grammatology*. Baltimore, MD: Johns Hopkins University Press.
Derrida, J. 1977. *Limited Inc: abc*. London: Johns Hopkins University Press.
Elliott, B. 2004. *Phenomenology and Imagination in Husserl and Heidegger*. London: Routledge.

Fanon, F 1982 [1952]. *Black Skin, White Masks*. London: Pluto.
Foucault, M. 1975. *Discipline and Punishment: The Birth of the Prison*. New York: Vintage Books.
Foucault, M. 1978. *History of Sexuality Vol 1*. New York: Vintage Books.
Fowler, B. 2003. Reading Pierre Bourdieu's Masculine Domination: Notes towards an Intersectional Analysis of Gender, Culture and Class. *Cultural Studies* **17**(3/4), pp.468–494.
Fraser, N. 1995. False Antitheses. In Benhabib, S., Butler, J., Cornell, D and Fraser, N. (eds) *Feminist Contentions: A Philosophical Exchange*. London: Routledge, pp.59–74.
Garratt, L. 2012. The Body, Masculinities and Racism: Social Relations between Migrant and Dominant Group Boys in Three Inner City Primary Schools in Dublin. Ph.D. thesis, Trinity College Dublin, Ireland.
Garratt, L. Forthcoming – a. Doubly Estranged, Embodying a Reflexive habitus: The Experience of Migrant Origin Boys in Three Inner City Primary Schools in Dublin, Ireland.
Garratt, L. Forthcoming – b. We're Just Ourselves, They're not Themselves': The Doxa of Authenticity in Young Boys' Inter-ethnic Relations.
Glaser, B. and Strauss, A. 2008 [1967]. *The Discovery of Grounded Theory: Strategies for Qualitative Research*. London: Aldine Transaction.
Goldberg, D.T. 1994. *Racist Culture: Philosophy and the Politics of Meaning*. Cambridge, MA: Blackwell.
Gramsci, A. 1995. *Further Selections from the Prison Notebooks*. London: Lawrence & Wishart.
Grosz, E. 1994. *Volatile Bodies: Towards a Corporeal Feminism*. Sydney, Australia: Allen & Unwin.
Hall, S. 1997. *Representations: Cultural Representations and Signifying Practices*. London: Sage.
Hughey, M.W. 2010. The (Dis)similarities of White Racial Identities: The Conceptual Framework of 'Hegemonic Whiteness'. *Ethnic and Racial Studies*. **33**, pp.1289–1309.
Kessler, S.J. and McKenna, W. 1978. *Gender: An Ethnomethodological Approach*. New York: Wiley.
Krais, B. 2006. Gender, Sociological Theory and Bourdieu's Sociology of Practice. *Theory Culture and Society*. **23**(6), pp.119–134.
Merleau-Ponty, M. 1962. *The Phenomenology of Perception*. London: RKP.
Merleau-Ponty, M. 1965. *The Structure of Behaviour*. London: Methuen.
Murji, K. and Solomos, J. 2005. Racialization in Theory and Practice. In Murji, K. and Solomos, J. (eds) *Racialization: Studies in Theory and Practice*. Oxford: Oxford University Press. pp.1–28.
Rottenberg, C. 2003. Passing: Race, Identification, and Desire. *Criticism*. **45**, pp.435–452.
Ryle, G. 1949. *The Concept of Mind*. London: Penguin.
Said, E. 1995 [1978]. *Orientalism: Western Conceptions of the Orient*. London: Penguin.
Sartre, J.-P. 1969. *Being and Nothingness*. London: Routledge.
Song, M. 2014. Challenging a Culture of Racial Equivalence. *British Journal of Sociology*. **65**(1), pp.107–129
Sorell, T. 2000. *Descartes: A Very Short Introduction*. Oxford: Oxford University Press.
Stoller, S. 2009. Phenomenology and the Poststructural Critique of Experience. *International Journal of Philosophical Studies*. **17**, pp.707–737.

Tyler, C. 1991. Boys Will Be Girls: The Politics of Gay Drag. In Fuss, D. (ed.) *Inside/Out: Lesbian Theories, Gay Theories*. London: Routledge, pp.32–70.

Vincent, L. 2006. Destined to Come to Blows?: Race and Constructions of 'Rational-Intellectual' Masculinity Ten Years after Apartheid. *Men and Masculinities*. **8**, pp.350–366.

Chapter 7

Migrating habitus
A comparative case study of Polish and South African migrants in the UK

Jenny Thatcher and Kristoffer Halvorsrud

Introduction

As two people who have both experienced migration to different societies – one from Norway to the UK and the other in the opposite direction – we have first-hand experience of the insecurities and internalised struggles that can occur when encountering unfamiliar fields. As researchers of migration we are aware that our habitus is in some way nationally and culturally bounded. We are reflexive of the negotiations that occur when we draw upon our own capital possession in new environments to legitimise our belonging. For us, Bourdieu's theorisation of habitus has aided us in understanding both how we position ourselves within these new fields as well as the challenges we face when encountering the unfamiliar and making decisions on whether to adapt to or resist our new host societies. By extension, we are reflexive and critical of the host societal mechanisms of exclusion that impose perceived social 'hierarchies' among its population, in particular the ways in which we might be automatically put in a privileged position compared to 'non-white' migrants and ethnic minorities simply due to our 'whiteness'.

The concept of habitus can be read as an attempt on Bourdieu's part to enable a sociological account that facilitated understanding of the complex and multifaceted interplay between actors and structures. That is, habitus can be interpreted as the learned dispositions actors acquire while growing up, or those practices and cultural competences that give actors a sense of the position they occupy in social space. Although habitus is a learned process, the majority of people tend most of the time to perceive themselves and their own social world and circles as the 'natural order of things', which is taken more or less for granted. This is a process of the reproduction of actors' social position. In this respect, the concept of habitus is a useful analytical tool, which facilitates an exploration of the way in which socio-economic inequalities are reproduced through the 'thoughtlessness' of habits and daily routines, enabling people to act without having to think and reflect on every move that they make (Bourdieu, 1977).

We suggest that situations whereby actors have experienced a socio-political transformation in their own society as well as undertaken migration from their societal order to another one, are both examples of situations in which individuals' habitus will be put to the test with regard to its durability and capability of withstanding external pressures. Derek Robbins (2005a; 2005b) argues Bourdieu's concepts must be embarked upon reflexively by acknowledging the origins of the concepts' development. Bourdieu wanted his concepts to be applied and extended to produce new social understandings. The experiences of migrants and the prior situation from their original countries – as reflected in the internalisations of their habitus – relate back to the issues Bourdieu was working on when he was looking at the social organisation of the Kabyle tribe in Algeria. Bourdieu and Sayad (1964) reasoned that the prior structure of culture was somehow internalised in the frame of thinking of the people who migrated or moved from one societal structure to another within Algeria. It is also worth noting that Algeria was experiencing political transformations caused by colonial repression and the war of national liberalisation. Silverstein (2004) argues that this process of uprooting has continued to inform the historical consciousness of the Kabyle diaspora. Of particular interest to Bourdieu was the Kabyle's rootedness in agricultural practices and the disruptions caused by the influx of capitalism. The Kabyle possessed a 'structural nostalgia' (Silverstein, 2004, p.556). The structural transformations that occurred in Algeria unsettled the Kabyle's symbolic system in which they experienced a process of hysteresis because of habitus-field disjuncture. Due to misrecognition, the Kabyle's doxa – meaning their pre-reflexive, intuitive knowledge – was locked in a cycle of reproduction in which they re-enacted their own practices and social norms during the transition.

Thus, Bourdieu's development of his conceptual framework was constructed under a study that displays many associations to our own investigation. We explore the processes of adaptation of a set of migrants coming from different political socio-economic and social-cultural systems that have undergone dramatic transformations in the last 25 years. Bourdieu's (2008) concept of a divided or cleft habitus here becomes useful, as it refers specifically to the mechanisms of the mind-sets of individuals who have experienced a considerable disjuncture between their present circumstances and the world in which these individuals were originally raised and socialised. Sam Friedman in Chapter 8, as well as Nicola Ingram and Jessie Abrahams in Chapter 10, discuss how agents experience a cleft habitus as they undergo social mobility. Their case studies offer examples of a habitus that has to constantly be negotiated with itself as the agents take on multiple identities in which they interweave between their working-class background and their present middle-class environments. Kirsty Morrin in Chapter 9 also discusses habitus-field disjuncture and the hysteresis experienced by educationally 'successful' working-class students at an entrepreneurial state secondary school academy. Morrin argues that this disjuncture can lead to heightened awareness and reflexivity of an agent's environment. We argue the result of this disjuncture can vary according to the specific situation, but may include emotions such as confusion and despair and countermeasures such as mobilisation (see Bourdieu, 1988; 1979). As Bourdieu understood habitus as a robust state of mind that would not necessarily change overnight, '[w]e can always say that individuals make choices, as long as we do not forget that they do not choose the principals [i.e. the habitus] of these choices' (cited in Wacquant, 1989, p.45).

This chapter applies the framework of habitus to the comparative case study of 'white' Polish and predominantly 'white' South African migrants living in the UK. The comparative case study will convey the different values and attitudes both sets of migrants assign toward 'whiteness' and social class in the host society and the influence of their home societal structures in shaping their views. Although South African and Polish migrants come from two societies with different orientations, the common applicability for the study of the migrants' habitus is brought into play by the fact that both societies have collapsed and have been in transition during the last 25 years. Both groups have had the concepts of class and stratum in their society challenged. Yet, the previous structures of their respective home societies are shown to still have considerable influence for both migrant groups. While the South African apartheid state's authoritarian and hierarchical racist societal structures perpetuated 'racial' inequalities for the reproduction of white-only domination, Poland's Soviet communist state denied the existence of stratification, intentionally shaping industrial working classes not to be 'class-conscious'.

We will first briefly outline the comparative features of the South African and Polish societies as shaped by socio-political and cultural transformations. This will provide the backdrop against which we will combine our individual materials from our respective qualitative interview studies in the UK with the two migrant groups and demonstrate the comparative value of these two studies. By revealing the comparative insights of the interview material relating to 'whiteness' and social class of the South African and Polish migrants, we argue that a comparison between migrants from two different societal backgrounds demonstrates the continuing relevance of Bourdieu's concept of habitus in understanding migrants' transnational consciousness as well as their 'assimilation' into British society.

The formation of the migrants' habitus

This section will briefly situate the past structures that influenced the migrants' habitus in the sense that previous structures from the 'exporting' societies (South Africa and Poland) can become embodied and affect the strategies of adaptation in the 'importing' society (the UK). Although it is around 25 years since apartheid was dismantled in South Africa and communism collapsed in Poland, all the participants from the two migrant groups were born under these respective regimes, as were many of their parents. Bourdieu (1958) pointed out that when there is a sudden rupture in the social organisation of a social unit, the habitus can often take time to readjust and 'catch up' to these changes. Burawoy and Verdery explain that '[w]hen we speak of transition, we think of a process connecting the past to the future. What we discover, however, are theories of transition often committed to some pregiven future or rooted in an unyielding past' (1999, p.4).

With reference to South Africa, the legacy of the 'white' apartheid regime cannot be ignored when trying to understand the habitus of 'white' South Africans. As 'racial'/ethnic groups were physically and mentally segregated by being confined to different geographical and social spaces, these divisions permeated everyday life in apartheid South Africa between 1948 and 1994.[1] Although the 'white' apartheid rulers argued that this was a 'natural' arrangement that would help 'non-white' communities develop 'on their own terms' without any interference from the 'white' community, there was nothing 'natural' about this arrangement (Steyn, 2001). It was by and large a construction on the part of the 'white' government, whereby 'the state formalized the category of "white" and classified those individuals who were light-skinned and straight-haired and had European ancestors as "white"' (MacDonald, 2012, p.61, inverted commas in original). Despite the legacy of the apartheid past and the 'racial' injustices inflicted upon 'non-white' people, the introduction of the first democratic elections in South Africa in 1994 and the election of the African National Congress (ANC) into power witnessed the post-apartheid state attempting to unify South Africans of all 'racial' and ethnic groups. This chapter will show the resilience of the 'apartheid habitus' that the interviewed 'white' South Africans were exposed to while growing up – even to the extent that it might follow them for a long time into the post-apartheid era and despite their relocation to the UK (Sallaz, 2010).

Similarly to South Africa, albeit with class as reference point rather than 'race', Polish society has been profoundly affected by political engineering and top-down decisions affecting ordinary people's habitus. By 1946, Poland was under Soviet military and political control and, two years later, Stalin had eliminated the nationalist fringe groups within the communist party of the Soviet Bloc. In Stalinist Poland, these transformations meant that the Soviet-backed Polish United Workers' Party would soon control all state institutions. In 1952, a new constitution declared that industrial workers were to be the principal class in Polish society in the newly-established Polish People's Republic. This built the foundations for a supposedly 'classless' society. However, social class still retained its importance in subtler forms with the reproduction of the class system through the cultural practices of the Polish intelligentsia (Lukowski & Zawadzki, 2006; Prażmowska, 2011). Although a new space for the everyday practices and micro-world of the people was created following the collapse of the state socialist political and economic structures – with the fall of the Berlin Wall in 1989[2] – the previous system continued to influence the emerging new structures as well as people's everyday lives. Burawoy and Verdery (1999) argue that the collapse of communism did not eliminate the various legacies inherited from the socialist regime, the main legacy of which was a cultural persistence of the elites. Drawing on Bourdieu and Weber, Burawoy (1999) tells us how a world in which strategic actors occupy a social space possessing different convertible capitals – such as economic, social and cultural – created a cultural bourgeoisie intelligentsia under communism. As such, in a post-communist capitalist society it is this cultural bourgeoisie who have used their cultural capital in pursuit of entrepreneurship to monopolise the creation of economic capital.

In addition to accounting for how the South African and Polish societies have been in transition, it is important to note that migration intersects with different 'regimes' and is affected by global-level socioeconomic and political transformations as part of wider global integration. The population of Central and Eastern Europe that had once been isolated from the global market could benefit from unrestricted travel after communism collapsed. EU accession in 2004 also gave Accession 8 countries,[3] including Poland, EU citizenship and the rights of permanent residence in Britain. Furthermore, the experienced structural reform problems associated with rapid integration such as widespread economic restructuring, privatisation and large flows of foreign direct investment – which Poland underwent after the collapse of communism – brought with it a redistribution and polarisation of income, increasing insecurity and unemployment in the labour market as well as extensive cuts in public welfare in Poland. This further encouraged migration out of Poland (Hardy, 2009, p.3). In South Africa, the post-apartheid era, which commenced in 1994, also coincided with a time of increased globalisation and international mobility. An increase in emigration from South Africa, including to the UK, was further encouraged by the opening up of borders as the authoritarian apartheid regime fell, and with the lifting of the international sanctions that had been imposed upon South Africa and upheld during apartheid (Nyamnjoh, 2006, Chapter 1).

Habitus: comparing Polish and South African migrants in the UK

Having drawn out the distinctive as well as overlapping characteristics of the transforming social structures in South Africa and Poland, we now explore the data material from around 30 qualitative in-depth interviews conducted with each migrant group, respectively. This builds on Thatcher's comparative research in London and Nottingham exploring Polish migrants' educational aspirations and school choice for their children, as well as Halvorsrud's research on the sense of belonging of mainly white South African migrants in the UK.

'Whiteness'

Doing a comparative analysis from the interviews with 'white' South African and Poles allows us to explore the impact of constructions of 'race'/ethnicity upon the participants' identity. The interview findings presented below show that both 'white' South African and Polish migrants might draw upon their own 'whiteness' in their everyday socialisation patterns in British society as part of a strategy to ensure their presumed assimilation into a 'white' majority context such as the UK. It is shown that this finding can be somewhat related to both the South African and Polish contextual conditions. In the former case, because of the apartheid policies of 'whiteness' and 'racial'/ethnic segregation, while in the latter, interestingly enough, the fact that the participants have not necessarily been overtly exposed to considerations of 'race'/ethnicity in Poland ushers in a sense of insecurity and some level of self-enclosure as they encounter a more multicultural setting especially in London.

For the Polish participants, their sense of 'whiteness' was often linked to broader constructions of perceived cultural similarity between Polish society and that of Britain and, in particular, Poland's historical relationship with Europe.

> It is easier to integrate when you are white because anywhere you will have more or less the same background and even the holidays that we celebrate together, and the way that you spend your life, what you are interested in, how you spend your summer holidays or any sort of holidays, Christmas or Easter – I think if you are white it's easier to integrate because you have more in common.
> (Michelina, 42, Polish, teaching assistant)

McDowell (2009) argues that there is an implicit difference between the new wave of EU economic migrants and previous post-war migration in a 'white' ethnic majority society marked by 'racial' discrimination such as Britain. As such, this new wave of migration is less visible; they are 'white' and have a European identity and Christian heritage to draw upon. According to McDowell (2009), 'whiteness' can act as a signifier of privilege in the labour market even in 'low-skilled' jobs. It must be remembered that being classified as 'white', in global terms, has secured certain privileges due to the manner in which discourses of 'whiteness' have been reproduced as an 'invisible' and taken-for-granted construction or 'norm' in society, as opposed to the manner in which the identities of 'racial' and ethnic minorities are construed as visible and 'problematic' (see Bonnett 2004; Dyer 1997).

Eade *et al.* (2007) found that one of the most significant methods of classification for Polish migrants in London was the positioning of themselves in a 'racial' and ethnic 'hierarchy' as 'whites' rather than Poles. Eade *et al.*'s (2007) research revealed that 54 per cent believed their 'whiteness' to be an important asset in British society in evading the 'racial' discrimination that 'non-white' migrants and ethnic minorities suffer. Poles drawing upon their 'whiteness' as a way to counteract the discrimination faced in British society, was a similar finding in our own research. Franciszka (37), for example, spoke about how her 'whiteness' was sometimes an advantage in British society: 'Many times I was thinking "oh thank god I'm white" so I don't have too much troubles, for example in my first home, the Jewish home, they were not accepting black people'. Franciszka's 'whiteness' was drawn upon as a way to counteract her down-ward mobility she had experienced upon migration. Previous to her migration, Franciszka had a high managerial role in the Polish health care system, but now she was working in the UK as a health care assistant in a nursing home on minimum wage. Franciszka reflected upon her different experiences in the UK when people had heard her Polish accent: 'it is such a shame sometimes there is a lot of Polish people and sometimes they don't speak Polish on the street because we don't want to let them know we are Polish'. As such, she believed that her 'whiteness' was only an asset in British society until people became aware of her 'Polishness' and, hence, immigrant status, embodied through other forms such as her accent.

Being classified as 'Polish migrants', they were likely to face the socially constructed categorisation of 'not yet "white" enough' (Bukowczyk, 1996, p.31). Take for example the case of Roza. Roza returned to university as a mature student in the UK, attending one of the top institutions in the country and gaining a degree in Sociology and Social Policy. Previous to this, she owned her own business. Yet, she talks about how her 'Polishness ' automatically results in native-born Britons categorising her not only in terms of her immigrant status, but also in terms of her presumed socio-economic position: 'I came here and I'm an immigrant and any time I open my mouth "Where are you from?" "Poland" "Oh, are you a cleaner?" so this attitude is very much there' (Roza, 33, Polish, legal and policy advisor for people on low income).

Fox *et al.* (2012) examine how Eastern European migration has been 'racialised' in immigration policy and in the media. They argue that the nature of institutional racism is incorporated into immigration policy by implying that 'whiteness' equates to inclusion in British society, securing Eastern European migrants residence status based on the visa-free agreement of EU membership. This is in sharp contrast to the tabloid media who focus on cultural differences, invoking a foundation for 'racial' differentiation, thereby ensuring that Eastern European migrants are excluded from the imagined 'British nation' in culturally racist ways despite their 'whiteness'.

It was found in this study that a 'racialised' discourse may be drawn upon as a reaction to the racism Polish migrants experienced from the 'white' British majority population, as a way to divert attention towards 'non-white' migrants and ethnic minorities. This was particularly revealed when the Polish interviewees had to engage with host societal institutions such as schools. A number of parents excluded schools from consideration because they cited the predominant black pupil intake of these schools. In a handful of cases, parents guestimated the percentage of the black student body of the schools. The guestimates of black pupil intake differed between participants, but were often in the 80–90 per cent mark. In real terms, this was an overestimation when we looked at the actual school statistics.[4] Ryan (2010) and McDowell (2009) have suggested that the relatively homogenous nature of Eastern European countries such as Poland and their relative lack of previous encounters with non-Europeans may contribute to racist attitudes towards 'non-white' people. Similarly, our research on 'white' South Africans shows that they subscribed to the idea of a 'racial hierarchy' operating in British society. Take the case of Zarah (21), a student at a high-ranking Russell Group university, whose parents had migrated to Britain with her in 1999. Despite living in Britain for over 10 years, she still placed herself within the migrant category, yet spoke about how her 'whiteness' was an advantage. The participant stated that because of her 'white' skin colour, 'I don't feel like I look any different to other people', before adding that 'I think if you're not white, your colour immediately gives you away'.

It is important to point out the disparities between groups of migrants and ethnic minorities that might subscribe to the idea of 'whiteness' as a resource in Britain. Derron Wallace in Chapter 4 is reflexive of the institutional racism that is experienced by Black[5] Caribbean adolescents in London. His description of 'Black' cultural capital as drawn upon by the adolescents offers an innovative insight into how stigmatised groups can invert the dominant 'white' discourses in British society. Wallace shows how the adolescents' possession of 'Black' cultural capital offers a means of reaffirming and performing their opposition to the everyday racism as experienced in the dominant spaces of wider British society.

In our own case study, the discrimination experienced by the Polish participants in Britain made them realise that 'whiteness' as a 'racial' category did not operate to every 'white' person's advantage, as did 'white' South Africans. Both migrant groups had to negotiate their inclusion as 'white' individuals who are 'deserving' of their inclusion in British society. The migrant status both sets of migrants had attached to them is not necessarily revealed when they carry out their everyday activities in British society. Being a 'migrant' is often impued with 'racialised' undertones and associated with being 'non-white' in tabloid media and the mind-set of some. For members of both migrant groups – even for 'white' South Africans among whom many spoke English as their first language – there was a reported experience of some level of resentment and discrimination while communicating in British society. This resentment was, as previously discussed by Polish migrants, also attributed to their non-British 'accents'. Thus, the migrants were conscious that they might get 'exposed' as migrants in situations which required communication:

> I get quite self-conscious about it, cause I know I've got a strong accent . . . there is a bit of a – I won't say xenophobia, is not as bad as that – but it is a bit embarrassing, I guess . . . when you ask someone for something and they, y'know, you get the feeling that they couldn't understand a word you just said.
>
> (Frederick, 35, 'white' South African, teacher)

Despite Frederick actually acquiring British citizenship by naturalisation, and therefore no longer retaining an immigrant status officially speaking, he still felt that his accent left him open to discrimination. He was also relatively high up in the socio-economic 'hierarchy' in British society, having obtained two Bachelor degrees and working as a teacher in London – although this did not seem to mediate the possibility of him getting exposed to some level of discrimination because of his 'South African accent'.

It should be considered the extent to which the 'white' South Africans reproduced the segregatory logic during apartheid that justified separate spaces for 'white' and 'non-white' people and permeated most aspects of South African everyday life. The setting in which this would most appropriately be assessed in British society is that of the global and multicultural city of London as a 'super-diverse' environment (Vertovec, 2007) – as opposed to the self-enclosed spaces that limited such diversity in 'white-only' spaces during the apartheid era in South Africa. Considering informal *practices* such as socialisation patterns – rather than simply the participants' attitudes in isolation from their possible consequences – speaks directly to the intended application of Bourdieu's concept of habitus. This is illustrated in the following quote, in which the participant talks about how his friendship group consisted of mainly 'white' South Africans from similar class background:

> If I'm going to be *very brutally honest*, the friends that I have over here – or whilst in South Africa – almost all white. I wish it was another way, but it's not. I've asked myself many times of *why* this is the case, why I hang out with them ... what I mean to say is that race and background are not a problem for me – if you're cool I will hang out with you. But it *frustrates* me and *puzzles* me that people I choose to hang out with – almost all the time – are white South African and of the same background as me.
> (Richard, 27, 'white' South African, freelance journalist)

As immigration and citizenship policies favour 'white' South Africans through ancestry and socio-economic status, around 90 per cent of South Africans who reside in the UK can be classified as 'white' (see Crawford, 2011) – as opposed to less than 9 percent among the population in South Africa itself (Statistics South Africa, 2012). Hence, some of the 'white' South African participants were quick to point out that it is only 'common sense' that another 'white' South African is easier to locate than a 'non-white' South African in the UK. However, this would not fully explain why this research found that the majority of 'white' South Africans interviewed did not socialise with British-born black and ethnic minorities as well as black South Africans from the same social background, despite some of these participants residing in the UK for over 20 years. It may be noteworthy to bring in the example of Thulasizwe – a highly-educated black South African working in the higher ranks of the civil service in Britain, who has been disappointed by his encounters with 'white' South Africans in the UK:

> Your white people here and your black people are like this [indicates separation with his hands] ... And again, it's that apartheid system that's causing that. It is that thing that is still causing that here. You find here, [white South Africans] doing their own thing, they are staying in certain areas. They

are opening these bars and they're calling them all sorts of names . . . there's a bar called Zulu Bar. And you, if you go – I'm a Zulu myself – and you would think that if it's called a Zulu Bar, then I would find other people like myself. You go there, you find you are the only one of this pigmentation. And people still look at you as if you are lost – you should be going somewhere. Which would have been the case then [during the apartheid era].
(Thulasizwe, 59, black South African, civil servant for a South African organisation in the UK)

Here we see that despite Thulasizwe's class position, he still feels excluded by 'white' South Africans. This, to some extent, can be linked to the 'racial' divisions that existed during the apartheid system. During the regime, the upper echelons of society were 'white' – as they still mostly are today due to social reproduction. This may explain Thulasizwe's account of feeling like a fish out of water because of the response he received from 'white' South Africans in upmarket bars aimed at affluent South Africans. It is interesting that Thulasizwe's description of his life in South Africa was one of happiness and comfort – despite his relatively underprivileged upbringing during apartheid – and that his justification for coming to Britain centred around the experience of going abroad. On the other hand, the majority of the 'white' South Africans interviewed for this research (who had come from privileged upbringings) spoke of 'fleeing' from South Africa to escape violence and affirmative action policies. By associating only with 'white' South Africans, they build enclaves based on ethnic classifications over that of social class – although we recognise social class is still very important to their friendship formations.

A 'classed' habitus?

In spite of some marked similarities in the experiences of the two migrant groups, the typical 'classed' circumstances for members of the respective groups reveal some qualitative and interesting differences/tensions. It is revealed that the two migrant groups benefit somewhat differently from the intersection of their 'racialised' and 'classed' dispositions while negotiating their inclusion in British society.

Among both groups, it seemed important for the participants to establish that they are 'hard workers' and are not claiming umemployment welfare while in the UK. This language could be linked to their migration to a British society in which neo-liberal undertones place considerable emphasis on the requirement that migrants should work in order to be 'deserving' of their residence in the country. However, we believe that particularly in the Polish case it is also relevant to trace such discourse back to their former society when ruled under communism. Joanka was a Polish participant from one of the poorest parts of Nottingham, with higher than average rates of unemployment in the UK. Her husband was a building labourer and she worked as a cleaner. Like many other Polish participants in the research, she spoke of how Polish people are 'hard working' and saw the unemployment of her neighbours as a cultural rather than a structural issue. A person's work status was for Joanka linked to their 'worth', reputation and social 'desirability', in similarity to the majority of Polish participants:

> I know my neighbours . . . no good family no working, they get only benefits and want every time more, more, more, so jealous if we have something, but we are really, really hard working. If I want to buy a car I need to be hard working . . . That is why sometimes I don't understand how he thinks. Don't want to go to work, what for? She has the same mother, no working. Nobody give me, I need to go to work . . . But sometimes I speak – it's a Polish shop and this gentleman lives here for 30 years, he's Polish but he lives here and he said 'Believe me, this is a no good family who live on benefits, from grandfather, father, son, grandson' they live only for benefits.
> (Joanka, 36, Polish, cleaner)

Stenning (2005) tells us that when Poland fell under Soviet control, there was much effort to produce a discursive construction of a socialist working class. Within this discourse was 'hard work' and the political value attached to such work. This construction was assisted by propaganda of the 'hero worker'. Particularly important to the discursive construction of the working class was industrialisation and urbanisation, which was seen to produce an 'urban' working class. Significantly, their status was established on their relationship to production. Work status and workplace also constructed workers' social lives. These workers developed a new sense of identity, one that was collective. These large-scale transformations and the creation of new social groups meant that working-class communities became the cornerstone of the socialist regimes. From the conception of a socialist working class, the political structure in socialist regimes necessitated its own legitimation by constructing the working class as 'moral' (Stenning, 2005).

In the case of 'white' South Africans, a 'hard working' rhetoric also seemed to have manifested itself. Although class never received the same attention as 'race'/ethnicity during apartheid South Africa, a classed discourse can be seen in the way in which 'white' South Africans take comfort in situating their achievements in the UK within a 'hard working' ethic. This, they claim, has been acquired as a consequence of the 'tough' conditions they grew up in. This discourse fails to mention how conditions were generally much tougher for 'non-white' people during apartheid South Africa. Take for example Patrick (35), a wealthy 'white' South African entrepreneur with several businesses in the UK and dual citizenship (British and South African). He acknowledges his parents were middle class, but still believed he had to fight for everything he had in life:

> I came here [to the UK] with no university education, with no contacts . . . And I battled, I absolutely battled. But my motivation was there, and it was to such a degree that nothing was gonna stop me . . . if you want it bad enough,

you will be successful. That's why I think a lot of South Africans have been successful over here [in the UK], because in South Africa, if you don't work, you don't eat.

Although many 'white' South Africans like Patrick could draw upon their ancestral ties to gain citizenship in the UK, there were others who had to apply for citizenship. Yet, members of both sets of 'white' South Africans showed resentment towards the visa-free access granted to EU-migrants. These participants would claim that, unlike EU-migrants, 'white' South Africans were supposedly not claiming any welfare, but rather 'contributing' to British society:

> [I]t irritates me that you see people coming in here [to the UK] . . . they can live off the dole . . . it's so much easier for other nationalities to come in when, y'know, we [South Africans] have to work. Obviously we don't mind working. But we have to work and pay all this money to, y'know, apply for citizenship or just to stay in the country.
> (Cathy, 29, 'white' South African, travel agent)

When asked to give any concrete examples of the 'other nationalities' that she was loosely referring to as 'abusing' the British welfare system, this participant mentioned Poles in particular. Eastern European migrants such as Poles may be particularly convenient targets, as the majority of them are working in lower-paid employment (Fox *et al.*, 2012). Some 'white' South Africans may buy into the myth that because of the position many Eastern Europeans occupy in the British labour market, they are not 'contributing' as much to the British economy as themselves.

This example shows how perceived social 'hierarchies' can be inverted. While Polish migrants used their 'whiteness' in an attempt to gain advantage in British society against black and ethnic minority groups, they increasingly become aware that they are excluded from the 'white' middle classes. In turn, they juxtapose themselves against the 'white' unemployed working classes to 'justify' their residence in Britain. Similarly, feeling disadvantaged by increasing anti-immigration discourse in Britain and experiencing the discrimination of the points-based immigration system, 'white' South Africans make a distinction between themselves and other migrant groups – who have 'benefitted' from EU-citizenship – as not 'deserving' of free migration movement due to language and cultural differences as well as belonging to lower socio-economic categorisations.

What about 'white' South Africans who are situated in the lower echelons of the British labour market themselves? Interestingly, the interview data indicated that some 'white' South African migrants occupying lower socio-economic positions engaged in the scapegoating of Eastern Europeans. These 'white' South Africans are tending to buy into an imagined 'hierarchy of nations', emphasising the British colonial/cultural connections of South Africa. The advantage of being 'white' South African in Britain would appear to be particularly important for those in lower class positions who have fewer other resources to draw upon than 'white' South Africans situated in higher-class positions. 'White' South Africans usually escape the adverse representations that Eastern Europeans are subject to in political and media rhetoric. Hence, 'white' South Africans in lower-class positions would be especially interested in contributing to the stereotypical notions of Eastern European migrants in order to perpetuate this form of discrimination, rather than getting any distorted attention on themselves during a time of recession (see Sveinsson and Gumuschian, 2008).

Drawing on Bourdieu's (1986) three forms of capital – social, economic and cultural – is helpful in investigating the Polish participants' comprehension of social class and divisions in British society. Moore (2008, p.102) tells us that Bourdieu extends the sense in which these three different forms of capitals can be used as part of a broader system of exchange in different fields. The possession, or the accumulation, of the different capitals is what defines the habitus of various social groups, in particular the acquisition of symbolic capital. We pointed out earlier that one legacy of the Soviet communist ideology was that of a 'classless society'. Although many of the Polish participants in this study acknowledged the existence of divisions during communism, they nevertheless pursued their educational aspirations for their children in the UK without comprehending the real structural barriers that they faced. A common narrative was that 'as long as you work hard, you can achieve anything'. Their knowledge of strategies, 'playing the game' and drawing on their cultural capital highlighted intergenerational social reproductions sometimes across several generations. Cultural capital refers to several things, including educational qualifications and knowledge, social confidence, assertiveness and possession of cultural goods. It can also exist in the embodied state in which agents' dispositions can give clues to their social background (Bourdieu, 1986).

The interviews revealed that lack of sufficient economic capital inhibited the pursuit of cultural and educational capital, placing their children at a disadvantage within a system they considered to be 'meritocratic'. The lingering 'classless' discourse also resulted in participants who were in a more advantaged socio-economic position in Britain sometimes being more likely to complain about 'disadvantages'. They were unable to position themselves within the social class 'hierarchy' operating in British society. Even those from the intelligentsia and former Polish aristocracy would define themselves as 'working class'. However, there was also a widely held acknowledgement that divisions in both the home and host societies could be predicated on an individual's holding of cultural capital, and that cultural capital to the Polish participants was sometimes seen as more important than economic capital. This, in part, may explain their positive attitude towards education.

Salomea from London was a third generation graduate from former Polish aristocracy. She was in the top socio-economic positions as categorised by the Standard Occupational Classification (2000). Despite both sides of her family having their wealth and assets seized under communism, their cultural capital continued to be reproduced. Salomea was given private Spanish and French lessons during the communist period. Salomea was able to reflect on her own social reproduction, in which once her family's wealth and title were taken away by the Communist Party, her intergenerational transition of the former family's social positional advantage was transmitted through education:

> Over here [UK] we've got a social circle, for example you belong to ... depending on how much money you've got, you live in the right area, you send your children to the right school, it doesn't really depend that much what you represent with yourself intellectually, you need to be fun and so on, have money and you will be accepted. Where I've been raised and brought up [Poland], you know, my parents for example were with higher education, they were intellectuals, they would have friends from similar intellectual circles, next door you could have the richest guy in the world but if he was not educated and he made his fortune in, I don't know, plumbing gadgets, he would not be accepted in that circle because the conversation with him apart from the odd job would not be at a certain level.
> (Salomea, 40, Polish, investment banker)

We can see how Salomea continues her intergenerational transmission of cultural capital through her son who attends one of the top public selective junior schools in the country and, despite being only 11 and a half years old, speaks English, Polish and French fluently, as well as learning Italian, Latin and Spanish. When Salomea was asked about the aspirations she has for her son, she said that he has just taken a pre-selection exam securing a place at another top private secondary school, which he will attend at 13 years of age.

Oliver and O'Reilly (2010) have explored migration to so-called 'classless' societies in which they applied a Bourdieusian framework. Looking at British migration to Spain, they explored the ways in which class was articulated under new conditions and the extent to which the migrants' habitus re-established itself upon encounters with new social fields. Narratives of different types of British migrants in Spain often took on a derogatory discourse replicating social class divisions in Britain. The reproduction of dominant cultural capital and distinctions retained greater value, especially as economic status could be disguised or in some cases seen as 'irrelevant'. Working-class migrants were often positioned as 'uncultured' Brits who were 'ignorant' of Spanish lifestyles and 'unwilling' to learn. In a new setting that was considered so-called 'egalitarian', Oliver and O'Reilly illustrated how Bourdieu's concepts of field, capital, habitus and distinction reproduced social stratification. Of particular importance was the process of distinction and the recognition of habitus. In the struggle for power in new fields, the habitus helps to position others. As they state, '[a] habitus finds similar habitus; one is thus attracted to those of one's own class, to avoid feeling like fish out of water' (2010, p.22).

Compare Salomea's account to other participants' lack of comprehension when it came to knowing how to 'play the game' in terms of education. They believed in 'meritocracy', stating that if their children really wanted to go to Oxford, for example, they could. Lopez Rodriguez (2010) has suggested that Polish mothers' 'meritocratic' perspective could possibly be linked back to their own experience of being at school both under the communist regime and in a time of transition. Szelenyi (1982) argued that antagonism existed between classes or strata in Eastern European state societies and that there was a class dichotomy between the working class and intelligentsia. The intelligentsia was advantaged by their knowledge and cultural resources; they understood how to 'play the system'. The intelligentsia would not recognise itself as a class and promoted the ideology of 'classlessness'. Yet, its interest in the social structure and system was a pre-condition for the creation of a class consciousness (Szelenyi, 1982).

There were also variations in how 'white' South Africans from different social class backgrounds viewed divisions in British society. Caroline left school at 15 in South Africa without any qualifications. She was currently working in a call centre in a disadvantaged UK town. Like the lack of acknowledgement of social class divisions expressed by the Polish migrants occupying lower socio-economic positions, Caroline saw these divisions as 'naturalised' human behaviour despite being excluded from certain sections of society herself:

> Social class, yeah. I think there's very much still cliques. In my office as such anyway. Y'know, the people upstairs who are the managers and the directors, they are still all cliquey. They'll have their birthday parties together and they'll have their little do's on their own and they'll go lunching together or they'll go Christmas-shopping together. And we won't be included on the first floor. But, y'know, I think that's people in general. I don't think that's a British or South African thing. I think that's just life, that's humans. Y'know, if you think that someone's below you, you're not gonna mingle with them. Simple as, you're gonna try and mix with your own.
> (Caroline, 36, 'white' South African)

Compare this with Frederick. He is highly educated, works in a traditional middle-class occupation and possesses a more legitimate form of cultural capital. He is aware of and observes divisions every day in British society:

> In the term of stereotype and et cetera, race et cetera . . . I think it works very negatively on the pupils I teach, because they, many of them don't see a future for themselves, because they live in some high-rise tower block . . . their brothers working in Sainsbury's and, y'know, Rymans – got menial jobs. They don't understand becoming investment bankers or going to Oxford and Cambridge and like that, whatever. And it's not entirely their fault . . . society has brought it.
> (Frederick, 35, 'white' South African, teacher)

It is telling that what Frederick is describing here would to many be divisions based on social class. Yet, Frederick still brings 'race' into his narrative. By looking at how both 'white' South African and Polish migrants in Britain perceive issues of 'race' and social class, we have shown the importance of intersectionality. Each society gave more importance to one form of social division over the other. Yet, there has always been a cross-over between 'race' and social class that is informing the participants' views.

Conclusion

In this chapter, we have suggested that situations whereby actors have experienced a socio-political transformation in their own society, as well as undertaken migration from their societal order to another one, are both examples of situations in which individuals' habitus will be put to the test with regard to its durability and capability of withstanding external pressures. Through the comparative case study of 'white' South African and Polish migrants in the UK, we have shown that the habitus is still historically specific and connected to a particular cultural, political and economic context – that of migrants' respective 'home societies'. When a country experiences an abrupt change of economic and political systems such as with the collapse of communism (in the case of Poland) and the collapse of apartheid (in the case of South Africa), the psychosocial cultural aspects of the nation's collective habitus takes some time to 'catch up' with these socio-structural changes. Even when combined with the process of migration, the two sets of migrants' national habitus may remain relatively intact – although it is important to acknowledge that the habitus may, of course, transform and adapt over time.

Through exploring two sets of migrants' experiences of adaption using Bourdieu, we have become more reflexive about how we deal with our everyday encounters in our host societies. Actions that would seem logical to ourselves may cause confusion and bemusement to others around us who are 'naturalised' into the cultural norms of the host society. Our enduring norms – that we bring with us as migrants – are used when mitigating ourselves, sometimes to frustrating ends. In order to integrate, we find our opposition to the unfamiliar weakens over time and our habitus slowly transcends, but never changes completely. As such, we become strangers in our home societies while not being fully accepted as a 'native' in our host society. We also recognise that our 'whiteness' and high levels of education mean that some 'natives' are more 'accepting' of us than of the 'traditional' post-colonial migrants who preceded a new wave of European migration. There is always an awkward moment at the dinner party when the topic of immigration comes up and people feel the need to turn to us in the respective host societies and state 'I don't mean you' – meaning that we somehow are more 'tolerated' than other types of migrants. For us, Bourdieu's concepts of habitus and capitals have aided in our understanding of not only our own position, but also that of other migrants as outlined in this chapter.

Notes

1. Although the peace process was initiated in 1990, many scholars assert that apartheid in South Africa did not come to a formal end before the first democratic elections in 1994 were being held (Neocosmos, 2006, p.20).
2. The fall of the Berlin Wall in 1989 saw the era of Soviet control over Eastern Europe dismantle. A Solidarity-led coalition government had already been formally elected in Poland in 1989, just before the fall of the Berlin Wall. On the first of January 1990, Poland was integrated into the international market through financial restructuration agreements with the IMF (Swain & Swain, 2003).
3. In 2004, citizens of eight countries joined the EU (Czech Republic, Estonia, Hungary, Latvia, Lithuania, Poland, Slovakia and Slovenia).
4. It should be noted that the longer Polish participants had been residing in Britain, the less 'racialised' discourse was used and, in many cases, Polish participants were reflexive and embarrassed of the racist views they first held when they came to Britain.
5. We have capitalised Black in the description of Wallace's work. This subscribes to his usage of Black as capitalised.

References

Bonnett, A. 2004. *The idea of the West: culture, politics and history*. Basingstoke: Palgrave Macmillan.
Bourdieu, P. 1958. *Sociologie d'Algerie*. Paris: PUF.
Bourdieu, P. 1977. *Outline of a theory of practice*. Cambridge: Cambridge University Press.
Bourdieu, P. 1979. *Algeria 1960*. Cambridge: Cambridge University Press.
Bourdieu, P. 1986. The forms of capital. In: Richardson, J. (ed.) *Handbook of theory and research for the sociology of education*. New York: Greenwood Press, pp.241–258.
Bourdieu, P. 1988. *Homo academicus*. Cambridge: Polity.
Bourdieu, P. 2008. *Sketch for a self-analysis*. Chicago, IL: University of Chicago Press.
Bourdieu, P. and Sayad, A. 1964. *Le deracinement, la crise de l'agriculture en Algerie*. Paris: Editions de Minuit.
Bukowczyk, J.J. 1996. Polish Americans, history writing, and the organization of memory. In: Bukowczyk, J.J. (ed.) *Polish Americans and their history, community, culture and politics*. Pittsburgh, PA: University of Pittsburgh, pp.1–38.
Burawoy, M. 1999. Afterword. In: Burawoy, M. and Verdery, K. (eds) *Uncertain transition: ethnographies of change in the postsocialist world*. Lanham, MD: Rowman & Littlefield, pp.301–311.
Burawoy, M. and Verdery, K. 1999. Introduction. In: Burawoy, M. and Verdery, K. (eds) *Uncertain transition: ethnographies of change in the postsocialist world*. Lanham, MD: Rowman & Littlefield, pp.1–17.
Crawford, R. 2011. *Bye the beloved country? South Africans in the UK 1994–2009*. Pretoria, South Africa: Unisa Press.
Dyer, R. 1997. *White: essays on race and culture*. London: Routledge.
Eade, J., Drinkwater, S. and Garapich, M. 2007. Class and ethnicity – Polish migrant workers in London: Full Research Report. *ESRC End of Award Report, RES-000-22-1294*. Swindon, UK: ESRC.
Fox, J.E., Morosanu, L. and Szilassy, E. 2012. The racialization of the new European migration to the UK. *Sociology*. **46**(4), pp.680–695.

Hardy, J. 2009. *Poland's new capitalism*. London: Pluto Press.
Lopez Rodriguez, M. 2010. Migration and a quest for 'normalcy'. Polish migrant mothers and the capitalization of meritocratic opportunities in the UK. *Social Identities*. **16**(3), pp.339–358.
Lukowski, J. and Zawadzki, H. 2006. *A concise history of Poland*. 2nd edn. Cambridge: Cambridge University Press.
MacDonald, M. 2012. *Why race matters in South Africa*. Cambridge, MA: Harvard University Press.
McDowell, L. 2009. Old and new European economic migrants: whiteness and managed migration polices. *Journal of Ethnic and Migration Studies*. **35**(1), pp.19–36.
Moore, R. 2008. Capital. In: Grenfell, M. (ed.) *Pierre Bourdieu: Key Concepts*. Durham, UK: Acumen, pp.101–117.
Neocosmos, M. 2006. *From 'foreign natives' to 'native foreigners': explaining xenophobia in post-apartheid South Africa: citizenship and nationalism, identity and politics*. Dakar, Senegal: CODESRIA Monograph Series.
Nyamnjoh, F.B. 2006. *Insiders and outsiders: citizenship and xenophobia in contemporary Southern Africa*. Dakar, Senegal: CODESRIA Books.
Oliver, C. and O'Reilly, K. 2010. A Bourdieusian analysis of class and migration: habitus and the individualizing process. *Sociology*. **44**(1), pp.49–66.
Prażmowska, A.J. 2011. *A history of Poland*. 2nd edn. Basingstoke: Palgrave Macmillan.
Robbins, D. 2005a. Introduction: Bourdieu's practical logic of the social sciences and its implications for international, cross-cultural understanding. In: Robbins, D. (ed.) 2000. *Pierre Bourdieu: four-volume set. Vol 2*. London: Sage, pp.ix–xliv.
Robbins, D. 2005b. The origins, early development and status of Bourdieu's concepts of 'cultural capital'. *The British Journal of Sociology*. **56**(1), pp.13–30.
Ryan, L. 2010. Becoming Polish in London: negotiating ethnicity through migration. *Social Identities*. **16**(3), pp.359–376.
Sallaz, J.J. 2010. Talking race, marketing culture: the racial habitus in and out of apartheid. *Social Problems*. **57**(2), pp.294–314.
Silverstein, P. 2004. Of rooting and uprooting: Kabyle habitus, domesticity, and structural nostalgia. *Ethnography*. **5**(4), pp.553–578.
Standard Occupational Classification (SOC). 2000. *Summary of structure*. [Online] [Accessed 18 July 2013] Available from: www.ons.gov.uk/ons/guide-method/classifications/archived-standard-classifications/standard-occupational-classification-2000/summary-of-structure.pdf
Statistics South Africa. 2012. *Census 2011: methodology and highlights of key results*. [Online] [Accessed 3 May 2013] Available from: http://unstats.un.org/unsd/demographic/sources/census/2010_PHC/South_Africa/ZAF06-Census2011.pdf
Stenning, A. 2005. Post-socialism and the changing geographies of the everyday in Poland. *Transactions of the Institute of British Geographers*. **30**(1), pp.113–127.
Steyn, M. 2001. *Whiteness just isn't what it used to be: white identity in a changing South Africa*. Albany, NY: State University of New York Press.
Sveinsson, K.P. and Gumuschian, A. 2008. Understanding diversity – South Africans in multi-ethnic Britain. *Runnymede Community Studies*. [Online] [Accessed 20 November 2009] Available from: www.runnymedetrust.org/uploads/publications/pdfs/UnderstandingDiversity-2008.pdf
Swain, G. and Swain, N. 2003. *Eastern Europe since 1945*. 3rd edn. Basingstoke: Palgrave Macmillan.

Szelenyi, I. 1982. The intelligentsia in the class structure of state socialist societies. *American Journal of Sociology*. **88**(Supplement), pp.287–326.

Vertovec, S. 2007. Super-diversity and its implications. *Ethnic and Racial Studies*. **30**(6), pp.1024–1054.

Wacquant, L. 1989. Towards a reflexive sociology. A workshop with Pierre Bourdieu. *Sociological Theory*. **7**(1), pp.26–63.

Chapter 8

The limits of capital gains
Using Bourdieu to understand social mobility into elite occupations

Sam Friedman

My mental tussles with the ideas of Pierre Bourdieu began long before I actually knew who he was. In school my best friend was a boy called Kieran whose parents came from a working-class coal mining family in South Wales. Kieran's parents had gone on to become successful ballroom dancers and later started a dance school that expanded into a profitable chain. When Kieran and I were 14, his parents decided to move the family from their modest new-build terrace on the outskirts of Bristol into a large five-bed town house on my leafy road in the city centre. But the thing that always perplexed me was that although Kieran's family had the money to move into my area, they never seemed comfortable in their new social habitat. Dinner table conversations continually revealed frustrations with unfriendly, uptight neighbours and their struggles to make a dance school work in the local area.

Certainly, Kieran's parents were different to everyone else on my street. They had different accents, wore different clothes, decorated their home differently and drove a different car. But at root Kieran's parents were lovely, sociable people who had done well and simply wanted to enjoy their upward mobility in a new area with new friends. Yet because their cultural identity was rooted in their working-class upbringing, their neighbours never fully accepted them. To me, the cultural differences were exciting – my parents would never let me eat at McDonalds, have TV on at the dinner table, or go on beach holidays to the Costa Del Sol. What I came to realise, though, was that it was precisely these practices that marked my friend's parents out as different, as being less 'sophisticated', as somehow having 'bad' taste. I even remember my Mum, normally a bastion of liberal tolerance, struggling to conceal her revulsion as Kieran's mum, Pam, showed us around their new living room, complete with zebra-skin rug and imitation crystal chandelier. Why did she continue to dodge Pam's invitations to the pub, I recall asking innocently one day: 'It's hard to explain, Sam, I just don't feel we have much in common . . .'

Now, as a teenager, this snobbery not only struck me as incredibly unfair but it also made me acutely aware of the often shadowy role that culture plays in marking out social class in Britain. It taught me that while nobody ever seems to talk about social class (it was never once mentioned in relation to Kieran's parents) its influence is nonetheless everywhere we look – in the way we speak, in the way we act, in what we like; in other words, in most of the things that we think of as natural and take for granted.

A few years later, during the second year of my sociology degree at the University of Edinburgh, I was introduced to *Distinction* (Bourdieu, 1984). As I read, adolescent memories flooded back. Bourdieu's analysis resonated deeply. It helped me make sense of my own biography – not just in terms of my friendship with Kieran and his family but also regarding my own privilege, my own 'natural' cultural confidence, and my own easy passage through the education system (compared to the struggles of many working-class friends).

Fast forward 10 years and the fascination with Bourdieusian social theory has only deepened. My PhD, for example, sought to engage directly with Bourdieu's work on cultural consumption, examining comedy taste and sense of humour as emerging sources of cultural capital (Friedman, 2014a). However, in this chapter, I want to explore more recent work that has brought me back to the experiences of people – such as Kieran's parents – who experience upward mobility in contemporary Britain.

The concept of social mobility has become one of the key motifs of the current political era, with politicians of left and right now championing it as a core policy objective (Payne, 2013). Yet most political debate and sociological research is focused on *rates* of social mobility, conceived as the absolute or relative numbers of those entering an occupational class different to that of their parents (Bukodi *et al.*, 2014; Milburn, 2013). To me, though, this emphasis on rates of occupational entry obscures a pivotal dimension of social mobility; progress *within* occupational groups. As the example of Kieran's parents illustrates, the upwardly mobile may well be successful in *becoming* professionals or entrepreneurs, but that doesn't necessarily mean they go on to achieve the highest levels of success, seniority or prestige. Indeed, they may – like Kieran's parents – continue to face powerful barriers once they've arrived at their destination class.

This chapter attempts to address this question of intra-occupational disadvantage by bringing together findings from two of my own research projects. In them, I have attempted to move beyond social mobility as occupational 'access' and instead provide a more Bourdieusian understanding of social mobility. The chapter proceeds in three steps. First, I outline what I mean by a Bourdieusian approach to social mobility and explain the way in which I draw upon Bourdieu's main thinking tools. Second, I seek to foreground the role that capitals play in structuring a person's ongoing mobility trajectory. Drawing on results from the BBC Great British Class Survey (GBCS), I demonstrate that even when those from working-class backgrounds enter elite occupations, they are less likely to accumulate the same economic, cultural and social capital as those from privileged backgrounds. In particular, I find that the mobile have considerably lower incomes, pointing toward the kind of 'glass ceiling' normally associated with women and ethnic minorities. Third, I aim to deepen this statistical analysis by using qualitative interviews to explore the *experience* of social mobility. In particular, I probe the social, cultural and emotional challenges the upwardly mobile face within elite occupations and how this might prevent them from achieving the highest incomes and seniority.

Bourdieu and social mobility

Although hugely influenced by Bourdieu, all of my work to date has stressed that Bourdieu's thinking needs renewal and extension, especially in light of historical shifts that have taken place since his death (see Friedman, 2014a, pp.169–172). I would also argue, alongside others (Bennett, 2007; Lawler, 1999), that social mobility remained a rather undertheorised area of Bourdieu's analysis. This view is normally associated with a critique of Bourdieu's notion of habitus, which many argue is almost antithetical to social mobility (Goldthorpe, 2007; De Landa, 2006; King, 2000). It is certainly true that Bourdieu (1984, p.101) saw the dispositions flowing from primary socialisation as so robust that in the vast majority of cases the habitus stayed unified over the lifecourse, meaning those with strong initial reserves of economic, social and cultural capital were statistically bound to accumulate further and vice versa (Bourdieu & Wacquant, 1992, p.133).

However, what many of Bourdieu's detractors fail to recognise is that his conception of social space was constructed along *three* dimensions – volume of capital, composition of capital *and* 'change in these properties over time' (Bourdieu, 1984, p.114). Thus, he had a theoretical conception of social mobility – albeit a somewhat limiting one – as a 'band of more or less probable trajectories' based on one's 'volume of inherited capital'. In this way, contrary to his critics, Bourdieu acknowledged that the dispositional architecture of the habitus was subject to change, according to both 'new experiences' (Bourdieu, 2000, p.161) and also via conscious, intentional self-fashioning or pedagogic effort. Yet, he saw the nature of this change as gradual and fundamentally limited by the childhood dispositions that always act as the 'scaffolding' of habitus (Wacquant, 2013, p.6). In other words, primary dispositions are 'long-lasting; they tend to perpetuate, to reproduce themselves, *but they are not eternal*' (Bourdieu, 2005, p.45).

In later works (2004; 1999; 1998), though, Bourdieu did (briefly) acknowledge that long-range mobility was more problematic for habitus. This was perhaps most powerfully illustrated in his own reminiscences in a *Sketch for a Self-Analysis* (2004). Raised by an uneducated postal worker and his wife, Bourdieu experienced extraordinary long-range upward mobility that eventually took him to the Chair of the prestigious Collège de France. However, the psychological price of this movement, he argued, was a painful feeling of double isolation from the fields of his origin and destination social class. At once the 'self-made Parvenu', forever lacking the embodied cultural capital to successfully acculturate into elite circles, Bourdieu also described an enduring disdain for a 'success that [he] conceived as a treachery' of his roots (Bourdieu, 2004, p.109). In other work (1999, pp.508–13) he developed this thinking further, noting that the limbo experienced by the extreme upwardly mobile (like himself) had profound psychic implications.

Drawing on the psychoanalytic notion of 'splitting of the self' (Steinmetz, 2006; Fourny, 2000), he noted that such hysteresis between habitus and field produced a painfully fragmented self, a habitus clivé 'torn by contradiction and internal division' (Bourdieu, 2004, p.161). Ingram and Abrahams further discuss the concept of habitus clivé in relation to social mobility in Chapter 10, highlighting the pain of this process for the socially mobile working classes as well as examining the potentially creative aspects of habitus change. Considering the disjuncture between habitus and field and the resulting hysteresis it can produce allows social mobility to be unpicked as a concept that is neither straightforwardly positive nor negative, as Morrin (Chapter 9) also shows in her work on unresolved class hauntings that endure through the mobility process.

While this notion of habitus clivé is forcefully invoked in Bourdieu's own self-analysis, long-range social mobility remains a concept only fleetingly explored in his empirical work. This was perhaps because its occurrence was relatively rare in 1970s and 1980s France, and therefore instances like his own could be interpreted as 'exceptions that proved the rule' in terms of the general stability of the primary habitus. However, in contemporary Britain, successive nationally representative studies (Bukodi et al., 2014; Bennett et al., 2008) indicate that long-range social mobility is more commonplace.[1] For some (Goldthorpe, 2007) this is therefore a fatal blow to the concept of habitus, fundamentally problematising its promise of a secure unity of dispositions over the lifecourse.

Yet, as noted in the introduction, conventional measures of social mobility tend to focus on occupational 'access'[2] and fail to consider how the upwardly mobile progress *within* occupations. Indeed it is here that I believe Bourdieu's trilogy of key concepts – capital, field and habitus – may be useful for providing a more nuanced understanding of mobility trajectories. A focus on capital and field – as I will shortly illustrate – allows us to see that even when the upwardly mobile do enter elite occupational fields, they generally fail to accumulate the same stocks of economic, cultural and social capital as those from privileged backgrounds. Habitus then helps us to unpick some of the reasons *why*. Not only does the durability of primary dispositions help to explain potentially debilitating feelings of insecurity among the upwardly mobile, but it also suggests that the mobile may be ambivalent about reaching 'the top' and often associate success with anxiety over abandoning familial ties and class-cultural origins.

Uncovering the 'class' ceiling[3]

The 2011 BBC Great British Class Survey (N =161,000) provides a unique data set from which to begin a Bourdieusian analysis of social mobility. It provides both detailed measures of cultural, social and economic capital and, while its self-selecting sample resulted in substantial skews, the main groups that were overrepresented are precisely those apposite for a more detailed examination of upward social mobility: *the occupationally successful*. Thus, drawing on the unusually large GBCS sample of respondents in elite[4] NS-SEC 1 occupations

(N = 40,077), I begin my analysis by investigating whether stocks of capital differ according to respondents' social origins.[5]

Before doing this, though, it is briefly worth outlining the measurement of the capitals that can be seen in contrast to Burke's measurement of capital (Chapter 2) from a small-scale qualitative approach. In terms of cultural capital, I use two measures. Following Savage et al.'s (2013) example, I first measure cultural capital in terms of engagement with 'legitimate culture' (i.e., classical music, attending stately homes, museums, art galleries, jazz, theatre, and French restaurants).[6] However, using a more conventional Bourdieusian (1984) frame, I also look at cultural capital in terms of educational attainment – specifically whether respondents have or have not attended university. In terms of social capital I draw on questions based on the Lin position generator (Lin et al., 2001), which asks whether the respondent knows someone socially in each of 34 occupations. Each of these are scored with the widely validated Cambridge Social Interaction and Stratification (CAMSIS) scale and the mean status score used as my measure of social capital. For economic capital, I look at three measures assessing household income, household savings and house price.

Table 8.1 demonstrates how the capital scores of respondents in elite occupations vary according to their social origin. This shows that stocks of cultural, social and economic capital are all considerably higher among those from higher professional and managerial backgrounds. Beginning with cultural capital, Table 8.1 shows that those from privileged backgrounds tend to engage more in highbrow

Table 8.1 Capitals by origin in elite occupations

	Senior managers and traditional professions	Lower managers and modern professions	Intermediate and technical occupations	Manual and never-worked	Average all in elite occupations
Average income	£71,090	£60,277	£56,955	£56,228	£63,834
Average savings	£58,085	£45,574	£46,956	£44,558	£50,975
Average house value	£243,883	£209,707	£211,894	£200,505	£223,545
Score on legitimate cultural participation	14.3	13.5	13.1	12.7	13.7
Average score of contacts	55.1	53.2	51.0	49.5	53.3
Went to independent/ fee-paying school	33%	17%	9%	7%	22%
Attended Oxford or Cambridge	11%	8%	4%	4%	8%
Has undergraduate degree (or more)	87%	84%	77%	75%	83%
N	16,841	12,200	7,079	3,959	40,077

culture and are more likely to have a degree than respondents who have been upwardly socially mobile. It also illustrates that they are more likely to have benefited from elite educational pathways, with a considerably higher proportion educated privately and/or attending Oxford or Cambridge universities. In terms of social capital they also have higher status social contacts. Finally, in terms of economic capital, Table 8.1 illustrates that those intergenerationally stable in elite occupations have on average £12,000 more in savings than their mobile counterparts, their houses are worth at least £33,000 more on average and their average incomes are between £11,000 and £15,000 higher.

Many of these differences in capitals point towards exactly the kind of intergenerational *transmission* of advantage highlighted by Bourdieu (1986). For example, parents in higher managerial and professional employment are likely to have higher status contacts themselves, which in turn they can directly pass on to their children. It is also probable they will transmit highbrow tastes, as well as inculcating valuable cultural dispositions such as aesthetic 'disinterestedness' (Bourdieu, 1984). Similarly, it may be that the greater savings and more valuable homes of the stable are the direct result of inheritance and/or informal 'gifting' of economic capital from parents who, because of their own occupational position, have greater economic resources (Piketty, 2014).

Yet processes of transmission or inheritance cannot explain the considerable differences in *income* demonstrated in Table 8.1. How, then, can we explain the fact that within elite occupations the upwardly mobile earn significantly less than those from intergenerationally stable backgrounds? In order to disentangle potential sources of this income disparity, Table 8.2 shows the results of a series of regressions of income among those in elite occupations.[7] Model 1 in Table 8.2 shows a simple base model where household income is predicted by the respondent's education (more or less than an undergraduate degree, with undergraduate degree the reference group), race/ethnicity (whites as reference group), gender (men as reference group) and NS-SEC category (higher managers as reference group), age, region (London and the Southeast vs the rest of the UK) and whether or not they are living with a partner (single people as reference group). All of these factors are clearly strongly associated with household income, and serve as controls in the next three models: in other words, any further differences by origin are above and beyond a 'London effect', age differences and differences in educational qualifications. Adding the respondents' class origin to the model shows that origins strongly predict income even net of these controls; those whose parents were not traditional professionals or higher managers have incomes between *£8178 and £10,760/year lower than otherwise-similar people in other elite occupations.*[8]

Next I add two types of elite schooling: having attended a private school, and having attended Oxford or Cambridge, or one of the other Russell Group universities. Both of these also strongly and substantively predict income; respondents who attended private schools have on average £9,570 more income than those who are otherwise similar but did not; those who attended Oxbridge

Table 8.2 Regression of income for all in elite occupations

Models	1	2	3	4
Education (vs undergraduate degree)				
Postgraduate degree	4,645	4,140	3,017	768
A-levels or less education	−8,367	−7,552	−4,997	−1,101
NS-SEC (vs 1.1)				
Higher professionals (ns-sec 1.2)	−19,337	−18,460	−18,231	−16,998
Lower managers (ns-sec 2)	−23,440	−22,132	−21,673	−19,810
Age	117	143	158	−0
Partnered	17,549	17,546	17,892	16,930
Not white	256	138	−95	−14
Female	−4,522	−4,658	−4,299	−6,338
Region (vs rest of UK)				
London	23,302	22,391	20,498	16,927
Southeast	10,523	10,029	9,479	8,067
Parents (vs higher mgmt and trad. profs)				
Modern prof. or lower mgmt		−8,178	−6,517	−5,191
Technical or intermediate		−10,721	−7,997	−4,863
Routine, semi-routine, never worked		−10,760	−7,801	−3,164
University attended (versus all others)				
Oxford or Cambridge			9,570	5,732
Any other Russell Group			4,412	2,470
Private/fee-paying school			9,507	6,795
Legitimate cultural participation (cultural capital)				23,879
Mean of contacts' scores (social capital)				77,323
Constant	69,475	73,564	54,550	3,599
N	38,973	38,973	38,973	38,973
r2	0.134	0.146	0.159	0.194
Adjusted r2	0.134	0.146	0.158	0.193

Source: The Great British Class Survey

have £9,507 more than those who attended non-Russell Group institutions. Further, it appears that some of the advantage in earnings for those from senior manager/traditional professional families operates through elite education: the coefficients for coming from lower-status occupation households are each reduced by around £1,500–£3,000 when education is added to the model.

In Model 4 in Table 8.2, measures of cultural and social capital (both transformed to range from 0 to 1) are added. While origins and schooling are clearly prior to current income, these capitals are associated both with current status *and* origins, so it is not necessarily surprising that they have associations with income. Nevertheless, the effects of social and cultural capital are striking. Together they account for up to nearly half (£1,700–£4,650) of the income advantage of those from privileged backgrounds.

What is important to emphasise, however, is that while the coefficients for origins shrink substantially with addition of capital measures to the model, they do not by any means disappear. This strongly implies that while some of the income disparity we see may be the effect of cultural and social capitals, these capitals (or at least our measures of them) do not explain the entire difference between the upwardly mobile and the children of upper professionals and managers. There are still considerable (nearly £3,200–£5,200) differences in annual household income by origins, even when a slew of other factors are held constant.

Together these findings underline the importance of looking beyond 'access' in social mobility research. In particular, they illustrate that even when the upwardly mobile are successful in entering elite fields they generally fail to achieve the same levels of success (in terms of cultural, social and economic capital) as those from more privileged backgrounds. Indeed, in terms of income, there is good reason to believe that a powerful class ceiling exists for people from lower-status occupational origins. Even when we control for schooling, education, age and capital volume, we find these respondents have considerably lower incomes than their higher-origin colleagues. If we are not willing to assume that people from lower-status backgrounds simply work less hard, the case for lingering, unfair disadvantage by class origin in the GBCS is strong.

The operation of cultural and social capital in everyday life

While the GBCS certainly points towards a powerful class ceiling, quantitative data can only provide limited insight into how this disadvantage actually plays out in everyday life. It cannot elucidate, for example, whether the mobile actually *feel* disadvantaged and uncomfortable in elite occupations, and/or whether they may be somehow ambivalent about the *illusio* (Bourdieu, 1993, pp.72–73) that dominates in the new occupational field they find themselves in. To tap these dimensions of social mobility, I turn to data from a separate qualitative project I conducted in 2012–2013 that specifically explored the subjective *experience* of social mobility. The project consisted of 52 life history interviews with a stratified sub-sample of mobile respondents drawn from the Cultural Capital and Social Exclusion Project (CCSE) survey (N = 1745). Interviewees were sampled to represent the contours of the representative survey sample – in terms of age, gender, region, ethnicity and range of social mobility. Here, in order to deepen the GBCS analysis, I focus on 25 interviews with respondents upwardly mobile into elite NS-SEC 1 occupations.

These interviews largely corroborated the GBCS results concerning the capital deficit of the upwardly mobile. However, they also acted to significantly nuance the GBCS's somewhat uni-dimensional measures of social and cultural capital. In particular, they demonstrated the more dynamic, micro-interactional way in which these resources actually functioned to generate advantages and disadvantages in social life. Helen (39), for example, had been brought up in South London and, after studying drama at university, had gone on to become a theatre director. Although she had enjoyed significant success – running her own theatre aged 26 – Helen said she had spent 'many unhappy years trying to be accepted by the theatre elite'. She attributed much of this to the way that cultural markers of her working-class background – her South-London accent, her large hooped earrings, her choice of sports trainers – were judged by others in the industry. She recounted a recent meeting with an agent:

> And at one point he went, 'I know a lot of producers; I can warn them that although you sound brash and uneducated, you've actually got a lot to say for yourself.' And I was like – 'Wow!'

Echoing the work of Lawler (1999) and Skeggs (1997), there was a sense here that the dominantly upper middle class – 'theatre world' – had marked Helen as 'other', as displaying the wrong type of taste and the wrong type of femininity. Moreover, Helen believed these unceasing judgments had had a direct effect on her career trajectory:

> Over the years a lot of people have tried to suggest that if I was to lose the 'Chav' earrings, or dress ... I dunno ... more appropriately, then I would somehow get on better. But it's just not me.

Karl, a 45-year-old engineering executive, was also acutely aware of his relative lack of cultural capital and its effect on his occupational status. Karl had spent 10 years gradually progressing through middle management before being promoted to a research and development team where the other staff were all graduates. Initially, the manager refused to grant Karl's promotion because he didn't have a degree, but eventually this was overruled. While Karl noted that he had now established himself in this environment, he described an abiding insecurity about his intellect:

KARL: Occasionally there's the odd situation where if it's about my work, that's fine, but you may be sat in a group and ... I just don't have the intellectual clout or capacity to react at their level sometimes.
XX: What do you mean by 'intellectual clout'?
KARL: I think it's probably more me, I'm not sure they even think that. Like you can get quite in-depth discussions on some quite technical aspects and it isn't accent, it's the language I use. I'm very much a kind of 'a spade is a spade', I don't use big words. English has never been a particularly strong subject of mine.

The accounts of Helen and Karl both demonstrate the more subtle ways that cultural capital – in terms of legitimate clothing and language – operates as a micro-political resource, shaping perceptions of one's 'appropriateness' to fulfil a role or their 'intellectual capacity' (Rivera, 2012). They also illustrate how these kinds of cultural competencies are hard to simply acquire (Bourdieu, 1984, pp.65–68). Helen and Brian do not see their clothing or language as a 'choice'. Instead they are essential to their sense of self. Indeed, they viewed purposive attempts at adaptation as phoney, inauthentic. As Helen noted, 'I could definitely play the game more, change my voice, but it's just not me. I'm never going to be in that club'. Similarly in Chapter 3 Mckenzie spoke of her participants' construction of self through their clothing and jewellery. For the women on the Nottingham council estate where Mckenzie conducted her ethnography, they were aware that their 'big gold hoop earrings' made them a target for middle-class mockery in wider media discourse. Yet, in the same way that legitimate clothing and language operates as a micro-political resource of 'appropriation' into middle-class society for those conforming to the norms of social mobility, the dress style of the women living on the council estate allowed them to occupy a site of resistance to middle-class values.

Interviews were also useful in demonstrating the interplay *between* different capitals and the way they often overlapped to generate cumulative advantages and disadvantages. Cerin (50, fiction writer), for example, described how her enduring sense of cultural inferiority had affected her ability to 'network':

> I don't have a lot of confidence so when it comes to networking in the writing world, I'm not very good at it. I tend to feel a bit gauche with a lot of things, when we're talking about socialising or eating habits . . . And god knows why, but I still feel the inclination to defer to people who speak with RP accents. Language lets me down. I'm not as articulate as I'd like to be.

Brian, a 38-year-old lawyer, explained a similar interaction between the cultural and the social in his work. In one telling example he compared his continuing fear of 'etiquette' at his firm's 'formal work dinners' with the 'ease' of more privileged colleagues:

> If you're from a certain background you just seem automatically comfortable with stuff . . . like my friend Jackie, from a really privileged background. I remember one dinner, at the Caprice [London restaurant]. I'd never been before, and I remember worrying so much that I was going to fuck up. And we're all waiting for our food and she just picks up her roll up and starts eating it like this [imitates stuffing food into his mouth] in front of all the partners (laughs). And you just think, actually, that's what it gives you the confidence to do. It's almost like learning to draw the figure before you can be an abstract artist. What a moneyed background gives you is that sense that you know all the right ways to do stuff, but because *you know*, it doesn't matter, you can do what the fuck you like.

Of course it is difficult to know how this sense of cultural and social deficit *directly* affected respondents' incomes or wider careers. The precise process of capital conversion is notoriously difficult to capture (Savage *et al.*, 2015), particularly from cultural and social *into* economic capital. Nonetheless, there was a consistent sense across interviewees that they lacked tacit advantages possessed by those with a 'natural' practical knowledge of the 'rules of the game' in elite occupational fields.

Of course interviews provide fundamentally subjective accounts and it may well be that respondents' sense of their own disadvantage were somewhat exaggerated or distorted. Yet this is telling in itself, as internal perceptions of deficit were clearly an active constituent of the notion of barriers to success. Here the pull of primary habitus, what Ingram (2011) neatly terms habitus tug, left many respondents with a paralytic suspicion that they somehow 'weren't good enough' (Mark, 42, script writer), a 'fraud' (Amy, 31, doctor), that a 'fall' was just around the corner (Helen) or that they were forever in danger of being 'caught out' (Usha, 41, graphic designer). In other words, the very real intra-occupational barriers described by the upwardly mobile were not always imposed by others, but sometimes represented *self-induced* anxieties about exceeding one's own 'field of possibles' (Bourdieu, 1984, p.110).

The ambivalences of upward trajectories

As I have demonstrated, the sense of disadvantage felt by many upwardly mobile respondents was a process in which they were, at least to some extent, active contributors. But this was not simply about the crippling insecurities of the parvenu. Indeed, there was often a powerful corresponding sense that they themselves did not fully *want to belong* in their field of destination. This frequently manifested through what Bourdieu calls 'self-elimination' (Bourdieu, 1984, p.379), where respondents consciously excluded themselves from certain legitimate social or cultural domains as a way of actively guarding against identity mutation. As Michelle (52), an architect, explained:

> I'm very much blinkered. My whole family is the kind of 'our kind of people don't do that kinda thing'. We impose limitations on ourselves. My brothers, my sisters, my parents, we're all kinda 'no, no, no, we don't do that, you can't wear anything fancy because we don't do that, don't get above yourselves, who do you think you are?' Whereas Keith [husband], as I say, he'll listen to any type of music. He would even go and watch a cricket match, whereas my family were always football, football, football. There's probably thousands of examples. There's a hotel on Refrew St, it's called Citizen M, all tinted glass and posh. And I would just never go in, because my type of person just doesn't go in there, you know? Keith would say – 'ah hell, they want our business, let's go in'. Whereas I tend to impose limitations.

The notion that some respondents, like Michelle, very consciously imposed 'limitations' on the cultural and social aspects of their upward trajectory further complicates the notion of a class ceiling. It suggests, in particular, a certain ambivalence towards the lifestyle that one is expected to adopt following occupational success, a conscious refusal to comply with all such rules of the game (*illusio*). My interview with Peter (45, arts PR executive) provided a particularly intriguing illustration of this ambivalence. I interviewed Peter in a famous private members' club in London, of which he was a member. At first I thought Peter's choice of venue was a way of signalling his success to me, a symbolic marker of his upward journey. But instead, over the course of our interview, it became clear that the club held a complex and quite contradictory role in Peter's mind. As we began the interview, he explained that he had always been 'very anti-clubs', that everyone in his industry used them for 'networking and entertaining clients' but that he didn't like the exclusivity, 'the snottiness', and besides he was 'scared of being rejected'. A few years ago, however, his husband (also in PR) had been 'asked to join' and had convinced him to try it too. Peter had now been a member for nearly a decade, but interestingly he still seemed decidedly uncertain, even suspicious, of the club. He was critical, for example, of the 'shady' way other members used it 'to do business' and instead proudly asserted his affinity with the staff:

> I like the people who work here. I treat them like normal people, which they are, and I think a lot of people who join these places, any club, there's a certain aggrandisement about you and I hate the way they talk down to the waiters. It took me years to turn up in a t-shirt here, but I remember one day someone who worked here said I love your tattoos, and I thought 'now I feel comfortable'.

This example may seem innocuous but in fact I think it neatly underlines the profound complexity of upward social mobility, and particularly the delicate renegotiation of habitus it demands. From deep suspicion to a paid up member, Peter's relationship to his private members' club mirrored his upward trajectory from, in his words, 'a little working-class boy from Romford' to a very successful director of an arts PR agency. Yet while the club gave Peter access to an elite environment perfect for cultivating professional relationships, he was keen to distance himself from these more instrumental or strategic uses. Instead, he delighted in mocking the 'posh' aesthetic and the 'uptight' members. In this way, it is possible to see the constant push and pull of habitus that takes place during upward mobility and what Bourdieu (2002, p.510) calls the 'contradictions of succession'. Elsewhere I have written about the psychological price attached to this mental juggling act, and how it can lead to a sense of dislocation and cultural homelessness (Friedman, 2015; 2012). Here, though, I see these findings more as a means of sounding a note of caution before reading the GBCS class ceiling as somehow a straightforward sign of discrimination or elite closure. Instead, a

Bourdieusian lens demands a more complex analysis, one that acknowledges how the emotional pull of class-cultural loyalties can entangle subjects in the affinities of the past, and why – despite prevailing political rhetoric – upward mobility may remain a state that not everyone unequivocally aspires to.

Conclusion

A short while ago, over a pint in a favourite Bristol pub, I made a garbled attempt to introduce Bourdieu to my old friend Kieran. He listened politely, humouring my passionate but long-winded explanations of habitus, field and symbolic violence. At the end, wishing to hammer my point home, I triumphantly introduced his parents, and recalled my mum's snobby comments about his living room. 'But Friedles', he said cooly. 'We were just as bad, my family used to rip the piss out of you all the time – the mouldy food, the TV rationing, the books no one in your family had actually *read*.'

At the time I was convinced Kieran hadn't understood my point. But the more I think about it the more I think his words demonstrate a very nuanced and very Bourdieusian understanding of social mobility. Fundamentally in this chapter I have tried to demonstrate that thinking with Bourdieu is particularly fruitful for moving beyond mobility as simply rates of occupational entry and instead helps to illuminate people's ongoing mobility *trajectories*, structured by both their volume and composition of capital. Indeed, a focus on capitals – using the GBCS – illustrates that those from lower-class backgrounds tend to face barriers even once they 'make it' into elite occupations, most notably in terms of a powerful earnings class ceiling.

Yet the chapter has also stressed the importance of reading such findings alongside a subjective exploration of how mobility is actually *experienced*. And it is here that Kieran's words are particularly telling. While my mum's taste snobbery toward Kieran's family are good examples of the very real cultural and social barriers that the upwardly mobile tend to face *within* elite domains, the family's astute counter-snobbery is a useful reminder that this is not a straightforwardly one-way process. As the accounts in this chapter illustrate, individual habituses always retain – at least in some shape or form – the symbolic baggage of the past and this means that most people do not necessarily fetishise upward mobility in the same way as politicians. As Kieran went on to tell me, his parents still feel detached from their 'posh' local community but at the same time they actively contribute to this detachment. They defiantly drive 10 miles to drink in their old local pub and proudly tell anyone who will listen that 'they are, and always will be, working class'.

It is worth noting a few brief caveats to the arguments advanced here. First, upward social mobility is highly complex and cannot, and should not, be reduced simply to the issues of deficit and disadvantage I have discussed here. As I have pointed out elsewhere (Friedman, 2015), the experience of mobility is significantly affected by the range, speed and direction of one's trajectory in social space, as well as their particular combination of class, gender and ethnicity. Second and connected to this, I would also note that my findings do not foreclose the possibility, as Abrahams and Ingram explore elsewhere in this book, that the changes in habitus implied by upward mobility are always associated with anxiety or ambivalence and may *simultaneously* yield significant insights and opportunities afforded by the ability to act as plural actors (Lahire, 2011).

However, despite these cautions, I feel these findings point toward the need to further interrogate the apparent social success of those who enter elite occupations from less privileged origins. While they may be held up by politicians as exemplars of meritocracy, this masks disadvantages (and ambivalences) that live on long after they have negotiated entry.

Notes

1 Most studies suggest approximately 20 per cent of those in professional and managerial jobs have been long-range upwardly mobile (Bukodi *et al.*, 2014; Bennett *et al.*, 2008).
2 Comparisons of two (or sometimes three) moments in a respondent's life (i.e. social origin, current job and occasionally also first job) (Erikson & Goldthorpe, 1992; Goldthorpe, 1980).
3 The analysis in this section was carried out with Daniel Laurison.
4 While it is difficult to define a set of uncontested 'elite occupations', here we primarily draw on the guidance of Rose (2013) who argues the best existing measure is provided by Class 1 of the National Statistics Socio-Economic Classification (NS-SEC). We also include a number of high-status occupations routinely associated in policy discourse with the British elite but not included in NS-SEC 1 (see Friedman *et al.*, 2015 for further detail).
5 Social mobility is usually defined by looking at comparable social class variables for one's social origin and destination. Here, while we are able to measure 'destination' using respondents' self-reported job title, an identical measure for 'origin' is not available. We therefore refer to the question asking respondents what work the 'main income earner' carried out when they were 14. While the nine possible answer categories do not exactly map onto the eight major NS-SEC categories, they come fairly close. We thus code responses into four groups; intergenerationally 'stable', 'short-range', 'mid-range' and 'long-range' upwardly mobile (see Friedman *et al.*, 2015 for further detail).
6 Rather than assuming a priori that certain culture is more "highbrow" than others, Savage *et al.* (2013) carried out an inductive analysis of cultural taste using multiple correspondence analysis (MCA) in order to assess the structuring of cultural divisions in Britain.
7 A few disclaimers: first, formal statistical inference is not possible, so I do not include measures of statistical significance. Second, many of the independent variables in these models (for example origins and schooling) are clearly correlated with one another. This will reduce the size of the observed effects of these variables, so if we still see strong relationships we can assume these are operating above and beyond their overlap with the other variables.
8 Although as noted the GBCS data is not representative, it is possible to benchmark these findings with data from the 2014 Labour Force Survey (LFS). The results of an LFS regression on income-origin differentials, controlling for educational qualifications, age, sex, ethnicity, region of the UK and whether the respondent worked part time, shows very similarly that the long-range upwardly mobile within NS-SEC 1 earn £7,997 less than the stable.

References

Abrahams, J. and Ingram, N. 2013. The chameleon habitus: exploring local students' negotiations of multiple fields. *Sociological Research Online.* **18**(4). [Online] Available from: www.socresonline.org.uk/18/4/21.html

Bennett, T. *et al.* 2008. *Class, culture, distinction.* London: Routledge.

Bourdieu, P. 1984. *Distinction: a social critique of the judgment of taste.* London: Routledge.

Bourdieu, P. 1990. *The logic of practice.* Stanford, CA: Stanford University Press.

Bourdieu, P. 1998. *The state nobility: elite schools in the field of power.* Stanford, CA: Stanford University Press.

Bourdieu, P. 1999. *The weight of the world.* London: Polity.

Bourdieu, P. 2004. *Esquisse pour une auto-analyse.* Paris: Editions Raisons D'Agir.

Bourdieu, P. 2005. Habitus. In: Hillier, J. and Rooksby, E. (eds) *Habitus: A sense of place.* Farnham, UK: Ashgate.

Bourdieu, P. and Wacquant, L. 1992. *An invitation to reflexive sociology.* Oxford: Polity Press.

Bukodi, E., Goldthorpe, J. H., Waller, L. and Kuha, J. 2015. The mobility problem in Britain: new findings from the analysis of birth cohort data. *The British Journal of Sociology.* **66**(1), pp.93–117.

Cabinet Office (2011) Opening doors, breaking barriers: a strategy for social mobility. *HM Government.* [Online] [Accessed 19 December 2014] Available from: www.gov.uk/government/uploads/system/uploads/attachment_data/file/61964/opening-doors-breaking-barriers.pdf

Friedman, S. 2012. Cultural omnivores or culturally homeless? Exploring the shifting cultural identities of the socially mobile. *Poetics.* **40**(5), pp.467–489.

Friedman, S. 2014a. *Comedy and distinction: the cultural currency of a 'good' sense of humour.* Abingdon, UK: Routledge.

Friedman, S. 2014b. The price of the ticket: rethinking the experience of social mobility. *Sociology.* **48**(2), pp.352–368.

Friedman, S. 2015. Habitus clivé and the emotional imprint of social mobility. *Sociological Review.* [Early view online.] DOI: 10.1111/1467–954X.12280

Friedman, S., Laurison, D. and Miles, A. 2015. Breaking the 'class' ceiling? Social mobility into Britain's elite occupations. *Sociological Review.* **63**(2), pp.259–290.

Fourny, J.F. 2000. Bourdieu's uneasy psychoanalysis. *SubStance.* **29**(3), pp.103–112.

Goldthorpe, J.H. 2007. 'Cultural capital': some critical observations. *Sociologica.* **2**. [Online] [Accessed 19 March 2015] Available from: www.sociologica.mulino.it/journal/article/index/Article/Journal:ARTICLE:100/Item/Journal:ARTICLE:100

Ingram, N. 2011. Within school and beyond the gate: the complexities of being educationally successful and working class. *Sociology.* **45**(2), pp.287–302.

King, A. 2000. Thinking with Bourdieu against Bourdieu: a 'practical' critique of the habitus. *Sociological Theory.* **18**(3), pp.417–433.

Lahire, B. 2011. *The plural actor.* Cambridge: Polity.

Lawler, S. 1999. Getting out and getting away: women's narratives of class mobility. *Feminist Review.* **63**(3), pp.3–24.

Lin, N., Fu, Y-C and Hsung, R-M. 2001. Position generator: a measurement for social capital. In: Lin, N., Coo, K. and Burt, R.S. (eds) *Social capital: theory and research.* Cambridge: Cambridge University Press, pp.51–87.

Milburn, A. 2013. Higher education: the fair access challenge. *Social Mobility and Child Poverty Commission*, pp.1–26. [Online] [Accessed 4 May 2015] Available from: www.gov.uk/government/uploads/system/uploads/attachment_data/file/206994/FINAL_Higher_Education_-_The_Fair_Access_Challenge.pdf

Payne, G. 2012. A new social mobility? The political redefinition of a sociological problem. *Contemporary Social Science*. **7**(1), pp.55–71.

Piketty, T. 2014. *Capital in the twenty-first century.* Cambridge, MA: Harvard University Press.

Rivera, L. 2012. Hiring as cultural matching: the case of elite professional service firms. *American Sociological Review*. 77(6), pp.999–1022.

Rose, D. 2013. Response to: The old new politics of class [by Mike Savage]. 14 May. *Stratification and Culture Research Network Blog*. [Online] [Accessed 19 May 2015] Available from: https://stratificationandculture.wordpress.com/2013/05/14/the-old-new-politics-of-classmike-savage-reflects/

Savage, M., Devine, F., Taylor, M., Friedman, S., Le Roux, B., Miles, A., Hjellbrekke, J. and Cunningham, N. 2013. A new model of social class: findings from the BBC's Great British Class Survey experiment. *Sociology*. **47**(2), pp.219–250.

Steinmetz, G. 2006. Bourdieu's disavowal of Lacan: psychoanalytic theory and the concepts of 'habitus' and 'symbolic capital'. *Constellations*. **13**(4), pp.445–464.

Wacquant, L. 2013. Homines in extremis: what fighting scholars teach us about habitus. *Body and Society*. **20**(2), pp.3–17.

Chapter 9

Unresolved reflections
Bourdieu, haunting and struggling with ghosts

Kirsty Morrin

Reflecting back on my childhood, I recall often staring out my bedroom window. My window looked out over the backyard; my dog Sasha would usually be there, barking at next-door's cat. Just beyond the end of my yard was a tall red brick wall. This belonged to a factory, at the time abandoned, soon to be converted into flats. Running alongside the factory was a railway track, and in the distance, beyond the tracks, an ornate factory chimney, the most prominent of all the buildings in the town. This image then framed in the centre of the window view, is now inscribed in my memory. These industrial landscapes are not only inscribed in my thoughts, but also in my biography. The ornate chimney attached to the factory that my parents worked in as I grew up, penned into ascription on my birth certificate; 'Mother: textile worker', 'Father: end of line operative'. On reflection this could be seen as having both a literal and symbolic meaning. The abandoned factory yard and the back alley behind my house are where my friends and I played as children, drawing hopscotch on the floor with old dried-out stones or trying out new tricks on our rollerblades. The backyard I looked upon, and the bedroom from which I was staring, one I shared with my sisters, once belonged to another family of factory workers. The purpose-built, two-up two-down terrace would not have existed but for Milltown's[1] (my hometown's) industrial past.

In the first section of this chapter I reflect on the industrial and cultural heritage of Milltown in order to critically consider the recent introduction of Milltown Community Academy. The academy in question has not only transformed the physical layout of the town through the building of a 49 million-pound 'superstructure' from which it operates, but has further attempted to instill a change in the psychic landscape of the townspeople through its 'entrepreneurial ethos'. I interrogate educational policies that led to the opening of the academy and critique them as initiatives that construct disadvantage in terms of a 'lack of aspiration', with modes of inequality cast as individual problems brought about by cultural 'deficits' rather than accounting for the impacts of material deprivation. Further, I counter the idea that the solution to past educational 'failures' within the academy and wider community are to be found in the introduction of a 'spirit of entrepreneurship'. I employ the Bourdieusian concept of doxa (1977) to assert that current policy reform attaches 'deficit' to culture, specifically working-class culture and 'solution' to enterprise, in this case, entrepreneurship in a 'taken-for-granted' manner. This reflects the way in which policy is part of a 'doxic practice', whereby questions of 'working class deficit' and entrepreneurial advantages go unquestioned. Bourdieu describes doxa as the 'pre-verbal taking-for-granted' of the world (Bourdieu, 1990, p.68). Doxa is said to generate practice through the *illusio* of practical sense. In other words, it is possible for individuals to have 'transposable dispositions' that adapt to attaining goals through generative practice, without 'presupposing' an aim or how to get there (Bourdieu, 1977, p.72). In this way, 'unthinkingness' is 'an active and creative relation to the world' (Bourdieu, 1992, p.122).

In 2007 and against the odds, I finished my A levels and left the town for university. Moving into and living in university halls was an unsettling experience; I found myself host to a variety of strange feelings. My accent was marked out as 'strong' and became a topic of conversation. The discussions I used to engage in at home, often about football, became less frequent. I felt distanced from what I had known. These 'out of place' (or 'out of time') feelings are well documented in sociological research on non-traditional university students, notably in Bourdieu's notion of hysteresis – as the emotional turmoil one might feel when habitus 'lags' (or 'tugs') temporally in relation to the field in which you are positioned (Bourdieu, 1977; 1984; 1990; 1996; 2000; Ngai, 2005; Reay *et al*, 2009; Ingram, 2011). It is no wonder, I suppose, that as the first in my family to not only attend university, but to attend an elite institution, I felt some biographical affinity when I first heard of Bourdieu's work during my undergraduate Sociology degree. Through Bourdieusian insights, learned in the lecture hall and seminar room, yet also experienced and 'felt' in the social, I began to feel as if the symbolic boundaries of my life were being redrawn. How I spoke, how I dressed – these 'things' were loaded with (new) symbolic meaning; distinctions of class, inscribed from birth, were now being reflected in the present. It is these thoughts and feelings that led me to think about and later formally research my 'home' in an undergraduate dissertation.

In this piece I not only want to consider when and how such 'unsettled feelings' arise, but the ways in which we might further reflect individually and theoretically on 'unsettledness'. Bourdieu's habitus-clivé has been discussed in Friedman's previous chapter, as well as the subsequent chapter by Ingram and Abrahams. Friedman in Chapter 8 explores the lingering effects of an individual's upbringing upon their habitus when they experience social mobility. Friedman shows how these individuals' resistance to the conformity of legitimate clothing and language of the middle classes who occupy the same employment field as them, can result in a stagnant career progression in which they encounter what Friedman terms 'the class ceiling'. Friedman similarly shows the discomfort experienced by middle-class people in possession of legitimate cultural capital when occupying predominantly working-class spaces. Ingram and Abrahams, in Chapter 10, discuss the sense of reflexivity that working-class students undergo in higher education when they 'achieve' social mobility. Both these chapters gave me a useful insight into other case studies of social mobility using Bourdieu's concept of cleft habitus. In addition, this chapter will be exploring not only what comes into play when we enter into a dialectic relationship with past experience and current practice, but also the possibilities of what 'comes to life' through practical action as a result of this. Beverley Skeggs (2011) notes that there are limitations in Bourdieu's conceptual framework, in its inability to set out working-class resistances against stigmatising judgements, underplaying people's ability to deflect and contest these. Similarly Mckenzie has shown how working-class women can invert stigmatisation by applying their own codes of recognition to working-class culture. Keeping working-class resistance in mind and reflecting on my own biography, in the final section of this chapter I analyse some of the interview narratives collated during my PhD fieldwork. The research was ethnographic work undertaken within and outside Milltown Community Academy. I document unsettled feelings (in the context of Bourdeiusian 'unsettledness') as well as accounting for subsequent reflexive practices present in the narratives of my respondents. I follow in the theoretical trajectory of the works of Crossley (2001) and more recently Atkinson (2010), who document phenomenological developments (or phenomenological hauntings) to Bourdieu's conceptual frameworks. I offer an additional reading of habitus-field relation to that of Bourdieu and the 'unsettled-hysteresis' effect, to consider how 'unsettledness' located in a habitus-field disjuncture, might lead to further feelings of 'unresolvedness' giving rise to strategy and resistance in narrative. I do so through Avery Gordon's (1997) phenomenological notion of 'social haunting'. Haunting, Gordon explains, is 'an emergent state' and tells of how the field carries with it residues of the past (Gordon, 2011, p.3). Further explaining that 'ghosts' are the signs of repression, Gordon talks about the visible premonitions of what 'has been' that arise when there is a rupture to the current (doxic) state: 'The ghost demands your attention. The present wavers. Something will happen' (ibid.). In this shift from noting the 'unsettled' to accounting for the 'unresolved', I consider a vital addition to the Bourdieusian toolbox.

Having finished my undergraduate dissertation, I found myself standing in my parents' kitchen, this time in a different room, in a new house, which was just around the corner from the old one. I was reading the local newspaper. Immediately one story caught my attention: 'Milltown Academy in Enterprise First: A Milltown high school has become the first in England to house business enterprise pods from which local start-ups and students can run their enterprises' (local newspaper). Although I had heard about the academy as it replaced the school just up the road from my house, and it had caused huge controversy during the construction of its new building, I had not been aware of the 'entrepreneurial specialism' it proposed. Not only was the school introducing business pods for students and new local businesses to operate from within the academy walls, it saw 'entrepreneurship' as a way of breaking the cycle of 'the poverty of aspiration' through the promotion of an 'entrepreneurial mindset'. In Milltown Community Academy, 'entrepreneurship' is not just good business sense but a set of cultural and social skills to be harnessed for future success in education and beyond. In the words of the academy sponsor, it is a 'way of life'. Having just refuted (with empirical evidence) that a 'lack of aspiration' or 'poverty-as a cultural facet' existed in the individuals I interviewed in the town for my undergraduate dissertation, I found myself now facing the same landscape of unfounded deficit. The 'new' model of education was built on nothing more than 'old' deficit models. Something had to be done.

Milltown Community Academy

In 2000, the New Labour government and the then Department for Education and Skills (now Department for Education (DfE)) laid out the means for the creation of city academies under The Learning and Skills Act (2000). City academies were renamed to the simpler 'academies' we recognise today under the Education Act (2002). The DfE stated all academies should be independent and largely funded by central government and a sponsor, rather than a local authority.[2] Initially only placed in urban areas of 'disadvantage', academies and academy sponsors were appointed with the task of 'reversing the cycle of failing schools' and 'helping articulate a clear educational vision that champions the ability of *all* children to achieve their potential' (www.dfe.gov.uk, emphasis added). The sponsors would also be expected to introduce a specialism at the academy in order to help them achieve the aims set out by the DfE. Furthermore, and of particular interest to this chapter, is the way in which the academies initiative was also proposed to tackle the so-called 'traditional ways of thinking ... achieve success, and break with *cultures of low aspiration*' (ibid., emphasis added). In this way, sponsors are said to be 'accountable for *progressive* and *sustainable* improvements to performance in their schools' (ibid., emphasis added).

In the case of Milltown Community Academy, its conversion to academy status took place in 2008.[3] Prior to this, the formerly-named Milltown High School had been placed in 'special measures' by Office for Standards in Education (OFSTED) after (among other things) in 2003 only 22 per cent of its pupils achieved five A*–C GCSE grades (including Maths and English). In 2004, the Lower Layer Super Output Area (LSOA) in which the high school stood was in the top 7 per cent of 'most deprived' in England (Office for National Statistics), marking the high school out as one 'prime' for academy conversion at the time. It was in 2004 that the now academy sponsor expressed an initial interest in academy takeover; sponsorship came in the form of an educational charitable foundation, founded by a billionaire businessman turned philanthropist. Documenting his own successes in the business world, the sponsor and his foundation claimed not only 'learning as central to the regeneration of the local economy and community' (Sponsor expression of interest document, 2004) but also the virtues of an 'entrepreneurial education' in leading such regeneration.

In the context of Milltown Community Academy, sponsors and official school documentation claim that 'entrepreneurship' is not just about having good business sense, but is a set of individual and social behaviours that if harnessed are said to act as a 'catalyst for social change' (academy sponsor website) and, in turn, creates a more 'successful' society:

> Our aim is to build a more successful society where regardless of their background, young people have the essential skills and entrepreneurial qualities they need to seize control of their own lives, and become contributing members of their local community.
>
> (Sponsor Brochure)

In 2010, and after delays (something I talk about later in this chapter), Milltown Community Academy moved into a new multi-million-pound building. The building, or 'superstructure' was costed to the sponsor for two million pounds, with government subsidising the further 47 million pounds. This made the building and additional resources the most expensive UK academy when it opened. The academy is a geometrically constructed, glass-fronted building, standing five storeys high and scaling 14,000 square metres in the centre of the town (architecture reports/website). The very site of the school and the building, it is claimed, reflects a socio-spatial embeddedness of the 'entrepreneurial ethos' as linked to be at the centre of 'progressive' education and to 'Milltown's future':

> The design is modern and contemporary and illustrates an ambition to take hold of the future . . . the site, town and usage of the building are opportune and appropriate. Education is the future.
>
> (Architectural design statement)

There are a number of things we should draw out here. First, what assumptions underlie the 'need' for an 'entrepreneurial education'? What is it about this period in time that makes the academy necessary in the eyes of the DfE and academy sponsor? Why Milltown? Finally, what impacts has the academy had on the physical and (if any) psychic landscape of the town and townspeople?

Through Bourdieusian insight, I contend that current 'neo-liberal'[4] educational policy initiatives have deficit models of working-class culture written into them. When we think about the link between policy and education, it is important to remember that in the mid-1960s, when Bourdieu was writing about the existing conservative educational ethos of French higher education, he was aware of the reciprocal relationships between the structures of society and that of institutional structures, as well as how an individual's biography would influence their educational trajectories. As Derek Robbins states:

> The educational system operated for society in the same way as a diary might for an individual. It offered clean sheets on which might be written both accounts of what has happened and projections of what might occur. It structurally guaranteed a continuity between the past and the future and

sustained the individual's sense of personal identity and was, therefore, conservative, but it embodied no predisposition in favour of either the past recollection or the future aspiration.

(1991, p.54)

Here I will identify this in terms of educational policy, but I will also go beyond this, exposing the general outlook and overwhelming acceptance that solutions-based 'enterprise culture' or 'entrepreneurship' are legitimate and equitable. In this respect, both 'deficit as cultural' and 'enterprise as solution', I argue, are part of a 'doxic' regime in current policy reform (Bourdieu 1977; Bourdieu & Wacquant 1992).

Recent educational policies (see Millburn Report, 2009, for example) have stated that in order to tackle 'blocked' social mobility and to close persistent attainment gaps there must be a focus on 'unleashing' and 'raising aspiration' within schools (Milburn Report, 2009) as well as 'encouraging' parents and carers to 'get involved' in their children's' education (DfES, 2006, p.23), further cementing the meritocratic narrative transmitted by successive (higher) educational policies discussed by Burke in Chapter 2. This focus illustrates that policy initiatives and subsequent academy-sponsorship schemes place the emphasis of previous educational 'failures' on issues of the 'cultural' poverty. By attributing such 'poverty' to a 'lack' of aspiration and/or a 'lack' of parental involvement, policy is not acknowledging the impact of structural and material deprivation; as typified by this quote from the (then) Department for Children and Families (now the DfE), 'children living in deprived communities face a *cultural barrier* which is in many ways a *bigger barrier than material poverty*' (DSCF, 2008, p.27, emphasis added).

Regardless of years of sociological research refuting the direct and absolute link between low 'aspirations' and educational 'under attainment' by students and parents alike (see Carter-Wall & Whitfield, 2012; Archer *et al.*, 2010), the message of the marked and detrimental impact of aspiration deficit persists in policy outlook.

In addition, we are increasingly seeing a promotion of enterprise culture within educational policy and reform, where it seems to have become 'common sense' or, I argue, 'doxic' (Bourdieu: 1977) to incorporate private sector principles (Cuban, 2004; Woods & Woods, 2011). Doing so is seen to instill 'a culture of ambition to replace the poverty of aspiration' in schooling (Adonis, 2008, p.15). While the entrepreneurial initiative at Milltown Community Academy is distinct and more overt in some of its practices, the underlying assumptions that an 'entrepreneurial ethos' acts as a foundation for a progressive model of education is not an isolated case, nor an entirely 'new' one. Enterprising initiatives in English schooling during in the 1980s were identified and dispelled as not successful in the works of Hollands (1990) and McDonald and Coffield (1991). However, there currently seems to be an 'ontological complicity' between the main UK political parties that the 'entrepreneurial solution' is one that will 'fix all'. Entrepreneurship has become a 'nation call', '*the* solution'; it will supposedly bridge the deficit in economy, labour market and education. In a speech given just after the formation of the Conservative-Liberal Democrats coalition government in 2010, David Cameron, the Prime Minister, stated: 'light the fires of entrepreneurialism in every corner of our country. That's what our coalition strategy for growth is all about' (Cameron, 2010). More recently the former Labour leader, Ed Miliband, called on entrepreneurs as though the nation's future rested in their hands and, more notably, on their 'ideas': 'I say to every entrepreneur we need your ideas and your enthusiasm' (Miliband, 2014). Moreover, in the 'Enterprise for All Report' (2014), Lord Young suggested that entrepreneurship should be embedded in all educational institutions, from primary school through to university.

Bourdieu outlines how 'the established cosmological and political order is perceived not as arbitrary, i.e. as one possible among others, but as a self-evident and natural order which goes without saying and therefore goes unquestioned' (Bourdieu, 1977, p.166). In this next part I will document two ways in which the current 'neo-liberal' deficit-solution doxa championed itself as so 'necessary' and part of 'natural progression' in the cultural-material space of Milltown. First, I will outline how the building of Milltown Community Academy came at the cost of a number of people's homes, which were cleared (against the will of some home occupiers) to make way for the building. Second, I consider the accelerated nature of claims to 'success' in the current doxic order, and document how since 2008 the academy sponsor has subsequently taken over a further 11 institutions, three of which are in Milltown.

Displaced and distracted

As mentioned, Milltown Community Academy was granted academy status in 2008, but it did not move into its new 49 million pound building until 2010. The initial plans were that Milltown Community Academy would be 'launched' in its new building. However, the building project was delayed due to contestation over the chosen site for the new building. When the plot of land was chosen, the new academy building was proposed back in 2003 as part of the Housing Market renewal Pathfinder scheme.[5] As well as being occupied by a variety of local residents, the earmarked land also had local businesses, a doctor's surgery and vacant properties on the site. After consultation between governing bodies, residents and business owners, an agreement on 'opportunity purchases' and 'housing relocation packages' could not be reached. This saw the parties involved enter a two-year battle with authorities over the placement of Compulsory Purchase Orders (CPOs) on their properties. CPOs are powers awarded to acquiring authorities to 'compulsorily purchase land to carry out a function which Parliament has decided is in the *public interest*' (Compulsory Purchase and Compensation document, 2004, p.7, emphasis added). It is in the notion and questioning of just what the 'public interest' is, that this piece situates itself. In the context of Milltown and the building of the academy, CPOs were initially granted to the governing bodies in 2005 and around 90 per cent of the buildings in the area were seized and demolished. A number of residents continued to fight the CPOs for a further two years, in which time the CPOs were overturned and retracted, and then reinstated seeing the remaining houses cleared for the building of the academy to take place. Importantly, the Milltown CPO procedure is now cited as an example of 'bad practice' in a 2010 Compulsory Purchase Order report and offers advice to governing authorities on how 'not to secure' CPOs in the future.

It is a salient point, however, that although the residents fighting to keep their homes were avidly against the proposed building site of the academy, they were not publicly against the academy itself. One contesting resident at the time sums up the sentiment of the campaign in a public letter published in the local newspaper in 2005:

> The campaign is not saying don't build the academy, it's only against the proposed site . . . people think the academy is a good idea, just not where they want to put it.
>
> (Milltown resident)

Although there was protest *en masse* from some of Milltown's residents around the building, there was no similar resistance documented on the entrepreneurial initiative it housed. Of note here is that 'public interest' is concurrent with the need for Milltown Community Academy as well as the entrepreneurial initiatives it proffers. In other words, 'public interest' has become bound up with market logic solutions in school, where the notion of 'progression' is to be established not only in an academy, but in an entrepreneurial academy. Many residents, campaigners and protesters documented (among other things) the sheer emotional costs of the process of re-homing, or displacement of the residents affected by the building project. One former resident complained that 'they're splitting up my family, my community and all my friends' (Milltown resident, 2006). Regardless, the 'public interest' as market logic doxa prevails.

Milltown Community Academy was the sponsor's flagship project and the first to open in the UK. Since then, the academy sponsor has gone from overseeing one school in Milltown to opening or taking over a further 11 educational institutions,[5] all of which have entrepreneurial education as their core ethos. Three of the further 11 institutions are in Milltown, to date, the town's *only* three secondary institutions: two converter academies, one Studio School. They are *all now* run by the same sponsor. The speed with which these institutions opened, year on year, without much time to evidence their 'success', notes the strength of the 'neo-liberal' agenda to produce and reproduce itself. One way in which Milltown Community Academy has moved from 'special measures' to a school that is currently graded 'good' by OFSTED, has been to increase the number of students achieving five A*–C GCSEs including Maths and English to that above the national average, which is currently 59 per cent. There was in fact a rise from 2009 of 23 per cent to a peak of 64 per cent in 2013. However, in 2014, there were changes to how the league table results were calculated. This involved taking the result of the student's first exam rather than their best result over a number of attempts. This change in how league tables were calculated, saw a drop in the number of students achieving five A*–C grades (including Maths and English) at Milltown Community Academy, plummeting from 64 per cent achieving the grades, to just 33 per cent. Regardless of whether this drop illustrates the faults in the implementation of this examination policy for calculating league table positions, or it predicts that we should be concerned about future 'one time only' examination policies, or even that the school was involved in 'game playing' that resulted in better GCSE grades recorded, the consequences were that Milltown Community Academy now plummeted into 'unsatisfactory' territory. However, this has not stopped the sponsor chain taking over further institutions since.

Given the controversy that surrounded the displacement of people to make room for the building of Milltown Community Academy, it is interesting that no-one negatively affected by this development seemed to question the deficit-solution model of this new academy, not to mention its 'entrepreneurial' initiative. Bourdieu's concept of doxa is a useful tool to explore why this may be. For Bourdieu, doxa contributed to the reproduction of social institutions and relations. Doxa as pre-reflexive, according to Bourdieu, means that a 'sense of limits' becomes internalised within agents (Deer, 2008, p.120). In this way, individualistic discourse of 'success' through business and 'one's own efforts' has become so entrenched in the mind-set of the people of Milltown, that the academy's 'entrepreneurial' ethos went unchallenged. As Bourdieu (1992, p.14) states, doxa is

> a formidable mechanism, like the imperial system – a wonderful instrument of ideology, much bigger and more powerful than television or propaganda

The 'naturalisation' of the sponsor's focus on entrepreneurship has resulted in sponsorship being spread across Milltown and into other areas of similar demography. This model of education has been portrayed as 'progressive' and 'successful'. It is the power of this doxic regime that displaces and distracts agents, which for me confirms the usefulness of the application of Bourdieu's theorising to empirical research.

So far in this chapter I have shown how Bourdieu identifies doxa as constitutive of a set of arbitrary and generative principles that largely go unquestioned by those subject to its rule because of its 'naturalised' position and, therefore, pre-reflexive nature, in which structures and relations are taken for granted. Moreover, I have described doxa as a useful conceptual tool for understanding current educational policy reforms that have led to the introduction of an 'entrepreneurial academy' in Milltown. In this way, it is possible to anticipate that through 'naturalised' notions of distinction, the 'issue of social inequality' may at times be rendered 'largely *invisible*' (Savage, 2000, p.159, emphasis in original). With the value placed on some voices over others in the 'public interest', and a perceived or prediction of a sharp fall in the student grades at Milltown Community Academy in 2014, the issue of inequality is clear to me, but just how apparent is it to those living it?

Inhabiting heterodoxy

As part of my PhD research, I conducted a 10-month ethnography of Milltown Community Academy and its surrounding area from 2013 to 2014. As well as everyday participant observations, focus groups and collating local newspapers (among other things), I spoke to around 150 people (inclusive of 40 formal recorded interviews) about their experiences and perceptions of the academy, from students to parents, teachers to librarians, staff serving lunch to the local entrepreneurs who run their businesses from inside the academy. My motivations for conducting the research might be considered 'heretical' or as former education secretary Michael Gove so warmly puts, in the blasphemous position of 'an enemy of promise'. If my own position is one built through learning the skills of 'reflexive sociology', a method Bourdieu defends as 'necessity of the critical intellectual', my research motives are also a condition of experiencing and 'feeling' the changing social condition of moving from Milltown to university. But what of the narratives, motivations and experiences of those affiliated with the shift from the old Milltown High School into Milltown Community Academy? Might these narratives also consist of 'feelings of change', and therefore give rise to questions of what happens to people in a time of transition?

Bourdieu (1977) talks about how a sudden rupture of external structures can affect agents: 'objective crisis, which, in breaking the immediate fit between the subjective structures and the objective structures, destroys self-evidence practically' (Bourdieu, 1977, p.168–69). Lizardo and Strand (2010) consider such an 'unsettledness' of habitus in Bourdieu's writing as one that can be both pre-reflexive state and one that can lead to reflexivity. The 'unsettled' feelings that operate below the level of consciousness can be theorised as part of the hysteresis effect (Bourdieu, 2000; 1996, p.157; 1990, p.59; 1984, p.142; 1977, p.77) where 'dispositions which are out of line with the field', experience negative internal sanctions (Bourdieu, 2000, p.160). Speaking to the temporal elements of hysteresis, it can further be defined as the lag in practical effect of the changing circumstances under which persons act. The latter reflexive elements of unsettled habitus as conceptualised in the 'Don Quixote' effect (Bourdieu, 1984, 1988, 1990) leads to a 'heightened awareness' of one's environment when habitus-field disjuncture arises. However, Bourdieu further claims that crisis is 'a necessary condition for a questioning of doxa but is not in itself a sufficient condition for the production of a critical discourse' (Bourdieu, 1977, p.169). So are we saying that an 'objective crisis', or habitus-field disjuncture, under the current Bourdieusian theorising, mean that the working-class people remain compliant?

To answer this I need to return to Beverley Skeggs' (2011) work and consider her critique of Bourdieu in which she argues his work is unable to set out working-class resistances against stigmatising judgements, and this underplays people's ability to deflect. I consider the critique that Bourdieu constrains working-class people by considering them as unable to 'think doxa' (or 'commit' heresy) and further as being immobilised by their illegitimated capitals, in a world of cultural arbitraries (Goldthorpe, 2007). Moreover, located in my findings and in the narratives of some of the respondents and participants in my study, I found some considered resistances. I argue therefore that Bourdieu's 'hysteresis', 'hysteresis-reflexivity' or 'Don Quixote' effects do not fully account for the ongoing, reflective and dialectic nature in which respondents engaged with my questions and their environment. It also does not account for 'what' kinds of reflexivity arose in the interview. As I contend there were not just moments of 'unsettledness', but further reflections on those feelings and narratives of defense that rose against them.

In *Outline of Theory and Practice*, Bourdieu offers a further theorising of the doxic regime, one that might offer a move away from modes of 'unthinkingness' and domination (thus reproduction), to the possibility of theorising for 'thoughtfulness' and breaks to the doxic regime. In Bourdieu's (1977) work, there are two ways in which doxa can enter thought; one is through the 'straightened opinion' of orthodoxy, which seeks to reinstate the purest form of doxa. The other is heterodoxy, which seeks to oppose; it is the 'choice-heresy-made possible by existence to competing possibilities and to the explicit critique of the sum of the total of the alternative not chosen that the established order implies' (Bourdieu, 1977, p.169).

In light of this I take a phenomenological (and spectral) turn towards Avery Gordon's notion of 'social haunting'. Haunting offers what is 'a very particular way of knowing what has happened or is happening'. Furthermore, it also adds a complimentary and developed reading of habitus-field relations in the context of my study (Gordon, 1997, p.8). Gordon asserts that haunting is

> an emergent state: the ghost arises, carrying the signs and portents of a repression in the past or the present that's no longer working. The ghost demands your attention. The present wavers. Something will happen.
> (Gordon, 2011, p.3)

This is the idea that those moments of crisis, or 'past repression' can lay dormant in the field itself, but when habitus-field relations rupture, according to the epistemology of haunting, the 'ghost' arises and demands our attention. Ghosts in this respect are the temporal residue in the field that creates dissonance. Not only might this lead to an unsettling of what we had known, but through haunting a further 'something-to-be-done' emerges as the ghost beckons us to listen.

Ghost hunting: from unsettled to unresolved

Gordon tells us 'to study social life one must confront the ghostly aspects of it' (1997, p.7). It is in the 'demanding' nature of ghosts that I found this alternative analytical tool for 'listening' to narratives in my fieldwork. In the narratives of my interviewees, I 'listen' to the spectre for resisting. As suggested previously, I consider two doxic modes of policy practice emplaced on the academy and those affiliated with it, one of 'working-class-as-deficit' (inclusive of Milltown's-past-as deficit) and second, 'entrepreneurship-as-solution'. The former I contend can be seen as a 'repressive former state' Gordon identifies. For example, during an interview with a student, I noted a deviation, further reflection and a struggle with a ghost in her response to a question about her aspirations for university.

Lydia, a 'star student', spoke about her aspirations for university. She documented that there is an absolute expectation from teachers, staff and her peers at Milltown Community Academy that she will not only go to university, but a 'good' university, therefore she would be focusing her attention on Oxbridge and Russell Group applications. However, after I had asked Lydia which universities specifically she was thinking of applying to, she paused for a few seconds, then gave the following four-fold response without any further questioning:

> But my mum and step dad, they're really supportive, kind people, they're just supporting me in whatever I do but they're saying just go as far as you can, they're just telling me to, go for it [pause] I don't know, I can't really describe it, they never tell me not to do something, and they never tell me to do something, they allow me to make my own mistakes, but support me in whatever I'm doing [pause] It's not just 'cos they don't want me to do it that they don't say 'do this do that' like the school it's just 'cos they're just nice people and like lovely and they went to college but that's it but that doesn't mean they don't help me or support me [pause] well they didn't go to university but that doesn't mean they don't want me to go.

I argue that Lydia is struggling with a 'ghost of deficit', as located not in her current educational success, but in the lingering effects of her habitus as reflected in her parents' educational past trajectories as they did not go to university. Lydia felt the need to reflect and defend her parents as just as 'aspirational' and supportive as the school, and not 'in deficit' just because their educational pasts did not map her perceived educational future in university. The visibility of 'ghost of deficit', I claim, actually led the student to do two things. First, it led Lydia to consider her position as relational to her parents and her future plans for university. This caused a feeling of unsettledness, a habitus-field disjuncture of 'what was' in her parents and 'what could be' in her own educational future. Second, it unearthed a feeling of something-to-be-done, something to further explain, something to defend, and, finally, the resistance itself, a defense of her parents – again a doxa (or a social haunting) of deficit.

It is important to be aware of both methodological or interviewer effect during this exchange with Lydia. It could be contented that my position as a PhD researcher from a Russell Group university produced this type of response. However, I would examine the overt relationship between the question 'so, what universities are you thinking of?' and the possibility of deciphering a parental involvement. Was the student Lydia aware and reflecting on the ways in which her parents had been brought into question by deficit attachment to the town and what stood before Milltown Community Academy? I would argue she was.

To begin with, there is a disruption between similar habitus, i.e that of Lydia's and her parents'. Here I contend that the ghost marks them out as distant from each other, their differences located in 'past' non-transition into Higher Education and 'present' expectation of a transition into university. However, what is defended here by Lydia, is against a 'ghost of deficit' and although that 'deficit' might be perceived as inside specific habitus (that of her parents in this case) the student is not recognising it as such. In this way she rejects the notion of 'lag' or that her parents are positioned as 'behind' because of their educational experiences and challenges that this might be put upon them. In this way the ghost is an 'out there' phenomenon located only in the field as she finds it, not in the habitus of her parents. She sees the ghost in the field itself and tussles with it there, resisting the 'ghost of deficit' as she goes. This offers a small example of resistance and a pattern of resistance to explore in all of my fieldwork. As Gordon foresaw, the present wavered. Something happened.

Concluding remarks: I haunted, he haunted, we haunted

> Through driving mists I seemed to see
> A Thing that smirked and smiled:
> And found that he was giving me
> A lesson in Biography,
> As if I were a child.
> (excerpt from Lewis Carroll's CANTO III: Scarmoges, 1911, p.25)

In this chapter, I have considered how my own biography is linked to much of Bourdieu's work, as a perpetual presence in my past and current work, engaging me in an 'ongoing dialogue' (Crossley, 2001, p.116) as an early career academic in an ever-expanding world of theory. Alongside this, I have given an insight into how the introduction of an entrepreneurial academy in my hometown reflects a current doxic mode of policy reform, where I contend that there is a 'working-class-deficit', 'entrepreneurship-solution' loop being played out as 'progressive', 'successful' and 'necessary'. I argue that this is the political discourse we need to critique.

Paralleled with my own autobiographical reflections in 'moments of crisis' or habitus-field disjuncture located in the narratives of my participants, I have further documented how Bourdieusian notions of 'unsettledness' might not fully explain the modes of resistance found in the working classes. In addition, I have proposed a phenomenological development of Bourdieu's habitus-field relation, and done so through Gordon's (1997) *Social Haunting*. Avery Gordon (1997), and more recently Elizabeth Silva (2014), have spoken of 'social haunting' as a 'sociological matter', proposing an epistemology of haunting that considers both socio-historical memory and their place and interrelations with the present. At various stages of his career, Bourdieu was influenced and haunted by phenomenological theory (Crossley, 2001; Robbins, 2000). In fact, the very doxa I have spoken about was attributed before Bourdieu, to the phenomenological thinker, Edmund Husserl (see Husserl, 1973, 1990, 1991). Scholars such as Myles (2004) have claimed Bourdieu's reading of Husserl to 'over- polarize' doxa and reflexivity (ibid., p.91). However, Robbins, Crossley and Myles have also affirmed that Bourdieu's conceptualisation of doxa and his theorising of habitus-field relations is not incompatible with more dialectic, phenomenological reasoning and development. I propose not to consider a re-reading Bourdieu's doxa in relation to Husserl, but move forward with another phenomenological concept, one that might make for further consideration of habitus-doxa, habitus-field relations. This is the notion of 'social haunting' (Gordon, 1997). These ruptures I document do not in and of themselves bring about change, but create space where the possibility of change arises (Spivak, 1988). It is this movement from unsettledness as 'bad feelings' to unresolvedness as 'something-to-be-done' that I think is vital for class analysis.

Bourdieu is not a ghost to be exorcised, but one to struggle with and reflect on. We need also need to look towards those who have continued a Bourdieusian approach to empirical research, for example Bev Skeggs and Diane Reay, David James, Derek Robbins, as well as the future generations of Bourdieusians to come. We should further consider the phenomenological and dialectic developments of Bourdieu's work, in order to understand how those positioned as 'powerless' in society might resist. In this case resistance came against the spectre of deficit, but what is salient is to consider how we might struggle with the ghosts of enterprise, or entrepreneurship – a spectre that is haunting Milltown, a spectre that is haunting Europe.

Thinking back to my childhood and my memories of looking out the bedroom window, I am now aware; I am aware of the history of the town and the changes it is undergoing. I am also aware that my view is now obscured. I would see the same backyard, the same factory-come-flats, the railways track remains and so does the ornate factory chimney, but there's something else in the distance, something catching the sun; it's the corner of Milltown Community Academy's roof, piercing the skyline, cementing its place firmly in my story, and firmly in the future of Milltown's (educational) landscape.

Something must be done!

Notes

1 Pseudonym used for town and from hereon in all names affiliated with the town. In addition, for reasons of anonymity, all inserts marked as 'quotes' from academy documentation, sponsor brochures and websites, architecture reports and websites and

local newspapers have been adapted to make them non-traceable sources. The context and words used are as similar as possible to avoid a change in meaning or emphasis.
2 Under early New Labour rules, sponsors were required to contribute 10 per cent of the capital costs of a new academy building, a cost capped at two million pounds. From 2009 onwards, it is no longer necessary for academy sponsors to make any financial contribution to their academy.
3 The school turned academy remains non-selective, but during conversion expanded from an 11–16 years institution to an 11–18 years academy and sixth form.
4 'Neo-liberalism' as defined by Bourdieu, but identified as a contested term, in both practice and theory. Here I do not have the room to elaborate but see for example Will Davies (2014) 'The limits of neo-liberalism: authority, sovereignty and the logic of competition', and Rajesh Venugopal's (2015) article, 'Neoliberalism as a concept'.
5 Operating from 2002 to 2011, the scheme set out to 'renew failing housing markets and reconnect them to regional markets, to improve neighbourhoods and to encourage people to live and work in these areas' (Wilson, 2013).

References

Adonis, A. 2008. *Academies and Social Mobility*, 7 February, London.
Archer, L., Hollingworth, S. and Mendick, H. 2010. *Urban Youth and Schooling: The Identities and Experiences of Educationally 'at Risk' Young People*. Buckingham, UK: Open University Press.
Atkinson, W. 2010 Phenomenological Additions to the Bourdieusian Toolbox: Two Problems for Bourdieu, Two Solutions from Schutz. *Sociological Theory*. **28**(1), pp.1–19.
Bourdieu, P. 1977. *Outline of a Theory of Practice*. Cambridge: Cambridge University Press.
Bourdieu, P. 1984. *Distinction: A Social Critique of the Judgement of Taste*. London: Routledge and Kegan and Paul.
Bourdieu, P. 1988. *Homo Academicus*. Stanford, CA: Stanford University Press.
Bourdieu, P. 1990. *The Logic of Practice*. Cambridge: Polity Press.
Bourdieu, P. 1996. *The Rules of Art*. Cambridge: Polity.
Bourdieu, P. 2000. *Pascalian Meditations*. Cambridge: Polity Press.
Bourdieu, P. and Eagleton, T. 1992. Doxa and Common Life. *New Left Review*. **191**, pp.111–121.
Bourdieu, P. and Wacquant, L. 1992. *An Invitation to Reflexive Sociology*. Chicago, IL: The University of Chicago Press.
Cameron, D. 2010. Transforming the British Economy Coalition Strategy for Economic Growth, 28 May, Cabinet Office, London.
Carroll, L. 1911. *Phantasmagoria and Other Poems*. Oxford: Oxford University Press.
Carter-Wall, C. and Whitfield, G. 2012. *The Role of Aspirations, Attitudes and Behaviour in Closing the Educational Attainment Gap*. York, UK: Joseph Rowntree Foundation.
Crossley, N. 2001. The Phenomenological Habitus and Its Construction. *Theory and Society*. **30**(1), pp.81–120.
Cuban, L. 2004. *The Blackboard and the Bottom Line: Why Schools Can't Be Businesses*. Cambridge, MA: Harvard University Press.
Davies, W. 2014. *The Limits of Neoliberalism Authority, Sovereignty and the Logic of Competition*. London: Sage.
Deer, C. 2008. Doxa. In: Grenfell, M. (ed.) *Pierre Bourdieu: Key Concepts*. Durham, UK: Acumen Publishing, pp.119–130.

Department for Education and Skills. 2006. *The Five Year Strategy for Children and Learners: Maintaining the Excellent Progress*. London: DfES.
Department for Education (2012) Education of Disadvantaged Children. [Online] [Accessed 22 December 2012] Available from: www.gov.uk/government/policies/education-of-disadvantaged-children?
Department of Children, School and Families. 2008. *The Extra Mile: How Schools Succeed in Raising Aspirations in Deprived Communities*. London: DCSF.
Goldthorpe, J. 2007. 'Cultural Capital': Some Critical Observations. *Sociologica.* 2, pp.1–23.
Gordon, A. 1997. *Ghostly Matters: Haunting and the Sociological Imagination*. Minneapolis, MN: University of Minnesota Press.
Gordon, A. 2011. Some Thoughts on Haunting and Futurity. *Borderlands.* **10**(2), pp.1–21.
Hollands, R. 1990. *The Long Transition: Class, Culture and Youth Training*. Basingstoke, UK: Palgrave: Macmillan.
Husserl, E. 1973. *Experience and Judgement*. London: Routledge and Kegan Paul.
Husserl, E. 1990. *Ideas Pertaining to a Pure Phenomenology and to a Phenomenological Philosophy. Second Book: Studies in the Phenomenology of Constitution*. Dordrecht, The Netherlands, and London: Kluwer.
Husserl, E. 1991. On the Phenomenology of the Consciousness of Internal Time (1893–1917). In: Bernet, R. (ed.) *Husserlinana Vol. 4*. Dordrecht, The Netherlands: Kluwer Academic Publishers.
Ingram, N. 2011. Within School and Beyond the Gate: The Complexities of Being Educationally Successful and Working Class. *Sociology.* **45**(2), pp.287–302.
Lizardo, O. and Strand, M. 2010. Skills, Toolkits, Contexts and Institutions: Clarifying the Relationship between Different Approaches to Cognition in Cultural Sociology. *Poetics.* **38**, pp.204–227.
Lord Young. (2014) *Enterprise for All: The Relevance of Enterprise in Education*. London: Cabinet Office.
McDonald, R.F. and Coffield, F. 1991. *Risky Business? Youth and Enterprise Culture*. London: Routledge.
Milburn, A. 2009. *Unleashing Aspiration: The Final Report on the Panel on Fair Access to the Professions*. London: Cabinet Office.
Miliband, E. (2014) *Labour Party Annual Conference, Leader's Speech*, 23 September, Manchester Convention Centre.
Myles, F. 2004. From Doxa to Experience: Issues in Bourdieu's Adoption of Husserlian Phenomenology. *Theory, Culture & Society.* **21**(2), pp.91–107.
Ngai, S. 2005. *Ugly Feelings*. Cambridge. MA: Harvard University Press.
Office for National Statistics (2012) *Neighbourhood Statistics*. [Online] [Accessed 13 December 2012] Available from: www.neighbourhood.statistics.gov.uk/dissemination/
Office of the Deputy Prime Minister. 2004. *Compulsory Purchase Procedure Compulsory Purchase and Compensation*. London: ODPM.
Reay, D., Crozier, G. and Clayton, J. 2009. Strangers in Paradise: Working Class Students in Elite Universities. *Sociology.* **43**(6), pp.1103–1121.
Robbins, D. 1991. *The Work of Pierre Bourdieu*. Buckingham, UK: Open University Press.
Robbins, D. 2000. *Bourdieu and Culture*. London: Sage.
Savage, M. 2000. *Class Analysis and Social Transformation*. Buckingham, UK: Open University Press.

Silva, E. 2014. Haunting in the Materials of Everyday Life. In: Harvey, P. *et al.* (eds) *Objects and Materials: A Routledge Companion.* CRESC. London: Routledge.
Skeggs, B. 2011. Imagining Personhood Differently: Person Value and Autonomist Working-Class Value Practices. *The Sociological Review.* **59**(3), pp.496–513.
Spivak, G.C. 1988. *In Other Worlds: Essays in Cultural Politics.* New York: Routledge.
The Education Act 2002. (c.32) London: The Stationery Office.
The Learning and Skills Act 2000. (c.21) London: The Stationery Office.
Venugopal, R. 2015. Neoliberalism as Concept. *Economy and Society.* **44**(2), pp.1–23.
Woods, P.A. and Woods, G.J. 2011. Lighting the Fires of Entrepreneurialism? Constructions of Meaning in an English Inner City Academy. *International Journal of Technology and Educational Marketing.* **1**(1), pp.1–24.
Wilson, W. 2013. *Housing Market Renewal Pathfinder.* London: House of Commons.

Chapter 10

Stepping outside of oneself
How a cleft-habitus can lead to greater reflexivity through occupying 'the third space'

Nicola Ingram and Jessie Abrahams

Introduction

Bourdieu discusses the way in which the habitus, defined as 'a system of *dispositions*, that is of permanent manners of being, seeing, acting and thinking, or a system of *long-lasting* (rather than permanent) schemes or schemata or structures of perception, conception and action' (Bourdieu, 2002, p.27, emphasis in original), is developed from the field of origin but can be altered by new experiences and pedagogic action. He talks about his own conflicted experiences of a cleft habitus and suggests that this comes about when the habitus encounters a new and contradictory field, causing an internalisation of divided structures (Bourdieu, 2002; 2000). Bourdieu considers this confrontation – a product of the process of social mobility – to be painful, which indeed it is for many who experience it. In Chapter 8 Sam Friedman discusses this process, exploring the way in which a person's habitus as structured by original social background retains prominence even when they experience life in a new social field. Importantly, he highlights how this can create painful negotiations. Bourdieu argues that at times a working-class originary habitus acts as a barrier to being fully accepted within a middle-class occupation/social world when a person is socially mobile (Bourdieu, 1990). Friedman (2015), following Bourdieu, discusses the psychological pains such a shift in field and habitus may cause individuals, arguing it generates a sense of being held back from middle-class acceptance or being torn between two competing worlds. His arguments echo the conclusions of earlier work by Diane Reay (2004; 2002) as well as our own previous work (Ingram, 2011), which discusses the psycho-social impacts of a cleft habitus. In this chapter we want to take this theorising forward by considering the powerful way in which this position can sometimes be a positive and empowering resource, without denying the potential pain it causes. Through drawing upon and incorporating Homi Bhabha's concept of the 'third space' we aim to extend Bourdieu's concept to consider the positive aspects of a marginal vantage point, a rearticulation of habitus (rather than a division), which contests the terms of two incommensurable fields to create a new space. In talking about the 'third space', Bhabha makes the argument that 'the transformational value of change lies in the rearticulation, or translation, of the elements that are neither the One . . . nor the Other . . . but something else besides which contests the terms and territories of both' (1994, p.28). For us the 'third space' is useful in that it helps us to think about ways of being neither working-class, nor middle-class but something else besides. It is quite an optimistic concept in a way because it works with the idea that this process is a creative one and is interesting to consider alongside Bourdieu's more negative framing of the divided habitus (Bourdieu, 2002).

We discuss how we were drawn to Bourdieu's work – and Bourdieu himself – due to a mutual experience of occupying this third space. This fractured lens has been the way in which we have come to view the world, and so the work of Bourdieu had immediate resonance with us both. We discuss our understanding of this awkward positioning and the theoretical and empirical insights it has afforded in our work as academic researchers. In this chapter we will consider the way in which occupying 'the third space' can lead to greater reflexivity; through drawing upon the work of Patricia Hill Collins we consider how this position renders us 'outsiders within' (Collins, 1986), as located within a marginalised yet inclusive place that enables us to experience 'epistemic privilege' of vantage point. Overall this chapter develops a discussion around working with Bourdieu in order to think about different ways in which working-class people negotiate class migration and social mobility. We consider ways of theorising the divisions and revisions of habitus and highlight the potential of those who are marginalised to disrupt the boundaries of social fields. In doing so we build upon and extend Bourdieu's concept of cleft habitus and account for greater complexity in understanding shifts in habitus and field.

Class migration

> My main problem is to try and understand what happened to me. My trajectory may be described as miraculous, I suppose – an ascension to a place where I don't belong. And so to be able to live in a world that is not mine I must try to understand both things: what it means to have an academic mind – how such is created – and at the same time what was lost in acquiring it. For that reason, even if my work – my full work – is a sort of auto-biography, it is a work for people who have the same sort of trajectory, and the same need to understand.
>
> (Bourdieu, 1992, p.117)

Despite the obscurity of Bourdieu's writing we have found his concepts to provide us with a clear framework for thinking about how we (and the participants of our research studies) have navigated the somewhat misaligned working-class and middle-class worlds we occupy; in particular we are fascinated by the question posed by Bourdieu – what does it mean to be able to live in a world that is not ours? To do so we have to think about how those separate worlds and our positions within them are created and what it means to be able to belong in two spaces at once.

We are both academics from working-class backgrounds. While we are at different stages in our career trajectories we share common ground in that often we feel as though we are occupying worlds that are not our own. This is in respect of both our originary working-class family/community field and the field of the academy. Having come to Bourdieu as part of our journey of social mobility we feel an alignment with him and his work. In the previous chapter, Kirsty Morrin also discusses the affinity she feels with Bourdieu. Morrin reflects upon her own hysteresis that the habitus-field disjuncture can produce for a working-class student such as herself occupying a middle-class space. Morrin refers to this as a 'social haunting' in which your background has a lasting and lingering effect on your actions and practices, including influencing what you choose to study as a sociologist. While we do not have the space in this chapter to adequately tell our stories we feel it necessary to contextualise the discussion to follow somewhat within our own personal narratives of class migration.

Nicola

I grew up in a deprived community in North Belfast where several generations of my family had been raised and where I was surrounded daily by grandparents, aunts, uncles and literally dozens of cousins. Despite the fact that my parents had to both work extremely hard to provide for the family we lived comfortably in our two up two down terrace. We didn't have many luxuries but we had food on our table, clothes on our backs and most importantly we generated a lot of happy memories. My existence was incredibly social and communal. My family dropped in and out of each other's houses on a daily basis, everyone looked after everyone else's children and if any work was required in relation to property there was always someone to call upon who would come and sort it out, whether it was plumbing, building, joinery, telephone maintenance, tiling, electrical work, curtain making, dress making, knitting or crocheting. No one ever thought to charge for their labour, it was just accepted that we sort each other out when in need. Neither of my parents were educated beyond the age of 16. My dad, who worked as a telephone engineer, had a couple of O Levels, and my mum, who worked in a garment factory, was barely literate, having left school at around 14, after years of being the bane of many teachers' existences. My mother is no longer alive but she was one of the most sensitive and clever people I have ever met, regardless of lack of qualification. She instilled in me the value of a good education from an early age and took pride in the fact that I excelled at school from the moment I stepped through the gates. My educational journey, supported by my family, took me to a world where I learned to value aspects of a culture that was outside that of my family cultural milieu. I went to an all-girls Catholic Grammar school and became the quintessential working-class grammar school kid. Later, when I came to read Jackson and Marsden's classic study of working-class success I felt that I could have walked straight out of the pages of their book. Like their participants from the 1950s, grammar schooling for me:

had meant a rejection at conscious or unconscious levels of the life of the 'neighbourhood'. This mattered less for some than others. But when the new manners, new friends, new accents, new knowledge, heightened the adolescent tensions of home life, security and sense of purpose shifted from any wide emotional life and located itself narrowly in schoolwork, in certificates, in *markability*.
(Jackson & Marsden, 1962, p.152, emphasis in original)

The experience of reorienting my way of seeing and being in the world through middle-class acculturation and educational success was quite a disturbing one. It threw me into state of heightened reflexivity where I questioned and analysed taken-for-granted ways of being, and left me feeling like I belonged nowhere. When I first came to Bourdieu's work as an adult I was struck by how his theories made sense to me and chimed with the complex amalgam of issues that I'd been trying to make sense of through my own life, which had taken me through university, into a career in teaching, into motherhood, out of the neighbourhood into a nice life in London, then back into the neighbourhood from where I'd once actively wanted to escape. Symbolic violence was the first concept that I was introduced to through the work of Paul Connolly. I was living back in Ardoyne, one of the most deprived areas of Belfast, and raising my kids and revaluing the culture I had left behind. My partner, who had an anthropology degree from Oxford and was doing a PhD at the time, brought home an academic article for me as it connected with things on which I had been reflecting. The concept of symbolic violence struck me as a powerful way to consider the significance of the denigration of working-class culture that is synonymous with the valuing of middle-class culture. It is an act of violence against the working classes whom, I had come to realise through my circuitous route through, out and back into working-class culture, had a great deal of value that the middle-classes lacked. I was hooked on exploring these ideas (I still am) and went on my journey into academia.

Jessie

I grew up in an ethnically diverse inner-city working-class neighbourhood with a single mother living on benefits. While we did not have much money and my mother had no formal educational qualifications, I would argue that she had developed cultural capital through radical feminist self-education. This had not enabled her to overcome poverty and 'be socially mobile' but had empowered her with the tools to understand and support my educational journey. Having spent my teenage years immersed within the social world of my area and attending the local comprehensive school, I first felt the impact of a habitus misaligned with the field when I attended the elite University of Bristol to study a degree in Sociology. In part I dealt with this through remaining solidly within my local community and refusing to adapt my habitus to suit the new field. This was majorly enabled through having a migration buddy (my boyfriend) who – coming from my local area – was also studying at the same institution at the same time. After finishing my degree I began working as a research assistant on the Paired Peers project in the Sociology department while continuing to further my education through a Masters. During this time the research team along with specific academics – who had themselves experienced social mobility – helped me to further develop my sociological imagination in a safe and supportive environment, free from judgement and symbolic violence. Following this I began my PhD, which is a painful and emotional journey as the focus of my study forces me to confront my own educational experiences and history; it is forcing my habitus to confront itself and all its contradictions. It is a place of extreme reflexivity where I have 'stepped outside of myself'. While this place is difficult to manage it is also productive and is nurtured with the support of others who have been through this. In particular through the supervision of Professor David James, who himself has a tale of class migration to tell (James, 2010), I am able to be comforted and feel at ease with the uncomfortableness that is my class migration. While this glimpse into my sociological journey does not do justice to my story, what I want to argue is that my journey is one of a habitus divided yet reconciled and that this is partially attributable to the support of others in a mutual position of dislocation. I am still on my journey of social mobility so for me this process is ongoing. At times it is more painful than others but it is the space of mutual understanding that acts as a haven, a safe place where I can be myself with others who are similarly in this space.

Coming back from our stories to Bourdieu, we are driven by the need to understand what is lost for working-class people in the experience of becoming socially mobile and living in two places in social space at the same time. Although Bourdieu touches upon these ideas in relation to a cleft habitus many times in his work (Bourdieu, 2008; 2002; 2000) we are frustrated by the lack of full development of this and theorising about the internalisation of incommensurate structures. While the seeds of these ideas appear in his work it is through the work of Diane Reay that we find them further developed and worked out (Reay, 2015; 2004; 2002).

However, there is more work to be done in fully theorising the idea of a cleft habitus and as a new generation of Bourdieusian scholars we are attempting to build upon the theoretical insights developed before us. We are particularly interested in thinking about the different ways in which people may navigate the internalised processing of structures from different fields. It is clear to us that not everyone will be affected by the assimilation of multiple structures in quite the same way. Within our work we have been developing ways of accounting for these differences and have been attempting to work through our ideas on both the negative and positive impact of the internalisation of seemingly incompatible structures. In doing so we have developed the concept of 'habitus tug' (Ingram, 2011), which denotes a multi-directional pull on the habitus rather than a division, and 'chameleon habitus' (Abrahams & Ingram, 2013), which helps us to think about the way the habitus can draw upon the internalisation of different structures to shift in accordance with the demands/expectations of different fields.

Conceptualising habitus interruptions

Our starting point has been Bourdieu's concept of habitus, his extension of this concept to thinking about a 'cleft habitus' and our own reflections on what it means to fit and to be in your place (or not). Bourdieu writes:

> It is likely that those who are 'in their right place' in the social world can abandon and entrust themselves more, and more completely to their dispositions (that is the 'ease' of the well-born) than those who occupy awkward positions, such as the parvenus and the declasses; and the latter are more likely to bring to consciousness that which, for others is taken for granted, because they are forced to keep watch on themselves and consciously correct the 'first movements' of a habitus that generates inappropriate or misplaced behaviours.
>
> (Bourdieu, 2000, p.163)

What Bourdieu is writing about here is feeling out of place, and finding yourself to be a wrong sort of person in a given situation. In particular he is considering how someone who has gained wealth but is from humble origins can be forced to consciously monitor their ways of being so as to ensure they fit within high society. We are drawn to this passage as it highlights what we have previously argued: that when a habitus is forced outside of the structures in which it developed, acute reflexivity can occur. Being forced into a new space makes you think not only of what is novel in that space but it creates a new lens to look at where you have come from. However, while we also understand and have felt the pull to 'correct' our habitus through some awkward experiences where we have felt ourselves judged because of our working classness, we have both used this reflexivity to refuse to 'correct' ourselves and instead suggest that it is the middle-class field that at times needs correcting. We are interested in considering what happens when a person's habitus is interrupted, and importantly what processes are involved in managing this. In doing this it will be necessary to consider the structural influences on the habitus, and how these influences can be produced by experiences in different fields. We wish to recognise that the habitus can be generated within multiple fields, some of which may help inform the originary habitus (including the family, community, and geographical location) and others that may act on the habitus later (including the institution of education and the world of employment). Bourdieu gives short shrift to consideration of the internalisation of the structures of multiple fields, although the formations of his ideas on this can be found in discussion of his concept of hysteresis. It could be argued that in these conditions the habitus is destabilised as it is caught in a tug between two conflicting social fields. Bourdieu writes of these conflicting external forces: 'Thus it can be observed that to contradictory positions, which tend to exert structural "double binds" on their occupants, there often correspond destabilized habitus, torn by contradiction and internal division, generating suffering' (2000, p.160).

In relation to a misalignment between habitus and field, Bourdieu writes, 'Where dispositions encounter conditions (including fields) different from those in which they were constructed and assembled, there is a "dialectical confrontation" between habitus as structured structure, and objective structures' (2002, p.31). It could be argued that the dialectical confrontation between habitus and field (other than the field of origin) results in a *degree* of accommodation where the habitus accepts the legitimacy of the new field's structure and is in turn structured by it, thus enabling a modification in the habitus. Yet the habitus is still constrained by the structuring forces of the field of origin. In this case the new habitus is made up of conflicting elements: the internalisation of new experiences and schemes of perception can lead to the internalisation of conflicting dispositions. This can be conceptualised as a 'habitus tug', where conflicting dispositions struggle for pole position and the individual can at times feel pulled in different directions. This may create a 'destabilised habitus' where the individual is not a 'fish in water' in either field. In some cases the conflicted habitus causes division, leaving an individual alienated from the practices within a field. Bourdieu describes this in terms of a *cleft habitus* resulting from contradictions of formation: 'I have many times pointed to the existence of cleft, tormented habitus bearing in the form of tensions and contradictions the mark of the contradictory conditions of formation of which they are the product' (2000, p.64). These contradictions are obvious when people are uprooted from one way of life and find themselves living in another part of the world, for example; or when the structure of society changes dramatically due to revolution. As an anthropologist, Bourdieu is able to highlight his ideas through radical examples. However, his theory should not be restricted to such radical changes in life. There are many other ways in which people can be confronted with lived cultural dissonance. Influenced by Bourdieu, Lahire (2011) argues that 'compulsory education leads children to be faced with forms of cultural apprenticeship, knowledge and social relations that are quite foreign to their original milieu' (p.x). They are then faced with contradictory forms of structural influences, which *can* lead to habitus changes. It must be cautioned though that, while habitus can be changed, it is mostly durable with changes unlikely to occur (Bourdieu & Wacquant, 1992, p.192). Indeed, the education system is more often a central cog in the process of production rather than a force for habitus change. However, change is possible and while durable the habitus is not static, despite arguments to the contrary from Bourdieu's critics (see for example Jenkins, 2002). We are interested in the tensions caused by habitus change.

The tension between habitus and fields and the notion of a habitus divided against itself (Bourdieu et al., 1999; Reay 2002) is central to our work where we often explore the pull between working-class identity and working-class educational achievement. A question on which we still feel unable to reach a clear conclusion is: is it possible to remain working-class and to be educationally successful? Bourdieu sums up these tensions in the following quotation, as part of his interview with Wacquant in *An Invitation to Reflexive Sociology*:

> If, to resist, I have no means other than to make mine and to claim aloud the very properties that mark me as dominated . . . in the manner of the sons of English proletarians proud to exclude themselves from school in the name of the ideal of masculinity borne by their class culture (Willis 1977), is that resistance? If so, on the other hand, I work to efface everything that is likely to reveal my origins, or to trap me in my social position (an accent, physical composure, family relations), should we then speak of submission?
>
> (Bourdieu & Wacquant, 1992, p.24)

We agree with Bourdieu that at times when there is a rupture in the seamless interconnection between habitus and field, a certain amount of reflexivity is enabled. This is not necessarily caused by crisis, as this rupture can be produced in ordinary life in any situation where habitus and field are not aligned. In order for this misalignment to occur the habitus needs to be confronted with a field that is not the originary field (the one to which it is attuned). In such cases it is possible for the habitus to internalise a degree of conflict. Lahire refers to the 'internal plurality of the actor' (2011, p.43) to describe how people can internalise and call forth different dispositions in response to different fields, relying on a person's ability to switch between and inhibit conflicting dispositions depending on the demands of the occasion. He writes:

> It is because the dispositions that make up each individual legacy of dispositions are not necessarily coherent or homogeneous among themselves, moreover, that each new situation experienced by the actor plays an important role as the filter, selector or trigger and is the occasion for an application or suspension, a flourishing or an inhibition of this or that part of the embodied dispositions.
>
> (Lahire, 2011, p.xii)

However, we are interested in presenting a more complex picture of the potential ways in which plural dispositions can operate as part of the habitus, as we think that as well as accounting for the divisiveness of internalising contradictory structures it is important to account for the potentially creative aspects of this process. We have developed the following typology of habitus interruptions to help us account for different ways of negotiating multiple fields. This is summarised Table 10.1 and the explanation that follows.

Table 10.1 provides a theoretical model for analysing the interaction between habitus and two different fields, i.e. the field of origin and a secondary field. It is applicable for analysing the interface between two strong, not wholly aligned fields

Table 10.1 Habitus interruptions typology

Disjunctive: originary field OR secondary field	Conjunctive: originary field AND secondary field
Abandoned habitus – divided from originary field. A person renegotiates their habitus in response to the structuring forces of the new field	Reconciled habitus – two fields are reconciled. A person can successfully navigate both fields. Can accommodate both structures despite opposition. Can induce a degree of reflexivity
Re-confirmed habitus – divided from new field. The new field is rejected and so its structures are not internalised	Destabilized habitus – person tries to incorporate the structuring forces of each field into their habitus but cannot achieve successful assimilation. Instead they oscillate between two dispositions and internalise conflict and division

in which an agent operates, especially when there is a transition between field influences. Working with Bourdieu's overall model of a theory of practice and relying on the conceptual tools of habitus and field, we accept that a person's primary habitus is formed through socialisation within the family and through experiences in early life (Bourdieu, 1977; Bourdieu & Passeron, 1990). This forms schemes of perceptions, conception and action; and as noted above, this in turn forms the basis on which all future experiences are built:

> Early experiences have particular weight because the habitus tends to ensure its own constancy and its defence against change through the selection it makes within new information by rejecting information capable of calling into question its accumulated information, if exposed to it accidentally or by force, and especially by avoiding exposure to such information.
> (Bourdieu, 1990, pp.60–61)

This can help account for why working-class people can reject schooling or forms of leisure activity where the middle classes dominate.

However, as children get older they become less dependent on the family as the main social space in which they operate, and are likely to experience life in other social spaces (fields) too. These new (or secondary) social fields then exert a strong force and impact on dispositions through the internalisation of structure. For most children school is an important secondary social space; important in the sense that they spend a lot of their time within this social space and so internalise the structuring influences based on their experiences of this field. For some children (particularly middle-class children) there is a high degree of congruence between the structures of perception produced by their early life experiences and the structures of perception produced by schools. It has been argued that schools purvey middle-class values and this creates resistance for working-class kids. However, there has been little discussion of how some working-class children accept the (so-called) middle-class values of the school and therefore incorporate the structures to produce schemes of perception that are congruent with the school field. Theoretically this is interesting because if the two fields exert opposing structural influences then the habitus must in some way be affected by this conflict. Is it possible for people to incorporate two separate schemes of perception, or must they reject one in favour of the other? With reference to Bourdieu's concept of habitus and the embodiment of reflexive dispositions in relation to multiple fields, Bernard Lahire argues:

> Sometimes contradictory socialising experience, can in/cohabit the same body; ... mental and behavioural dispositions, internalized to a greater or lesser extent, can manifest themselves or be put on standby at different moments in social life (according to the area of practices) or the course of a biography.
> (2008, p.186)

This implies that a social agent can simply swap and change their habitus and practice, pulling out dispositions in accordance to fields. We find this an interesting idea but too simplistic for accounting for the complexities of contradictory social experience. Lahire's thinking is perhaps more akin to the idea of the cultural omnivore (Peterson & Kern 1996). It suggests a smooth process of 'picking up and putting down' tastes and practices at will. It is our contention that the process of internalisation of contradictory structures creates something much more complex than dispositions shifting between a state of latency and manifestation. We perceive something much more messy than omnivouressness and less straightforward than cultural mobility as a natural accompaniment to social mobility. In our research we have worked with the idea that two contradictory fields – the home and the school/university – can have differing structuring influences, which may indeed be in opposition. We have shown this through work on the way working-class teenage boys attempt to reconcile their educational success with their sense of working-class masculine identity (Ingram, 2011; 2009) and through considering working-class local students experience of an elite Higher Education institution, and the way that they develop a chameleon habitus, that although shifts in accordance to fields, does so in a bumpy way that is both positive and negative for the students (Abrahams & Ingram, 2013).This model is applicable as a toolbox for analysing the processes involved when a person is caught between the influences of any two opposing fields. We recognise that within school, the home and the school field may in fact be aligned. In this case the model is not applicable.

Table 10.1 is divided into four separate sections, each pertaining to a relationship between the habitus and the two fields. Each section represents a separate possibility for the habitus in terms of how it incorporates the structures of the fields. In the left-hand column the two possibilities are based on the incorporation of the schemes of perception from only one field and the rejection of the other. In the right-hand column the two possibilities are based on the incorporation of the schemes of perception of both fields. This is a heuristic device and as such is an approximate and not a perfect measure. We understand that to some degree in all cases schemes of perception from both fields will be incorporated. However, the degree of incorporation of each set of schemes may vary and it is this that we find interesting to theorise. We provide an explanation of each of these four potential responses, first explaining the disjunctive responses and then the conjunctive responses. The disjunctive responses pertain to situations when the habitus incorporates one or other of the fields' schemes of perception, conception and action. The two sets of schemes are seen (not necessarily in a fully conscious sense) as alternatives. The conjunctive responses pertain to situations where the habitus attempts to incorporate both schemes of perception and attempts to find a way of accommodating the contradictions. We offer two options within each type of response, i.e. two disjunctive and two conjunctive responses.

Disjunctive responses

Abandoned habitus

The abandoned habitus is divided from its originary field. As the secondary field of the school exerts a structuring force on a person's habitus they have difficulties in accommodating both sets of incongruent structures. Over a period of time the structures of the new field become internally dominant as part of the habitus, and the old/originary structures are usurped or overwritten. Through a complex interaction between structure and agency a person renegotiates their habitus in response to the structuring forces of the new field. An example of this may be when a working-class child adopts the manners and attitudes of his/her middle-class peers and becomes attuned to behaving 'appropriately' and performing well in school, but in doing so becomes less attuned to the 'appropriate' manners and ways of being when at home or in his/her community.

Re-confirmed habitus

The re-confirmed habitus is divided from a new/secondary field. Again, as the secondary field of the habitus exerts a structuring force on the habitus a person will experience difficulties in accommodating both sets of incongruent structures. As the new schemes filter through the habitus they become diluted by the strength of the old schemes. At times this may be partly conscious, when an agent considers the ways of viewing the world offered by each of the fields' structures. However, often this will be part of the non-conscious operations of the habitus, and the new field's structures simply find no means of being received by and assimilated into the originary schemes. The new structures do not then become part of the internalised dispositions of the habitus. The new field is rejected and so its structures are not internalised: the person's original habitus is re-confirmed (re-confirmed, rather than confirmed, because the habitus that is not exposed to a new field may be considered confirmed on a daily basis, through its encounters with the field of which it is the product; a re-confirmed habitus has encountered and rejected an alternative field and therefore alternative dispositions, conceptions and perceptions). This may lead to symbolic violence, reproduction, misrecognition and may be best exemplified by Willis' (1977) 'lads', who thoroughly reject school in favour of their own working-class male subculture.

Conjunctive responses

Reconciled habitus

The reconciled habitus occurs when the two fields, although opposing, are integrated. Despite the oppositional structuring of the secondary field the agent is able to reconcile the internalisation of both fields' schemes of perception. This is reminiscent of Lahire's discussion of contradictory socialising experiences cohabiting the same body (Lahire, 2011; 2003). A person can successfully navigate both fields by drawing on these different aspects of habitus depending on which field they are in, i.e. they are responsive to each field and have a 'feel for each game' and behave accordingly. The agent behaves 'naturally' in each of the divergent fields, i.e. in attunement with the field's accepted norms of behaviour and disposition. In this way a person can accommodate both field structures despite the opposition between them. It could be argued that in these circumstances, because of the incongruence of the schemes of perception and the differing ways in which a person acts in the separate fields, a high degree of reflexivity is generated. The reconciled habitus is a more positive framing of habitus interruption and accords with the concept of the third space where something new is generated from the process of internalising incommensurate structures.

Destabilised habitus

A destabilised habitus is when the structuring forces of each field are incorporated into the habitus but cannot be reconciled. Instead the two separate schemes of perception vie for dominance. The person tries to incorporate the structuring forces of each field into their habitus, but cannot achieve successful assimilation. Instead they oscillate between two dispositions and internalise conflict and division. The participants of Friedman's work (2015; 2014) are often good examples of this form of habitus interruption and indeed his work builds from Bourdieu's theorising of habitus clivé. We also have spoken to this form of habitus disruption in our own work (Ingram, 2011).

We offer these forms of habitus interruptions as a model for thinking about multiple ways in which the internalisation of dissonant fields can be negotiated by individuals. In our research we have found the idea of a divided habitus to be both useful and limiting in thinking about different ways of navigating social mobility. There is a need for a model to account for those who have left behind their class without pain, those who have found it painful, those who refuse to erode their identity and those who find a way to reconcile the differences. The model we offer is attemtping to offer this complexity with the recognition that a person's habitus type is not static.

Conclusions

'Third space travel'

> The borderline work of culture demands an encounter with 'newness' that is not part of the continuum of past and present . . . it renews the past, refiguring it as a contingent 'in-between' space, that innovates and interrupts the performance of the present.
>
> (Bhabha, 1994, p.10)

In this chapter we have considered the ways in which Bourdieu conceptualised the divided habitus and discussed the usefulness and the limitations of his thinking on this with reference to his, our own and others' work. We have argued for the need to move beyond the idea of divisiveness in relation to the internalisation of contradictory structures in order to give way to thinking of the potentially creative aspects of the process of bringing sets of structures together that don't belong. We have set this out in our typology of 'habitus interruptions' and have provided a way of theorising the process of encountering different structures through living and being in different fields. We want to finish by drawing further on the work of Bhabha and of Hill-Collins to think about the positive aspects of a cleft habitus, which is an area of Bourdieu's theory that requires expansion.

Bhabha's concept of the third space provides us with a useful way of thinking about what can be created from the painful experience of a cleft habitus, and what can be generated from the process of being forced to step outside of oneself. We have described what we are calling a 'reconciled habitus' wherein the structures of different fields have somehow been accommodated. We do not conceive of this as being about finding the common ground of different structures, but about something entirely new being created in their fusion. In passing through workingclass and middle-class worlds we have become class and cultural hybrids, belonging in neither and both places at once. We have been displaced to the third space and have recognised this displacement in our research participants too.

But for me the importance of hybridity is not to be able to trace two original moments from which the third emerges; rather, hybridity to me is the 'third space', which enables other positions to emerge. This 'third space' displaces the histories that constitute it and sets up new structures of authority, new political initiatives, which are inadequately understood through received wisdom (Bhabha, 1994, p.211).

There is an interesting creativity in not belonging fully in different fields because it allows us to contest the boundaries. Through a displacement of habitus we need to operate in a space outside of the fields in which we function. Bhabha's concepts of hybridity and the third space have helped us to take Bourdieu's concept of the cleft habitus further (Abrahams & Ingram, 2013). His theoretical work is borne out of ways of thinking about and understanding identities in relation to migration and although our work is not considering migration in the geographical sense we are interested in what we call 'class migration', a movement across and through social space. In doing this we take our histories and the structures that shape our habitus and find ways of creating our own 'structures of authority' that go beyond integration or assimilation. The 'third space' does not emerge from combining two dominant social fields and picking and choosing aspects of both to fuse together; it is the development of something new altogether in relation to the confrontation of the incommensurate aspects of two fields.

Outsiders within

Overall we have argued that, through experiences of a cleft-habitus, socially mobile individuals, while potentially feeling much pain and anxiety over their location, are able to generate much creativity and insight through occupying a position within the third space. Friedman in an earlier chapter talks about his school friend Kieran and the symbolic violence his family encountered as their tastes and practices were not accepted. Despite moving in social space into the economic elite, they did not possess the 'right' cultural capital to be socially and culturally accepted in that world. However, he concludes by highlighting the complexity of this, discussing how Kieran's parents in fact made fun of his own family's tastes, and how they adamantly claim position within the working-class community culturally despite their economic mobility. Kieran's parents arguably occupy a powerful position within the third space. Rather than rejecting one world in favour of the other and attempting to adapt their habitus to suit that world, they creatively contest the rigid boundaries of these two supposedly incommensurable fields. Laughing at the pretentious practices of the cultural elite, something they do not necessarily want to be part of, they attempt to generate a new position for themselves; they appear to exist within two fields or, as we argue, in a third space. From this position they can step outside of themselves and view both social fields from a distance, allowing them greater reflexivity.

Academics researching social class and inequality who have experienced social mobility and find themselves in the 'third space' arguably occupy a privileged position from which to research and view the world. This resonates with standpoint epistemological arguments made by feminists. In opposition to positivistic assertions that social scientists should be objective and value free, standpoint epistemology reclaims the importance of using one's own experiences as valuable research tools (Smith, 1992; 1988; Harding, 1987; Stanley & Wise, 1983). It is argued that science is blind to its own subjectivity and that notions of objectivity are in fact merely male subjectivity (Caplan, 1988). Thus, feminists have argued for the need to be honest about one's bias and specific standpoint. Collins argues that admitting the knowledge we construct is partial renders it more trustworthy than knowledge that is partial but presents itself as universally true (Collins, 1990). Bourdieu argues 'experience linked to one's social past can and must be mobilised in research' (Bourdieu, 2004, p.113).

Patricia Hill-Collins provides an excellent and directive analysis of the benefits of what she calls 'outsider within status', which echoes the discourse of standpoint epistemology, in that it is about using the 'experiences' of marginalised groups as a foundation for sociological research (Collins, 1986). We contend that there is another element to this, which relates back to the Marxist idea of the bourgeoisie controlling the production of knowledge; that is, sociological knowledge has been primarily constructed through the standpoint of white middle-class males. Collins argues that black feminists have directed sociology through their status as 'outsiders within' (Collins, 1986); we argue that working-class academics can similarly utilise *their* status as 'outsiders within' or third space occupants. Collins defines outsider within status in the following way:

> At its best, outsider within status seems to offer its occupants a powerful balance between the strengths of their sociological training and the offerings of their personal and cultural experiences. Neither is subordinated to the other. Rather experienced reality is used as a valid source of knowledge for critiquing sociological facts and theories while sociological thought offers new ways of seeing that experienced reality.
> (Collins, 1986, pp.29–30)

'Outsiders within' can expose elements of reality that are concealed by orthodox approaches to analysis. They are more likely to notice anomalies that have been ignored due to taken-for-granted assumptions imminent in traditional sociologists' belief that they have a 'normal world view' (Collins, 1986).

Merton argues that 'outsiders', due to their exploited and dominated position in the social structure, once trained as social scientists occupy a privileged position. This is because they have been sensitised to the problems within the social system and can thus see things taken for granted by groups who have benefitted rather than having been disadvantaged by it (Merton, 1972). There is something about having a similar experience of oppression or disadvantage that can serve to enhance one's knowledge or direct knowledge. That is, although the experience of 'class' is relational, what all members of the working-class seem to share is an experience of having been disadvantaged in one way or another by a social system that does not benefit them. If they migrate from a position of disadvantage to a position of advantage in a middle-class world they see this world with different eyes to those who have only known the privilege of that world. Being outsiders within they understand that world but from the vantage point of the third space, which disrupts the 'normalising' world view.

Those of us occupying the third space are 'outsiders within', our class of origin often preventing us from being complete 'insiders' within the middle-class academic world. However, while feeling or indeed being made to feel like 'outsiders' in the academy, we *are* in fact existing and working within it, rendering us 'outsiders within'. Moreover, we consider that within the working-class field of origin we operate as 'insiders without', having grown up in such a community our knowledge and loyalties remain strongly rooted within that culture but we are no longer fully 'within' it; thus we would coin this concept to capture such a position. This position is helpful when attempting to conduct research within such communities and we often find ourselves moving with ease into such fields, understanding the taken-for-granted norms and symbols within such a space. Many academics before us have experienced and spoken openly about how a shared background can result in greater access and understandings within the research process. For example, Mohony and Zmroczek (1997) draw upon these issues in their influential edited collection *Class Matters: Working-Class Women's Perspectives on Social Class*.

In relation to our own work we have found our personal biographies to be both a useful source of experiential knowledge, a helpful tool for gaining access to marginalised communities and also a motivation to focus on specific issues of inequality. We are drawn to Bourdieu as we, like him, occupy the third space and are outsiders within; this shared experience engenders a strong connection. We, like him, experience immense tensions at times and feelings of isolation and dislocation. Yet, like Bourdieu, we are able to channel this into insight and understandings of those in marginal positions. We are drawn to Bourdieu's work as he 'gets it' – his insights seem to reflect our reality, and seem to be borne of occupying a similar position between two contrasting social fields. By testing the boundaries of the middle-class academy through our outsider within status and refusing to accept the rules of the field and adapt our habitus to suit them, we are aiming to claim a new space, a 'third space', one where those caught between two worlds are accepted and feel at home. The third space offers a small but significant resistance against the pull of an academy that privileges and supports the cultural reproduction of the dominant class.

References

Abrahams, J. and Ingram, N. 2013. The chameleon habitus: local students' negotiations of a multiple fields. *Sociological Review Online*. **18**(4), 2 [Online] [Accessed on 15 May 2014] Available from: www.socresonline.org.uk/18/4/21.html

Bhabha, H. 1994. *The Location of Culture*. New York: Routledge.

Bourdieu, P. 1977. *Outline of a Theory of Practice*. Cambridge: Cambridge University Press.

Bourdieu, P. 1990. *The Logic of Practice*. Cambridge: Polity.

Bourdieu, P. 1999. *The Weight of the World: Social Suffering in Contemporary Society*. Stanford, CA: Stanford University Press.

Bourdieu, P. 2000. *Pascalian Meditations*. Stanford, CA: Stanford University Press.

Bourdieu, P. 2002. Habitus. In: Hillier, J. and Rooksby, E. (eds) *Habitus: A sense of place*. Aldershot: Ashgate, pp.27–34.

Bourdieu, P. 2004. *Science of Science and Reflexivity*. Cambridge: Polity.

Bourdieu, P. 2008. *Sketch for a Self-Analysis*. Cambridge: Polity.
Bourdieu, P. and Eagleton, T. 1992. Doxa and common life. *New Left Review*. **191**, pp.111–121.
Bourdieu, P. and Passeron, J-C. 1990. *Reproduction in Education, Society and Culture*, (2nd edn) London: Sage.
Bourdieu, P. and Wacquant, L. 1992. *An Invitation to Reflexive Sociology*. Cambridge: Polity Press.
Caplan, P. 1988. Engendering knowledge: the politics of ethnography, part 1. *Anthropology Today*. **4**(5), pp.8–12.
Harding, S. 1987. *Feminism and Methodology*. Milton Keynes, UK: Open University Press.
Friedman, S. 2015.Habitus clivé and the emotional imprint of social mobility. *Sociological Review*. [Online] [Accessed 14 May 2015] Available from: http://onlinelibrary.wiley.com/doi/10.1111/1467-954X.12280/abstract.
Ingram, N. 2011. Within school and beyond the gate: the difficulties of being educationally successful and working-class. *Sociology*. **45**(7), pp.287–302.
Ingram, N. 2009. Working-class boys, educational success and the misrecognition of working-class culture. *British Journal of Sociology of Education*. **30**(4), pp.421–434.
Jackson, B. and Marsden, D. 1962. *Education and the Working Class*. London: Routledge & Kegan Paul.
James, D. 2010. *From Borders Lane to Bourdieu: A sociological journey*. Inaugural Professorial Lecture. 18 March 2010, University of the West of England, Bristol, UK.
Jenkins, R. 2002. *Pierre Bourdieu*. London: Routledge.
Lahire, B. 2003. From the habitus to an individual heritage of dispositions. Towards a sociology at the level of the individual. *Poetics*. **31**, pp.329–355.
Lahire, B. 2008. The individual and the mixing of genres: Cultural dissonance and self-distinction. *Poetics*. **36**, pp.166–188.
Lahire, B. 2011. *The Plural Actor*. Cambridge: Polity.
Mahoney, P. and Zmroczek, C. 1997. *Class Matters: 'Working Class' Women's Perspectives On Social Class*. London: Taylor & Francis.
Merton, R.K. 1972. Insiders and outsiders: a chapter in the sociology of knowledge. *American Journal of Sociology*. **78**(1), pp.9–47.
Peterson, R.A. and Kern, R.M. 1996. Changing highbrow taste: from snob to omnivore. *American Sociological Review*. **61**(5), pp.900–907.
Smith, D.E. 1988. *The Everyday World as Problematic: A Feminist Sociology*. Milton Keynes, UK: Open University Press.
Smith, D.E. 1992. Sociology from women's experience: a reaffirmation. *Sociological Theory*. **10**(1), pp.88–98.
Stanley, L. and Wise, S. 1983. *Breaking Out: Feminist Consciousness and Feminist Research*. London: Routledge & Kegan Paul.
Reay, D. 2002. Shaun's story: troubling discourses of white working-class masculinities. *Gender and Education*. **14**(3), pp.221–234.
Reay, D. 2004. 'It's all becoming a habitus': beyond the habitual use of habitus in educational research. *British Journal of Sociology of Education*. **25**(4), pp.431–444.
Reay, D. 2013. Social mobility, a panacea for austere times: tales of emperors, frogs, and tadpoles. *British Journal of Sociology of Education*. **34**(5–6), pp.660–677.
Reay, D. 2015. Habitus and the psychosocial: Bourdieu with feelings. *Cambridge Journal of Education*. **45**(1), pp.9–23.
Willis, P.E. 1977. *Learning to Labour: How Working Class Kids Get Working Class Jobs*. Farnborough, UK: Saxon House.

Chapter 11

Conclusion

Bourdieu – the next generation

Jessie Abrahams, Nicola Ingram,
Jenny Thatcher and Ciaran Burke

> The main thing for me is that Bourdieu's 'thinking tools' are especially sharp. At the risk of over-doing the analogy, these tools were made from good philosophical metal in the first place, and were refined and honed via empirical work over a long period. They have a high degree of complementarity and mutual, interlocking dependency. Even so, they do not - and do not claim - to give us a finished theoretical edifice (though there are some regularities in how the social world looks when they are used). Rather, I feel there is something more modest in Bourdieu, which is an invitation to use the tools oneself.
>
> (James, 2015, personal correspondence)

This book makes the case for the relevance of Bourdieusian theory for a generation of contemporary sociological researchers interested in inequalities. Every chapter exemplifies an approach to Bourdieu that engages with conceptual thinking that is neither habitual (Reay, 2004) nor superficial (Hey, 2003). We are interested in what is at the heart of Bourdieu's theory without reifying his concepts or idolising the thinker. Importantly, we gain value from using Bourdieu to think through the complexities of contemporary social inequalities.

We have learnt from and been influenced by the first generation of anglophile scholars who have taken up Bourdieusian concepts. As we reflect on our own journeys with Bourdieu, we realise the influence of Diane Reay, Bev Skeggs, David James, Derek Robbins, Val Hey and Paul Connolly – academics who have been our mentors, supervisors, examiners, role models, friends and colleagues. The way that we have come to 'know' Bourdieu is grounded in their thinking, as much as the first hand reading of his texts. As a new generation of Bourdieusians we are thus less tied to the direct influence of his writing, which may give us the freedom to take his theory in new directions.

This book is a product of many years of ongoing engagement and conversations among Bourdieusian scholars often brought together by the BSA Bourdieu Study Group. Inspired by feminist approaches to research, we promote a way of doing and using Bourdieusian theory, which is about community, collegiality and collaboration. We are attempting to resist the neoliberal marketisation of the higher education landscape through supporting each generation and building on each other's work. We are inspired by and are inspiring each other. Diane Reay writes of the way in which our 'academic freedom' has been challenged in the name of capitalism:

> Just as insidious is the conversion of knowledge into something to be sold, traded and consumed. We no longer have independent knowledge underpinned by academic freedom, but a knowledge economy where the value of knowledge is decided by political elites on the basis of its utility to them.
> (Reay, 2014, para. 7)

She continues that this has resulted in a situation whereby the academy is now 'servicing the status quo'. As a study group we are attempting to use Bourdieusian theory to break away from this, reinstating critique and challenging the status quo. We are trying to reclaim our academic freedom and come together for intellectual debate; this book is truly the fruit of such collaboration. As a study group we often host debates around the themes within this book and argue that these debates and disagreements are crucial to the development of the field as we work at times in different directions to make sense of the entanglement that is Bourdieusian theory. In this conclusion though we draw together some of the central and complementary themes running through the book and engage in a conversation with them. We want to highlight the way in which they speak to each other and are – in part – a product of this shared thought. We do this through the lens of capitals and then habitus and social mobility, considering the way in which each chapter contributes to building on these concepts and situating them as of relevance within contemporary British society.

Capitals

> The inability to trade one's cultural capital because it has only limited value or is not recognised in the places where value can be accrued is a substantial disadvantage to and sign of being born working-class.
> (Skeggs, 1997, p.129)

As was aforementioned, Bev Skeggs is a thinker who has been largely influential in introducing many of the authors in this collection to Bourdieu's concepts. As such this quote has a deep and powerful resonance with the themes in this book around the valuing and devaluing of certain capitals and the painful process this can cause. Chapters 2, 3, 4, 5, 6 and 7 build on the concept of capital in different ways, but crucially they all speak to each other and together they push forward debates among the scholarly community. In this section we tease out some mutual and complementary points emerging from each chapter and thread them together in an attempt to highlight some central themes.

In Chapter 2, in response to the recent popularity of a focus on habitus as the key to understanding the experiences of inequality in contemporary society, Ciaran Burke makes a call for the re-centralising of capitals within Bourdieu's theory of practice. Following this up, Lisa Mckenzie in Chapter 3 demonstrates the power of using the concept of capital alongside an awareness of field and the metaphor of 'the game' to understand the way in which disadvantaged and marginalised communities have come to be so through a devaluing of their forms of culture. She argues that working-class culture and practices are devalued as they are understood in relation to mainstream values alone and disconnected from 'the game' within which they function. She argues thus, for the importance of contextualising practices, something Bourdieusian theory can help us to do very well. Derron Wallace's Chapter 4 similarly argues that a de-contextualising or simplification of the concept of capital has resulted in political denigration of ethnic minorities and their culture and practices are seen as 'lacking'. Lindsey Garratt in Chapter 6 provides us with insight into how this may occur through the body and bodily practice. She argues that Bourdieusian theory and in particular the concepts of habitus, embodied cultural capital and hexis can help us to understand the process through which bodily phenotypes are constructed as objects of value – or as valueless, but concurrently how this construction is inculcated within our bodies as the site of practice.

Wallace extends Prudence Carter's (2003) notion of 'Black' cultural capital by showing how 'blackness' can be a form of capital within a peer group of working-class Afro-Caribbean young men in London. Wallace's chapter offers an interesting comparison to Thatcher and Halvorsrud's chapter in which they argue that the Polish and 'white' South African migrants would draw on their 'whiteness' as a form of capital in an attempt to avoid the 'racial' discrimination that 'non-white' migrants and ethnic minorities suffer in British society. They draw on Bourdieu's capitals as a way to understand their Polish and South African participants' comprehension of social class and divisions in British society. The participants brought with them knowledge of strategies to 'play the game', drawing on their cultural capital in order to assure intergenerational social reproductions for their children in Britain, which involved a privileging of whiteness. Relatedly, both Wallace and McKenzie show how stigmatised groups can invert values as they create their own value system within their community. As such, in Wallace's chapter 'blackness' becomes a capital possession for the black students in London, whereas for McKenzie the residents living on the St Ann's estate in Nottingham abide by their own code system that gives them status and symbolic legitimation on the estate as a way to shield them from the stigma they receive from wider society. Bourdieu is often used to talk about legitimated forms of cultural capital; what these studies bring to the debate is an understanding of the workings of alternative forms of capital. Moreover through their work we come to understand the ways in which the legitimisation process is contextual and operates differently at different levels of social space. Some capitals only have 'value' in certain spaces.

As an interesting follow-on to the discussion of the re-valuing of devalued capitals, Tamsin Bowers-Brown in Chapter 5 demonstrates how it is not always easy to create forms of resistance to symbolic domination. Her study of secondary school girls' understandings of achievement and educational choices shows the force of legitimated cultural capital in constructing the rules of the game. She argues the girls attempted to deliberately generate forms of 'useful' capital for CV building purposes only. In this way they were inadvertently maintaining the status quo and reproducing the illusio by continuing to value and legitimate what is arbitrarily considered important. Furthermore, the over-emphasis on the hierarchy of 'core' subjects meant that not all interests and talents were recognised as equally valuable. The girls asserted that anything other than progression to higher education was deemed 'a failure'. These symbolically violent practices are often internalised with pupils accepting personal responsibility for both their achievements and their 'failures'. This demonstrates how the legitimacy of the hierarchy is maintained. She thus argues that Bourdieu's theory is crucial as it centralises the political and school contexts when unpacking experiences of educationally successful young people.

The need to appreciate the temporality and contextual application of some capitals can also be seen in Burke's argument (Chapter 2). He demonstrates ways in which seemingly socially mobile individuals' trajectories are influenced by access and use of context-specific forms of capital – in particular, social capital accessed through family. He argues that this context-specific capital can be used as a one-off investment to gain a return of a 'graduate job'; however, once this capital is spent, it cannot be used again. Burke questions the extent to which these individuals have become socially mobile as their positions are capped and their options limited due to a return to previous forms of capital.

Overall these chapters come together to form a collective discussion of the functioning of 'the forms of capital' today in the lives of marginalised and often silenced groups in the UK (young people, migrants and those living in 'de-valued' communities). The next section, through weaving together Chapters 7 to 10, turns to the concept of 'habitus' and its relation to the process of social mobility in contemporary British society.

Habitus and social mobility

> Social mobility is a wrenching process. It rips working-class young people out of communities that need to hold on to them, and it *rips valuable aspects of self out of the socially mobile themselves* as they are forced to discard qualities and dispositions that do not accord with the dominant middle-class culture that is increasingly characterized by selfish individualism and hyper-competition.
>
> (Reay, 2013, p.667, emphasis added)

Without using the term habitus, Reay provides a Bourdieusian analysis of the painful process of social mobility. The description of having the valuable aspects ripped from the self, accords with some of our experiences and provides the impetus for much of our research. Bourdieu's theoretical framework is evident here and Diane works with the notion of the habitus divided against itself (Bourdieu *et al*., 1999), providing a vivid image of what that division can do to working-class people as they leave behind their roots and accept middle-class culture. Chapters 7 to 10 all engage with this idea in some way or another through using Bourdieu's concept of habitus clivé, divided, or cleft habitus. Sam Friedman in Chapter 8, for example, uses habitus clivé to explore the painful dimensions of social mobility. His work importantly reminds us that social mobility, as a common sense political discourse much mobilised by successive governments of all persuasions, requires critical scepticism and challenge. This is an example of Bourdieusian sociology in action, where seemingly sensible ideas can be unpicked through the use of his tools to reveal the inequalities that inhere within. As Bourdieu argues that 'what is essential goes without saying because it comes without saying: the tradition is silent, not least about itself as a tradition' (Bourdieu, 1977, p.167). Friedman provides an example of the traditional application of Bourdieu in the contemporary. His work shows the continued relevance of Bourdieusian theory as a means to challenge what is often unquestioned.

Kirsty Morrin in Chapter 9 takes the notion of unearthing inequalities that lie beneath accepted wisdom a stage further in her consideration of both her research and her position within it. She employs Bourdieu's notion of doxa to think about the ways in which policies embed within the education system and restructure the habitus of actors in this field. Creatively bringing Gordon's (1997) concept of 'social hauntings' to the Bourdieusian toolbox, she is able to then account for the ghostly traces of the originary habitus and how it manifests to form small resistances. Instead of thinking of the habitus as divided, Morrin conceives of a restructured habitus always being haunted by its past structures. This is an interesting development of Bourdieusian theory, showing a fruitful breaking away from purist adherence to his concepts but thinking with the theorist nonetheless. Even Bourdieu's strongest critics admit that he is good to think with and against (Jenkins, 2002) even if they challenge his concepts. Morrin shows a confidence to engage with Bourdieu on her own terms – both with and against. Her work connects to both that of Friedman (Chapter 8) and Ingram and Abrahams (Chapter 10) in that she uses 'social hauntings' to talk about something that has traditionally been considered as a cleft habitus, and in doing so brings a fresh way of conceptualising habitus revisions. While Bourdieu has written on the cleft habitus, his theoretical work on this is frustratingly under-developed. He does, however, provide us with the genesis of thoughts for taking this concept forward and Diane Reay in particular has led the way on this throughout her body of work. This book takes up this engagement with ways in which habitus can be used to understand attempts to reconcile the internalisation of structures from two incommensurate fields and in concert with Reay this work is part of the ongoing conversation about the contribution of Bourdieu, including the limitations of his work and its application.

Thatcher and Halvorsrud (in Chapter 7) take this discussion forward in their comparative study of two sets of migrants – Polish and South African. They explore what happens to members of a society when that society is disrupted by political and economic transformation, but also when people migrate to a new society. They argue that such an investigation relates back to the issues Bourdieu was working on when he was studying the social organisation of the Kabyle tribe in Algeria. Drawing on Bourdieu's concept of a divided or cleft habitus (which has it origin in Bourdieu's study of the Kabyle), they show how migrants experience a disjuncture between their present circumstances and the world in which these individuals were originally raised and socialised. Through an exploration of their adaptation into British society, the distinct character of each set of migrant group can be shown as internalised by them yet always transitioning. The habitus is shown to be fluid and subject to revision through new structures. This very much connects with the final chapter of our book, which although considering a different empirical issue, that of social class mobility, also interrogates the notion of habitus change. Ingram and Abrahams refer to this as 'class migration' and similar to Morrin introduce another theorist to the Bourdieusian conversation. Through drawing upon Homi Bhabha's concept of the 'third space' (Bhabha, 1994), Ingram and Abrahams think through the flipside of habitus division; that of the creative energy that can be released through such a negative process. The process may be compared with nuclear fission, where splitting the atom causes division yet releases energy and resulting fragments that are different to the matter that produced them.

Final thoughts

Although this book has included chapters from a small group of people, we are all part of a wider community of early career Bourdieusian researchers who have made connections with each other through our published work and collegial engagement at academic conferences and ongoing BSA Bourdieu Study Group events. We wish to recognise the value of these ongoing conversations. As the editors, we cannot ignore the increasing popularity of Bourdieu among early career researchers in Britain. Bourdieu is primarily a social theorist whose ideas have spread across many disciplines. The continuing relevance of Bourdieu's theoretical framework is often best verified through practical application of his concepts, which may explain his popularity among empirical researchers. The authors in this collection come from a variety of backgrounds, but nevertheless this new generation of researchers feel a deep affinity to Bourdieu. This book provides a glimpse into the reasons for this through critically centralising the authors personally, situating them within their own trajectories and stories. In an attempt to engage with one of Bourdieu's central ideas – that of reflexivity – each author was asked to describe their own journey to and with Bourdieu. They thus reflect on the impact their own experiences have had on their research interests but also discuss what it was that initially drew them to the work of the French thinker. In so doing each author has exposed themselves by recounting childhood memories and structural conditions that led them to Bourdieu. Professor David James in personal correspondence to the editors describes what we consider a central reason for the popularity of the thinker to this new generation of researchers who are beginning their careers in an age of austerity:

> Bourdieu's work insists on a relational approach and a strong form of reflexivity. It promotes a respect for people as individuals, whilst nevertheless championing an analysis at the level of the social. In a socio-economic context that appears to demand the worship of individualism (and in which, therefore, individualistic economic or psychological models might themselves feel especially 'natural'), a Bourdieusian perspective can seem like a radical refusal of the Anglo-Saxon way of seeing the world. In my view it gives us some hope of understanding and then challenging 'what goes without saying'. We owe it to our fellow human beings – especially those that suffer the most and have the least by way of voice or power – to at least try.
>
> (James, 2015, personal correspondence)

We continue to live in an unequal society, where inequalities, although at times challenged, refuse to be uprooted. Bourdieu has been found useful, by the authors in this book, and by other Bourdieusian scholars for interrogating forms of inequality. To argue, as some do, that new theories need to be engaged with because Bourdieu has simply become too popular, entirely misses the importance of his usefulness in the face of entrenched injustice. Just as Bourdieu should not be used on the basis of fashion or popularity, so should he not be dismissed on the same grounds. No theory will ever provide the answer to everything, but as a way to engage critically with an unequal world Bourdieu's tools are some of the sharpest we have.

References

Bhabha, H. 1994. *The Location of Culture.* New York: Routledge.
Bourdieu, P. 1977. *Outline of a Theory of Practice.* Cambridge: Cambridge University Press.
Bourdieu, P., *et al.* 1999. *The Weight of the World: Social Suffering in Contemporary Society.* Stanford, CA: Stanford University Press.
Gordon, A. 1997. *Ghostly Matters: Haunting and the Sociological Imagination.* Minneapolis, MN: University of Minnesota Press.
James, D. 2015 Why is Bourdieu still relevant and important today? Some thoughts. *Personal Correspondence*, 27 April 2015.
Jenkins, R. 2002. *Pierre Bourdieu: Key Sociologists.* Abingdon, UK: Routledge.
Hey, V. 2003. Identification and mortification in late modernity: New Labour; alpha femininities and their dis/contents. Keynote address at the 2003 *International Conference of Gender & Education*, University of Sheffield, UK.

Reay, D. 2004. 'It's all becoming a habitus': beyond the habitual use of habitus in educational research. *British Journal of Sociology of Education.* **25**(4), pp.31–444.

Reay, D. 2013. Social mobility, a panacea for austere times: tales of emperors, frogs, and tadpoles. *British Journal of Sociology of Education.* **34**(5–6), pp.660–677.

Reay, D. (2014) 'From academic freedom to academic capitalism', *Discover Society.* [Online] [Accessed on 26 April 2015] Available from: www.discoversociety.org/2014/02/15/on-the-frontline-from-academic-freedom-to-academic-capitalism/

Index

Abrahams, J. 1–7, 89, 120, 124, 140–155, 157–163
academies 123, 125–131
Adams, M. 10
Alexander, C. 47
Algeria 29, 89, 162
Allen, K. 57
anamnesis 81
apartheid 90–93, 96–97, 103
Archer, L. 12, 62
Atkinson, W. 20–21, 125
austerity 68, 163
authenticity 41–42, 46–49, 51, 74

Back, L. 75
Baker, J. 68
Ball, S.J. 61, 70
Bathmaker, A.-M. 59, 65
Bhabha, H. 140, 152, 162
Blair, T. 28
Bornholt, L. 69
Bowers-Brown, T. 27, 55–71, 160
Bradley, H. 14, 69
Burawoy, M. 90–91
Burke, C. 1–22, 26, 55, 58, 80, 111, 128, 157–163
Burkitt, I. 80
Butin, D.W. 55
Butler, J. 77
Byrom, T. 66–67

Cameron, D. 28, 129
capital 2, 8–10, 17, 20–22, 28–29, 34, 91, 158–159; and the body 76, 81–82; education choice 55, 57–58; migration 100–101, 103; social mobility 108, 110–114; *see also* economic capital; social capital; symbolic capital
capital accumulation 31, 34, 63
capitalism 32, 92, 100, 158
Carter, P. 39–41, 47, 49–50
Cartesian dualism *see* dualism
Chambers, S.A. 77
class *see* social class
cleft habitus 110, 124, 140–141, 145–147, 151–155, 161
Coffield, F. 128
cold-knowledge 61, 70
colonialism 89, 99
communism 90–92, 97, 100–103
Compulsory Purchase Orders (CPOs) 129–130
Connolly, P. 143, 157
context-specific capital 20, 160
council estates 27–30
Crossley, N. 9, 125, 136
cultural capital 14–16, 38, 41, 100–102, 115–117, 143; black 39–40, 44, 46–48, 50–52, 95, 159; class inequality 27, 31, 33–35; education choice 58–59, 61, 64, 69; embodied 74, 76, 82–84, 100, 159

Davies, J. 68
De Beauvoir, S. 77
Derrida, J. 77
Descartes, R. 76–79
determinism 8, 34
de-valuing 27, 29, 35
doxa 11, 82, 89, 123–124, 128–129, 131, 133–134, 136, 161

dualism 74, 76–79
Dublin 73

Eade, J. 93
economic capital 12–13, 31, 58–59, 68–69, 100
education 33, 101–102, 112, 126–128, 131–132, 134–135, 147–148, 160; choice 55–57, 64, 66–69; educational capital 64, 100
employment strategies 17–18
entrepreneurship 92, 98, 108, 123–131, 135–136
ethnicity 37–38, 75, 91–93, 95, 97–99, 159
ethnography 29, 35, 39, 116, 125, 132
European Union 92, 94, 99
existentialism 74, 76, 78

feminism 56, 77, 143, 153, 157
field 2–3, 10, 55, 61, 81, 101, 110, 119, 159; cleft habitus 146–147, 149–151, 153; social haunting 133, 135–136
Foucault, M. 75
Fox, J.E. 94
Friedman, S. 9, 30, 89, 107–120, 124, 140, 151, 161

Garratt, L. 73–84, 90, 159
gender 34, 48, 56–57, 74, 77–78, 82, 154–155
Gilroy, P. 50
Goldberg, D.T. 75
Gordon, A. 133, 135, 161
Gouldner, A. 6
Gove, M. 132
Greenbank, P. 60

habitus 2, 9–11, 17, 19, 22, 143, 148, 150, 158–162; and the body 74, 76, 80–83; class inequality 28, 32, 35; cleft 110, 124, 140–141, 145–147, 151–155, 161; educational choice 55–56, 59, 61–62, 67, 70; migration 88–90, 92, 97, 101, 103; social haunting 124, 133, 135–136; social mobility 109–110, 118–119
habitus tug 117, 144, 146
Halvorsrud, K. 9, 51, 88–103, 159, 162
Haylett, C. 32

Heath, A. 11
Hepworth, S. 60
heterodoxy 132–133
hexis 74, 76, 81, 83
Hey, V. 157
Hill-Collins, P. 152, 154
Hodkinson, P. 70
Hollands, R. 128
hot-knowledge 61, 70
Husserl, E. 136
hysteresis 124, 132–133

Icarus Effect 21
illusio 64, 70, 81–82, 114, 124
immigration *see* migration
Ingram, N. 1–7, 89, 117, 120, 124, 140–155, 157–163
intersectionality 51, 56, 82, 103
Ireland *see* Republic of Ireland
Irwin, S. 60

Jackson, B. 142
James, D. 144, 157, 163
Jenkins, R. 61

knowledge economy 11, 21, 158

labour market 12, 17, 20, 93, 99
Lahire, B. 146–147, 149
Lawler, S. 33, 115
Levi-Strauss, C. 8
Lightfoot, N. 66–67
Lizardo, O. 132
London 42–44, 47–48, 95–96, 100, 159
Lopez Rodriguez, M. 102

McDonald, R.F. 128
McDowell, L. 93–94
Mckenzie, L. 14, 25–35, 39, 56, 116, 125, 159
McRobbie, A. 56
market-driven education 56, 130, 157–158
Marsden, D. 142
Marx, K. 154
masculinities 74, 77, 81, 147, 149
meritocracy 11, 21, 100, 102
Merleau-Ponty, M. 8, 79–80
Meszaros, P.S. 61

micro-aggressions 50, 103
middle classes 15–16, 27, 33–35, 37, 41, 44; cleft habitus 140–141, 143, 145, 148–149
migration 52, 73–75, 81, 88–91, 94–96, 98–101, 153, 162
Miliband, E. 129
Moore, R. 100
Morrin, K. 35, 39, 57, 89, 110, 123–136, 142, 161
multiculturalism 93, 96
Murji, K. 75
Myles, F. 136

narrative 25–35
Nash, R. 1
neoliberalism 56–57, 157
New York 37, 39, 42
Northern Ireland 8, 142–143
Norway 88
Nottingham 27, 30, 33, 39, 92, 97, 116, 159

Office for Standards in Education (OFSTED) 58, 70, 126, 130
Oliver, C. 101
O'Reilly, K. 101

Passeron, J.-C. 62
peer groups 40, 44–47
phenomenology 2, 78–79, 81, 125, 133, 136
Poland 90–94, 97–98, 100–103, 159, 162
power relations 32, 39, 57–58, 83
Pygmalion Dilemma 20–21

race 35, 37–52, 82, 84, 90–93, 98, 102–103
racialisation 37–40, 46, 74–76, 78, 90, 94, 97
racism 73–75, 77–78, 81–82, 93, 159
rationality 11, 75–76, 78, 84
Raty, H. 61–62
Reay, D. 1, 10, 55, 63, 140, 157–158, 160–161
reflexivity 3, 10–11, 70, 145, 147, 151, 162
Republic of Ireland 73, 81

Robbins, D. 1, 6, 89, 127, 136, 157
Ryan, L. 94
Ryle, G. 78–79

Savage, M. 111
Sayad, A. 89
Sayer, A. 11
Scott, J. 14
Shilling, C. 83
Silva, E. 136
Silverstein, P. 89
Skeggs, B. 26–27, 34–35, 115, 125, 132, 157–159
social capital 13–14, 18–19, 58–60, 66, 69–70
social class 3, 14–18, 97, 102–103, 107, 124, 136; black cultural capital 37, 41; class ceiling 110–114, 118, 124; class consciousness 38, 102; class migration 141–145, 153, 162; educational choices 55, 59, 63; hierarchies 27, 33, 38; inequality 25, 28, 34–35, 62
social haunting 125, 133–136, 142, 161
socialism 91, 98
social mobility 3, 11–12, 20, 31, 69, 107–120, 124, 158, 160–162; cleft habitus 140, 143, 153; migration 89, 93
social reproduction 2, 62, 66, 70, 159
Solomos, J. 75
South Africa 90–92, 94, 96, 98, 102–103, 159, 162
Stalin, J. 91
Stenning, A. 98
Strand, M. 132
structural determinism 10–11, 80
Structuralism 2, 8
symbolic capital 31, 33, 35, 57, 83
symbolic violence 29, 34, 46, 119, 143, 151, 153, 160
Szelenyi, I. 102

Thatcher, J. 1–7, 9, 51, 88–103, 157–163
Thatcher, M. 28
third space 6, 140–141, 151–155, 162
Thompson, P. 3

UCAS 64, 70
USA 37, 39, 42

Verdery, K. 90–91
Vincent, C. 61, 70

Wacquant, L. 82, 147
Wallace, D. 35, 74, 95, 159
Webb, D. 58
Weber, M. 33, 91
whiteness 38, 92–94, 98–99
Willis, P.E. 151

Winterton, M.T. 60
working class culture 123–125, 146, 151, 159
working classes 12–13, 15, 57, 98, 100, 154; black cultural capital 41, 51; cleft habitus 140–142, 148–149; converted 17–22; inequality 27–28, 30, 32, 34–35; social haunting 124, 132–134; social mobility 107, 119